Today's New International V

BEGINNING THE JOURNEY

A GUIDE FOR THE SPIRITUALLY CURIOUS

ZONDERVAN™

Beginning the Journey: A Guide for the Spiritually Curious

Published by Zondervan
Grand Rapids, Michigan 49530, U.S.A.

www.zondervan.com

Library of Congress Catalog Card Number 2004116874

Printed in the United States of America

05 06 07 08 09 10 /❖ DCI/ 10 9 8 7 6 5 4 3 2 1

You will be pleased to know that a portion of the purchase price of your new NIV Bible has been provided to International Bible Society to help spread the gospel of Jesus Christ around the world!

International Bible Society

www.ibs.org

The purpose and passion of International Bible Society is to faithfully translate, publish and reach out with God's Word so that people around the world may become disciples of Jesus Christ and members of his Body.

Contents

What's a "Spiritual Seeker"?

If you've picked up this book, you may very well be a "spiritual seeker"—someone who is looking for truth. If someone gave this book to you, apparently that person thinks you're a seeker, or hopes you'll soon become one. To be a seeker in the spiritual realm is to seriously consider—or reconsider—what God means to you.

Maybe the success you've enjoyed in your life isn't as satisfying as you thought it would be. Maybe the fun is starting to feel routine. Maybe things you used to deal with are starting to deal with you. Maybe you just want your "good" life to be good at a deeper, more meaningful level. Whatever the case, if you're trying to discover spiritual truth, you're qualified to call yourself a "seeker."

As a seeker, you're open to the possibility that God might be real and able to make a definite difference. Things in your life don't have to be really rotten to make you become a seeker—you don't have to be desperate. But you're looking for something more, and you've stopped pretending to have it all together. You know you don't know—but you want to know.

So here you are, a seeker, and here is your intrduction to Christianity, taken from the Bible itself. Given the time it was written and the cultural differences between then and now, how are you going to understand the Bible's message? Fewer and fewer people have been exposed to it through formal education. Yet seekers want to know what's in these pages—not only because the Bible has sold more copies than any other book in history, but because so many people claim they've met God as they've read its pages and embraced its message. In light of the Bible's enduring reputation, can a person be open-minded and not give it at least some consideration?

Several features make *Beginning the Journey* "user-friendly" for those trying to comprehend the Bible for the first time. To begin with, it contains an accurate and easily understandable translation of the Bible called *Today's New International Version*—one of the newest English-language translations of Scripture. Paired with this excellent translation are informational notes that highlight passages of spiritual interest to seekers. These notes fall into six categories:

- Discovering God
- Reasons to Believe
- Addressing Questions
- Knowing Yourself
- Strengthening Relationships
- Managing Resources

Be careful not to confuse the comments of our writers and editors with the actual texts of the Bible. In these notes we hoped to address those areas of life most often questioned by people engaged in a spiritual search.

Bible book introductions summarize the central ideas and give general information about the various books, and introductory articles use everyday illustrations to help you "dig in" to the text. There's also some fairly helpful information in the beginning of the Bible—this article, for example!

So what's the best way to begin? Do you just start reading at page 1? Do you indiscriminately flip pages hoping God will mystically talk to you? Because the Bible is actually a collection of several dozen individual books, we've designed *Beginning the Journey* to give you an overview by reading from a few books; then you can go back and read the rest of the Bible. For this purpose, we've developed a reading plan that focuses on five key Bible books: Genesis (page 2), Deuteronomy (page 70), John (page 116), Acts (page 156) and Romans (page 198). By reading them, you will get a fairly comprehensive view of the main themes of the whole Bible. (See page x for a one-month reading plan that guides you through these books.)

If you'd like an even quicker summary, we suggest that you begin by reading the Gospel of John (it begins on page 116). There you'll find out about Jesus, the One who's at the center of everything else that's written in the Bible.

A word of caution: Be careful not to read into the Bible things it doesn't really say. Opening the Bible and pointing to a verse for inspiration—sort of a "flip-and-sip" method of studying the Bible—can lead to deceptive interpretations. Always take into account a verse's context. Study themes within the Bible, not just unrelated statements here and there. Determine that when you don't understand something, you'll use some of the helps in this Bible to get at the meaning. Also, talk to somebody who is familiar with the Bible's teaching. It's okay to ask questions—that's what a seeker is supposed to do!

Understand that the book you hold in your hands offers the potential for a lifetime of learning. While you may eventually "graduate" to a complete Bible, the book you have here is an excellent beginning point. It's designed to set you on a course we hope you'll continue on for the rest of your life.

That, in a nutshell, is what *Beginning the Journey* is all about. We sincerely hope you'll understand and benefit from it.

There is one other thing we should tell you up front: You're not the only seeker in this process. No, we're not talking about all the other spiritual inquirers out there. We're talking about someone who is seeking *you.*

You see, Jesus Christ is the ultimate "seeker." He once said his whole purpose was "to seek and to save what was lost" (Luke chapter 19, verse 10). So as you read, remember: *The Bible isn't so much a book about people's search for God as it is a record of God's search for us.* It's the story of God's repeated refusal to allow humanity to wander away from him unchallenged. In this book, you'll see how God made possible "life in the opposite direction"—a life he offers you.

As a seeker, we think you'll end up finding what you're looking for! Jesus went so far as to promise you actually would (see Matthew chapter 7, verses 7 and 8). If you're not willing to let that happen, reconsider before you get in too deep! This is not a "safe" book—its message is a life-changing one. And it's fine if you don't yet believe that message. God's promise to you today is simply this: "You will seek me and find me when you seek me with all your heart" (Jeremiah chapter 29, verse 13).

How to Seek God

Are you a seeker? If so, we offer you some good news and some bad news. The good news is that God is not lost in the woods. The bad news is, *you are.*

This realization can be painful. It involves facing your own finite nature and recognizing that some of your life choices have been less than "enlightened." It's okay to admit that you're not sure of God, but if you're a true seeker, you'll admit that you're not so sure of yourself, either. Rest assured that you don't have to go it alone—God wants to help you find the right path through the forest of your life.

Becoming a genuine seeker means you've begun to open yourself up to a different way of living—one that includes God in the loop. That thought contains great possibilities, and some potentially frightening implications. Clearly, if you become convinced that God exists and you choose to follow him, you'll never be the same again. And change is hard for most of us.

So what are you supposed to do as a seeker? How can you go about this all-important task of pursuing God and his truth? Well, the steps below don't claim to be the final and authoritative word on the subject. But with a humble recognition that the stakes are sky-high—and believing you are very precious to God—here are four questions to help you in your search. They aren't the map to your ultimate destination, but they may keep you from getting waylaid while you make your journey.

1. WHY DO YOU WANT TO KNOW GOD—WHAT DO YOU HOPE TO GET FROM HIM?

People seek God for a variety of reasons. Some think their search will lead to a more fulfilling life or a greater sense of purpose. Others are looking for relief from their pain. Still others are curious and just want to find out what's true. What is your reason? You should be aware of your aspirations and motivations, because you may be looking for the wrong thing.

Perhaps you're a seeker, for example, because you want to find greater happiness. What if you do find God, but your life circumstances lead to *less* happiness? Will you feel cheated? Believers often report that God gives them greater joy, meaning and purpose in life. But nearly every believer will also admit to experiencing periods of difficulty.

So this is a good question to ask yourself: What am I looking for? And, conversely, What does God offer me? As you read this book you'll discover how much he's already given. But he may not give you exactly what you've anticipated. So expect the unexpected, and make it your goal to find God, no matter what the outcome or perks. The bottom line is that a true seeker seeks the Giver of life, not just his gifts.

2. ARE YOU PLACING LIMITATIONS ON WHAT GOD CAN ASK FROM YOU?

Two people who have fallen deeply in love don't go into a marriage with the intention of ignoring each other's wishes after the wedding ceremony. Such a commitment involves adjusting personal priorities in the interest of building the relationship. When they establish their residence, for example, a couple will usually discuss at length the furnishings, wall hangings, and other touches that will make their house (or apartment) a home. In the same way, it would be absurd for a seeker to open up to God but give no thought to the possibility that God may want to rearrange a few pieces of furniture when he moves in.

Of course, some people are fearful that God wants to throw out all the furniture and condemn their house as uninhabitable. They think that God is just waiting to stifle their every pleasure and ridicule their every action. But nothing could be further from the truth! God created us to be in relationship with him and with each other. Through creation, through the Bible, and through Jesus Christ, God tells us that he wants us to enjoy this life in a way that's in line with his purpose for us.

But the question remains: Do you realize that God wants to be a powerful presence in your life, not just an idea in your head? Following him means following his *leadership*. So let's be honest—accepting that leadership will affect your lifestyle.

Here is where many seekers' searches find the ditch. They declare intellectual reasons for dismissing the claims of the Bible, but in truth they are not willing to give up some activity they know is offensive to God. If that's you, you need to know that God will take you as you are, but he doesn't want to leave you as you are. He wants you to let him make you into what he wants you to be.

3. WHAT DO YOU THINK ABOUT JESUS?

A spiritual seeker may think the proper order of inquiry is to first decide if there's a God (a philosophical question) and then figure out who Jesus is (a historical question). But another and possibly even more exciting way would be to reverse the order, or at least work through the questions in tandem.

Many seekers discover that when they deal with the person of Jesus, at the same time they find answers to many of their other questions.

- Is there a God? (Yes, and he came to earth in human form in the person of Jesus Christ. See John chapter 16, verse 28 [page 145].)
- Does God love me? (Yes! Look at what he did to show that love. See John chapter 3, verses 16–17 [page 121]).
- What religion is the right one? (Reconsider that question in light of the fact that God wants a relationship with *you*, not your religious affiliation. See Romans 10:9–13 [page 213].)
- What do I have to do to live forever? (Accept Jesus as your forgiver and your leader. See John chapter 3, verse 36 [page 123].)
- How can I experience meaning and purpose in life? (By following Jesus and by cultivating your relationships with God and with other people. See Deuteronomy chapter 6, verse 5 [page 81] and Romans chapter 13, verse 9 [page 217].)

According to the Bible, until a seeker comes to terms with Jesus, he or she hasn't dealt with the issue that's most important in starting a relationship with God.

Consider this reality: Jesus is the most influential person in history. This poor itinerant preacher, the son of a carpenter but also the Son of God, changed the entire course of world history. How can any serious spiritual search overlook him? For example, look at any calendar. Today's date is based on a reckoning that hinges on Jesus' life. Because of him, people were moved to split world history into two eras—"before him" and "after him" (B.C. and A.D.).

4. HOW WILL YOU RESPOND TO JESUS?

It's not enough to intellectually agree with Jesus' claims. If you read through this book and recognize Jesus as the true Son of God, a man who walked the earth, lived a perfect life, died, and rose again from the dead, you must choose to cross the line of faith and receive him. This is a once-for-all decision—a "crisis." A "process" follows, but you have to start by inviting him into your life and accepting that he paid the debt you owe for your sin but could never pay yourself.

Salvation in Jesus is a totally free gift, and receiving it is as easy as saying, "Jesus, I acknowledge my sin and your payment for it on the cross. I now ask you to be my forgiver and leader." But you must respond personally and deliberately or the gift will remain unopened and unenjoyed.

SOME PRACTICAL HELPS

Keeping in mind the above questions, here are some practical ideas to guide you in your spiritual search:

- Ask God to reveal himself to you if you're not sure he's there.
- Read what is contained within these pages.
- Talk to people who display a genuine relationship with God; those who obviously love him and who live their lives by a different set of principles.
- Spend time in nature, observing and experiencing God's creation.
- Listen to older people who have walked with God for a long time.
- Question things everybody seems to take for granted—be a lover of truth.
- Ask God-followers *why* they believe, what they believe and how they know their beliefs are true.
- Recognize that following God must make sense: Truth may go beyond reason, but not against it.
- Read what other believers say about Christianity—spend time scouring the shelves at a Christian bookstore or church library for credible authors, or ask your Christian friends for a list of authors who have inspired them in their walk with God.
- Write down your questions, especially about what you read in the Bible, and take them to a knowledgeable Christian who respects your seeking process.
- Expect ongoing questions and some doubts along the way.
- Know your presuppositions—the things you already believe—and try not to let them interfere with your quest for the truth.
- Stay open to actually finding what you're looking for—fear of commitment and change can keep you from finding the truth.
- Keep a journal of your thoughts and feelings during your search.
- Know your personal issues—your past will profoundly influence your present ability to be objective.
- Remember that you don't have to know everything to know something.
- Determine to seek for a specific period of time, and continually evaluate your progress. Then try to reach an appropriate conclusion.
- *Act* on what you decide.

"Ask and it will be given to you; seek and you will find; knock and the door will be opened to you. For everyone who asks receives; those who seek find; and to those who knock, the door will be opened."

—Jesus (Matthew chapter 7, verses 7–8)

Your Guide to the Journey

A One-Month Reading Plan Covering Five Books That Contain the Essential Teachings of the Bible

The Reading Plan

(See page xii for book summaries and main themes.)

Day 1 **Genesis 1–4**
God creates a perfect world, but humanity falls into sin.

Day 2 **Genesis 5–9**
God destroys the evil world with a flood but spares Noah and his family. The rainbow is the sign of God's promise to recreate instead of obliterate humanity.

Day 3 **Genesis 10–14**
Humanity rebels against God again at the tower of Babel; God calls Abram to start a "new community."

Day 4 **Genesis 15–19**
God pledges to bless the whole world through Abram; he destroys Sodom and Gomorrah, showing his resolve to restrain human sin.

Day 5 **Genesis 20–24**
Isaac, the son of God's promise, is born. God provides him with a family, and so expands his covenant people.

Day 6 **Genesis 25–28**
Jacob deceives his twin brother Esau and his father Isaac, but experiences God's kindness in spite of his scheming.

Day 7 **Genesis 29–36**
The story of Jacob's family life and reconciliation with Esau.

Day 8 **Genesis 37–41**
Joseph earns his brothers' envy and is betrayed. Through a fascinating series of events, Joseph goes from being a slave and prisoner to being second in command under Egypt's Pharaoh.

Day 9 **Genesis 42–45**
Joseph's brothers come to Egypt looking for food, and discover that God has turned their treachery into triumph for Joseph.

Day 10 **Genesis 46–50**
Jacob's entire family moves to Egypt, and the nation of Israel flourishes.

Day 11 **Deuteronomy 1–6**
Moses, God's chosen leader over Israel, prepares God's people to enter the promised land by reviewing God's commands (including the Ten Commandments).

Day 12 **Deuteronomy 7–10**
Moses makes predictions of prosperity for an obedient Israel and gives them warnings from their past.

Day 13 **Deuteronomy 11–15**
Moses gives the people God's rules for worship, cleanliness and respect for each other in the promised land.

Day 14 **Deuteronomy 16–20**
The Israelites hear God's rules about worship festivals, establishing a government and legal system, and going to war.

Day 15 **Deuteronomy 21–25**
These chapters contain instructions for keeping the people of Israel from evil influences.

Day 16 **Deuteronomy 26–30**

God gives Israel a choice: "Obey me and live, or disobey and be destroyed."

Day 17 **Deuteronomy 31–34**

Moses appoints a successor, blesses the tribes of Israel, and gets a final look at God's promised land before he dies.

Day 18 **John 1–5**

After waiting many centuries, Israel gets its first look at its Messiah, Jesus, who shows his divinity through various signs.

Day 19 **John 6–11**

Jesus affirms his identity as the Messiah and performs convincing miracles. The Jewish leaders refuse to accept Jesus' claims and plot to have him killed.

Day 20 **John 12–16**

Jesus enters Jerusalem in triumph and predicts his coming suffering and death. He promises that the Holy Spirit will come to take his place when he returns to heaven.

Day 21 **John 17–21**

Jesus prays for all his followers throughout all time and resolutely faces his execution. Three days later he appears to them alive—victorious forever over the power of death!

Day 22 **Acts 1–5**

Christ ascends to heaven and, as promised, the Holy Spirit comes. The church grows by leaps and bounds, and Jewish opposition heats up.

Day 23 **Acts 6–10**

Persecution scatters believers so that Christ's message is heard in non-Jewish regions. Saul's conversion and Peter's vision serve to sharpen the new church's focus on reaching all people everywhere.

Day 24 **Acts 11–15**

Church leaders in Jerusalem debate Jewish custom as it relates to non-Jewish believers. Meanwhile, the apostles continue their bold stand for Christ in faraway cities.

Day 25 **Acts 16–20**

Paul and the apostles travel to various cities where they preach and experience opposition, persecution, prison, and even a riot. Still, the church grows in each city.

Day 26 **Acts 21–28**

This is the action-packed account of Paul's arrest and journey to stand trial in Rome; eventually he carries the word of Christ's resurrection to the leaders of this leading capital city of the ancient world.

Day 27 **Romans 1–4**

Paul begins this letter by emphasizing the "bad news" that all the world has sinned, but then shares the "good news" that reconciliation with God is available through faith in Jesus Christ.

Day 28 **Romans 5–8**

Paul tells us that even though sin is pervasive and powerful, we can have the assurance that all of our sin is covered by Christ's death and resurrection. A new life is available through a relationship with Jesus Christ.

Day 29 **Romans 9–11**

Paul explains that God, in his grace, chooses disobedient people to become his followers—just as he did with the Israelites of long ago. Only because of God's work can anyone be rescued from sin.

Day 30 **Romans 12–16**

Paul gives guidelines for living the kind of life that pleases God day by day.

Book Summaries and Main Themes

Genesis

What It's About

This book, written by the prophet Moses, outlines the "beginnings" of God's work in this world. It describes the perfect creation—including humans—that God made out of nothing. Unfortunately, the relationship between the first people and God was broken by rebellion. But God refused to give up, and the rest of the book outlines how God reached out to various individuals, promising to be their God if they in turn would promise to serve him exclusively. These people—Noah, Abraham, Isaac, Jacob and Joseph—were the ancestors of the Jews. Out of this family line, God eventually brought Jesus Christ into the world—the one who would repair the brokenness between us and God forever.

What to Look For

- One God, who is a person and who created the universe.
- Humanity's rejection of God—the "fall."
- God's kindness in reaching out to people and promising to be their God.
- How God works out his purposes even through imperfect people.

Deuteronomy

What It's About

This book represents Moses' last words to the people of Israel. Throughout its pages Moses summarizes God's laws for his people's lives. He also encourages Israel to follow these laws because of the benefits such obedience will bring. God's love for his people shines through this book, and many of the principles that govern that relationship apply across the board in every generation. Although we will encounter trials and struggles throughout our lives (as did the Israelites), God promises to remain faithful because of his everlasting love.

What to Look For

- God's love and concern for his people.
- God's rules, which reveal his holy character.
- The common sense contained in God's laws.
- The call to remain true to God, no matter what.

John

What It's About

In this book, John looks deeply into the meaning behind Jesus' life on this earth. He introduces Jesus Christ as the miracle-working Son of God, the Savior who was promised to Abraham, Isaac, and Jacob. This truth is laid out in the very first paragraph of the book, when John declares that Jesus Christ—the "Word"—participated in creating the universe. Even though some of these ideas are complex, John brings them all together in chapter 3, verse 16 (page 121), where he provides the Bible's most concise explanation of the plan of salvation. Later in the book John sums up his goals for his work: "These are written that you may believe that Jesus is the Messiah, the Son of God, and that by believing you may have life in his name" (chapter 20, verse 31 [page 152]).

What to Look For

- Evidence that Jesus Christ is God's unique Son, and that he was present with his heavenly Father even at creation.

- The details of John's eyewitness account, which focus on the significance of Jesus' miracles and teaching.
- Jesus' work in the world described by images of life, light, water, bread and fruit.
- The direct way that John explains Jesus' mission on earth.

Acts

What It's About

This exciting book was written by Luke, the author of one of the four Biblical books about Jesus' life. This book's main focus is the story of how the good news of Jesus' victory over death spread like wildfire throughout the Mediterranean region. Luke's readers follow the trail of the disciples as they perform amazing miracles and preach to multitudes of people. They also meet Paul, a missionary who once persecuted Jesus' followers. The account of Paul's conversion—including a flash of light from the sky and Christ's own voice—is one of the most dramatic stories in the book. Acts follows the apostles on a whirlwind tour of many cities where the word of Christ's resurrection was first heard and believed, even in the midst of persecution. The last few chapters tell the story of Paul's trip to Rome—delayed by a fierce storm and a violent shipwreck—to stand trial before Caesar himself. Each of the apostles experienced trouble and danger as they spoke to others about their faith. But Christ never left them, for he was at work in them through the Spirit—exactly as he is in his followers today.

What to Look For

- The amazing power of the Holy Spirit to change the lives of individuals.
- The spread of the church and the incredible numbers of new believers in Jesus.
- How the apostles responded to Christ's directives, even though they suffered for their faithfulness.
- The strong message that Jesus and the new life he offers is for all people.

Romans

What It's About

"Well, nobody's perfect." This common phrase has been true since the beginning of human history. The third chapter of this book picks up that theme as it sums up this letter from Paul to the church in Rome (perhaps before you jump into the reading plan you'd like to skim that chapter first). In it Paul explains that we all disobey God, no matter how good we think we are. That's what it means to be a "sinner." The good news of Romans is that God had provided a way that we can be forgiven and experience a new quality of life. In chapter 8, one of the Bible's most powerful passages, Paul tells us that the only life worth living is the one that has been captured by God's Spirit and is being led by him. Paul suffered his fair share of persecution, but God's goodness carried him through every hardship. Paul wants us to know, "If a guy like me can do it, so can you."

What to Look For

- The clear message that we're forgiven—"saved"—by trust in God, not by our own efforts.
- Paul's response when faced with challenges and his admission that he's no superman.
- Paul's frank discussion of his own inner struggles.
- The power that we can tap into when we live our lives with the help of the Spirit.

Beginning the Journey

Genesis

Deuteronomy

John

Acts

Romans

Genesis Introduction

THE BOTTOM LINE

This book answers some of life's deepest questions, such as "Where did everything come from?" and "Why are we here?" In it you'll find out about your maker, the powerful being we call "God." You'll also find out why our world is in such a mess today—because of sin, committed by people who were remarkably like us. As you read through this book, you'll discover the good news that God hasn't given up on us. Long ago he began a plan that unfolds throughout the rest of the Bible—and continues today—to restore what was lost in the beginning.

CENTRAL IDEAS

- God created the universe and is its only rightful ruler.
- People—not God—have spoiled the perfect creation that God made.
- God worked through his chosen people (e.g., Noah, Abraham) to spread the news of his desire to close the gap between himself and people.
- God used ordinary people to accomplish his purposes in this world.

OUTLINE

1. Creation history (1:1—11:26)
   - A. Adam and Eve (2:4–25)
   - B. Sin enters the world (chap. 3)
   - C. Sin's progress (4:1–16)
   - D. Genealogies (4:17—5:2)
   - E. The great flood (6:1—9:29)
   - F. Spread of the nations (10:1—11:26)

2. Human History (11:27—50:26)
   - A. Abraham (11:27—25:18)
   - B. Jacob (25:19—35:29)
   - C. Esau (36:1—37:1)
   - D. Joseph (37:2—50:26)

TITLE

Genesis means "beginnings"—the beginning of the universe, of human history, and of God's dealings with humankind.

AUTHOR AND READERS

Moses, leader of the Israelites in the ancient world, wrote this book. Although it gives an account of our human ancestors, the truths it contains are for every person on earth.

On my eighth birthday my parents gave me a BB gun. Its cold steel barrel and carved wooden stock made it a thing of beauty. The gun and I formed a deadly partnership. Cans, bottles, road signs—nothing was safe from us.

Well, almost nothing. One afternoon I raised my gun and aimed at a bird perched in the willow tree in our backyard. Just as I was about to squeeze the trigger, my older sister, Patsy, ran into the yard waving her arms and yelling. As the bird fluttered away, Patsy looked at me and smiled. She said nothing, but her smug face taunted, "See, I have more power than you!"

In that moment something inside of me took control. I lowered the barrel and aimed at my sister. A look of horror replaced her smug confidence, and she took off at a full run. I aimed at the part of her I considered most heavily padded and thought, "Sit on this!" as I pulled the trigger. The BB found its mark, and she grabbed her posterior and yelped. She darted into the house screaming, "I've been shot! I've been shot!" For a brief moment I wondered what had made me do something so cruel—then I realized how much I enjoyed it.

I lowered the barrel and aimed at my sister.

After my dad disciplined me, he confiscated my gun. But while he had the power to take away the tools I used for evil, he wasn't able to take away that dark part of my personality that enjoyed doing wrong.

All of us have areas in our lives in which we have, at best, mixed motives. We know to do the right thing, yet we end up doing what is wrong. The particulars of our inner battles may be different, but we all struggle with duplicity. We all have enjoyed doing what we know we shouldn't. We've all groveled before some authority, justifying our excesses, promising reform, and pleading for mercy. And we've all gone right out and done the same thing over again.

The Bible is the only book in the world that adequately explains the source of this universal phenomenon. It doesn't shy away from describing a wide assortment of human failures, and it contains ample illustrations of sinful people in action. This first book, Genesis, makes it clear that after God made the world good, something happened that spoiled it. Humans are the original "moral polluters" (and over the years we've added other forms of pollution as well!). But God has this "thing" for people. He has this thing for *you.*

Want to find out how it all began? That's what Genesis means—"Beginnings." Turn to page 8 and read chapter 3 to find out how our problems with God and with each other started. Maybe you'll see something of yourself in the behavior of humankind's "first couple." It's not a pretty picture. But don't despair. Even though this book contains a lot of bad news, Genesis chapter 3, verse 15 (page 9) promises that there's great news coming!

GENESIS

The Beginning

1 In the beginning God created the heavens and the earth. 2Now the earth was form-
less and empty, darkness was over the surface of the deep, and the Spirit of God was
hovering over the waters.

3And God said, "Let there be light," and there was light. 4God saw that the light was good,
and he separated the light from the darkness. 5God called the light "day," and the
darkness he called "night." And there was evening, and there was morning—the first
day.

6And God said, "Let there be a vault between the waters to separate water from water."
7So God made the vault and separated the water under the vault from the water above
it. And it was so. 8God called the vault "sky." And there was evening, and there was
morning—the second day.

9And God said, "Let the water under the sky be gathered to one place, and let dry ground
appear." And it was so. 10God called the dry ground "land," and the gathered waters
he called "seas." And God saw that it was good.

11Then God said, "Let the land produce vegetation: seed-bearing plants and trees on
the land that bear fruit with seed in it, according to their various kinds." And it was
so. 12The land produced vegetation: plants bearing seed according to their kinds and
trees bearing fruit with seed in it according to their kinds. And God saw that it was
good. 13And there was evening, and there was morning—the third day.

14And God said, "Let there be lights in the vault of the sky to separate the day from the
night, and let them serve as signs to mark seasons and days and years, 15and let them
be lights in the vault of the sky to give light on the earth." And it was so. 16God made
two great lights—the greater light to govern the day and the lesser light to govern the
night. He also made the stars. 17God set them in the vault of the sky to give light on

Discovering God

1:1 // The God Who Is There. The Bible opens with the assumption that God exists. He is the all-knowing and all-powerful being who created everything from nothing. While we humans have the capability to imagine things that don't exist, we can't *create* something from nothing. We can only create something from something, combining different elements into things that never existed before. God is vastly different from us in that he literally spoke into being the basic elements of the universe—space, time and matter—and then fashioned everything that exists.

Can we prove God's existence? Throughout history, many individuals have expended much energy developing "arguments for the existence of God." Such arguments help some people, while leaving other people unconvinced. The Bible never tries to *prove* God's existence. It simply affirms that God exists. And it assumes that anyone who seeks God will find him, because he is the One who is always there, eager to meet any who look for him (Hebrews chapter 11, verse 6).

Enough evidence is available, however, to draw a reasonable conclusion about God's existence. For example, could something as ordered as the universe come into being by chance? That's like a car coming together (with a full tank of gas and the key in the ignition) as a result of an earthquake in Detroit! Likewise, how can we explain mere matter becoming self-aware without a pre-existing intelligent and conscious cause?

Universal order and human intelligence are two of many phenomena that point to an all-knowing and all-powerful Creator. The very fact that the universe exists and that we human creatures exist points to the source of those realities; that is, to God. Whether or not those arguments are persuasive is an issue each of us may want to debate.

In the end, however, the Bible simply invites its readers to take an honest and careful look at God and at Jesus, the one who claims that he is the way to God (see John chapter 14, verse 6 [page 141]). We are challenged to find out for ourselves whether Jesus is who he claims to be.

the earth, 18to govern the day and the night, and to separate light from darkness. And
God saw that it was good. 19And there was evening, and there was morning—the
fourth day.
20And God said, "Let the water teem with living creatures, and let birds fly above the earth
across the vault of the sky." 21So God created the great creatures of the sea and every
living and moving thing with which the water teems, according to their kinds, and
every winged bird according to its kind. And God saw that it was good. 22God blessed
them and said, "Be fruitful and increase in number and fill the water in the seas, and
let the birds increase on the earth." 23And there was evening, and there was morn-
ing—the fifth day.
24And God said, "Let the land produce living creatures according to their kinds: livestock,
creatures that move along the ground, and wild animals, each according to its kind."
And it was so. 25God made the wild animals according to their kinds, the livestock ac-
cording to their kinds, and all the creatures that move along the ground according to
their kinds. And God saw that it was good.
26Then God said, "Let us make human beings in our image, in our likeness, so that
they may rule over the fish in the sea and the birds in the sky, over the livestock and
all the wild animals,[a] and over all the creatures that move along the ground."

27So God created human beings in his own image,
in the image of God he created them;
male and female he created them.

28God blessed them and said to them, "Be fruitful and increase in number; fill the
earth and subdue it. Rule over the fish in the sea and the birds in the sky and over ev-
ery living creature that moves on the ground."
29Then God said, "I give you every seed-bearing plant on the face of the whole earth
and every tree that has fruit with seed in it. They will be yours for food. 30And to all the
beasts of the earth and all the birds in the sky and all the creatures that move on the
ground—everything that has the breath of life in it—I give every green plant for food."
And it was so.
31God saw all that he had made, and it was very good. And there was evening, and
there was morning—the sixth day.

Knowing Yourself

1:27–31 // A New Identity. God created both woman and man in his image and appointed them as equal caretakers over the earth. Notice that the first human couple were created in God's *image*. God blessed them and gave them special responsibilities.

As you reflect on your own worth, consider the fact that God made you in his image—capable of reasoning, relating and ruling. These gifts are meant to be affirmed and expressed throughout your life.

Note also that according to the Bible, sexism—or any other form of discrimination—did not originate with God but with people. *All* individuals, whatever our gender or race, are made in his image. God's intention for us is that we respect his imprint in every human being we meet.

Addressing Questions

1:31 // God. Did God create everything in six literal 24-hour days? Certainly an all-powerful God could have. Yet is that what the text really says? Is that what other evidence points to? Scientists and theologians who have examined both the Bible and assorted scientific data don't agree on how we should interpret the meaning of "days." As a seeker, you may wish to study this issue further. The good news is that God, the creator of the universe, wants a relationship with you even while you're trying to sort this out!

[a] *26* Probable reading of the original Hebrew text (see Syriac); Masoretic Text *the earth*

2 Thus the heavens and the earth were completed in all their vast array.

2 By the seventh day God had finished the work he had been doing; so on the seventh day he rested from all his work. 3 Then God blessed the seventh day and made it holy, because on it he rested from all the work of creating that he had done.

Adam and Eve

4 This is the account of the heavens and the earth when they were created, when the LORD God made the earth and the heavens.

5 Now no shrub had yet appeared on the earth[a] and no plant had yet sprung up, for the LORD God had not sent rain on the earth and there was no one to work the ground, 6 but streams[b] came up from the earth and watered the whole surface of the ground. 7 Then the LORD God formed a man[c] from the dust of the ground and breathed into his nostrils the breath of life, and the man became a living being.

8 Now the LORD God had planted a garden in the east, in Eden; and there he put the man he had formed. 9 The LORD God made all kinds of trees grow out of the ground—trees that were pleasing to the eye and good for food. In the middle of the garden were the tree of life and the tree of the knowledge of good and evil.

10 A river watering the garden flowed from Eden; from there it was separated into four headwaters. 11 The name of the first is the Pishon; it winds through the entire land of Havilah, where there is gold. 12 (The gold of that land is good; aromatic resin[d] and onyx are also there.) 13 The name of the second river is the Gihon; it winds through the entire land of Cush.[e] 14 The name of the third river is the Tigris; it runs along the east side of Ashur. And the fourth river is the Euphrates.

15 The LORD God took the man and put him in the Garden of Eden to work it and take care of it. 16 And the LORD God commanded the man, "You are free to eat from any tree in the garden; 17 but you must not eat from the tree of the knowledge of good and evil, for when you eat of it you will certainly die."

18 The LORD God said, "It is not good for the man to be alone. I will make a helper suitable for him."

19 Now the LORD God had formed out of the ground all the wild animals and all the birds in the sky. He brought them to the man to see what he would name them; and whatever the man called each living creature, that was its name. 20 So the man gave names to all the livestock, the birds in the sky and all the wild animals.

But for Adam[f] no suitable helper was found. 21 So the LORD God caused the man to fall into a deep sleep; and while he was sleeping, he took one of the man's ribs[g] and then closed up the place with flesh. 22 Then the LORD God made a woman from the rib[h] he had taken out of the man, and he brought her to the man.

23 The man said,

> "This is now bone of my bones
>   and flesh of my flesh;

Discovering God

2:1–2 // The God Who Is There. The Bible claims that God is the source of the universe and of all life. He is not merely "one with" the universe, as some Eastern religions teach. Nor is he just "one among" many gods, as ancient mythology and contemporary Mormonism teach. He is the "one and only" God who made everything, who had no beginning, and who will have no end.

As a seeker, make this God the starting point of your investigation. If he does exist, any other so-called god is irrelevant.

[a] 5 Or *land;* also in verse 6 [b] 6 Or *mist* [c] 7 The Hebrew for *man (adam)* sounds like and may be related to the Hebrew for *ground (adamah);* it is also the name *Adam* (see Gen. 2:20). [d] 12 Or *good; pearls* [e] 13 Possibly southeast Mesopotamia [f] 20 Or *the man* [g] 21 Or *took part of the man's side* [h] 22 Or *part*

she shall be called 'woman,'
for she was taken out of man."

[24]For this reason a man will leave his father and mother and be united to his wife, and they will become one flesh.
[25]The man and his wife were both naked, and they felt no shame.

Knowing Yourself

3:1–21 // Sin. The account of Adam and Eve in the garden of Eden is bursting with insight into human and spiritual realities. Setting aside all the scientific questions of creation versus evolution for a moment, this simple story is actually a multilayered drama unparalleled in ancient literature. Compared to other ancient creation stories, this narrative is surprisingly free of mythological elements. And the universal nature of the main characters might make you think it was written yesterday.

In this chapter we discover the origins of human suffering. Here we find two people living in an ideal environment unscarred by hatred or conflict. They enjoy an open relationship with God and with each other. Yet that's not the way real life is for any of us. So what happened to make the world the way it is today?

The story revolves around one simple request that God made to the first couple: Eat all you want from anywhere you want, but don't eat from this one certain tree (chapter 2, verses 16–17 [page 6]). Not that the fruit of that tree was bad; on the contrary, like everything God made, it was undoubtedly good. But the Creator gave Adam and Eve freedom to choose—even if that meant they could choose what was wrong. The command about the fruit served as a test of their willingness to obey God.

Enter the talking serpent, later identified as the devil. The Bible describes the devil as a real being. He was originally a good angel who, along with many other angels, rejected God and was banished from heaven and sent to earth (Revelation chapter 12, verses 7–9). The earthly form he took in this instance may well have been snake-like.

Why did he go after these two people? Because corrupting the highest achievement of God's creation was the best way for the devil to continue his rebellion against God. And this crafty father and angel knew exactly how to break down Adam and Eve's resistance.

First, the devil called into question the accuracy of what God had said (verse 1). By misquoting God's instructions, he planted a seed of doubt in Eve's mind. Second, he maligned God's character (verse 4), questioning God's goodness and convincing Eve that God was keeping something beneficial from her. Finally, he promised that something wonderful would occur if she would simply take a bite (verse 5). This final step painted a distorted picture of sinful actions, as if they contained only pleasure with no undesirable side effects. This is the same "one-two-three punch" that Satan often uses to break down people today.

The strategy worked. The more Eve looked at the fruit, the more appealing it became. She took a bite, and then she urged Adam to try it. Shame, guilt, and fear followed. Instead of having a close relationship with God and with each other, Adam and Eve were reduced to hiding and blaming.

Make no mistake about it: The Bible says that we are spiritual as well as physical beings, which means that both natural and supernatural forces affect our experience. In that first act of disobedience, Adam and Eve set a corrupted pattern that we all follow. At virtually every stage of life, we all "miss the mark" and know firsthand the pain of guilt and shame.

Fortunately, this story also holds a pledge from God that the damage done will not last forever. God predicts the serpent's eventual destruction (verse 15). He does so with a curious phrase, assuring the serpent that an offspring of Eve—though wounded temporarily by the serpent—will ultimately crush his head.

This first promise of the devil's eventual overthrow comes into clearer focus as the Bible's message unfolds. Much later, in an obscure village in Palestine, a descendant of Eve—Jesus himself—was born as the Savior of the world. When Jesus died by crucifixion, the devil gloated over his apparent victory. But Jesus arose from the dead! He shrugged off his temporary wounds and delivered a fatal blow to the serpent's head. Jesus' conquering act assures us that the devil's plans are doomed to fail.

The Fall

3 Now the serpent was more crafty than any of the wild animals the LORD God had
made. He said to the woman, "Did God really say, 'You must not eat from any tree
in the garden'?"
2The woman said to the serpent, "We may eat fruit from the trees in the garden, 3but God
did say, 'You must not eat fruit from the tree that is in the middle of the garden, and you
must not touch it, or you will die.' "
4"You will not certainly die," the serpent said to the woman. 5"For God knows that when
you eat of it your eyes will be opened, and you will be like God, knowing good and evil."
6When the woman saw that the fruit of the tree was good for food and pleasing to the
eye, and also desirable for gaining wisdom, she took some and ate it. She also gave some
to her husband, who was with her, and he ate it. 7Then the eyes of both of them were
opened, and they realized they were naked; so they sewed fig leaves together and made cov-
erings for themselves.
8Then the man and his wife heard the sound of the LORD God as he was walking in the
garden in the cool of the day, and they hid from the LORD God among the trees of the gar-
den. 9But the LORD God called to the man, "Where are you?"
10He answered, "I heard you in the garden, and I was afraid because I was naked; so I hid."
11And he said, "Who told you that you were naked? Have you eaten from the tree that I
commanded you not to eat from?"
12The man said, "The woman you put here with me—she gave me some fruit from the
tree, and I ate it."

Addressing Questions

3:24 // Human Experience. Why did God create Adam and Eve when he knew they were going to sin? This is an often-asked question with deep emotional undertones. Was this some kind of setup? Did God enjoy the prospect of creating people he could later condemn?

First, let's address the emotional side of this question. Whatever answer we come up with, be assured that everything else the Bible teaches about God leads us to believe in his goodness and wisdom. The very fact that he works hard to win back the people he has created must mean that he doesn't want people to separate themselves from him (Ezekiel chapter 18, verse 23). If, as a seeker, you're afraid you'll find a cruel and judgmental God at the end of your search, you need to explore the multitude of Biblical references that clearly reveal his kindness (see, for example, Psalm 16, Jeremiah chapter 29, verses 11 and 12 and John chapter 3, verse 16 [page 121]).

So why did God make people if he knew they would sin? As we answer this question keep in mind an important distinction: God didn't make people who *would* reject him, he made people who *could* reject him. There's a difference.

Maybe an analogy will help. A couple who decides to have a child doesn't do so because they believe that child will be perfect. They have the child so that they can give her their love and be loved in return. Even though they know their child will invariably disappoint them, they still desire that relationship.

In other words, *the potential for love exists only alongside the potential for rejection.* If you take away the freedom to refuse love, you take away love itself. In the same way, God knew in advance that some people would reject him. He also knew that some people would accept his love. And the value of having a relationship with those who would turn to him far outweighed the loss of those who wouldn't.

A relationship of love is possible because God gave us the dignity of choice, in spite of how we would abuse it. What a relief it is to know that our foolish preference for distance from God is not greater than his relentless pursuit of us.

Don't miss an important detail as you consider how this story answers the question of why God created us. Note that after Adam and Eve sinned, they became "seekers." What they were seeking, however, was distance from God! In contrast, God, the original seeker, came looking and calling for them (verse 9). Adam and Eve could have ignored God's initiative and stayed in the woods. Instead, they responded to God's call. After that, God initiated their restoration.

God still seeks to bring wandering people to himself today. How will you respond?

13 Then the LORD God said to the woman, "What is this you have done?"
The woman said, "The serpent deceived me, and I ate."
14 So the LORD God said to the serpent, "Because you have done this,

"Cursed are you above all livestock
  and all wild animals!
You will crawl on your belly
  and you will eat dust
  all the days of your life.
15 And I will put enmity
  between you and the woman,
  and between your offspring[a] and hers;
he will crush[b] your head,
  and you will strike his heel."

16 To the woman he said,

"I will make your pains in childbearing very severe;
  with pain you will give birth to children.
Your desire will be for your husband,
  and he will rule over you."

17 To Adam he said, "Because you listened to your wife and ate from the tree about which
I commanded you, 'You must not eat of it,'

"Cursed is the ground because of you;
  through painful toil you will eat of it
  all the days of your life.
18 It will produce thorns and thistles for you,
  and you will eat the plants of the field.
19 By the sweat of your brow
  you will eat your food
until you return to the ground,
  since from it you were taken;
for dust you are
  and to dust you will return."

20 Adam[c] named his wife Eve,[d] because she would become the mother of all the living.
21 The LORD God made garments of skin for Adam and his wife and clothed them. 22 And
the LORD God said, "The man has now become like one of us, knowing good and evil. He
must not be allowed to reach out his hand and take also from the tree of life and eat, and
live forever." 23 So the LORD God banished him from the Garden of Eden to work the ground
from which he had been taken. 24 After he drove them out, he placed on the east side[e] of
the Garden of Eden cherubim and a flaming sword flashing back and forth to guard the
way to the tree of life.

Cain and Abel

4 Adam[e] made love to his wife Eve, and she became pregnant and gave birth to Cain.[f]
She said, "With the help of the LORD I have brought forth[g] a man." 2 Later she gave
birth to his brother Abel.
Now Abel kept flocks, and Cain worked the soil. 3 In the course of time Cain brought
some of the fruits of the soil as an offering to the LORD. 4 But Abel also brought an offering—
fat portions from some of the firstborn of his flock. The LORD looked with favor on Abel
and his offering, 5 but on Cain and his offering he did not look with favor. So Cain was very
angry, and his face was downcast.

---

[a] 15 Or *seed* [b] 15 Or *strike* [c] 20, 1 Or *The man* [d] 20 *Eve* probably means *living.*
[e] 24 Or *placed in front* [f] 1 *Cain* sounds like the Hebrew for *brought forth* or *acquired.*
[g] 1 Or *have acquired*

6 Then the LORD said to Cain, "Why are you angry? Why is your face downcast? 7 If you
do what is right, will you not be accepted? But if you do not do what is right, sin is crouch-
ing at your door; it desires to have you, but you must rule over it."
8 Now Cain said to his brother Abel, "Let's go out to the field."[a] While they were in the
field, Cain attacked his brother Abel and killed him.
9 Then the LORD said to Cain, "Where is your brother Abel?"
"I don't know," he replied. "Am I my brother's keeper?"
10 The LORD said, "What have you done? Listen! Your brother's blood cries out to me from
the ground. 11 Now you are under a curse and driven from the ground, which opened its
mouth to receive your brother's blood from your hand. 12 When you work the ground, it will
no longer yield its crops for you. You will be a restless wanderer on the earth."
13 Cain said to the LORD, "My punishment is more than I can bear. 14 Today you are driv-
ing me from the land, and I will be hidden from your presence; I will be a restless wander-
er on the earth, and whoever finds me will kill me."
15 But the LORD said to him, "Not so[b]; anyone who kills Cain will suffer vengeance seven
times over." Then the LORD put a mark on Cain so that no one who found him would kill him.
16 So Cain went out from the LORD's presence and lived in the land of Nod,[c] east of Eden.
17 Cain made love to his wife, and she became pregnant and gave birth to Enoch. Cain
was then building a city, and he named it after his son Enoch. 18 To Enoch was born Irad,
and Irad was the father of Mehujael, and Mehujael was the father of Methushael, and Me-
thushael was the father of Lamech.
19 Lamech married two women, one named Adah and the other Zillah. 20 Adah gave birth
to Jabal; he was the father of those who live in tents and raise livestock. 21 His brother's
name was Jubal; he was the father of all who play stringed instruments and pipes. 22 Zillah
also had a son, Tubal-Cain, who forged all kinds of tools out of[d] bronze and iron. Tubal-
Cain's sister was Naamah.
23 Lamech said to his wives,

"Adah and Zillah, listen to me;
  wives of Lamech, hear my words.
I have killed a man for wounding me,
  a young man for injuring me.
24 If Cain is avenged seven times,
  then Lamech seventy-seven times."

25 Adam made love to his wife again, and she gave birth to a son and named him Seth,[e]
saying, "God has granted me another child in place of Abel, since Cain killed him." 26 Seth
also had a son, and he named him Enosh.
At that time people began to call on[f] the name of the LORD.

Knowing Yourself

4:4–5 // Sin. This passage shows us that it's possible to be the wrong kind of seeker. Both Cain and Abel approached God, but he only accepted one of them. Why?

The key is found in verse 5. The problem wasn't just the offering. The verses that follow show the murderous results of Cain's anger. Clearly, Cain's offering wasn't presented in the right spirit; he had a "spiritual dysfunction."

Throughout the Bible we discover that God looks beyond our actions and considers our motives. A person can't just go through the motions with God. God knows what's inside each of us and is unimpressed by rituals that have no sincerity or substance behind them.

As you continue to seek God, know that he cannot be fooled. Honestly face your spiritual "shadows," and come to God admitting that they exist. In that way you'll not only be seeking the God who is real, you'll seek him by being real.

---

[a] 8 Samaritan Pentateuch, Septuagint, Vulgate and Syriac; Masoretic Text does not have *"Let's go out to the field."* [b] 15 Septuagint, Vulgate and Syriac; Hebrew *Very well* [c] 16 *Nod* means *wandering* (see verses 12 and 14). [d] 22 Or *who instructed all who work in* [e] 25 *Seth* probably means *granted.* [f] 26 Or *to proclaim*

From Adam to Noah

5 This is the written account of Adam's family line.

When God created human beings, he made them in the likeness of God. 2 He creat-
ed them male and female and blessed them. And when they were created, he called them
"human beings."
3 When Adam had lived 130 years, he had a son in his own likeness, in his own image;
and he named him Seth. 4 After Seth was born, Adam lived 800 years and had other sons
and daughters. 5 Altogether, Adam lived a total of 930 years, and then he died.
6 When Seth had lived 105 years, he became the father[a] of Enosh. 7 After he became the
father of Enosh, Seth lived 807 years and had other sons and daughters. 8 Altogether, Seth
lived a total of 912 years, and then he died.
9 When Enosh had lived 90 years, he became the father of Kenan. 10 After he became the
father of Kenan, Enosh lived 815 years and had other sons and daughters. 11 Altogether,
Enosh lived a total of 905 years, and then he died.
12 When Kenan had lived 70 years, he became the father of Mahalalel. 13 After he became
the father of Mahalalel, Kenan lived 840 years and had other sons and daughters. 14 Alto-
gether, Kenan lived a total of 910 years, and then he died.
15 When Mahalalel had lived 65 years, he became the father of Jared. 16 After he became
the father of Jared, Mahalalel lived 830 years and had other sons and daughters. 17 Altogeth-
er, Mahalalel lived a total of 895 years, and then he died.
18 When Jared had lived 162 years, he became the father of Enoch. 19 After he became the
father of Enoch, Jared lived 800 years and had other sons and daughters. 20 Altogether, Ja-
red lived a total of 962 years, and then he died.
21 When Enoch had lived 65 years, he became the father of Methuselah. 22 After he be-
came the father of Methuselah, Enoch walked faithfully with God 300 years and had oth-
er sons and daughters. 23 Altogether, Enoch lived a total of 365 years. 24 Enoch walked
faithfully with God; then he was no more, because God took him away.
25 When Methuselah had lived 187 years, he became the father of Lamech. 26 After he be-
came the father of Lamech, Methuselah lived 782 years and had other sons and daughters.
27 Altogether, Methuselah lived a total of 969 years, and then he died.
28 When Lamech had lived 182 years, he had a son. 29 He named him Noah[b] and said, "He
will comfort us in the labor and painful toil of our hands caused by the ground the LORD
has cursed." 30 After Noah was born, Lamech lived 595 years and had other sons and daugh-
ters. 31 Altogether, Lamech lived a total of 777 years, and then he died.
32 After Noah was 500 years old, he became the father of Shem, Ham and Japheth.

Wickedness in the World

6 When human beings began to increase in number on the earth and daughters were
born to them, 2 the sons of God saw that these daughters were beautiful, and they
married any of them they chose. 3 Then the LORD said, "My Spirit will not contend
with[c] human beings forever, for they are mortal[d]; their days will be a hundred and twenty
years."
4 The Nephilim were on the earth in those days—and also afterward—when the sons of
God went to the daughters of the human beings and had children by them. They were the
heroes of old, men of renown.
5 The LORD saw how great the wickedness of the human race had become on the earth,
and that every inclination of the thoughts of the human heart was only evil all the time.
6 The LORD regretted that he had made human beings on the earth, and his heart was deep-
ly troubled. 7 So the LORD said, "I will wipe from the face of the earth the human race I have
created—and with them the animals, the birds and the creatures that move along the
ground—for I regret that I have made them." 8 But Noah found favor in the eyes of the LORD.

---

[a] 6 *Father* may mean *ancestor*; also in verses 7-26. [b] 29 *Noah* sounds like the Hebrew for *comfort.* [c] 3 Or *My spirit will not remain in* [d] 3 Or *corrupt*

Noah and the Flood

9This is the account of Noah and his family.

Noah was a righteous man, blameless among the people of his time, and he walked faithfully with God. 10Noah had three sons: Shem, Ham and Japheth.

11Now the earth was corrupt in God's sight and was full of violence. 12God saw how corrupt the earth had become, for all the people on earth had corrupted their ways. 13So God said to Noah, "I am going to put an end to all people, for the earth is filled with violence because of them. I am surely going to destroy both them and the earth. 14So make yourself an ark of cypress[a] wood; make rooms in it and coat it with pitch inside and out. 15This is how you are to build it: The ark is to be three hundred cubits long, fifty cubits wide and thirty cubits high.[b] 16Make a roof for it, leaving below the roof an opening one cubit[c] high all around.[d] Put a door in the side of the ark and make lower, middle and upper decks. 17I am going to bring floodwaters on the earth to destroy all life under the heavens, every creature that has the breath of life in it. Everything on earth will perish. 18But I will establish my covenant with you, and you will enter the ark—you and your sons and your wife and your sons' wives with you. 19You are to bring into the ark two of all living creatures, male and female, to keep them alive with you. 20Two of every kind of bird, of every kind of animal and of every kind of creature that moves along the ground will come to you to be kept alive. 21You are to take every kind of food that is to be eaten and store it away as food for you and for them."

22Noah did everything just as God commanded him.

7 The LORD then said to Noah, "Go into the ark, you and your whole family, because I have found you righteous in this generation. 2Take with you seven pairs of every kind of clean animal, a male and its mate, and one pair of every kind of unclean animal, a male and its mate, 3and also seven pairs of every kind of bird, male and female, to keep their various kinds alive throughout the earth. 4Seven days from now I will send rain on the earth for forty days and forty nights, and I will wipe from the face of the earth every living creature I have made."

5And Noah did all that the LORD commanded him.

6Noah was six hundred years old when the floodwaters came on the earth. 7And Noah and his sons and his wife and his sons' wives entered the ark to escape the waters of the flood. 8Pairs of clean and unclean animals, of birds and of all creatures that move along the ground, 9male and female, came to Noah and entered the ark, as God had commanded Noah. 10And after the seven days the floodwaters came on the earth.

11In the six hundredth year of Noah's life, on the seventeenth day of the second month—on that day all the springs of the great deep burst forth, and the floodgates of the heavens were opened. 12And rain fell on the earth forty days and forty nights.

Discovering God

6:13 // Life with God. Before you conclude from this passage that God decided to wipe out humanity while in a fit of rage, note that before the flood people were described as *exceptionally* evil, yet God was patient. God allowed Noah to build the ark, during which time Noah must have warned his neighbors and others of the destruction to come. Apparently, nobody responded.

Both this passage and history as a whole are full of the tension between God's love for his creatures and his grief over how sin corrupts them. Basically, our sin is like a heavy ball and chain that each of us carries with us throughout our lives. God hates sin, and offers to forgive us and release us from its weight in our lives. However, if we ignore that call and refuse to be set free, God will honor our decision and allow us to carry our sin all alone. If we choose to "go swimming" with that weight, what happens next is our responsibility, not God's.

What's the alternative? Seek God as Noah did and walk daily in God's presence (verse 9).

---

[a] *14* The meaning of the Hebrew for this word is uncertain. [b] *15* That is, about 450 feet long, 75 feet wide and 45 feet high or about 135 meters long, 22.5 meters wide and 13.5 meters high [c] *16* That is, about 18 inches or about 45 centimeters [d] *16* The meaning of the Hebrew for this clause is uncertain.

[13]On that very day Noah and his sons, Shem, Ham and Japheth, together with his wife and the wives of his three sons, entered the ark. [14]They had with them every wild animal according to its kind, all livestock according to their kinds, every creature that moves along the ground according to its kind and every bird according to its kind, everything with wings. [15]Pairs of all creatures that have the breath of life in them came to Noah and entered the ark. [16]The animals going in were male and female of every living thing, as God had commanded Noah. Then the LORD shut him in.

[17]For forty days the flood kept coming on the earth, and as the waters increased they lifted the ark high above the earth. [18]The waters rose and increased greatly on the earth, and the ark floated on the surface of the water. [19]They rose greatly on the earth, and all the high mountains under the entire heavens were covered. [20]The waters rose and covered the mountains to a depth of more than fifteen cubits.[a,b] [21]Every living thing that moved on the earth perished—birds, livestock, wild animals, all the creatures that swarm over the earth, and the entire human race. [22]Everything on dry land that had the breath of life in its nostrils died. [23]Every living thing on the face of the earth was wiped out; human beings and animals and the creatures that move along the ground and the birds were wiped from the earth. Only Noah was left, and those with him in the ark.

[24]The waters flooded the earth for a hundred and fifty days.

8 But God remembered Noah and all the wild animals and the livestock that were with him in the ark, and he sent a wind over the earth, and the waters receded. [2]Now the springs of the deep and the floodgates of the heavens had been closed, and the rain had stopped falling from the sky. [3]The water receded steadily from the earth. At the end of the hundred and fifty days the water had gone down, [4]and on the seventeenth day of the seventh month the ark came to rest on the mountains of Ararat. [5]The waters continued to recede until the tenth month, and on the first day of the tenth month the tops of the mountains became visible.

[6]After forty days Noah opened a window he had made in the ark [7]and sent out a raven, and it kept flying back and forth until the water had dried up from the earth. [8]Then he sent out a dove to see if the water had receded from the surface of the ground. [9]But the dove could find nowhere to perch because there was water over all the surface of the earth; so it returned to Noah in the ark. He reached out his hand and took the dove and brought it back to himself in the ark. [10]He waited seven more days and again sent out the dove from the ark. [11]When the dove returned to him in the evening, there in its beak was a freshly plucked olive leaf! Then Noah knew that the water had receded from the earth. [12]He waited seven more days and sent the dove out again, but this time it did not return to him.

[13]By the first day of the first month of Noah's six hundred and first year, the water had dried up from the earth. Noah then removed the covering from the ark and saw that the surface of the ground was dry. [14]By the twenty-seventh day of the second month the earth was completely dry.

Discovering God

7:23 // Life with God. God's method of delivering Noah and his family provides us with a profound lesson in how salvation works.

Basically, Noah had no hope of saving himself from the coming flood. God didn't simply give Noah swimming lessons and a life jacket. Noah needed resources that extended far beyond his own abilities to survive, and that's why God gave him specific instructions for building the ark. As a result of God's direction, Noah and his family literally "rose above" the calamity. By being in the boat, they enjoyed all its benefits.

Likewise, God's plan for rescuing you is to place you spiritually "into" Jesus Christ. Jesus delivers you like the ark delivered Noah. By being "in Christ," all his perfection becomes yours. You don't become sinless, but Jesus' sinless perfection covers your sin in God's eyes. (See Romans chapter 8, verses 1 and 2, [page 209] for more information.)

And the benefits extend into eternity. As God rescued Noah from the flood's judgment, Christ can deliver you from the coming day when God will separate good and evil forever.

---

[a] *20* That is, about 22 feet or about 6.8 meters [b] *20* Or *rose more than fifteen cubits, and the mountains were covered*

15 Then God said to Noah, 16 "Come out of the ark, you and your wife and your sons and
their wives. 17 Bring out every kind of living creature that is with you—the birds, the animals,
and all the creatures that move along the ground—so they can multiply on the earth and be
fruitful and increase in number on it."
18 So Noah came out, together with his sons and his wife and his sons' wives. 19 All the an-
imals and all the creatures that move along the ground and all the birds—everything that
moves on the earth—came out of the ark, one kind after another.
20 Then Noah built an altar to the LORD and, taking some of all the clean animals and
clean birds, he sacrificed burnt offerings on it. 21 The LORD smelled the pleasing aroma and
said in his heart: "Never again will I curse the ground because of human beings, even
though[a] every inclination of the human heart is evil from childhood. And never again will
I destroy all living creatures, as I have done.

22 "As long as the earth endures,
seedtime and harvest,
cold and heat,
summer and winter,
day and night
will never cease."

God's Covenant With Noah

9 Then God blessed Noah and his sons, saying to them, "Be fruitful and increase in
number and fill the earth. 2 The fear and dread of you will fall on all the beasts of the
earth and all the birds in the sky, on every creature that moves along the ground,
and on all the fish in the sea; they are given into your hands. 3 Everything that lives and
moves will be food for you. Just as I gave you the green plants, I now give you everything.
4 "But you must not eat meat that has its lifeblood still in it. 5 And for your lifeblood I will
surely demand an accounting. I will demand an accounting from every animal. And from
each human being, too, I will demand an accounting for the life of another human being.

6 "Whoever sheds human blood,
by human beings shall their blood be shed;
for in the image of God
has God made humankind.

7 As for you, be fruitful and increase in number; multiply on the earth and increase upon it."
8 Then God said to Noah and to his sons with him: 9 "I now establish my covenant with
you and with your descendants after you 10 and with every living creature that was with
you—the birds, the livestock and all the wild animals, all those that came out of the ark
with you—every living creature on earth. 11 I establish my covenant with you: Never again
will all life be destroyed by the waters of a flood; never again will there be a flood to de-
stroy the earth."
12 And God said, "This is the sign of the covenant I am making between me and you and
every living creature with you, a covenant for all generations to come: 13 I have set my rain-
bow in the clouds, and it will be the sign of the covenant between me and the earth.
14 Whenever I bring clouds over the earth and the rainbow appears in the clouds, 15 I will re-
member my covenant between me and you and all living creatures of every kind. Never
again will the waters become a flood to destroy all life. 16 Whenever the rainbow appears in
the clouds, I will see it and remember the everlasting covenant between God and all liv-
ing creatures of every kind on the earth."
17 So God said to Noah, "This is the sign of the covenant I have established between me
and all life on the earth."

The Sons of Noah

18 The sons of Noah who came out of the ark were Shem, Ham and Japheth. (Ham was
the father of Canaan.) 19 These were the three sons of Noah, and from them came the peo-
ple who were scattered over the whole earth.

---

[a] *21* Or *human beings, for*

20 Noah, a man of the soil, proceeded[a] to plant a vineyard. 21 When he drank some of its
wine, he became drunk and lay uncovered inside his tent. 22 Ham, the father of Canaan,
saw his father's nakedness and told his two brothers outside. 23 But Shem and Japheth took
a garment and laid it across their shoulders; then they walked in backward and covered
their father's nakedness. Their faces were turned the other way so that they would not see
their father's nakedness.

24 When Noah awoke from his wine and found out what his youngest son had done to
him, 25 he said,

> "Cursed be Canaan!
> The lowest of slaves
> will he be to his brothers."

26 He also said,

> "Praise be to the LORD, the God of Shem!
> May Canaan be the slave of Shem.
> 27 May God extend Japheth's[b] territory;
> may Japheth live in the tents of Shem,
> and may Canaan be the slave of Japheth."

28 After the flood Noah lived 350 years. 29 Noah lived a total of 950 years, and then he
died.

The Table of Nations

10 This is the account of Shem, Ham and Japheth, Noah's sons, who themselves had sons after the flood.

The Japhethites

2 The sons[c] of Japheth:
Gomer, Magog, Madai, Javan, Tubal, Meshek and Tiras.
3 The sons of Gomer:
Ashkenaz, Riphath and Togarmah.
4 The sons of Javan:
Elishah, Tarshish, the Kittites and the Rodanites.[d] 5 (From these the maritime
peoples spread out into their territories by their clans within their nations, each with
its own language.)

Knowing Yourself

9:20–25 // Sin. Here is a man earlier singled out as the most blameless person in all the earth, and now he's lying drunk in his tent! What happened?

Noah had just ended a stressful period in his life with a spiritual "high." God had spared him and his family from a terrible calamity. But Noah also undoubtedly felt anguish—his whole world had been destroyed. Did Noah miss friends now gone? We'll never know. For whatever reason, this man of God turned to alcohol as a source of comfort.

Among other things, this story points out the destructive power of alcohol. It can affect an otherwise righteous man and bring him to ruin. It can drastically change the relationship between a good father and the next generation.

If you don't think you could ever fall into a similar situation, take a warning from the life of Noah. Nobody is immune from the snare or from the dangerous effects of substance abuse.

---

[a] 20 Or *soil, was the first* [b] 27 *Japheth* sounds like the Hebrew for *extend.* [c] 2 *Sons* may mean *descendants* or *successors* or *nations*; also in verses 3, 4, 6, 7, 20-23, 29 and 31. [d] 4 Some manuscripts of the Masoretic Text and Samaritan Pentateuch (see also Septuagint and 1 Chron. 1:7); most manuscripts of the Masoretic Text *Dodanites*

The Hamites

[6]The sons of Ham:
Cush, Egypt, Put and Canaan.
[7]The sons of Cush:
Seba, Havilah, Sabtah, Raamah and Sabteka.
The sons of Raamah:
Sheba and Dedan.

[8]Cush was the father[a] of Nimrod, who became a mighty warrior on the earth. [9]He was
a mighty hunter before the LORD; that is why it is said, "Like Nimrod, a mighty hunter be-
fore the LORD." [10]The first centers of his kingdom were Babylon, Uruk, Akkad and Kalneh,
in[b] Shinar.[c] [11]From that land he went to Assyria, where he built Nineveh, Rehoboth Ir,[d] Ca-
lah [12]and Resen, which is between Nineveh and Calah—which is the great city.

[13]Egypt was the father of
the Ludites, Anamites, Lehabites, Naphtuhites, [14]Pathrusites, Kasluhites (from
whom the Philistines came) and Caphtorites.
[15]Canaan was the father of
Sidon his firstborn,[e] and of the Hittites, [16]Jebusites, Amorites, Girgashites, [17]Hivites,
Arkites, Sinites, [18]Arvadites, Zemarites and Hamathites.

Later the Canaanite clans scattered [19]and the borders of Canaan reached from Sidon to-
ward Gerar as far as Gaza, and then toward Sodom, Gomorrah, Admah and Zeboyim, as far
as Lasha.
[20]These are the sons of Ham by their clans and languages, in their territories and na-
tions.

The Semites

[21]Sons were also born to Shem, whose older brother was[f] Japheth; Shem was the ances-
tor of all the sons of Eber.

[22]The sons of Shem:
Elam, Ashur, Arphaxad, Lud and Aram.
[23]The sons of Aram:
Uz, Hul, Gether and Meshek.[g]
[24]Arphaxad was the father of[h] Shelah,
and Shelah the father of Eber.
[25]Two sons were born to Eber:
One was named Peleg,[i] because in his time the earth was divided; his brother was
named Joktan.
[26]Joktan was the father of
Almodad, Sheleph, Hazarmaveth, Jerah, [27]Hadoram, Uzal, Diklah, [28]Obal,
Abimael, Sheba, [29]Ophir, Havilah and Jobab. All these were sons of Joktan.

[30]The region where they lived stretched from Mesha toward Sephar, in the eastern hill
country.
[31]These are the sons of Shem by their clans and languages, in their territories and na-
tions.

[32]These are the clans of Noah's sons, according to their lines of descent, within their na-
tions. From these the nations spread out over the earth after the flood.

---

[a] 8 *Father* may mean *ancestor* or *predecessor* or *founder*; also in verses 13, 15, 24 and 26.
[b] 10 Or *Uruk and Akkad—all of them in* [c] 10 That is, Babylonia [d] 11 Or *Nineveh with its city squares* [e] 15 Or *of the Sidonians, the foremost* [f] 21 Or *Shem, the older brother of*
[g] 23 See Septuagint and 1 Chron. 1:17; Hebrew *Mash.* [h] 24 Hebrew; Septuagint *father of Cainan, and Cainan was the father of* [i] 25 *Peleg* means *division.*

The Tower of Babel

11 Now the whole world had one language and a common speech. 2As people moved
eastward,[a] they found a plain in Shinar[b] and settled there.
3They said to each other, "Come, let's make bricks and bake them thoroughly."
They used brick instead of stone, and tar for mortar. 4Then they said, "Come, let us build
ourselves a city, with a tower that reaches to the heavens, so that we may make a name
for ourselves and not be scattered over the face of the whole earth."
5But the LORD came down to see the city and the tower that they were building. 6The
LORD said, "If as one people speaking the same language they have begun to do this, then
nothing they plan to do will be impossible for them. 7Come, let us go down and confuse
their language so they will not understand each other."
8So the LORD scattered them from there over all the earth, and they stopped building
the city. 9That is why it was called Babel[c]—because there the LORD confused the language
of the whole world. From there the LORD scattered them over the face of the whole earth.

From Shem to Abram

10This is the account of Shem's family line.

Two years after the flood, when Shem was 100 years old, he became the father[d] of Ar-
phaxad. 11And after he became the father of Arphaxad, Shem lived 500 years and had oth-
er sons and daughters.
12When Arphaxad had lived 35 years, he became the father of Shelah. 13And after he became
the father of Shelah, Arphaxad lived 403 years and had other sons and daughters.[e]
14When Shelah had lived 30 years, he became the father of Eber. 15And after he became
the father of Eber, Shelah lived 403 years and had other sons and daughters.
16When Eber had lived 34 years, he became the father of Peleg. 17And after he became
the father of Peleg, Eber lived 430 years and had other sons and daughters.
18When Peleg had lived 30 years, he became the father of Reu. 19And after he became the
father of Reu, Peleg lived 209 years and had other sons and daughters.
20When Reu had lived 32 years, he became the father of Serug. 21And after he became
the father of Serug, Reu lived 207 years and had other sons and daughters.
22When Serug had lived 30 years, he became the father of Nahor. 23And after he became
the father of Nahor, Serug lived 200 years and had other sons and daughters.

Strengthening Relationships

11:1–9 // Social. A lot of good causes exist to which people can give time and effort. But sometimes people get the idea that they can build a better world and leave God out of it.

That's what happened to this ancient civilization. There was nothing wrong with working together to build a beautiful tower. But these people built it as a monument to their autonomy. Their ambition made them think they could function completely without God's approval.

Perhaps you've never thought about it, but is your life like a tower of Babel? As you work each day and try to make a name for yourself, do you ever give God any credit for the good things he's given you? Do you recognize his right to have a place in your life?

The people spoken of in this passage didn't. To be sure, they became famous—but not in the way they had planned. Without God they became "Babel" (from which we get our word "babble"). Their dreams were left unfinished; their ambitions went unfulfilled.

[a] 2 Or *from the east*; or *in the east* [b] 2 That is, Babylonia [c] 9 That is, Babylon; *Babel* sounds like the Hebrew for *confused.* [d] 10 *Father* may mean *ancestor*; also in verses 11-25.
[e] 12,13 Hebrew; Septuagint (see also Luke 3:35, 36 and note at Gen. 10:24) *35 years, he became the father of Cainan. 13And after he became the father of Cainan, Arphaxad lived 430 years and had other sons and daughters, and then he died. When Cainan had lived 130 years, he became the father of Shelah. And after he became the father of Shelah, Cainan lived 330 years and had other sons and daughters*

24 When Nahor had lived 29 years, he became the father of Terah. 25 And after he became
the father of Terah, Nahor lived 119 years and had other sons and daughters.
26 After Terah had lived 70 years, he became the father of Abram, Nahor and Haran.

Abram's Family

27 This is the account of Terah's family line.

Terah became the father of Abram, Nahor and Haran. And Haran became the father of
Lot. 28 While his father Terah was still alive, Haran died in Ur of the Chaldeans, in the land
of his birth. 29 Abram and Nahor both married. The name of Abram's wife was Sarai, and the
name of Nahor's wife was Milkah; she was the daughter of Haran, the father of both Mil-
kah and Iskah. 30 Now Sarai was childless because she was not able to conceive.
31 Terah took his son Abram, his grandson Lot son of Haran, and his daughter-in-law Sa-
rai, the wife of his son Abram, and together they set out from Ur of the Chaldeans to go to
Canaan. But when they came to Harran, they settled there.
32 Terah lived 205 years, and he died in Harran.

The Call of Abram

12 The LORD had said to Abram, "Go from your country, your people and your fa-
ther's household to the land I will show you.

2 "I will make you into a great nation,
    and I will bless you;
I will make your name great,
    and you will be a blessing.[a]
3 I will bless those who bless you,
    and whoever curses you I will curse;
and all peoples on earth
    will be blessed through you."[b]

4 So Abram went, as the LORD had told him; and Lot went with him. Abram was seven-
ty-five years old when he set out from Harran. 5 He took his wife Sarai, his nephew Lot, all
the possessions they had accumulated and the people they had acquired in Harran, and
they set out for the land of Canaan, and they arrived there.
6 Abram traveled through the land as far as the site of the great tree of Moreh at She-
chem. At that time the Canaanites were in the land. 7 The LORD appeared to Abram and

Discovering God

12:1–20 // Life with God. This chapter marks a significant step in God's dealings with the human race. With God's call to this man Abram (whose name God later changed to "Abraham"), God began to build a new community of people who would reach the rest of the world with God's love.

Note that God's intent was not just to make a nation out of Abraham's family but to be a blessing to all the people on earth (verse 3). Abraham's descendants, the Hebrew people, were to fill this role in the ancient world.

The high point of this plan was to take place many years in the future, when the most famous Hebrew in all history would give up his life—not just for one nation, but for all the world's people. That well-known descendant of Abraham was Jesus of Nazareth, whom we read about in the book of John (page 116).

From this point on, God identifies a growing group of individuals as his people. In that sense, this chapter marks the end of the beginning and the dawn of a new era.

---

[a] 2 Or *great, / and you will be seen as blessed* [b] 3 Or *earth / will use your name in blessings* (see Gen. 48:20)

said, "To your offspring[a] I will give this land." So he built an altar there to the LORD, who had appeared to him.

8From there he went on toward the hills east of Bethel and pitched his tent, with Bethel on the west and Ai on the east. There he built an altar to the LORD and called on the name of the LORD.

9Then Abram set out and continued toward the Negev.

Abram in Egypt

10Now there was a famine in the land, and Abram went down to Egypt to live there for a while because the famine was severe. 11As he was about to enter Egypt, he said to his wife Sarai, "I know what a beautiful woman you are. 12When the Egyptians see you, they will say, 'This is his wife.' Then they will kill me but will let you live. 13Say you are my sister, so that I will be treated well for your sake and my life will be spared because of you."

14When Abram came to Egypt, the Egyptians saw that Sarai was a very beautiful woman. 15And when Pharaoh's officials saw her, they praised her to Pharaoh, and she was taken into his palace. 16He treated Abram well for her sake, and Abram acquired sheep and cattle, male and female donkeys, male and female servants, and camels.

17But the LORD inflicted serious diseases on Pharaoh and his household because of Abram's wife Sarai. 18So Pharaoh summoned Abram. "What have you done to me?" he said. "Why didn't you tell me she was your wife? 19Why did you say, 'She is my sister,' so that I took her to be my wife? Now then, here is your wife. Take her and go!" 20Then Pharaoh gave orders about Abram to his men, and they sent him on his way, with his wife and everything he had.

Abram and Lot Separate

13 So Abram went up from Egypt to the Negev, with his wife and everything he had, and Lot went with him. 2Abram had become very wealthy in livestock and in silver and gold.

3From the Negev he went from place to place until he came to Bethel, to the place between Bethel and Ai where his tent had been earlier 4and where he had first built an altar. There Abram called on the name of the LORD.

5Now Lot, who was moving about with Abram, also had flocks and herds and tents. 6But the land could not support them while they stayed together, for their possessions were so great that they were not able to stay together. 7And quarreling arose between Abram's herders and the herders of Lot. The Canaanites and Perizzites were also living in the land at that time.

8So Abram said to Lot, "Let's not have any quarreling between you and me, or between your herders and mine, for we are close relatives. 9Is not the whole land before you? Let's part company. If you go to the left, I'll go to the right; if you go to the right, I'll go to the left."

10Lot looked around and saw that the whole plain of the Jordan was well watered, like the garden of the LORD, like the land of Egypt, toward Zoar. (This was before the LORD destroyed Sodom and Gomorrah.) 11So Lot chose for himself the whole plain of the Jordan and set out toward the east. The two men parted company: 12Abram lived in the land of Canaan, while Lot lived among the cities of the plain and pitched his tents near Sodom. 13Now the people of Sodom were wicked and were sinning greatly against the LORD.

14The LORD said to Abram after Lot had parted from him, "Look around from where you are, to the north and south, to the east and west. 15All the land that you see I will give to you and your offspring[b] forever. 16I will make your offspring like the dust of the earth, so that if anyone could count the dust, then your offspring could be counted. 17Go, walk through the length and breadth of the land, for I am giving it to you."

18So Abram went to live near the great trees of Mamre at Hebron, where he pitched his tents. There he built an altar to the LORD.

---

[a] 7 Or *seed*   [b] 15 Or *seed*; also in verse 16

Abram Rescues Lot

14 At the time when Amraphel was king of Shinar,[a] Arioch king of Ellasar, Kedorlaomer king of Elam and Tidal king of Goyim, [2]these kings went to war against Bera king of Sodom, Birsha king of Gomorrah, Shinab king of Admah, Shemeber king of Zeboyim, and the king of Bela (that is, Zoar). [3]All these latter kings joined forces in the Valley of Siddim (that is, the Dead Sea Valley). [4]For twelve years they had been subject to Kedorlaomer, but in the thirteenth year they rebelled.

[5]In the fourteenth year, Kedorlaomer and the kings allied with him went out and defeated the Rephaites in Ashteroth Karnaim, the Zuzites in Ham, the Emites in Shaveh Kiriathaim [6]and the Horites in the hill country of Seir, as far as El Paran near the desert. [7]Then they turned back and went to En Mishpat (that is, Kadesh), and they conquered the whole territory of the Amalekites, as well as the Amorites who were living in Hazezon Tamar.

[8]Then the king of Sodom, the king of Gomorrah, the king of Admah, the king of Zeboyim and the king of Bela (that is, Zoar) marched out and drew up their battle lines in the Valley of Siddim [9]against Kedorlaomer king of Elam, Tidal king of Goyim, Amraphel king of Shinar and Arioch king of Ellasar—four kings against five. [10]Now the Valley of Siddim was full of tar pits, and when the kings of Sodom and Gomorrah fled, some of the men fell into them and the rest fled to the hills. [11]The four kings seized all the goods of Sodom and Gomorrah and all their food; then they went away. [12]They also carried off Abram's nephew Lot and his possessions, since he was living in Sodom.

[13]A man who had escaped came and reported this to Abram the Hebrew. Now Abram was living near the great trees of Mamre the Amorite, a brother[b] of Eshkol and Aner, all of whom were allied with Abram. [14]When Abram heard that his relative had been taken captive, he called out the 318 trained men born in his household and went in pursuit as far as Dan. [15]During the night Abram divided his men to attack them and he routed them, pursuing them as far as Hobah, north of Damascus. [16]He recovered all the goods and brought back his relative Lot and his possessions, together with the women and the other people.

[17]After Abram returned from defeating Kedorlaomer and the kings allied with him, the king of Sodom came out to meet him in the Valley of Shaveh (that is, the King's Valley).

[18]Then Melchizedek king of Salem brought out bread and wine. He was priest of God Most High, [19]and he blessed Abram, saying,

> "Blessed be Abram by God Most High,
> Creator of heaven and earth.
> [20]And praise be to God Most High,
> who delivered your enemies into your hand."

Then Abram gave him a tenth of everything.

[21]The king of Sodom said to Abram, "Give me the people and keep the goods for yourself."

[22]But Abram said to the king of Sodom, "With raised hand I have sworn an oath to the LORD, God Most High, Creator of heaven and earth, [23]that I will accept nothing belonging to you, not even a thread or the thong of a sandal, so that you will never be able to say, 'I made Abram rich.' [24]I will accept nothing but what my men have eaten and the share that belongs to the men who went with me—to Aner, Eshkol and Mamre. Let them have their share."

God's Covenant With Abram

15 After this, the word of the LORD came to Abram in a vision:

> "Do not be afraid, Abram.
> I am your shield,[c]
> your very great reward.[d]"

---

[a] 1 That is, Babylonia; also in verse 9 [b] 13 Or *a relative;* or *an ally* [c] 1 Or *sovereign*
[d] 1 Or *shield; / your reward will be very great*

2But Abram said, "Sovereign LORD, what can you give me since I remain childless and the one who will inherit[a] my estate is Eliezer of Damascus?" 3And Abram said, "You have given me no children; so a servant in my household will be my heir."

4Then the word of the LORD came to him: "This man will not be your heir, but a son coming from your own body will be your heir." 5He took him outside and said, "Look up at the heavens and count the stars—if indeed you can count them." Then he said to him, "So shall your offspring[b] be."

6Abram believed the LORD, and he credited it to him as righteousness.

7He also said to him, "I am the LORD, who brought you out of Ur of the Chaldeans to give you this land to take possession of it."

8But Abram said, "Sovereign LORD, how can I know that I will gain possession of it?"

9So the LORD said to him, "Bring me a heifer, a goat and a ram, each three years old, along with a dove and a young pigeon."

10Abram brought all these to him, cut them in two and arranged the halves opposite each other; the birds, however, he did not cut in half. 11Then birds of prey came down on the carcasses, but Abram drove them away.

12As the sun was setting, Abram fell into a deep sleep, and a thick and dreadful darkness came over him. 13Then the LORD said to him, "Know for certain that for four hundred years your descendants will be strangers in a country not their own and that they will be enslaved and mistreated there. 14But I will punish the nation they serve as slaves, and afterward they will come out with great possessions. 15You, however, will go to your ancestors in peace and be buried at a good old age. 16In the fourth generation your descendants will come back here, for the sin of the Amorites has not yet reached its full measure."

17When the sun had set and darkness had fallen, a smoking firepot with a blazing torch appeared and passed between the pieces. 18On that day the LORD made a covenant with Abram and said, "To your descendants I give this land, from the Wadi[c] of Egypt to the great river, the Euphrates— 19the land of the Kenites, Kenizzites, Kadmonites, 20Hittites, Perizzites, Rephaites, 21Amorites, Canaanites, Girgashites and Jebusites."

Hagar and Ishmael

16 Now Sarai, Abram's wife, had borne him no children. But she had an Egyptian servant named Hagar; 2so she said to Abram, "The LORD has kept me from having children. Go, sleep with my servant; perhaps I can build a family through her."

Abram agreed to what Sarai said. 3So after Abram had been living in Canaan ten years, Sarai his wife took her Egyptian servant Hagar and gave her to her husband to be his wife. 4He slept with Hagar, and she conceived.

When she knew she was pregnant, she began to despise her mistress. 5Then Sarai said to Abram, "You are responsible for the wrong I am suffering. I put my servant in your arms,

Discovering God

15:5–6 // Life with God. When Abram looked up at the night sky, he remembered and believed God's promise to bless him with as many descendants as the stars he saw. Abram and Sarai had no children, and they were quite old. Abram could only base his assurance on God's ability to do the miraculous.

That's a good definition of faith. It's trusting in God's promises even though they may look impossible. It's not belief *in spite of* the facts; it's belief that must go *beyond* the facts.

And notice God's response. Abram wasn't a perfect man (see chapter 12, verses 10–20 [page 19] for an example); he needed forgiveness and a right standing with God, just as each one of us does. Abram's faith—his trust in God—gave him that standing.

The same is true for you today. As you seek God, you'll do well to follow Abram's example and trust God as best you can to lead you step by step. In the end you'll find that his promises are trustworthy, and that true faith has definite rewards.

[a] 2 The meaning of the Hebrew for this phrase is uncertain. [b] 5 Or *seed.* [c] 18 Or *river*

and now that she knows she is pregnant, she despises me. May the LORD judge between you
and me."
6"Your servant is in your hands," Abram said. "Do with her whatever you think best."
Then Sarai mistreated Hagar; so she fled from her.
7The angel of the LORD found Hagar near a spring in the desert; it was the spring that is
beside the road to Shur. 8And he said, "Hagar, servant of Sarai, where have you come from,
and where are you going?"
"I'm running away from my mistress Sarai," she answered.
9Then the angel of the LORD told her, "Go back to your mistress and submit to her." 10The
angel added, "I will increase your descendants so much that they will be too numerous to
count."
11The angel of the LORD also said to her:

"You are now pregnant
  and you will give birth to a son.
You shall name him Ishmael,[a]
  for the LORD has heard of your misery.
12He will be a wild donkey of a man;
  his hand will be against everyone
  and everyone's hand against him,
and he will live in hostility
  toward[b] all his brothers."

13She gave this name to the LORD who spoke to her: "You are the God who sees me," for
she said, "I have now seen[c] the One who sees me." 14That is why the well was called Beer
Lahai Roi[d]; it is still there, between Kadesh and Bered.
15So Hagar bore Abram a son, and Abram gave the name Ishmael to the son she had
borne. 16Abram was eighty-six years old when Hagar bore him Ishmael.

The Covenant of Circumcision

17 When Abram was ninety-nine years old, the LORD appeared to him and said, "I
am God Almighty[e]; walk before me faithfully and be blameless. 2Then I will make
my covenant between me and you and will greatly increase your numbers."
3Abram fell facedown, and God said to him, 4"As for me, this is my covenant with you:
You will be the father of many nations. 5No longer will you be called Abram[f]; your name
will be Abraham,[g] for I have made you a father of many nations. 6I will make you very fruit-
ful; I will make nations of you, and kings will come from you. 7I will establish my covenant
as an everlasting covenant between me and you and your descendants after you for the
generations to come, to be your God and the God of your descendants after you. 8The whole
land of Canaan, where you now reside as a foreigner, I will give as an everlasting posses-
sion to you and your descendants after you; and I will be their God."
9Then God said to Abraham, "As for you, you must keep my covenant, you and your de-
scendants after you for the generations to come. 10This is my covenant with you and your
descendants after you, the covenant you are to keep: Every male among you shall be cir-
cumcised. 11You are to undergo circumcision, and it will be the sign of the covenant be-
tween me and you. 12For the generations to come every male among you who is eight days
old must be circumcised, including those born in your household or bought with money
from a foreigner—those who are not your offspring. 13Whether born in your household or
bought with your money, they must be circumcised. My covenant in your flesh is to be an
everlasting covenant. 14Any uncircumcised male, who has not been circumcised in the
flesh, will be cut off from his people; he has broken my covenant."
15God also said to Abraham, "As for Sarai your wife, you are no longer to call her Sarai;
her name will be Sarah. 16I will bless her and will surely give you a son by her. I will bless
her so that she will be the mother of nations; kings of peoples will come from her."
17Abraham fell facedown; he laughed and said to himself, "Will a son be born to a man

---

[a] 11 *Ishmael* means *God hears.* [b] 12 Or *live to the east / of* [c] 13 Or *seen the back of* [d] 14 *Beer Lahai Roi* means *well of the Living One who sees me.* [e] 1 Hebrew *El-Shaddai* [f] 5 *Abram* means *exalted father.* [g] 5 *Abraham* probably means *father of many.*

a hundred years old? Will Sarah bear a child at the age of ninety?" 18And Abraham said to
God, "If only Ishmael might live under your blessing!"

19Then God said, "Yes, but your wife Sarah will bear you a son, and you will call him
Isaac.[a] I will establish my covenant with him as an everlasting covenant for his descen-
dants after him. 20And as for Ishmael, I have heard you: I will surely bless him; I will make
him fruitful and will greatly increase his numbers. He will be the father of twelve rulers,
and I will make him into a great nation. 21But my covenant I will establish with Isaac, whom
Sarah will bear to you by this time next year." 22When he had finished speaking with Abra-
ham, God went up from him.

23On that very day Abraham took his son Ishmael and all those born in his household or
bought with his money, every male in his household, and circumcised them, as God told
him. 24Abraham was ninety-nine years old when he was circumcised, 25and his son Ishma-
el was thirteen; 26Abraham and his son Ishmael were both circumcised on that same day.
27And every male in Abraham's household, including those born in his household or bought
from a foreigner, was circumcised with him.

The Three Visitors

18 The LORD appeared to Abraham near the great trees of Mamre while he was sit-
ting at the entrance to his tent in the heat of the day. 2Abraham looked up and
saw three men standing nearby. When he saw them, he hurried from the en-
trance of his tent to meet them and bowed low to the ground.

3He said, "If I have found favor in your eyes, my lord,[b] do not pass your servant by. 4Let
a little water be brought, and then you may all wash your feet and rest under this tree. 5Let
me get you something to eat, so you can be refreshed and then go on your way—now that
you have come to your servant."

"Very well," they answered, "do as you say."

6So Abraham hurried into the tent to Sarah. "Quick," he said, "get three seahs[c] of the fin-
est flour and knead it and bake some bread."

7Then he ran to the herd and selected a choice, tender calf and gave it to a servant, who
hurried to prepare it. 8He then brought some curds and milk and the calf that had been
prepared, and set these before them. While they ate, he stood near them under a tree.

9"Where is your wife Sarah?" they asked him.

"There, in the tent," he said.

10Then the LORD[d] said, "I will surely return to you about this time next year, and Sarah
your wife will have a son."

Addressing Questions

18:1–15 // God. This unusual meeting between Abraham and three men is actually a divine encounter in which God takes on human form. On rare occasions in the Old Testament, God appears in some physical way to get his point across. (This kind of communication culminated 2000 years later when Jesus of Nazareth was born; one of his titles was "Immanuel," which means "God with us.")

Perhaps you're thinking that you'd have no problem believing in God if he were to appear to you miraculously. But neither Abraham nor Sarah viewed this encounter as a summit meeting with God. As a matter of fact, Sarah was quick with a doubter's laugh (as Abraham had been; see Genesis 17, verse 17 [page 22]) and even lied right to God's face.

Be cautious of the unusual or bizarre in the spiritual realm. Faith that is built primarily on such infrequent "happenings" doesn't have a very solid foundation. God certainly can and sometimes will do unexpected things that will affect you personally. But as you seek out God's direction in your life, you'll also discover him at work in the everyday occurrences. And it's the perception of God's hand in everything you do that provides the firmest foundation for building up your faith.

[a] *19* *Isaac* means *he laughs.* [b] *3* Or *eyes, Lord* [c] *6* That is, probably about 36 pounds or about 16 kilograms [d] *10* Hebrew *Then he*

Now Sarah was listening at the entrance to the tent, which was behind him. 11Abraham and Sarah were already very old, and Sarah was past the age of childbearing. 12So Sarah laughed to herself as she thought, "After I am worn out and my lord is old, will I now have this pleasure?"

13Then the LORD said to Abraham, "Why did Sarah laugh and say, 'Will I really have a child, now that I am old?' 14Is anything too hard for the LORD? I will return to you at the appointed time next year and Sarah will have a son."

15Sarah was afraid, so she lied and said, "I did not laugh."

But he said, "Yes, you did laugh."

Abraham Pleads for Sodom

16When the men got up to leave, they looked down toward Sodom, and Abraham walked along with them to see them on their way. 17Then the LORD said, "Shall I hide from Abraham what I am about to do? 18Abraham will surely become a great and powerful nation, and all nations on earth will be blessed through him.[a] 19For I have chosen him, so that he will direct his children and his household after him to keep the way of the LORD by doing what is right and just, so that the LORD will bring about for Abraham what he has promised him."

20Then the LORD said, "The outcry against Sodom and Gomorrah is so great and their sin so grievous 21that I will go down and see if what they have done is as bad as the outcry that has reached me. If not, I will know."

22The men turned away and went toward Sodom, but Abraham remained standing before the LORD.[b] 23Then Abraham approached him and said: "Will you sweep away the righteous with the wicked? 24What if there are fifty righteous people in the city? Will you really sweep it away and not spare[c] the place for the sake of the fifty righteous people in it? 25Far be it from you to do such a thing—to kill the righteous with the wicked, treating the righteous and the wicked alike. Far be it from you! Will not the Judge of all the earth do right?"

26The LORD said, "If I find fifty righteous people in the city of Sodom, I will spare the whole place for their sake."

27Then Abraham spoke up again: "Now that I have been so bold as to speak to the Lord, though I am nothing but dust and ashes, 28what if the number of the righteous is five less than fifty? Will you destroy the whole city for lack of five people?"

"If I find forty-five there," he said, "I will not destroy it."

29Once again he spoke to him, "What if only forty are found there?"

He said, "For the sake of forty, I will not do it."

30Then he said, "May the Lord not be angry, but let me speak. What if only thirty can be found there?"

He answered, "I will not do it if I find thirty there."

31Abraham said, "Now that I have been so bold as to speak to the Lord, what if only twenty can be found there?"

He said, "For the sake of twenty, I will not destroy it."

32Then he said, "May the Lord not be angry, but let me speak just once more. What if only ten can be found there?"

He answered, "For the sake of ten, I will not destroy it."

33When the LORD had finished speaking with Abraham, he left, and Abraham returned home.

Sodom and Gomorrah Destroyed

19 The two angels arrived at Sodom in the evening, and Lot was sitting in the gateway of the city. When he saw them, he got up to meet them and bowed down with his face to the ground. 2"My lords," he said, "please turn aside to your servant's house. You can wash your feet and spend the night and then go on your way early in the morning."

"No," they answered, "we will spend the night in the square."

3But he insisted so strongly that they did go with him and entered his house. He prepared a meal for them, baking bread without yeast, and they ate. 4Before they had gone to

---

[a] 18 Or *will use his name in blessings* (see Gen. 48:20) [b] 22 Masoretic Text; an ancient Hebrew scribal tradition *but the LORD remained standing before Abraham* [c] 24 Or *forgive*; also in verse 26

bed, all the men from every part of the city of Sodom—both young and old—surrounded
the house. 5They called to Lot, "Where are the men who came to you tonight? Bring them
out to us so that we can have sex with them."
6Lot went outside to meet them and shut the door behind him 7and said, "No, my
friends. Don't do this wicked thing. 8Look, I have two daughters who have never slept with
a man. Let me bring them out to you, and you can do what you like with them. But don't
do anything to these men, for they have come under the protection of my roof."
9"Get out of our way," they replied. "This fellow came here as a foreigner, and now he
wants to play the judge! We'll treat you worse than them." They kept bringing pressure on
Lot and moved forward to break down the door.
10But the men inside reached out and pulled Lot back into the house and shut the door.
11Then they struck the men who were at the door of the house, young and old, with blind-
ness so that they could not find the door.
12The two men said to Lot, "Do you have anyone else here—sons-in-law, sons or daugh-
ters, or anyone else in the city who belongs to you? Get them out of here, 13because we are
going to destroy this place. The outcry to the LORD against its people is so great that he has
sent us to destroy it."
14So Lot went out and spoke to his sons-in-law, who were pledged to marry[a] his daugh-
ters. He said, "Hurry and get out of this place, because the LORD is about to destroy the
city!" But his sons-in-law thought he was joking.
15With the coming of dawn, the angels urged Lot, saying, "Hurry! Take your wife and
your two daughters who are here, or you will be swept away when the city is punished."
16When he hesitated, the men grasped his hand and the hands of his wife and of his two
daughters and led them safely out of the city, for the LORD was merciful to them. 17As soon
as they had brought them out, one of them said, "Flee for your lives! Don't look back, and
don't stop anywhere in the plain! Flee to the mountains or you will be swept away!"
18But Lot said to them, "No, my lords,[b] please! 19Your[c] servant has found favor in your[c]
eyes, and you[c] have shown great kindness to me in sparing my life. But I can't flee to the
mountains; this disaster will overtake me, and I'll die. 20Look, here is a town near enough
to run to, and it is small. Let me flee to it—it is very small, isn't it? Then my life will be
spared."
21He said to him, "Very well, I will grant this request too; I will not overthrow the town
you speak of. 22But flee there quickly, because I cannot do anything until you reach it."
(That is why the town was called Zoar.[d])
23By the time Lot reached Zoar, the sun had risen over the land. 24Then the LORD rained
down burning sulfur on Sodom and Gomorrah—from the LORD out of the heavens. 25Thus
he overthrew those cities and the entire plain, destroying all those living in the cities—
and also the vegetation in the land. 26But Lot's wife looked back, and she became a pillar
of salt.

Strengthening Relationships

19:4–8 // Social. Most people who've heard about Sodom and Gomorrah associate those places with unrestrained lust. In this part of the story, the men of Sodom intended to commit homosexual rape. Truly this passage demonstrates humanity at its worst, with unbridled appetites directing human behavior.

Note how this wickedness affected Lot and his family. With such overt displays of immorality, their moral sensibilities had dulled. Was Lot all that much better for offering his daughters to these men in place of the human-like angels who were visiting? His behavior is reprehensible—a telling story of how Lot slowly conformed to the company he kept. In the end, it's hard for readers to tell who "the good guy" is in this story.

What's the lesson in this passage? Choose your associates carefully. You could easily become like them.

---

[a] *14* Or *were married to* [b] *18* Or *No, Lord;* or *No, my lord* [c] *19* The Hebrew is singular.
[d] *22* *Zoar* means *small.*

[27]Early the next morning Abraham got up and returned to the place where he had stood
before the LORD. [28]He looked down toward Sodom and Gomorrah, toward all the land of the
plain, and he saw dense smoke rising from the land, like smoke from a furnace.
[29]So when God destroyed the cities of the plain, he remembered Abraham, and he
brought Lot out of the catastrophe that overthrew the cities where Lot had lived.

Lot and His Daughters

[30]Lot and his two daughters left Zoar and settled in the mountains, for he was afraid to
stay in Zoar. He and his two daughters lived in a cave. [31]One day the older daughter said
to the younger, "Our father is old, and there is no man around here to give us children—
as is the custom all over the earth. [32]Let's get our father to drink wine and then sleep with
him and preserve our family line through our father."
[33]That night they got their father to drink wine, and the older daughter went in and slept
with him. He was not aware of it when she lay down or when she got up.
[34]The next day the older daughter said to the younger, "Last night I slept with my fa-
ther. Let's get him to drink wine again tonight, and you go in and sleep with him so we
can preserve our family line through our father." [35]So they got their father to drink wine that
night also, and the younger daughter went in and slept with him. Again he was not aware
of it when she lay down or when she got up.
[36]So both of Lot's daughters became pregnant by their father. [37]The older daughter had
a son, and she named him Moab[a]; he is the father of the Moabites of today. [38]The younger
daughter also had a son, and she named him Ben-Ammi[b]; he is the father of the Ammon-
ites[c] of today.

Abraham and Abimelek

20 Now Abraham moved on from there into the region of the Negev and lived be-
tween Kadesh and Shur. For a while he stayed in Gerar, [2]and there Abraham
said of his wife Sarah, "She is my sister." Then Abimelek king of Gerar sent for
Sarah and took her.
[3]But God came to Abimelek in a dream one night and said to him, "You are as good as
dead because of the woman you have taken; she is a married woman."
[4]Now Abimelek had not gone near her, so he said, "Lord, will you destroy an innocent
nation? [5]Did he not say to me, 'She is my sister,' and didn't she also say, 'He is my broth-
er'? I have done this with a clear conscience and clean hands."
[6]Then God said to him in the dream, "Yes, I know you did this with a clear conscience,
and so I have kept you from sinning against me. That is why I did not let you touch her.
[7]Now return the man's wife, for he is a prophet, and he will pray for you and you will live.
But if you do not return her, you may be sure that you and all who belong to you will die."
[8]Early the next morning Abimelek summoned all his officials, and when he told them
all that had happened, they were very much afraid. [9]Then Abimelek called Abraham in and
said, "What have you done to us? How have I wronged you that you have brought such
great guilt upon me and my kingdom? You have done things to me that should never be
done." [10]And Abimelek asked Abraham, "What was your reason for doing this?"
[11]Abraham replied, "I said to myself, 'There is surely no fear of God in this place, and
they will kill me because of my wife.' [12]Besides, she really is my sister, the daughter of my
father though not of my mother; and she became my wife. [13]And when God had me wan-
der from my father's household, I said to her, 'This is how you can show your love to me:
Everywhere we go, say of me, "He is my brother." ' "
[14]Then Abimelek brought sheep and cattle and male and female slaves and gave them
to Abraham, and he returned Sarah his wife to him. [15]And Abimelek said, "My land is be-
fore you; live wherever you like."
[16]To Sarah he said, "I am giving your brother a thousand shekels[d] of silver. This is to cov-
er the offense against you before all who are with you; you are completely vindicated."

---

[a] 37 *Moab* sounds like the Hebrew for *from father.* [b] 38 *Ben-Ammi* means *son of my father's people.* [c] 38 Hebrew *Bene-Ammon* [d] 16 That is, about 25 pounds or about 11.5 kilograms

17 Then Abraham prayed to God, and God healed Abimelek, his wife and his female slaves
so they could have children again, 18 for the LORD had kept all the women in Abimelek's
household from conceiving because of Abraham's wife Sarah.

The Birth of Isaac

21 Now the LORD was gracious to Sarah as he had said, and the LORD did for Sarah
what he had promised. 2 Sarah became pregnant and bore a son to Abraham in his
old age, at the very time God had promised him. 3 Abraham gave the name Isaac[a]
to the son Sarah bore him. 4 When his son Isaac was eight days old, Abraham circumcised
him, as God commanded him. 5 Abraham was a hundred years old when his son Isaac was
born to him.

6 Sarah said, "God has brought me laughter, and everyone who hears about this will laugh
with me." 7 And she added, "Who would have said to Abraham that Sarah would nurse chil-
dren? Yet I have borne him a son in his old age."

Hagar and Ishmael Sent Away

8 The child grew and was weaned, and on the day Isaac was weaned Abraham held a
great feast. 9 But Sarah saw that the son whom Hagar the Egyptian had borne to Abraham
was mocking, 10 and she said to Abraham, "Get rid of that slave woman and her son, for
that slave woman's son will never share in the inheritance with my son Isaac."

11 The matter distressed Abraham greatly because it concerned his son. 12 But God said to
him, "Do not be so distressed about the boy and your servant. Listen to whatever Sarah
tells you, because it is through Isaac that your offspring[b] will be reckoned. 13 I will make
the son of the servant into a nation also, because he is your offspring."

14 Early the next morning Abraham took some food and a skin of water and gave them
to Hagar. He set them on her shoulders and then sent her off with the boy. She went on
her way and wandered in the Desert of Beersheba.

15 When the water in the skin was gone, she put the boy under one of the bushes. 16 Then
she went off and sat down about a bowshot away, for she thought, "I cannot watch the boy
die." And as she sat there, she[c] began to sob.

17 God heard the boy crying, and the angel of God called to Hagar from heaven and said
to her, "What is the matter, Hagar? Do not be afraid; God has heard the boy crying as he
lies there. 18 Lift the boy up and take him by the hand, for I will make him into a great na-
tion."

19 Then God opened her eyes and she saw a well of water. So she went and filled the skin
with water and gave the boy a drink.

20 God was with the boy as he grew up. He lived in the desert and became an archer.
21 While he was living in the Desert of Paran, his mother got a wife for him from Egypt.

The Treaty at Beersheba

22 At that time Abimelek and Phicol the commander of his forces said to Abraham, "God
is with you in everything you do. 23 Now swear to me here before God that you will not deal
falsely with me or my children or my descendants. Show to me and the country where you
now reside as a foreigner the same kindness I have shown to you."

24 Abraham said, "I swear it."

25 Then Abraham complained to Abimelek about a well of water that Abimelek's servants
had seized. 26 But Abimelek said, "I don't know who has done this. You did not tell me, and
I heard about it only today."

27 So Abraham brought sheep and cattle and gave them to Abimelek, and the two men
made a treaty. 28 Abraham set apart seven ewe lambs from the flock, 29 and Abimelek asked
Abraham, "What is the meaning of these seven ewe lambs you have set apart by them-
selves?"

30 He replied, "Accept these seven lambs from my hand as a witness that I dug this well."

31 So that place was called Beersheba,[d] because the two men swore an oath there.

---

[a] 3 *Isaac* means *he laughs.* [b] 12 Or *seed* [c] 16 Hebrew; Septuagint *the child* [d] 31 *Beersheba* can mean *well of seven* or *well of the oath.*

[32]After the treaty had been made at Beersheba, Abimelek and Phicol the commander of
his forces returned to the land of the Philistines. [33]Abraham planted a tamarisk tree in Be-
ersheba, and there he called on the name of the LORD, the Eternal God. [34]And Abraham
stayed in the land of the Philistines for a long time.

Abraham Tested

22 Some time later God tested Abraham. He said to him, "Abraham!"
"Here I am," he replied.
[2]Then God said, "Take your son, your only son, whom you love—Isaac—and go
to the region of Moriah. Sacrifice him there as a burnt offering on a mountain I will show
you."
[3]Early the next morning Abraham got up and loaded his donkey. He took with him two
of his servants and his son Isaac. When he had cut enough wood for the burnt offering, he
set out for the place God had told him about. [4]On the third day Abraham looked up and saw
the place in the distance. [5]He said to his servants, "Stay here with the donkey while I and
the boy go over there. We will worship and then we will come back to you."
[6]Abraham took the wood for the burnt offering and placed it on his son Isaac, and he
himself carried the fire and the knife. As the two of them went on together, [7]Isaac spoke
up and said to his father Abraham, "Father?"
"Yes, my son?" Abraham replied.
"The fire and wood are here," Isaac said, "but where is the lamb for the burnt offering?"
[8]Abraham answered, "God himself will provide the lamb for the burnt offering, my son."
And the two of them went on together.
[9]When they reached the place God had told him about, Abraham built an altar there
and arranged the wood on it. He bound his son Isaac and laid him on the altar, on top of
the wood. [10]Then he reached out his hand and took the knife to slay his son. [11]But the an-
gel of the LORD called out to him from heaven, "Abraham! Abraham!"
"Here I am," he replied.

Discovering God

22:1–2, 12–18 // Life with God. What is going on here? Why would God make Abraham wait years for his promised son, only to turn around and make this heart-wrenching request?

If all we knew of God was from a quick reading of these few verses, we'd be left with more questions than answers. But some important points emerge after closer examination that can help you understand who God is and what he wants to do in your life if you respond to him.

First, Abraham needed to be reminded that his son Isaac was a gift from God. Ultimately, everything we have belongs to God and must be held before him with an open hand.

Second, Abraham had God's promise that Isaac would have descendants. The current situation, however, appeared to contradict that assurance. So Abraham could either trust God in the midst of confusion or reject God because of unanswered questions. After decades of knowing God's character, of observing his love and kindness, and of being delivered from difficult situations, Abraham knew he could trust God with these new questions based on God's previous trustworthiness. The same holds true for us.

Third, much more was going on here than meets the eye. Had Abraham looked only at the short term, he might have taken Isaac and run away. But by obeying God, he gave us a picture of a time when another "only Son" would walk up a hill and lie down to die. That's what Jesus did for us. In that case, however, God didn't spare him—the knife fell, so to speak, when Jesus was crucified. Because of that sacrifice, we all can have new life.

Finally, as Abraham took his son back with him, he gave us a picture of Jesus' resurrection. In both instances a situation of death led to unexpected life.

It's not easy to embark on a life where God gets to be God. Times of testing will come. But let Abraham's example be yours. You can say as he did in verse 8, "God himself will provide."

12“Do not lay a hand on the boy,” he said. “Do not do anything to him. Now I know that
you fear God, because you have not withheld from me your son, your only son.”
13Abraham looked up and there in a thicket he saw a ram[a] caught by its horns. He went
over and took the ram and sacrificed it as a burnt offering instead of his son. 14So Abraham
called that place The LORD Will Provide. And to this day it is said, “On the mountain of the
LORD it will be provided.”
15The angel of the LORD called to Abraham from heaven a second time 16and said, “I
swear by myself, declares the LORD, that because you have done this and have not withheld
your son, your only son, 17I will surely bless you and make your descendants as numerous
as the stars in the sky and as the sand on the seashore. Your descendants will take posses-
sion of the cities of their enemies, 18and through your offspring[b] all nations on earth will
be blessed,[c] because you have obeyed me.”
19Then Abraham returned to his servants, and they set off together for Beersheba. And
Abraham stayed in Beersheba.

Nahor’s Sons

20Some time later Abraham was told, “Milkah is also a mother; she has borne sons to your
brother Nahor: 21Uz the firstborn, Buz his brother, Kemuel (the father of Aram), 22Kesed,
Hazo, Pildash, Jidlaph and Bethuel.” 23Bethuel became the father of Rebekah. Milkah bore
these eight sons to Abraham’s brother Nahor. 24His concubine, whose name was Reumah,
also had sons: Tebah, Gaham, Tahash and Maakah.

The Death of Sarah

23 Sarah lived to be a hundred and twenty-seven years old. 2She died at Kiriath
Arba (that is, Hebron) in the land of Canaan, and Abraham went to mourn for
Sarah and to weep over her.
3Then Abraham rose from beside his dead wife and spoke to the Hittites.[d] He said, 4“I
am a foreigner and stranger among you. Sell me some property for a burial site here so I
can bury my dead.”
5The Hittites replied to Abraham, 6“Sir, listen to us. You are a mighty prince among us.
Bury your dead in the choicest of our tombs. None of us will refuse you his tomb for bury-
ing your dead.”
7Then Abraham rose and bowed down before the people of the land, the Hittites. 8He
said to them, “If you are willing to let me bury my dead, then listen to me and intercede
with Ephron son of Zohar on my behalf 9so he will sell me the cave of Machpelah, which
belongs to him and is at the end of his field. Ask him to sell it to me for the full price as a
burial site among you.”
10Ephron the Hittite was sitting among his people and he replied to Abraham in the hear-
ing of all the Hittites who had come to the gate of his city. 11“No, my lord,” he said. “Lis-
ten to me; I give[e] you the field, and I give[e] you the cave that is in it. I give[e] it to you in the
presence of my people. Bury your dead.”
12Again Abraham bowed down before the people of the land 13and he said to Ephron in
their hearing, “Listen to me, if you will. I will pay the price of the field. Accept it from me
so I can bury my dead there.”
14Ephron answered Abraham, 15“Listen to me, my lord; the land is worth four hundred
shekels[f] of silver, but what is that between me and you? Bury your dead.”
16Abraham agreed to Ephron’s terms and weighed out for him the price he had named
in the hearing of the Hittites: four hundred shekels of silver, according to the weight cur-
rent among the merchants.

---

[a] *13* Many manuscripts of the Masoretic Text, Samaritan Pentateuch, Septuagint and Syriac; most manuscripts of the Masoretic Text *a ram behind ⌞him⌟* [b] *18* Or *seed* [c] *18* Or *and all nations on earth will use the name of your offspring in blessings* (see Gen. 48:20) [d] *3* Or *the descendants of Heth*; also in verses 5, 7, 10, 16, 18 and 20 [e] *11* Or *sell* [f] *15* That is, about 10 pounds or about 4.6 kilograms

[17]So Ephron's field in Machpelah near Mamre—both the field and the cave in it, and all the trees within the borders of the field—was deeded [18]to Abraham as his property in the presence of all the Hittites who had come to the gate of the city. [19]Afterward Abraham buried his wife Sarah in the cave in the field of Machpelah near Mamre (which is at Hebron) in the land of Canaan. [20]So the field and the cave in it were deeded to Abraham by the Hittites as a burial site.

Isaac and Rebekah

24 Abraham was now very old, and the LORD had blessed him in every way. [2]He said to the senior servant in his household, the one in charge of all that he had, "Put your hand under my thigh. [3]I want you to swear by the LORD, the God of heaven and the God of earth, that you will not get a wife for my son from the daughters of the Canaanites, among whom I am living, [4]but will go to my country and my own relatives and get a wife for my son Isaac."

[5]The servant asked him, "What if the woman is unwilling to come back with me to this land? Shall I then take your son back to the country you came from?"

[6]"Make sure that you do not take my son back there," Abraham said. [7]"The LORD, the God of heaven, who brought me out of my father's household and my native land and who spoke to me and promised me on oath, saying, 'To your offspring[a] I will give this land'—he will send his angel before you so that you can get a wife for my son from there. [8]If the woman is unwilling to come back with you, then you will be released from this oath of mine. Only do not take my son back there." [9]So the servant put his hand under the thigh of his master Abraham and swore an oath to him concerning this matter.

[10]Then the servant left, taking with him ten of his master's camels loaded with all kinds of good things from his master. He set out for Aram Naharaim[b] and made his way to the town of Nahor. [11]He had the camels kneel down near the well outside the town; it was toward evening, the time the women go out to draw water.

[12]Then he prayed, "LORD, God of my master Abraham, make me successful today, and show kindness to my master Abraham. [13]See, I am standing beside this spring, and the daughters of the townspeople are coming out to draw water. [14]May it be that when I say to a girl, 'Please let down your jar that I may have a drink,' and she says, 'Drink, and I'll water your camels too'—let her be the one you have chosen for your servant Isaac. By this I will know that you have shown kindness to my master."

[15]Before he had finished praying, Rebekah came out with her jar on her shoulder. She was the daughter of Bethuel son of Milkah, who was the wife of Abraham's brother Nahor. [16]The girl was very beautiful, a virgin; no man had ever slept with her. She went down to the spring, filled her jar and came up again.

Strengthening Relationships

24:3–4 // Marriage. The Bible doesn't endorse any one approach to finding a mate, but it does set forth a clear prerequisite—shared spiritual viewpoints. God's people are advised against marrying others who don't have the same desire to put God first in every area of life. When two people are first committed to following God's plan for their lives, they will experience the oneness and fulfillment God intended for the lifelong union of marriage.

If you're married but are having difficulties, could it be that some of them come from not sharing a common spiritual foundation? If you're contemplating marriage, realize that there may be heartache ahead if the two of you don't agree on what will be the final authority in your marriage before you say "I do."

God's purpose isn't to limit your choices—he wants to extend your joys. The best marriage counseling advice you can get is this: Work together to build your relationship on the solid ground of God and the teaching of the Bible.

[a] *7* Or *seed* [b] *10* That is, Northwest Mesopotamia

[17]The servant hurried to meet her and said, "Please give me a little water from your jar."

[18]"Drink, my lord," she said, and quickly lowered the jar to her hands and gave him a drink.

[19]After she had given him a drink, she said, "I'll draw water for your camels too, until they have had enough to drink." [20]So she quickly emptied her jar into the trough, ran back to the well to draw more water, and drew enough for all his camels. [21]Without saying a word, the man watched her closely to learn whether or not the LORD had made his journey successful.

[22]When the camels had finished drinking, the man took out a gold nose ring weighing a beka[a] and two gold bracelets weighing ten shekels.[b] [23]Then he asked, "Whose daughter are you? Please tell me, is there room in your father's house for us to spend the night?"

[24]She answered him, "I am the daughter of Bethuel, the son that Milkah bore to Nahor." [25]And she added, "We have plenty of straw and fodder, as well as room for you to spend the night."

[26]Then the man bowed down and worshiped the LORD, [27]saying, "Praise be to the LORD, the God of my master Abraham, who has not abandoned his kindness and faithfulness to my master. As for me, the LORD has led me on the journey to the house of my master's relatives."

[28]The girl ran and told her mother's household about these things. [29]Now Rebekah had a brother named Laban, and he hurried out to the man at the spring. [30]As soon as he had seen the nose ring, and the bracelets on his sister's arms, and had heard Rebekah tell what the man said to her, he went out to the man and found him standing by the camels near the spring. [31]"Come, you who are blessed by the LORD," he said. "Why are you standing out here? I have prepared the house and a place for the camels."

[32]So the man went to the house, and the camels were unloaded. Straw and fodder were brought for the camels, and water for him and his men to wash their feet. [33]Then food was set before him, but he said, "I will not eat until I have told you what I have to say."

"Then tell us," Laban said.

[34]So he said, "I am Abraham's servant. [35]The LORD has blessed my master abundantly, and he has become wealthy. He has given him sheep and cattle, silver and gold, male and female servants, and camels and donkeys. [36]My master's wife Sarah has borne him a son in her old age, and he has given him everything he owns. [37]And my master made me swear an oath, and said, 'You must not get a wife for my son from the daughters of the Canaanites, in whose land I live, [38]but go to my father's family and to my own clan, and get a wife for my son.'

[39]"Then I asked my master, 'What if the woman will not come back with me?'

[40]"He replied, 'The LORD, before whom I have walked faithfully, will send his angel with you and make your journey a success, so that you can get a wife for my son from my own clan and from my father's family. [41]Then, when you go to my clan, you will be released from my oath even if they refuse to give her to you—you will be released from my oath.'

[42]"When I came to the spring today, I said, 'LORD, God of my master Abraham, if you will, please grant success to the journey on which I have come. [43]See, I am standing beside this spring. If a young woman comes out to draw water and I say to her, "Please let me drink a little water from your jar," [44]and if she says to me, "Drink, and I'll draw water for your camels too," let her be the one the LORD has chosen for my master's son.'

[45]"Before I finished praying in my heart, Rebekah came out, with her jar on her shoulder. She went down to the spring and drew water, and I said to her, 'Please give me a drink.'

[46]"She quickly lowered her jar from her shoulder and said, 'Drink, and I'll water your camels too.' So I drank, and she watered the camels also.

[47]"I asked her, 'Whose daughter are you?'

"She said, 'The daughter of Bethuel son of Nahor, whom Milkah bore to him.'

"Then I put the ring in her nose and the bracelets on her arms, [48]and I bowed down and worshiped the LORD. I praised the LORD, the God of my master Abraham, who had led me

---

[a] *22* That is, about 1/5 ounce or about 5.7 grams [b] *22* That is, about 4 ounces or about 115 grams

on the right road to get the granddaughter of my master's brother for his son. 49Now if you
will show kindness and faithfulness to my master, tell me; and if not, tell me, so I may
know which way to turn."

50Laban and Bethuel answered, "This is from the LORD; we can say nothing to you one
way or the other. 51Here is Rebekah; take her and go, and let her become the wife of your
master's son, as the LORD has directed."

52When Abraham's servant heard what they said, he bowed down to the ground before
the LORD. 53Then the servant brought out gold and silver jewelry and articles of clothing
and gave them to Rebekah; he also gave costly gifts to her brother and to her mother.
54Then he and the men who were with him ate and drank and spent the night there.

When they got up the next morning, he said, "Send me on my way to my master."

55But her brother and her mother replied, "Let the girl remain with us ten days or so;
then you[a] may go."

56But he said to them, "Do not detain me, now that the LORD has granted success to my
journey. Send me on my way so I may go to my master."

57Then they said, "Let's call the girl and ask her about it." 58So they called Rebekah and
asked her, "Will you go with this man?"

"I will go," she said.

59So they sent their sister Rebekah on her way, along with her nurse and Abraham's ser-
vant and his men. 60And they blessed Rebekah and said to her,

"Our sister, may you increase
  to thousands upon thousands;
may your offspring possess
  the cities of their enemies."

61Then Rebekah and her attendants got ready and mounted their camels and went back
with the man. So the servant took Rebekah and left.

62Now Isaac had come from Beer Lahai Roi, for he was living in the Negev. 63He went
out to the field one evening to meditate,[b] and as he looked up, he saw camels approach-
ing. 64Rebekah also looked up and saw Isaac. She got down from her camel 65and asked
the servant, "Who is that man in the field coming to meet us?"

"He is my master," the servant answered. So she took her veil and covered herself.

66Then the servant told Isaac all he had done. 67Isaac brought her into the tent of his
mother Sarah, and he married Rebekah. So she became his wife, and he loved her; and
Isaac was comforted after his mother's death.

The Death of Abraham

25 Abraham had taken another wife, whose name was Keturah. 2She bore him Zim-
ran, Jokshan, Medan, Midian, Ishbak and Shuah. 3Jokshan was the father of She-
ba and Dedan; the descendants of Dedan were the Ashurites, the Letushites and
the Leummites. 4The sons of Midian were Ephah, Epher, Hanok, Abida and Eldaah. All
these were descendants of Keturah.

5Abraham left everything he owned to Isaac. 6But while he was still living, he gave gifts
to the sons of his concubines and sent them away from his son Isaac to the land of the
east.

7Abraham lived a hundred and seventy-five years. 8Then Abraham breathed his last and
died at a good old age, an old man and full of years; and he was gathered to his people. 9His
sons Isaac and Ishmael buried him in the cave of Machpelah near Mamre, in the field of
Ephron son of Zohar the Hittite, 10the field Abraham had bought from the Hittites.[c] There
Abraham was buried with his wife Sarah. 11After Abraham's death, God blessed his son
Isaac, who then lived near Beer Lahai Roi.

---

[a] *55* Or *she* [b] *63* The meaning of the Hebrew for this word is uncertain. [c] *10* Or *the descendants of Heth*

Ishmael's Sons

12This is the account of the family line of Abraham's son Ishmael, whom Sarah's ser-
vant, Hagar the Egyptian, bore to Abraham.

13These are the names of the sons of Ishmael, listed in the order of their birth: Nebaioth
the firstborn of Ishmael, Kedar, Adbeel, Mibsam, 14Mishma, Dumah, Massa, 15Hadad, Tema,
Jetur, Naphish and Kedemah. 16These were the sons of Ishmael, and these are the names
of the twelve tribal rulers according to their settlements and camps. 17Ishmael lived a hun-
dred and thirty-seven years. He breathed his last and died, and he was gathered to his peo-
ple. 18His descendants settled in the area from Havilah to Shur, near the eastern border of
Egypt, as you go toward Ashur. And they lived in hostility toward[a] all the tribes related to
them.

Jacob and Esau

19This is the account of the family line of Abraham's son Isaac.

Abraham became the father of Isaac, 20and Isaac was forty years old when he married
Rebekah daughter of Bethuel the Aramean from Paddan Aram[b] and sister of Laban the Ar-
amean.

21Isaac prayed to the LORD on behalf of his wife, because she was childless. The LORD
answered his prayer, and his wife Rebekah became pregnant. 22The babies jostled each
other within her, and she said, "Why is this happening to me?" So she went to inquire of
the LORD.

23The LORD said to her,

"Two nations are in your womb,
  and two peoples from within you will be separated;
one people will be stronger than the other,
  and the older will serve the younger."

24When the time came for her to give birth, there were twin boys in her womb. 25The
first to come out was red, and his whole body was like a hairy garment; so they named him
Esau.[c] 26After this, his brother came out, with his hand grasping Esau's heel; so he was
named Jacob.[d] Isaac was sixty years old when Rebekah gave birth to them.

27The boys grew up, and Esau became a skillful hunter, a man of the open country, while
Jacob was content to stay at home among the tents. 28Isaac, who had a taste for wild game,
loved Esau, but Rebekah loved Jacob.

29Once when Jacob was cooking some stew, Esau came in from the open country, fam-
ished. 30He said to Jacob, "Quick, let me have some of that red stew! I'm famished!" (That
is why he was also called Edom.[e])

31Jacob replied, "First sell me your birthright."

Addressing Questions

25:8 // Unseen Realities. The Bible doesn't try to prove the existence of life after death or of heaven or hell. The Scriptures simply assume that people live on after they die and that God has some sort of reward and punishment system.

The details of life after death unfold as the Scriptures unfold. But even here in the first book of the Bible we find a phrase that hints at this reality by telling us that Abraham was "gathered to his people." Physically, he was a long way off from the burial sites of his ancestors, so surely this cannot refer to actually laying his body among those of his extended family. The phrase "gathered to his people," however, does point to some sort of existence beyond this life. As you continue to look through this book, you may want to search out more clues to what the afterlife will be like.

---

[a] 18 Or *lived to the east of* [b] 20 That is, Northwest Mesopotamia [c] 25 *Esau* may mean *hairy*.
[d] 26 *Jacob* means *he grasps the heel*, a Hebrew idiom for *he deceives*. [e] 30 *Edom* means *red*.

32“Look, I am about to die,” Esau said. “What good is the birthright to me?”
33But Jacob said, “Swear to me first.” So he swore an oath to him, selling his birthright
to Jacob.
34Then Jacob gave Esau some bread and some lentil stew. He ate and drank, and then
got up and left.
So Esau despised his birthright.

Isaac and Abimelek

26 Now there was a famine in the land—besides the previous famine in Abraham’s
time—and Isaac went to Abimelek king of the Philistines in Gerar. 2The LORD ap-
peared to Isaac and said, “Do not go down to Egypt; live in the land where I tell
you to live. 3Stay in this land for a while, and I will be with you and will bless you. For to
you and your descendants I will give all these lands and will confirm the oath I swore to
your father Abraham. 4I will make your descendants as numerous as the stars in the sky and
will give them all these lands, and through your offspring[a] all nations on earth will be
blessed,[b] 5because Abraham obeyed me and did everything I required of him, keeping my
commands, my decrees and my instructions.” 6So Isaac stayed in Gerar.
7When the men of that place asked him about his wife, he said, “She is my sister,” be-
cause he was afraid to say, “She is my wife.” He thought, “The men of this place might kill
me on account of Rebekah, because she is beautiful.”
8When Isaac had been there a long time, Abimelek king of the Philistines looked down
from a window and saw Isaac caressing his wife Rebekah. 9So Abimelek summoned Isaac
and said, “She is really your wife! Why did you say, ‘She is my sister’?”
Isaac answered him, “Because I thought I might lose my life on account of her.”
10Then Abimelek said, “What is this you have done to us? One of the men might well
have slept with your wife, and you would have brought guilt upon us.”
11So Abimelek gave orders to all the people: “Anyone who harms this man or his wife
shall surely be put to death.”
12Isaac planted crops in that land and the same year reaped a hundredfold, because the
LORD blessed him. 13The man became rich, and his wealth continued to grow until he be-
came very wealthy. 14He had so many flocks and herds and servants that the Philistines
envied him. 15So all the wells that his father’s servants had dug in the time of his father
Abraham, the Philistines stopped up, filling them with earth.
16Then Abimelek said to Isaac, “Move away from us; you have become too powerful
for us.”
17So Isaac moved away from there and encamped in the Valley of Gerar, where he set-
tled. 18Isaac reopened the wells that had been dug in the time of his father Abraham, which
the Philistines had stopped up after Abraham died, and he gave them the same names his
father had given them.
19Isaac’s servants dug in the valley and discovered a well of fresh water there. 20But the
herders of Gerar quarreled with those of Isaac and said, “The water is ours!” So he named
the well Esek,[c] because they disputed with him. 21Then they dug another well, but they
quarreled over that one also; so he named it Sitnah.[d] 22He moved on from there and dug
another well, and no one quarreled over it. He named it Rehoboth,[e] saying, “Now the LORD
has given us room and we will flourish in the land.”
23From there he went up to Beersheba. 24That night the LORD appeared to him and said,
“I am the God of your father Abraham. Do not be afraid, for I am with you; I will bless you
and will increase the number of your descendants for the sake of my servant Abraham.”
25Isaac built an altar there and called on the name of the LORD. There he pitched his
tent, and there his servants dug a well.
26Meanwhile, Abimelek had come to him from Gerar, with Ahuzzath his personal advis-
er and Phicol the commander of his forces. 27Isaac asked them, “Why have you come to me,
since you were hostile to me and sent me away?”

---

[a] 4 Or *seed* [b] 4 Or *and all nations on earth will use the name of your offspring in blessings* (see Gen. 48:20) [c] *20 Esek* means *dispute.* [d] *21 Sitnah* means *opposition.* [e] *22 Rehoboth* means *room.*

28They answered, "We saw clearly that the LORD was with you; so we said, 'There ought
to be a sworn agreement between us'—between us and you. Let us make a treaty with you
29that you will do us no harm, just as we did not harm you but always treated you well and
sent you away peacefully. And now you are blessed by the LORD."
30Isaac then made a feast for them, and they ate and drank. 31Early the next morning
the men swore an oath to each other. Then Isaac sent them on their way, and they went
away peacefully.
32That day Isaac's servants came and told him about the well they had dug. They said,
"We've found water!" 33He called it Shibah,[a] and to this day the name of the town has been
Beersheba.[b]

Jacob Takes Esau's Blessing

34When Esau was forty years old, he married Judith daughter of Beeri the Hittite, and
also Basemath daughter of Elon the Hittite. 35They were a source of grief to Isaac and Re-
bekah.

27 When Isaac was old and his eyes were so weak that he could no longer see, he
called for Esau his older son and said to him, "My son."
"Here I am," he answered.
2Isaac said, "I am now an old man and don't know the day of my death. 3Now then, get
your equipment—your quiver and bow—and go out to the open country to hunt some wild
game for me. 4Prepare me the kind of tasty food I like and bring it to me to eat, so that I
may give you my blessing before I die."
5Now Rebekah was listening as Isaac spoke to his son Esau. When Esau left for the open
country to hunt game and bring it back, 6Rebekah said to her son Jacob, "Look, I overheard
your father say to your brother Esau, 7'Bring me some game and prepare me some tasty
food to eat, so that I may give you my blessing in the presence of the LORD before I die.'
8Now, my son, listen carefully and do what I tell you: 9Go out to the flock and bring me
two choice young goats, so I can prepare some tasty food for your father, just the way he
likes it. 10Then take it to your father to eat, so that he may give you his blessing before he
dies."
11Jacob said to Rebekah his mother, "But my brother Esau is a hairy man while I have
smooth skin. 12What if my father touches me? I would appear to be tricking him and would
bring down a curse on myself rather than a blessing."
13His mother said to him, "My son, let the curse fall on me. Just do what I say; go and
get them for me."
14So he went and got them and brought them to his mother, and she prepared some
tasty food, just the way his father liked it. 15Then Rebekah took the best clothes of Esau
her older son, which she had in the house, and put them on her younger son Jacob. 16She
also covered his hands and the smooth part of his neck with the goatskins. 17Then she hand-
ed to her son Jacob the tasty food and the bread she had made.
18He went to his father and said, "My father."
"Yes, my son," he answered. "Who is it?"
19Jacob said to his father, "I am Esau your firstborn. I have done as you told me. Please
sit up and eat some of my game, so that you may give me your blessing."
20Isaac asked his son, "How did you find it so quickly, my son?"
"The LORD your God gave me success," he replied.
21Then Isaac said to Jacob, "Come near so I can touch you, my son, to know whether
you really are my son Esau or not."
22Jacob went close to his father Isaac, who touched him and said, "The voice is the voice
of Jacob, but the hands are the hands of Esau." 23He did not recognize him, for his hands
were hairy like those of his brother Esau; so he proceeded to bless him. 24"Are you really
my son Esau?" he asked.
"I am," he replied.

---

[a] 33 *Shibah* can mean *oath* or *seven.* [b] 33 *Beersheba* can mean *well of the oath* or *well of seven.*

25 Then he said, "My son, bring me some of your game to eat, so that I may give you my
blessing."
Jacob brought it to him and he ate; and he brought some wine and he drank. 26 Then his
father Isaac said to him, "Come here, my son, and kiss me."
27 So he went to him and kissed him. When Isaac caught the smell of his clothes, he
blessed him and said,

"Ah, the smell of my son
  is like the smell of a field
  that the LORD has blessed.
28 May God give you of heaven's dew
  and of earth's richness—
  an abundance of grain and new wine.
29 May nations serve you
  and peoples bow down to you.
Be lord over your brothers,
  and may the sons of your mother bow down to you.
May those who curse you be cursed
  and those who bless you be blessed."

30 After Isaac finished blessing him, and Jacob had scarcely left his father's presence, his
brother Esau came in from hunting. 31 He too prepared some tasty food and brought it to
his father. Then he said to him, "My father, please sit up and eat some of my game, so that
you may give me your blessing."
32 His father Isaac asked him, "Who are you?"
"I am your son," he answered, "your firstborn, Esau."
33 Isaac trembled violently and said, "Who was it, then, that hunted game and brought
it to me? I ate it just before you came and I blessed him—and indeed he will be blessed!"
34 When Esau heard his father's words, he burst out with a loud and bitter cry and said
to his father, "Bless me—me too, my father!"
35 But he said, "Your brother came deceitfully and took your blessing."
36 Esau said, "Isn't he rightly named Jacob[a]? This is the second time he has taken advan-
tage of me: He took my birthright, and now he's taken my blessing!" Then he asked,
"Haven't you reserved any blessing for me?"
37 Isaac answered Esau, "I have made him lord over you and have made all his relatives
his servants, and I have sustained him with grain and new wine. So what can I possibly do
for you, my son?"
38 Esau said to his father, "Do you have only one blessing, my father? Bless me too, my
father!" Then Esau wept aloud.
39 His father Isaac answered him,

"Your dwelling will be
  away from the earth's richness,
  away from the dew of heaven above.
40 You will live by the sword
  and you will serve your brother.
But when you grow restless,
  you will throw his yoke
  from off your neck."

41 Esau held a grudge against Jacob because of the blessing his father had given him. He
said to himself, "The days of mourning for my father are near; then I will kill my brother
Jacob."
42 When Rebekah was told what her older son Esau had said, she sent for her younger son
Jacob and said to him, "Your brother Esau is planning to avenge himself by killing you.

---

[a] 36 *Jacob* means *he grasps the heel*, a Hebrew idiom for *he takes advantage of* or *he deceives*.

43 Now then, my son, do what I say: Flee at once to my brother Laban in Harran. 44 Stay with him for a while until your brother's fury subsides. 45 When your brother is no longer angry with you and forgets what you did to him, I'll send word for you to come back from there. Why should I lose both of you in one day?"

46 Then Rebekah said to Isaac, "I'm disgusted with living because of these Hittite women. If Jacob takes a wife from among the women of this land, from Hittite women like these, my life will not be worth living."

28 So Isaac called for Jacob and blessed him. Then he commanded him: "Do not marry a Canaanite woman. 2 Go at once to Paddan Aram,[a] to the house of your mother's father Bethuel. Take a wife for yourself there, from among the daughters of Laban, your mother's brother. 3 May God Almighty[b] bless you and make you fruitful and increase your numbers until you become a community of peoples. 4 May he give you and your descendants the blessing given to Abraham, so that you may take possession of the land where you now reside as a foreigner, the land God gave to Abraham." 5 Then Isaac sent Jacob on his way, and he went to Paddan Aram, to Laban son of Bethuel the Aramean, the brother of Rebekah, who was the mother of Jacob and Esau.

6 Now Esau learned that Isaac had blessed Jacob and had sent him to Paddan Aram to take a wife from there, and that when he blessed him he commanded him, "Do not marry a Canaanite woman," 7 and that Jacob had obeyed his father and mother and had gone to Paddan Aram. 8 Esau then realized how displeasing the Canaanite women were to his father Isaac; 9 so he went to Ishmael and married Mahalath, the sister of Nebaioth and daughter of Ishmael son of Abraham, in addition to the wives he already had.

Jacob's Dream at Bethel

10 Jacob left Beersheba and set out for Harran. 11 When he reached a certain place, he stopped for the night because the sun had set. Taking one of the stones there, he put it under his head and lay down to sleep. 12 He had a dream in which he saw a stairway[c] resting on the earth, with its top reaching to heaven, and the angels of God were ascending and descending on it. 13 There above it[d] stood the LORD, and he said: "I am the LORD, the God of your father Abraham and the God of Isaac. I will give you and your descendants the land on which you are lying. 14 Your descendants will be like the dust of the earth, and you will spread out to the west and to the east, to the north and to the south. All peoples on earth will be blessed through you and your offspring.[e] 15 I am with you and will watch over you wherever you go, and I will bring you back to this land. I will not leave you until I have done what I have promised you."

16 When Jacob awoke from his sleep, he thought, "Surely the LORD is in this place, and I was not aware of it." 17 He was afraid and said, "How awesome is this place! This is none other than the house of God; this is the gate of heaven."

18 Early the next morning Jacob took the stone he had placed under his head and set it up as a pillar and poured oil on top of it. 19 He called that place Bethel,[f] though the city used to be called Luz.

Knowing Yourself

28:10–15 // A New Identity. If our relationship with God were based on our own goodness, none of us would have a chance. Yet in this passage, as in our time, God is the seeker. He doesn't look for virtue; in fact, Jacob is just one example in a long line of far-from-perfect individuals that God sought out to do his work. After searching us out, God makes and fulfills promises—even when we do a bad job of keeping our commitments to him. He remakes us by his power—not because we're good, but because he is.

Centuries later, Jesus referred to this story as he described himself as the ladder between God and man (see John chapter 1, verse 51 [page 120]). He is the ultimate expression of God's seeking heart.

---

[a] 2 That is, Northwest Mesopotamia; also in verses 5, 6 and 7 [b] 3 Hebrew *El-Shaddai*
[c] 12 Or *ladder* [d] 13 Or *There beside him* [e] 14 Or *will use your name and the name of your offspring in blessings* (see Gen. 48:20) [f] 19 *Bethel* means *house of God.*

[20]Then Jacob made a vow, saying, "If God will be with me and will watch over me on this journey I am taking and will give me food to eat and clothes to wear [21]so that I return safely to my father's household, then the LORD[a] will be my God [22]and[b] this stone that I have set up as a pillar will be God's house, and of all that you give me I will give you a tenth."

Jacob Arrives in Paddan Aram

29 Then Jacob continued on his journey and came to the land of the eastern peoples. [2]There he saw a well in the open country, with three flocks of sheep lying near it because the flocks were watered from that well. The stone over the mouth of the well was large. [3]When all the flocks were gathered there, the shepherds would roll the stone away from the well's mouth and water the sheep. Then they would return the stone to its place over the mouth of the well.

[4]Jacob asked the shepherds, "My brothers, where are you from?"

"We're from Harran," they replied.

[5]He said to them, "Do you know Laban, Nahor's grandson?"

"Yes, we know him," they answered.

[6]Then Jacob asked them, "Is he well?"

"Yes, he is," they said, "and here comes his daughter Rachel with the sheep."

[7]"Look," he said, "the sun is still high; it is not time for the flocks to be gathered. Water the sheep and take them back to pasture."

[8]"We can't," they replied, "until all the flocks are gathered and the stone has been rolled away from the mouth of the well. Then we will water the sheep."

[9]While he was still talking with them, Rachel came with her father's sheep, for she was their shepherd. [10]When Jacob saw Rachel daughter of Laban, his mother's brother, and Laban's sheep, he went over and rolled the stone away from the mouth of the well and watered his uncle's sheep. [11]Then Jacob kissed Rachel and began to weep aloud. [12]He had told Rachel that he was a relative of her father and a son of Rebekah. So she ran and told her father.

[13]As soon as Laban heard the news about Jacob, his sister's son, he hurried to meet him. He embraced him and kissed him and brought him to his home, and there Jacob told him all these things. [14]Then Laban said to him, "You are my own flesh and blood."

Jacob Marries Leah and Rachel

After Jacob had stayed with him for a whole month, [15]Laban said to him, "Just because you are a relative of mine, should you work for me for nothing? Tell me what your wages should be."

[16]Now Laban had two daughters; the name of the older was Leah, and the name of the younger was Rachel. [17]Leah had weak[c] eyes, but Rachel had a lovely figure and was beautiful. [18]Jacob was in love with Rachel and said, "I'll work for you seven years in return for your younger daughter Rachel."

[19]Laban said, "It's better that I give her to you than to some other man. Stay here with me." [20]So Jacob served seven years to get Rachel, but they seemed like only a few days to him because of his love for her.

[21]Then Jacob said to Laban, "Give me my wife. My time is completed, and I want to make love to her."

[22]So Laban brought together all the people of the place and gave a feast. [23]But when evening came, he took his daughter Leah and brought her to Jacob, and Jacob made love to her. [24]And Laban gave his servant Zilpah to his daughter as her attendant.

[25]When morning came, there was Leah! So Jacob said to Laban, "What is this you have done to me? I served you for Rachel, didn't I? Why have you deceived me?"

[26]Laban replied, "It is not our custom here to give the younger daughter in marriage before the older one. [27]Finish this daughter's bridal week; then we will give you the younger one also, in return for another seven years of work."

---

[a] 20,21 Or *Since God . . . father's household, the* LORD [b] 21,22 Or *household, and the* LORD *will be my God,* [22]*then* [c] 17 Or *delicate*

28 And Jacob did so. He finished the week with Leah, and then Laban gave him his daugh-
ter Rachel to be his wife. 29 Laban gave his servant Bilhah to his daughter Rachel as her at-
tendant. 30 Jacob made love to Rachel also, and his love for Rachel was greater than his love
for Leah. And he worked for Laban another seven years.

Jacob's Children

31 When the LORD saw that Leah was not loved, he enabled her to conceive, but Rachel
remained childless. 32 Leah became pregnant and gave birth to a son. She named him Reu-
ben,[a] for she said, "It is because the LORD has seen my misery. Surely my husband will love
me now."

33 She conceived again, and when she gave birth to a son she said, "Because the LORD
heard that I am not loved, he gave me this one too." So she named him Simeon.[b]

34 Again she conceived, and when she gave birth to a son she said, "Now at last my husband
will become attached to me, because I have borne him three sons." So he was named Levi.[c]

35 She conceived again, and when she gave birth to a son she said, "This time I will praise
the LORD." So she named him Judah.[d] Then she stopped having children.

30 When Rachel saw that she was not bearing Jacob any children, she became jeal-
ous of her sister. So she said to Jacob, "Give me children, or I'll die!"
2 Jacob became angry with her and said, "Am I in the place of God, who has kept
you from having children?"

3 Then she said, "Here is Bilhah, my servant. Sleep with her so that she can bear children
for me and I too can build a family through her."

4 So she gave him her servant Bilhah as a wife. Jacob slept with her, 5 and she became
pregnant and bore him a son. 6 Then Rachel said, "God has vindicated me; he has listened
to my plea and given me a son." Because of this she named him Dan.[e]

7 Rachel's servant Bilhah conceived again and bore Jacob a second son. 8 Then Rachel
said, "I have had a great struggle with my sister, and I have won." So she named him Naph-
tali.[f]

9 When Leah saw that she had stopped having children, she took her servant Zilpah and
gave her to Jacob as a wife. 10 Leah's servant Zilpah bore Jacob a son. 11 Then Leah said,
"What good fortune!"[g] So she named him Gad.[h]

12 Leah's servant Zilpah bore Jacob a second son. 13 Then Leah said, "How happy I am!
The women will call me happy." So she named him Asher.[i]

14 During wheat harvest, Reuben went out into the fields and found some mandrake
plants, which he brought to his mother Leah. Rachel said to Leah, "Please give me some
of your son's mandrakes."

15 But she said to her, "Wasn't it enough that you took away my husband? Will you take
my son's mandrakes too?"

"Very well," Rachel said, "he can sleep with you tonight in return for your son's man-
drakes."

16 So when Jacob came in from the fields that evening, Leah went out to meet him. "You
must sleep with me," she said. "I have hired you with my son's mandrakes." So he slept
with her that night.

17 God listened to Leah, and she became pregnant and bore Jacob a fifth son. 18 Then Leah
said, "God has rewarded me for giving my servant to my husband." So she named him Is-
sachar.[j]

19 Leah conceived again and bore Jacob a sixth son. 20 Then Leah said, "God has present-
ed me with a precious gift. This time my husband will treat me with honor, because I have
borne him six sons." So she named him Zebulun.[k]

---

[a] 32 *Reuben* sounds like the Hebrew for *he has seen my misery;* the name means *see, a son.*
[b] 33 *Simeon* probably means *one who hears.* [c] 34 *Levi* sounds like and may be derived from the Hebrew for *attached.* [d] 35 *Judah* sounds like and may be derived from the Hebrew for *praise.*
[e] 6 *Dan* here means *he has vindicated.* [f] 8 *Naphtali* means *my struggle.* [g] 11 Or *"A troop is coming!"* [h] 11 *Gad* can mean *good fortune* or *a troop.* [i] 13 *Asher* means *happy.* [j] 18 *Issachar* sounds like the Hebrew for *reward.* [k] 20 *Zebulun* probably means *honor.*

[21]Some time later she gave birth to a daughter and named her Dinah.
[22]Then God remembered Rachel; he listened to her and enabled her to conceive. [23]She
became pregnant and gave birth to a son and said, "God has taken away my disgrace."
[24]She named him Joseph,[a] and said, "May the LORD add to me another son."

Jacob's Flocks Increase

[25]After Rachel gave birth to Joseph, Jacob said to Laban, "Send me on my way so I can
go back to my own homeland. [26]Give me my wives and children, for whom I have served
you, and I will be on my way. You know how much work I've done for you."
[27]But Laban said to him, "If I have found favor in your eyes, please stay. I have learned
by divination that the LORD has blessed me because of you." [28]He added, "Name your wag-
es, and I will pay them."
[29]Jacob said to him, "You know how I have worked for you and how your livestock has
fared under my care. [30]The little you had before I came has increased greatly, and the LORD
has blessed you wherever I have been. But now, when may I do something for my own
household?"
[31]"What shall I give you?" he asked.
"Don't give me anything," Jacob replied. "But if you will do this one thing for me, I will
go on tending your flocks and watching over them: [32]Let me go through all your flocks to-
day and remove from them every speckled or spotted sheep, every dark-colored lamb and
every spotted or speckled goat. They will be my wages. [33]And my honesty will testify for me
in the future, whenever you check on the wages you have paid me. Any goat in my posses-
sion that is not speckled or spotted, or any lamb that is not dark-colored, will be considered
stolen."
[34]"Agreed," said Laban. "Let it be as you have said." [35]That same day he removed all the
male goats that were streaked or spotted, and all the speckled or spotted female goats (all
that had white on them) and all the dark-colored lambs, and he placed them in the care of
his sons. [36]Then he put a three-day journey between himself and Jacob, while Jacob con-
tinued to tend the rest of Laban's flocks.
[37]Jacob, however, took fresh-cut branches from poplar, almond and plane trees and
made white stripes on them by peeling the bark and exposing the white inner wood of the
branches. [38]Then he placed the peeled branches in all the watering troughs, so that they
would be directly in front of the flocks when they came to drink. When the flocks were in
heat and came to drink, [39]they mated in front of the branches. And they bore young that
were streaked or speckled or spotted. [40]Jacob set apart the young of the flock by them-
selves, but made the rest face the streaked and dark-colored animals that belonged to La-
ban. Thus he made separate flocks for himself and did not put them with Laban's animals.
[41]Whenever the stronger females were in heat, Jacob would place the branches in the
troughs in front of the animals so they would mate near the branches, [42]but if the animals
were weak, he would not place them there. So the weak animals went to Laban and the
strong ones to Jacob. [43]In this way the man grew exceedingly prosperous and came to own
large flocks, and female and male servants, and camels and donkeys.

Discovering God

31:34 // Spiritual Fraud. Superstition ran rampant among the people of Canaan. Its influence was such that even some of God's people who lived in Canaan clung to the local idols. Even today it's not uncommon to find people who believe in God but still rely on other spiritually deceptive practices (such as horoscopes) for daily advice.

What about you? Do you fear certain days or numbers? Do you treat certain inanimate objects as if they had power? If you hold to God, you hold to the greatest power in the universe. All other so-called powers are pretenders. As you search out God's ways, you'll find that he deserves your loyalty. And if you put your trust in him, he will be faithful to you.

[a] 24 *Joseph* means *may he add.*

Jacob Flees From Laban

31 Jacob heard that Laban's sons were saying, "Jacob has taken everything our fa-
ther owned and has gained all this wealth from what belonged to our father."
2And Jacob noticed that Laban's attitude toward him was not what it had been.
3Then the LORD said to Jacob, "Go back to the land of your fathers and to your relatives,
and I will be with you."
4So Jacob sent word to Rachel and Leah to come out to the fields where his flocks were.
5He said to them, "I see that your father's attitude toward me is not what it was before, but
the God of my father has been with me. 6You know that I've worked for your father with
all my strength, 7yet your father has cheated me by changing my wages ten times. How-
ever, God has not allowed him to harm me. 8If he said, 'The speckled ones will be your
wages,' then all the flocks gave birth to speckled young; and if he said, 'The streaked ones
will be your wages,' then all the flocks bore streaked young. 9So God has taken away your
father's livestock and has given them to me.
10"In breeding season I once had a dream in which I looked up and saw that the male
goats mating with the flock were streaked, speckled or spotted. 11The angel of God said to
me in the dream, 'Jacob.' I answered, 'Here I am.' 12And he said, 'Look up and see that all
the male goats mating with the flock are streaked, speckled or spotted, for I have seen all
that Laban has been doing to you. 13I am the God of Bethel, where you anointed a pillar and
where you made a vow to me. Now leave this land at once and go back to your native land.' "
14Then Rachel and Leah replied, "Do we still have any share in the inheritance of our fa-
ther's estate? 15Does he not regard us as foreigners? Not only has he sold us, but he has
used up what was paid for us. 16Surely all the wealth that God took away from our father
belongs to us and our children. So do whatever God has told you."
17Then Jacob put his children and his wives on camels, 18and he drove all his livestock
ahead of him, along with all the goods he had accumulated in Paddan Aram,[a] to go to his
father Isaac in the land of Canaan.
19When Laban had gone to shear his sheep, Rachel stole her father's household gods.
20Moreover, Jacob deceived Laban the Aramean by not telling him he was running away.
21So he fled with all he had, crossed the Euphrates River, and headed for the hill country
of Gilead.

Laban Pursues Jacob

22On the third day Laban was told that Jacob had fled. 23Taking his relatives with him,
he pursued Jacob for seven days and caught up with him in the hill country of Gilead.
24Then God came to Laban the Aramean in a dream at night and said to him, "Be careful
not to say anything to Jacob, either good or bad."
25Jacob had pitched his tent in the hill country of Gilead when Laban overtook him, and
Laban and his relatives camped there too. 26Then Laban said to Jacob, "What have you
done? You've deceived me, and you've carried off my daughters like captives in war. 27Why
did you run off secretly and deceive me? Why didn't you tell me, so I could send you away
with joy and singing to the music of timbrels and harps? 28You didn't even let me kiss my
grandchildren and my daughters good-by. You have done a foolish thing. 29I have the pow-
er to harm you; but last night the God of your father said to me, 'Be careful not to say any-
thing to Jacob, either good or bad.' 30Now you have gone off because you longed to return
to your father's household. But why did you steal my gods?"
31Jacob answered Laban, "I was afraid, because I thought you would take your daughters
away from me by force. 32But if you find anyone who has your gods, that one shall not live.
In the presence of our relatives, see for yourself whether there is anything of yours here
with me; and if so, take it." Now Jacob did not know that Rachel had stolen the gods.
33So Laban went into Jacob's tent and into Leah's tent and into the tent of the two female
servants, but he found nothing. After he came out of Leah's tent, he entered Rachel's tent.
34Now Rachel had taken the household gods and put them inside her camel's saddle and
was sitting on them. Laban searched through everything in the tent but found nothing.

---

[a] *18* That is, Northwest Mesopotamia

[35]Rachel said to her father, "Don't be angry, my lord, that I cannot stand up in your presence; I'm having my period." So he searched but could not find the household gods.

[36]Jacob was angry and took Laban to task. "What is my crime?" he asked Laban. "How have I wronged you that you hunt me down? [37]Now that you have searched through all my goods, what have you found that belongs to your household? Put it here in front of your relatives and mine, and let them judge between the two of us.

[38]"I have been with you for twenty years now. Your sheep and goats have not miscarried, nor have I eaten rams from your flocks. [39]I did not bring you animals torn by wild beasts; I bore the loss myself. And you demanded payment from me for whatever was stolen by day or night. [40]This was my situation: The heat consumed me in the daytime and the cold at night, and sleep fled from my eyes. [41]It was like this for the twenty years I was in your household. I worked for you fourteen years for your two daughters and six years for your flocks, and you changed my wages ten times. [42]If the God of my father, the God of Abraham and the Fear of Isaac, had not been with me, you would surely have sent me away empty-handed. But God has seen my hardship and the toil of my hands, and last night he rebuked you."

[43]Laban answered Jacob, "The women are my daughters, the children are my children, and the flocks are my flocks. All you see is mine. Yet what can I do today about these daughters of mine, or about the children they have borne? [44]Come now, let's make a covenant, you and I, and let it serve as a witness between us."

[45]So Jacob took a stone and set it up as a pillar. [46]He said to his relatives, "Gather some stones." So they took stones and piled them in a heap, and they ate there by the heap. [47]Laban called it Jegar Sahadutha, and Jacob called it Galeed.[a]

[48]Laban said, "This heap is a witness between you and me today." That is why it was called Galeed. [49]It was also called Mizpah,[b] because he said, "May the LORD keep watch between you and me when we are away from each other. [50]If you mistreat my daughters or if you take any wives besides my daughters, even though no one is with us, remember that God is a witness between you and me."

[51]Laban also said to Jacob, "Here is this heap, and here is this pillar I have set up between you and me. [52]This heap is a witness, and this pillar is a witness, that I will not go past this heap to your side to harm you and that you will not go past this heap and pillar to my side to harm me. [53]May the God of Abraham and the God of Nahor, the God of their father, judge between us."

So Jacob took an oath in the name of the Fear of his father Isaac. [54]He offered a sacrifice there in the hill country and invited his relatives to a meal. After they had eaten, they spent the night there.

*[55]Early the next morning Laban kissed his grandchildren and his daughters and blessed them. Then he left and returned home.

Jacob Prepares to Meet Esau

32 *Jacob also went on his way, and the angels of God met him. [2]When Jacob saw them, he said, "This is the camp of God!" So he named that place Mahanaim.[c]

[3]Jacob sent messengers ahead of him to his brother Esau in the land of Seir, the country of Edom. [4]He instructed them: "This is what you are to say to my lord Esau: 'Your servant Jacob says, I have been staying with Laban and have remained there till now. [5]I have cattle and donkeys, sheep and goats, male and female servants. Now I am sending this message to my lord, that I may find favor in your eyes.' "

[6]When the messengers returned to Jacob, they said, "We went to your brother Esau, and now he is coming to meet you, and four hundred men are with him."

[7]In great fear and distress Jacob divided the people who were with him into two groups,[d] and the flocks and herds and camels as well. [8]He thought, "If Esau comes and attacks one group,[e] the group[e] that is left may escape."

---

[a] 47 The Aramaic *Jegar Sahadutha* and the Hebrew *Galeed* both mean *witness heap.* [b] 49 *Mizpah* means *watchtower.* [c] 2 *Mahanaim* means *two camps.* [d] 7 Or *camps* [e] 8 Or *camp*

*31:55 is numbered 32:1 in Hebrew texts. *32:1-32 is numbered 32:2-33 in Hebrew texts.

[9]Then Jacob prayed, "O God of my father Abraham, God of my father Isaac, LORD, you
who said to me, 'Go back to your country and your relatives, and I will make you prosper,'
[10]I am unworthy of all the kindness and faithfulness you have shown your servant. I had
only my staff when I crossed this Jordan, but now I have become two camps. [11]Save me, I
pray, from the hand of my brother Esau, for I am afraid he will come and attack me, and
also the mothers with their children. [12]But you have said, 'I will surely make you prosper
and will make your descendants like the sand of the sea, which cannot be counted.' "

[13]He spent the night there, and from what he had with him he selected a gift for his
brother Esau: [14]two hundred female goats and twenty male goats, two hundred ewes and
twenty rams, [15]thirty female camels with their young, forty cows and ten bulls, and twen-
ty female donkeys and ten male donkeys. [16]He put them in the care of his servants, each
herd by itself, and said to his servants, "Go ahead of me, and keep some space between the
herds."

[17]He instructed the one in the lead: "When my brother Esau meets you and asks, 'Who
do you belong to, and where are you going, and who owns all these animals in front of
you?' [18]then you are to say, 'They belong to your servant Jacob. They are a gift sent to my
lord Esau, and he is coming behind us.' "

[19]He also instructed the second, the third and all the others who followed the herds:
"You are to say the same thing to Esau when you meet him. [20]And be sure to say, 'Your ser-
vant Jacob is coming behind us.' " For he thought, "I will pacify him with these gifts I am
sending on ahead; later, when I see him, perhaps he will receive me." [21]So Jacob's gifts
went on ahead of him, but he himself spent the night in the camp.

Jacob Wrestles With God

[22]That night Jacob got up and took his two wives, his two female servants and his elev-
en sons and crossed the ford of the Jabbok. [23]After he had sent them across the stream, he
sent over all his possessions. [24]So Jacob was left alone, and a man wrestled with him till
daybreak. [25]When the man saw that he could not overpower him, he touched the socket of
Jacob's hip so that his hip was wrenched as he wrestled with the man. [26]Then the man said,
"Let me go, for it is daybreak."

But Jacob replied, "I will not let you go unless you bless me."

[27]The man asked him, "What is your name?"

"Jacob," he answered.

[28]Then the man said, "Your name will no longer be Jacob, but Israel,[a] because you have
struggled with God and with human beings and have overcome."

[29]Jacob said, "Please tell me your name."

But he replied, "Why do you ask my name?" Then he blessed him there.

[30]So Jacob called the place Peniel,[b] saying, "It is because I saw God face to face, and yet
my life was spared."

[31]The sun rose above him as he passed Peniel,[c] and he was limping because of his hip.
[32]Therefore to this day the Israelites do not eat the tendon attached to the socket of the hip,
because the socket of Jacob's hip was touched near the tendon.

Jacob Meets Esau

33 Jacob looked up and there was Esau, coming with his four hundred men; so he
divided the children among Leah, Rachel and the two female servants. [2]He put
the female servants and their children in front, Leah and her children next, and
Rachel and Joseph in the rear. [3]He himself went on ahead and bowed down to the ground
seven times as he approached his brother.

[4]But Esau ran to meet Jacob and embraced him; he threw his arms around his neck and
kissed him. And they wept. [5]Then Esau looked up and saw the women and children. "Who
are these with you?" he asked.

Jacob answered, "They are the children God has graciously given your servant."

---

[a] *28* *Israel* probably means *he struggles with God.* [b] *30* *Peniel* means *face of God.* [c] *31* Hebrew *Penuel,* a variant of *Peniel*

6Then the female servants and their children approached and bowed down. 7Next, Leah and her children came and bowed down. Last of all came Joseph and Rachel, and they too bowed down.

8Esau asked, "What do you mean by all these flocks and herds I met?"

"To find favor in your eyes, my lord," he said.

9But Esau said, "I already have plenty, my brother. Keep what you have for yourself."

10"No, please!" said Jacob. "If I have found favor in your eyes, accept this gift from me. For to see your face is like seeing the face of God, now that you have received me favorably. 11Please accept the present that was brought to you, for God has been gracious to me and I have all I need." And because Jacob insisted, Esau accepted it.

12Then Esau said, "Let us be on our way; I'll accompany you."

13But Jacob said to him, "My lord knows that the children are tender and that I must care for the ewes and cows that are nursing their young. If they are driven hard just one day, all the animals will die. 14So let my lord go on ahead of his servant, while I move along slowly at the pace of the flocks and herds before me and the pace of the children, until I come to my lord in Seir."

15Esau said, "Then let me leave some of my men with you."

"But why do that?" Jacob asked. "Just let me find favor in the eyes of my lord."

16So that day Esau started on his way back to Seir. 17Jacob, however, went to Sukkoth, where he built a place for himself and made shelters for his livestock. That is why the place is called Sukkoth.[a]

18After Jacob came from Paddan Aram,[b] he arrived safely at the[c] city of Shechem in Canaan and camped within sight of the city. 19For a hundred pieces of silver,[d] he bought from the sons of Hamor, the father of Shechem, the plot of ground where he pitched his tent. 20There he set up an altar and called it El Elohe Israel.[e]

Dinah and the Shechemites

34 Now Dinah, the daughter Leah had borne to Jacob, went out to visit the women of the land. 2When Shechem son of Hamor the Hivite, the ruler of that area, saw her, he took her and raped her. 3His heart was drawn to Dinah daughter of Jacob; he loved the young woman and spoke tenderly to her. 4And Shechem said to his father Hamor, "Get me this young woman as my wife."

5When Jacob heard that his daughter Dinah had been defiled, his sons were in the fields with his livestock; so he did nothing about it until they came home.

6Then Shechem's father Hamor went out to talk with Jacob. 7Meanwhile, Jacob's sons had come in from the fields as soon as they heard what had happened. They were shocked and furious, because Shechem had done an outrageous thing in[f] Israel by sleeping with Jacob's daughter—a thing that should not be done.

8But Hamor said to them, "My son Shechem has his heart set on your daughter. Please give her to him as his wife. 9Intermarry with us; give us your daughters and take our daughters for yourselves. 10You can settle among us; the land is open to you. Live in it, trade[g] in it, and acquire property in it."

11Then Shechem said to Dinah's father and brothers, "Let me find favor in your eyes, and I will give you whatever you ask. 12Make the price for the bride and the gift I am to bring as great as you like, and I'll pay whatever you ask me. Only give me the young woman as my wife."

13Because their sister Dinah had been defiled, Jacob's sons replied deceitfully as they spoke to Shechem and his father Hamor. 14They said to them, "We can't do such a thing; we can't give our sister to a man who is not circumcised. That would be a disgrace to us. 15We will enter into an agreement with you on one condition only: that you become like us

---

[a] 17 *Sukkoth* means *shelters.* [b] 18 That is, Northwest Mesopotamia [c] 18 Or *arrived at Shalem, a* [d] 19 Hebrew *hundred kesitahs*; a kesitah was a unit of money of unknown weight and value. [e] 20 *El Elohe Israel* can mean *El is the God of Israel* or *mighty is the God of Israel.* [f] 7 Or *against* [g] 10 Or *move about freely*; also in verse 21

by circumcising all your males. 16Then we will give you our daughters and take your daughters for ourselves. We'll settle among you and become one people with you. 17But if you will not agree to be circumcised, we'll take our sister and go."

18Their proposal seemed good to Hamor and his son Shechem. 19The young man, who was the most honored of all his father's family, lost no time in doing what they said, because he was delighted with Jacob's daughter. 20So Hamor and his son Shechem went to the gate of their city to speak to the men of their city. 21"These men are friendly toward us," they said. "Let them live in our land and trade in it; the land has plenty of room for them. We can marry their daughters and they can marry ours. 22But the men will agree to live with us as one people only on the condition that our males be circumcised, as they themselves are. 23Won't their livestock, their property and all their other animals become ours? So let us agree to their terms, and they will settle among us."

24All the men who went out of the city gate agreed with Hamor and his son Shechem, and every male in the city was circumcised.

25Three days later, while all of them were still in pain, two of Jacob's sons, Simeon and Levi, Dinah's brothers, took their swords and attacked the unsuspecting city, killing every male. 26They put Hamor and his son Shechem to the sword and took Dinah from Shechem's house and left. 27The sons of Jacob came upon the dead bodies and looted the city where[a] their sister had been defiled. 28They seized their flocks and herds and donkeys and everything else of theirs in the city and out in the fields. 29They carried off all their wealth and all their women and children, taking as plunder everything in the houses.

30Then Jacob said to Simeon and Levi, "You have brought trouble on me by making me obnoxious to the Canaanites and Perizzites, the people living in this land. We are few in number, and if they join forces against me and attack me, I and my household will be destroyed."

31But they replied, "Should he have treated our sister like a prostitute?"

Jacob Returns to Bethel

35 Then God said to Jacob, "Go up to Bethel and settle there, and build an altar there to God, who appeared to you when you were fleeing from your brother Esau."

2So Jacob said to his household and to all who were with him, "Get rid of the foreign gods you have with you, and purify yourselves and change your clothes. 3Then come, let us go up to Bethel, where I will build an altar to God, who answered me in the day of my distress and who has been with me wherever I have gone." 4So they gave Jacob all the foreign gods they had and the rings in their ears, and Jacob buried them under the oak at Shechem. 5Then they set out, and the terror of God fell on the towns all around them so that no one pursued them.

6Jacob and all the people with him came to Luz (that is, Bethel) in the land of Canaan. 7There he built an altar, and he called the place El Bethel,[b] because it was there that God revealed himself to him when he was fleeing from his brother.

8Now Deborah, Rebekah's nurse, died and was buried under the oak below Bethel. So it was named Allon Bakuth.[c]

9After Jacob returned from Paddan Aram,[d] God appeared to him again and blessed him. 10God said to him, "Your name is Jacob,[e] but you will no longer be called Jacob; your name will be Israel.[f]" So he named him Israel.

11And God said to him, "I am God Almighty[g]; be fruitful and increase in number. A nation and a community of nations will come from you, and kings will come from your body. 12The land I gave to Abraham and Isaac I also give to you, and I will give this land to your descendants after you." 13Then God went up from him at the place where he had talked with him.

---

[a] 27 Or *because* [b] 7 *El Bethel* means *God of Bethel.* [c] 8 *Allon Bakuth* means *oak of weeping.* [d] 9 That is, Northwest Mesopotamia; also in verse 26 [e] 10 *Jacob* means *he grasps the heel,* a Hebrew idiom for *he deceives.* [f] 10 *Israel* probably means *he struggles with God.* [g] 11 Hebrew *El-Shaddai*

[14]Jacob set up a stone pillar at the place where God had talked with him, and he poured
out a drink offering on it; he also poured oil on it. [15]Jacob called the place where God had
talked with him Bethel.[a]

The Deaths of Rachel and Isaac

[16]Then they moved on from Bethel. While they were still some distance from Ephrath,
Rachel began to give birth and had great difficulty. [17]And as she was having great difficul-
ty in childbirth, the midwife said to her, "Don't despair, for you have another son." [18]As she
breathed her last—for she was dying—she named her son Ben-Oni.[b] But his father named
him Benjamin.[c]
[19]So Rachel died and was buried on the way to Ephrath (that is, Bethlehem). [20]Over her
tomb Jacob set up a pillar, and to this day that pillar marks Rachel's tomb.
[21]Israel moved on again and pitched his tent beyond Migdal Eder. [22]While Israel was liv-
ing in that region, Reuben went in and slept with his father's concubine Bilhah, and Isra-
el heard of it.

Jacob had twelve sons:
[23]The sons of Leah:
Reuben the firstborn of Jacob,
Simeon, Levi, Judah, Issachar and Zebulun.
[24]The sons of Rachel:
Joseph and Benjamin.
[25]The sons of Rachel's servant Bilhah:
Dan and Naphtali.
[26]The sons of Leah's servant Zilpah:
Gad and Asher.
These were the sons of Jacob, who were born to him in Paddan Aram.

[27]Jacob came home to his father Isaac in Mamre, near Kiriath Arba (that is, Hebron),
where Abraham and Isaac had stayed. [28]Isaac lived a hundred and eighty years. [29]Then he
breathed his last and died and was gathered to his people, old and full of years. And his sons
Esau and Jacob buried him.

Esau's Descendants

36 This is the account of the family line of Esau (that is, Edom).
[2]Esau took his wives from the women of Canaan: Adah daughter of Elon the
Hittite, and Oholibamah daughter of Anah and granddaughter of Zibeon the Hivite—
[3]also Basemath daughter of Ishmael and sister of Nebaioth.
[4]Adah bore Eliphaz to Esau, Basemath bore Reuel, [5]and Oholibamah bore Jeush,
Jalam and Korah. These were the sons of Esau, who were born to him in Canaan.

Knowing Yourself

35:10 // A New Identity. Throughout the Bible God renamed key individuals. For example, God changed the name of Abram (meaning "exalted father") to Abraham ("father of many"; see chapter 17, verse 5 [page 22]). Here God changed the name of Jacob (meaning "he deceives") to Israel ("he struggles with God").

In Biblical times, a person's name often reflected that person's character. A change in a name meant that the person had changed—either internally or in relationship with another person. Today, when a person decides to put his or her complete trust in Christ, God sees that person in a new light. In a sense, God changes that person's "name" to reflect the change in the relationship between himself and that person.

As he did with Abram and Jacob, he's ready to offer you a new spiritual identity.

---

[a] 15 *Bethel* means *house of God.* [b] 18 *Ben-Oni* means *son of my trouble.* [c] 18 *Benjamin* means *son of my right hand.*

[6]Esau took his wives and sons and daughters and all the members of his household, as well as his livestock and all his other animals and all the goods he had acquired in Canaan, and moved to a land some distance from his brother Jacob. [7]Their
possessions were too great for them to remain together; the land where they were staying could not support them both because of their livestock. [8]So Esau (that is,
Edom) settled in the hill country of Seir.

[9]This is the account of the family line of Esau the father of the Edomites in the hill country of Seir.

[10]These are the names of Esau's sons:
Eliphaz, the son of Esau's wife Adah, and Reuel, the son of Esau's wife Basemath.
[11]The sons of Eliphaz:
Teman, Omar, Zepho, Gatam and Kenaz.
[12]Esau's son Eliphaz also had a concubine named Timna, who bore him Amalek. These were grandsons of Esau's wife Adah.
[13]The sons of Reuel:
Nahath, Zerah, Shammah and Mizzah. These were grandsons of Esau's wife Basemath.
[14]The sons of Esau's wife Oholibamah daughter of Anah and granddaughter of Zibeon, whom she bore to Esau:
Jeush, Jalam and Korah.

[15]These were the chiefs among Esau's descendants:
The sons of Eliphaz the firstborn of Esau:
Chiefs Teman, Omar, Zepho, Kenaz,
[16]Korah,[a] Gatam and Amalek. These were the chiefs descended from Eliphaz in Edom; they were grandsons of Adah.
[17]The sons of Esau's son Reuel:
Chiefs Nahath, Zerah, Shammah and Mizzah. These were the chiefs descended from Reuel in Edom; they were grandsons of Esau's wife Basemath.
[18]The sons of Esau's wife Oholibamah:
Chiefs Jeush, Jalam and Korah. These were the chiefs descended from Esau's wife Oholibamah daughter of Anah.
[19]These were the sons of Esau (that is, Edom), and these were their chiefs.

[20]These were the sons of Seir the Horite, who were living in the region:
Lotan, Shobal, Zibeon, Anah,
[21]Dishon, Ezer and Dishan. These sons of Seir in Edom were Horite chiefs.
[22]The sons of Lotan:
Hori and Homam.[b] Timna was Lotan's sister.
[23]The sons of Shobal:
Alvan, Manahath, Ebal, Shepho and Onam.
[24]The sons of Zibeon:
Aiah and Anah. This is the Anah who discovered the hot springs[c] in the desert while he was grazing the donkeys of his father Zibeon.
[25]The children of Anah:
Dishon and Oholibamah daughter of Anah.
[26]The sons of Dishon[d]:
Hemdan, Eshban, Ithran and Keran.
[27]The sons of Ezer:
Bilhan, Zaavan and Akan.
[28]The sons of Dishan:
Uz and Aran.

---

[a] *16* Masoretic Text; Samaritan Pentateuch (see also Gen. 36:11 and 1 Chron. 1:36) does not have *Korah.* [b] *22* Hebrew *Hemam,* a variant of *Homam* (see 1 Chron. 1:39) [c] *24* Vulgate; Syriac *discovered water;* the meaning of the Hebrew for this word is uncertain. [d] *26* Hebrew *Dishan,* a variant of *Dishon*

[29] These were the Horite chiefs:
Lotan, Shobal, Zibeon, Anah, [30] Dishon, Ezer and Dishan. These were the Horite
chiefs, according to their divisions, in the land of Seir.

The Rulers of Edom

[31] These were the kings who reigned in Edom before any Israelite king reigned:
[32] Bela son of Beor became king of Edom. His city was named Dinhabah.
[33] When Bela died, Jobab son of Zerah from Bozrah succeeded him as king.
[34] When Jobab died, Husham from the land of the Temanites succeeded him as king.
[35] When Husham died, Hadad son of Bedad, who defeated Midian in the country of
Moab, succeeded him as king. His city was named Avith.
[36] When Hadad died, Samlah from Masrekah succeeded him as king.
[37] When Samlah died, Shaul from Rehoboth on the river succeeded him as king.
[38] When Shaul died, Baal-Hanan son of Akbor succeeded him as king.
[39] When Baal-Hanan son of Akbor died, Hadad[a] succeeded him as king. His city was
named Pau, and his wife's name was Mehetabel daughter of Matred, the daughter
of Me-Zahab.

[40] These were the chiefs descended from Esau, by name, according to their clans and regions:
Timna, Alvah, Jetheth, [41] Oholibamah, Elah, Pinon, [42] Kenaz, Teman, Mibzar, [43] Mag-
diel and Iram. These were the chiefs of Edom, according to their settlements
in the land they occupied.

This was Esau the father of the Edomites.

Joseph's Dreams

37 Jacob lived in the land where his father had stayed, the land of Canaan.

[2] This is the account of Jacob's family line.

Joseph, a young man of seventeen, was tending the flocks with his brothers, the sons of Bilhah and the sons of Zilpah, his father's wives, and he brought their father a bad report about them.

[3] Now Israel loved Joseph more than any of his other sons, because he had been born to him in his old age; and he made a richly ornamented[b] robe for him. [4] When his brothers saw that their father loved him more than any of them, they hated him and could not speak a kind word to him.

[5] Joseph had a dream, and when he told it to his brothers, they hated him all the more.
[6] He said to them, "Listen to this dream I had: [7] We were binding sheaves of grain out in the field when suddenly my sheaf rose and stood upright, while your sheaves gathered around mine and bowed down to it."

[8] His brothers said to him, "Do you intend to reign over us? Will you actually rule us?" And they hated him all the more because of his dream and what he had said.

Strengthening Relationships

37:3 // Parenting. Playing favorites with your children is dangerous. One of the keys to successful parenting is to affirm the unique character in each of your children without being preferential to one in particular.

While Jacob was growing up, his mother favored him while his father favored his twin brother, Esau (see chapter 25, verse 28 [page 33]). Their favoritism led to all kinds of competition and trouble. In this passage Jacob (called Israel) favors Joseph, his youngest son. And the sibling rivalry that this favoritism inspires will soon break Jacob's heart.

[a] 39 Many manuscripts of the Masoretic Text, Samaritan Pentateuch and Syriac (see also 1 Chron. 1:50); most manuscripts of the Masoretic Text *Hadar* [b] 3 The meaning of the Hebrew for *richly ornamented* is uncertain; also in verses 23 and 32.

[9]Then he had another dream, and he told it to his brothers. "Listen," he said, "I had another dream, and this time the sun and moon and eleven stars were bowing down to me."

[10]When he told his father as well as his brothers, his father rebuked him and said, "What is this dream you had? Will your mother and I and your brothers actually come and bow down to the ground before you?" [11]His brothers were jealous of him, but his father kept the matter in mind.

Joseph Sold by His Brothers

[12]Now his brothers had gone to graze their father's flocks near Shechem, [13]and Israel said to Joseph, "As you know, your brothers are grazing the flocks near Shechem. Come, I am going to send you to them."

"Very well," he replied.

[14]So he said to him, "Go and see if all is well with your brothers and with the flocks, and bring word back to me." Then he sent him off from the Valley of Hebron.

When Joseph arrived at Shechem, [15]a man found him wandering around in the fields and asked him, "What are you looking for?"

[16]He replied, "I'm looking for my brothers. Can you tell me where they are grazing their flocks?"

[17]"They have moved on from here," the man answered. "I heard them say, 'Let's go to Dothan.' "

So Joseph went after his brothers and found them near Dothan. [18]But they saw him in the distance, and before he reached them, they plotted to kill him.

[19]"Here comes that dreamer!" they said to each other. [20]"Come now, let's kill him and throw him into one of these cisterns and say that a ferocious animal devoured him. Then we'll see what comes of his dreams."

[21]When Reuben heard this, he tried to rescue him from their hands. "Let's not take his life," he said. [22]"Don't shed any blood. Throw him into this cistern here in the wilderness, but don't lay a hand on him." Reuben said this to rescue him from them and take him back to his father.

[23]So when Joseph came to his brothers, they stripped him of his robe—the richly ornamented robe he was wearing— [24]and they took him and threw him into the cistern. The cistern was empty; there was no water in it.

[25]As they sat down to eat their meal, they looked up and saw a caravan of Ishmaelites coming from Gilead. Their camels were loaded with spices, balm and myrrh, and they were on their way to take them down to Egypt.

[26]Judah said to his brothers, "What will we gain if we kill our brother and cover up his blood? [27]Come, let's sell him to the Ishmaelites and not lay our hands on him; after all, he is our brother, our own flesh and blood." His brothers agreed.

[28]So when the Midianite merchants came by, his brothers pulled Joseph up out of the cistern and sold him for twenty shekels[a] of silver to the Ishmaelites, who took him to Egypt.

[29]When Reuben returned to the cistern and saw that Joseph was not there, he tore his clothes. [30]He went back to his brothers and said, "The boy isn't there! Where can I turn now?"

[31]Then they got Joseph's robe, slaughtered a goat and dipped the robe in the blood. [32]They took the ornamented robe back to their father and said, "We found this. Examine it to see whether it is your son's robe."

[33]He recognized it and said, "It is my son's robe! Some ferocious animal has devoured him. Joseph has surely been torn to pieces."

[34]Then Jacob tore his clothes, put on sackcloth and mourned for his son many days. [35]All his sons and daughters came to comfort him, but he refused to be comforted. "No," he said, "in mourning will I go down to the grave to my son." So his father wept for him.

[36]Meanwhile, the Midianites[b] sold Joseph in Egypt to Potiphar, one of Pharaoh's officials, the captain of the guard.

---

[a] *28* That is, about 8 ounces or about 230 grams [b] *36* Samaritan Pentateuch, Septuagint, Vulgate and Syriac (see also verse 28); Masoretic Text *Medanites*

Judah and Tamar

38 At that time, Judah left his brothers and went down to stay with a man of Adul-
lam named Hirah. 2There Judah met the daughter of a Canaanite man named
Shua. He married her and made love to her; 3she became pregnant and gave
birth to a son, who was named Er. 4She conceived again and gave birth to a son and named
him Onan. 5She gave birth to still another son and named him Shelah. It was at Kezib that
she gave birth to him.
6Judah got a wife for Er, his firstborn, and her name was Tamar. 7But Er, Judah's first-
born, was wicked in the LORD's sight; so the LORD put him to death.
8Then Judah said to Onan, "Sleep with your brother's wife and fulfill your duty to her as
a brother-in-law to raise up offspring for your brother." 9But Onan knew that the child
would not be his; so whenever he slept with his brother's wife, he spilled his semen on the
ground to keep from providing offspring for his brother. 10What he did was wicked in the
LORD's sight; so he put him to death also.
11Judah then said to his daughter-in-law Tamar, "Live as a widow in your father's house-
hold until my son Shelah grows up." For he thought, "He may die too, just like his broth-
ers." So Tamar went to live in her father's household.
12After a long time Judah's wife, the daughter of Shua, died. When Judah had recovered
from his grief, he went up to Timnah, to the men who were shearing his sheep, and his
friend Hirah the Adullamite went with him.
13When Tamar was told, "Your father-in-law is on his way to Timnah to shear his sheep,"
14she took off her widow's clothes, covered herself with a veil to disguise herself, and then
sat down at the entrance to Enaim, which is on the road to Timnah. For she saw that,
though Shelah had now grown up, she had not been given to him as his wife.
15When Judah saw her, he thought she was a prostitute, for she had covered her face.
16Not realizing that she was his daughter-in-law, he went over to her by the roadside and
said, "Come now, let me sleep with you."
"And what will you give me to sleep with you?" she asked.
17"I'll send you a young goat from my flock," he said.
"Will you give me something as a pledge until you send it?" she asked.
18He said, "What pledge should I give you?"
"Your seal and its cord, and the staff in your hand," she answered. So he gave them to
her and slept with her, and she became pregnant by him. 19After she left, she took off her
veil and put on her widow's clothes again.
20Meanwhile Judah sent the young goat by his friend the Adullamite in order to get his
pledge back from the woman, but he did not find her. 21He asked the men who lived there,
"Where is the shrine prostitute who was beside the road at Enaim?"
"There hasn't been any shrine prostitute here," they said.
22So he went back to Judah and said, "I didn't find her. Besides, the men who lived there
said, 'There hasn't been any shrine prostitute here.' "
23Then Judah said, "Let her keep what she has, or we will become a laughingstock. Af-
ter all, I did send her this young goat, but you didn't find her."

Addressing Questions

38:9–10 // God. Why did God strike Onan dead? Apart from its culture and context, this Bible passage could easily be misunderstood.

In Bible times a woman was commonly cared for by her father if she was unmarried or by her husband if she was married. If a woman's husband died, her adult children took over the responsibility to care for her. A widow who had no children, then, was destitute. To insure the future well-being of such women, one of the deceased husband's brothers was compelled to marry the childless widow so she could bear children and ensure her future support (see Deuteronomy chapter 25, verses 5–6 [page 99]).

Against this background, the story of Onan begins to make sense. God has a special place in his heart for disadvantaged and forgotten individuals in society, which appears to be why Onan's sin especially grieved God.

24About three months later Judah was told, "Your daughter-in-law Tamar is guilty of pros-
titution, and as a result she is now pregnant."
Judah said, "Bring her out and have her burned to death!"
25As she was being brought out, she sent a message to her father-in-law. "I am pregnant
by the man who owns these," she said. And she added, "See if you recognize whose seal
and cord and staff these are."
26Judah recognized them and said, "She is more righteous than I, since I wouldn't give
her to my son Shelah." And he did not sleep with her again.
27When the time came for her to give birth, there were twin boys in her womb. 28As she
was giving birth, one of them put out his hand; so the midwife took a scarlet thread and
tied it on his wrist and said, "This one came out first." 29But when he drew back his hand,
his brother came out, and she said, "So this is how you have broken out!" And he was
named Perez.[a] 30Then his brother, who had the scarlet thread on his wrist, came out and
he was given the name Zerah.[b]

Joseph and Potiphar's Wife

39 Now Joseph had been taken down to Egypt. Potiphar, an Egyptian who was one
of Pharaoh's officials, the captain of the guard, bought him from the Ishmael-
ites who had taken him there.
2The LORD was with Joseph so that he prospered, and he lived in the house of his Egyp-
tian master. 3When his master saw that the LORD was with him and that the LORD gave him
success in everything he did, 4Joseph found favor in his eyes and became his attendant.
Potiphar put him in charge of his household, and he entrusted to his care everything he
owned. 5From the time he put him in charge of his household and of all that he owned, the
LORD blessed the household of the Egyptian because of Joseph. The blessing of the LORD was
on everything Potiphar had, both in the house and in the field. 6So Potiphar left everything
he had in Joseph's care; with Joseph in charge, he did not concern himself with anything
except the food he ate.
Now Joseph was well-built and handsome, 7and after a while his master's wife took no-
tice of Joseph and said, "Come to bed with me!"
8But he refused. "With me in charge," he told her, "my master does not concern him-
self with anything in the house; everything he owns he has entrusted to my care. 9No one
is greater in this house than I am. My master has withheld nothing from me except you,
because you are his wife. How then could I do such a wicked thing and sin against God?"
10And though she spoke to Joseph day after day, he refused to go to bed with her or even
be with her.
11One day he went into the house to attend to his duties, and none of the household ser-
vants was inside. 12She caught him by his cloak and said, "Come to bed with me!" But he
left his cloak in her hand and ran out of the house.
13When she saw that he had left his cloak in her hand and had run out of the house, 14she
called her household servants. "Look," she said to them, "this Hebrew has been brought
to us to make sport of us! He came in here to sleep with me, but I screamed. 15When he
heard me scream for help, he left his cloak beside me and ran out of the house."
16She kept his cloak beside her until his master came home. 17Then she told him this
story: "That Hebrew slave you brought us came to me to make sport of me. 18But as soon
as I screamed for help, he left his cloak beside me and ran out of the house."
19When his master heard the story his wife told him, saying, "This is how your slave
treated me," he burned with anger. 20Joseph's master took him and put him in prison, the
place where the king's prisoners were confined.
But while Joseph was there in the prison, 21the LORD was with him; he showed him kind-
ness and granted him favor in the eyes of the prison warden. 22So the warden put Joseph
in charge of all those held in the prison, and he was made responsible for all that was done

---

[a] 29 *Perez* means *breaking out.* [b] 30 *Zerah* can mean *scarlet* or *brightness.*

there. 23The warden paid no attention to anything under Joseph's care, because the LORD was with Joseph and gave him success in whatever he did.

The Cupbearer and the Baker

40 Some time later, the cupbearer and the baker of the king of Egypt offended their master, the king of Egypt. 2Pharaoh was angry with his two officials, the chief cupbearer and the chief baker, 3and put them in custody in the house of the captain of the guard, in the same prison where Joseph was confined. 4The captain of the guard assigned them to Joseph, and he attended them.

After they had been in custody for some time, 5each of the two men—the cupbearer and the baker of the king of Egypt, who were being held in prison—had a dream the same night, and each dream had a meaning of its own.

6When Joseph came to them the next morning, he saw that they were dejected. 7So he asked Pharaoh's officials who were in custody with him in his master's house, "Why do you look so sad today?"

8"We both had dreams," they answered, "but there is no one to interpret them."

Then Joseph said to them, "Do not interpretations belong to God? Tell me your dreams."

9So the chief cupbearer told Joseph his dream. He said to him, "In my dream I saw a vine in front of me, 10and on the vine were three branches. As soon as it budded, it blossomed, and its clusters ripened into grapes. 11Pharaoh's cup was in my hand, and I took the grapes, squeezed them into Pharaoh's cup and put the cup in his hand."

12"This is what it means," Joseph said to him. "The three branches are three days. 13Within three days Pharaoh will lift up your head and restore you to your position, and you will put Pharaoh's cup in his hand, just as you used to do when you were his cupbearer. 14But when all goes well with you, remember me and show me kindness; mention me to Pharaoh and get me out of this prison. 15I was forcibly carried off from the land of the Hebrews, and even here I have done nothing to deserve being put in a dungeon."

16When the chief baker saw that Joseph had given a favorable interpretation, he said to Joseph, "I too had a dream: On my head were three baskets of bread.[a] 17In the top basket were all kinds of baked goods for Pharaoh, but the birds were eating them out of the basket on my head."

18"This is what it means," Joseph said. "The three baskets are three days. 19Within three days Pharaoh will lift off your head and impale your body on a pole. And the birds will eat away your flesh."

20Now the third day was Pharaoh's birthday, and he gave a feast for all his officials. He lifted up the heads of the chief cupbearer and the chief baker in the presence of his officials: 21He restored the chief cupbearer to his position, so that he once again put the cup into Pharaoh's hand— 22but he impaled the chief baker, just as Joseph had said to them in his interpretation.

Knowing Yourself

39:1–23 // Character. Joseph's refusal to sleep with Potiphar's wife is a great example of strong moral character. Joseph turned down the woman's repeated solicitations at great personal cost: He was falsely accused and thrown into prison.

But notice what followed. God made Joseph's prison experience tolerable and allowed him to use his leadership abilities in that horrible place. God worked through a chain of events to give Joseph an opportunity to speak to Pharaoh and to become a powerful leader (see chapter 41, verses 9–14 [page 53]).

If you take a strong stand against immorality, you will probably be among a small minority in our society. You may be labeled as some kind of prude. You may even pay an unfair price, as Joseph did. In the end, however, you'll find out that God's standards of morality are worth following. He can help you as you work to maintain your moral integrity. And if your stand appears to make things worse in the short term, remember that, in the long run, God honors and affirms faithful people.

---

[a] 16 Or *three wicker baskets*

23The chief cupbearer, however, did not remember Joseph; he forgot him.

Pharaoh's Dreams

41 When two full years had passed, Pharaoh had a dream: He was standing by the
Nile, 2when out of the river there came up seven cows, sleek and fat, and they
grazed among the reeds. 3After them, seven other cows, ugly and gaunt, came up
out of the Nile and stood beside those on the riverbank. 4And the cows that were ugly and
gaunt ate up the seven sleek, fat cows. Then Pharaoh woke up.
5He fell asleep again and had a second dream: Seven heads of grain, healthy and good,
were growing on a single stalk. 6After them, seven other heads of grain sprouted—thin and
scorched by the east wind. 7The thin heads of grain swallowed up the seven healthy, full
heads. Then Pharaoh woke up; it had been a dream.
8In the morning his mind was troubled, so he sent for all the magicians and wise men
of Egypt. Pharaoh told them his dreams, but no one could interpret them for him.
9Then the chief cupbearer said to Pharaoh, "Today I am reminded of my shortcomings.
10Pharaoh was once angry with his servants, and he imprisoned me and the chief baker in
the house of the captain of the guard. 11Each of us had a dream the same night, and each
dream had a meaning of its own. 12Now a young Hebrew was there with us, a servant of the
captain of the guard. We told him our dreams, and he interpreted them for us, giving each
man the interpretation of his dream. 13And things turned out exactly as he interpreted them
to us: I was restored to my position, and the other man was impaled."
14So Pharaoh sent for Joseph, and he was quickly brought from the dungeon. When he
had shaved and changed his clothes, he came before Pharaoh.
15Pharaoh said to Joseph, "I had a dream, and no one can interpret it. But I have heard
it said of you that when you hear a dream you can interpret it."
16"I cannot do it," Joseph replied to Pharaoh, "but God will give Pharaoh the answer he
desires."
17Then Pharaoh said to Joseph, "In my dream I was standing on the bank of the Nile,
18when out of the river there came up seven cows, fat and sleek, and they grazed among
the reeds. 19After them, seven other cows came up—scrawny and very ugly and lean. I had
never seen such ugly cows in all the land of Egypt. 20The lean, ugly cows ate up the seven
fat cows that came up first. 21But even after they ate them, no one could tell that they had
done so; they looked just as ugly as before. Then I woke up.
22"In my dream I saw seven heads of grain, full and good, growing on a single stalk. 23Af-
ter them, seven other heads sprouted—withered and thin and scorched by the east wind.

Addressing Questions

41:16 // Unseen Realities. Joseph made it clear to Pharaoh that he wasn't psychic. The Bible actually condemns the practices of fortune-telling and divination (see Deuteronomy chapter 18, verses 10–13 [page 93]). Joseph claimed that he was merely relaying a message from God—as a prophet, rather than a fortune-teller.

The Bible does not teach that all dreams foretell future events. Current research indicates that dreams are the mind's way of processing strong feelings and experiences. The Bible does teach, however, that a dream may have significance beyond our immediate personal experience. The difficulty is knowing when any particular dream has divine origins.

If you sense that God is leading you in some unusual way, the Bible recommends taking a variety of steps:

- Carefully research the issue (Proverbs chapter 14, verse 15).
- Ask God for wisdom (James chapter 1, verse 5).
- Seek out the counsel of advisors (Proverbs chapter 15, verse 22).
- Make sure that what you propose doesn't violate a Scriptural command (Joshua chapter 22, verse 5).
- Make sure your plans include God (Psalm 127, verse 1; Proverbs chapter 3, verses 5–6).

[24]The thin heads of grain swallowed up the seven good heads. I told this to the magicians,
but none of them could explain it to me."

[25]Then Joseph said to Pharaoh, "The dreams of Pharaoh are one and the same. God has
revealed to Pharaoh what he is about to do. [26]The seven good cows are seven years, and the
seven good heads of grain are seven years; it is one and the same dream. [27]The seven lean,
ugly cows that came up afterward are seven years, and so are the seven worthless heads
of grain scorched by the east wind: They are seven years of famine.

[28]"It is just as I said to Pharaoh: God has shown Pharaoh what he is about to do. [29]Sev-
en years of great abundance are coming throughout the land of Egypt, [30]but seven years of
famine will follow them. Then all the abundance in Egypt will be forgotten, and the fam-
ine will ravage the land. [31]The abundance in the land will not be remembered, because the
famine that follows it will be so severe. [32]The reason the dream was given to Pharaoh in
two forms is that the matter has been firmly decided by God, and God will do it soon.

[33]"And now let Pharaoh look for a discerning and wise man and put him in charge of the
land of Egypt. [34]Let Pharaoh appoint commissioners over the land to take a fifth of the har-
vest of Egypt during the seven years of abundance. [35]They should collect all the food of
these good years that are coming and store up the grain under the authority of Pharaoh,
to be kept in the cities for food. [36]This food should be held in reserve for the country, to be
used during the seven years of famine that will come upon Egypt, so that the country may
not be ruined by the famine."

[37]The plan seemed good to Pharaoh and to all his officials. [38]So Pharaoh asked them,
"Can we find anyone like this man, one in whom is the spirit of God[a]?"

[39]Then Pharaoh said to Joseph, "Since God has made all this known to you, there is no
one so discerning and wise as you. [40]You shall be in charge of my palace, and all my peo-
ple are to submit to your orders. Only with respect to the throne will I be greater than you."

Joseph in Charge of Egypt

[41]So Pharaoh said to Joseph, "I hereby put you in charge of the whole land of Egypt."
[42]Then Pharaoh took his signet ring from his finger and put it on Joseph's finger. He dressed
him in robes of fine linen and put a gold chain around his neck. [43]He had him ride in a
chariot as his second-in-command,[b] and people shouted before him, "Make way[c]!" Thus
he put him in charge of the whole land of Egypt.

[44]Then Pharaoh said to Joseph, "I am Pharaoh, but without your word no one will lift
hand or foot in all Egypt." [45]Pharaoh gave Joseph the name Zaphenath-Paneah and gave
him Asenath daughter of Potiphera, priest of On,[d] to be his wife. And Joseph went through-
out the land of Egypt.

[46]Joseph was thirty years old when he entered the service of Pharaoh king of Egypt. And
Joseph went out from Pharaoh's presence and traveled throughout Egypt. [47]During the sev-
en years of abundance the land produced plentifully. [48]Joseph collected all the food pro-
duced in those seven years of abundance in Egypt and stored it in the cities. In each city
he put the food grown in the fields surrounding it. [49]Joseph stored up huge quantities of
grain, like the sand of the sea; it was so much that he stopped keeping records because it
was beyond measure.

[50]Before the years of famine came, two sons were born to Joseph by Asenath daughter
of Potiphera, priest of On. [51]Joseph named his firstborn Manasseh[e] and said, "It is because
God has made me forget all my trouble and all my father's household." [52]The second son
he named Ephraim[f] and said, "It is because God has made me fruitful in the land of my
suffering."

[53]The seven years of abundance in Egypt came to an end, [54]and the seven years of fam-
ine began, just as Joseph had said. There was famine in all the other lands, but in the whole

---

[a] *38* Or *of the gods* [b] *43* Or *in the chariot of his second-in-command*; or *in his second chariot*
[c] *43* Or *Bow down* [d] *45* That is, Heliopolis; also in verse 50 [e] *51* *Manasseh* sounds like and
may be derived from the Hebrew for *forget.* [f] *52* *Ephraim* sounds like the Hebrew for *twice
fruitful.*

land of Egypt there was food. [55]When all Egypt began to feel the famine, the people cried to Pharaoh for food. Then Pharaoh told all the Egyptians, "Go to Joseph and do what he tells you."

[56]When the famine had spread over the whole country, Joseph opened all the storehouses and sold grain to the Egyptians, for the famine was severe throughout Egypt. [57]And all the world came to Egypt to buy grain from Joseph, because the famine was severe everywhere.

Joseph's Brothers Go to Egypt

42 When Jacob learned that there was grain in Egypt, he said to his sons, "Why do you just keep looking at each other?" [2]He continued, "I have heard that there is grain in Egypt. Go down there and buy some for us, so that we may live and not die."

[3]Then ten of Joseph's brothers went down to buy grain from Egypt. [4]But Jacob did not send Benjamin, Joseph's brother, with the others, because he was afraid that harm might come to him. [5]So Israel's sons were among those who went to buy grain, for the famine was in the land of Canaan also.

[6]Now Joseph was the governor of the land, the person who sold grain to all its people. So when Joseph's brothers arrived, they bowed down to him with their faces to the ground. [7]As soon as Joseph saw his brothers, he recognized them, but he pretended to be a stranger and spoke harshly to them. "Where do you come from?" he asked.

"From the land of Canaan," they replied, "to buy food."

[8]Although Joseph recognized his brothers, they did not recognize him. [9]Then he remembered his dreams about them and said to them, "You are spies! You have come to see where our land is unprotected."

[10]"No, my lord," they answered. "Your servants have come to buy food. [11]We are all the sons of one man. Your servants are honest men, not spies."

[12]"No!" he said to them. "You have come to see where our land is unprotected."

[13]But they replied, "Your servants were twelve brothers, the sons of one man, who lives in the land of Canaan. The youngest is now with our father, and one is no more."

[14]Joseph said to them, "It is just as I told you: You are spies! [15]And this is how you will be tested: As surely as Pharaoh lives, you will not leave this place unless your youngest brother comes here. [16]Send one of your number to get your brother; the rest of you will be kept in prison, so that your words may be tested to see if you are telling the truth. If you are not, then as surely as Pharaoh lives, you are spies!" [17]And he put them all in custody for three days.

[18]On the third day, Joseph said to them, "Do this and you will live, for I fear God: [19]If you are honest men, let one of your brothers stay here in prison, while the rest of you go and take grain back for your starving households. [20]But you must bring your youngest brother to me, so that your words may be verified and that you may not die." This they proceeded to do.

[21]They said to one another, "Surely we are being punished because of our brother. We saw how distressed he was when he pleaded with us for his life, but we would not listen; that's why this distress has come on us."

[22]Reuben replied, "Didn't I tell you not to sin against the boy? But you wouldn't listen! Now we must give an accounting for his blood." [23]They did not realize that Joseph could understand them, since he was using an interpreter.

[24]He turned away from them and began to weep, but then came back and spoke to them again. He had Simeon taken from them and bound before their eyes.

[25]Joseph gave orders to fill their bags with grain, to put each man's silver back in his sack, and to give them provisions for their journey. After this was done for them, [26]they loaded their grain on their donkeys and left.

[27]At the place where they stopped for the night one of them opened his sack to get feed for his donkey, and he saw his silver in the mouth of his sack. [28]"My silver has been returned," he said to his brothers. "Here it is in my sack."

Their hearts sank and they turned to each other trembling and said, "What is this that God has done to us?"

[29]When they came to their father Jacob in the land of Canaan, they told him all that had
happened to them. They said, [30]"The man who is lord over the land spoke harshly to us
and treated us as though we were spying on the land. [31]But we said to him, 'We are honest
men; we are not spies. [32]We were twelve brothers, sons of one father. One is no more, and
the youngest is now with our father in Canaan.'

[33]"Then the man who is lord over the land said to us, 'This is how I will know whether
you are honest men: Leave one of your brothers here with me, and take food for your starv-
ing households and go. [34]But bring your youngest brother to me so I will know that you are
not spies but honest men. Then I will give your brother back to you, and you can trade[a] in
the land.' "

[35]As they were emptying their sacks, there in each man's sack was his pouch of silver!
When they and their father saw the money pouches, they were frightened. [36]Their father Ja-
cob said to them, "You have deprived me of my children. Joseph is no more and Simeon is
no more, and now you want to take Benjamin. Everything is against me!"

[37]Then Reuben said to his father, "You may put both of my sons to death if I do not bring
him back to you. Entrust him to my care, and I will bring him back."

[38]But Jacob said, "My son will not go down there with you; his brother is dead and he is
the only one left. If harm comes to him on the journey you are taking, you will bring my
gray head down to the grave in sorrow."

The Second Journey to Egypt

43 Now the famine was still severe in the land. [2]So when they had eaten all the
grain they had brought from Egypt, their father said to them, "Go back and buy
us a little more food."

[3]But Judah said to him, "The man warned us solemnly, 'You will not see my face again
unless your brother is with you.' [4]If you will send our brother along with us, we will go
down and buy food for you. [5]But if you will not send him, we will not go down, because the
man said to us, 'You will not see my face again unless your brother is with you.' "

[6]Israel asked, "Why did you bring this trouble on me by telling the man you had anoth-
er brother?"

[7]They replied, "The man questioned us closely about ourselves and our family. 'Is your
father still living?' he asked us. 'Do you have another brother?' We simply answered his
questions. How were we to know he would say, 'Bring your brother down here'?"

[8]Then Judah said to Israel his father, "Send the boy along with me and we will go at
once, so that we and you and our children may live and not die. [9]I myself will guarantee

Addressing Questions

42:21–22 // Human Experience. Like Joseph's brothers, people who carry guilt feelings often see adverse circumstances as some kind of payback for the wrong they've done. But the Bible does not endorse this simplistic, cause-and-effect rationale. Sometimes innocent people suffer while guilty people get away with evil—at least for the time being. In the future, this will change. When Jesus returns, all deeds will be seen for what they are. Only at that future time will faithfulness be completely rewarded and evil be thoroughly punished (see Revelation chapter 20, verses 11–13 for an illustration of this principle).

However, the Bible does teach that we experience consequences in a general sense. Eventually bad actions *do* produce bad results in our lives. For example, the body can only take so many years of alcohol abuse; eventually the internal organs will begin to malfunction. High-integrity living often gives one peace of mind and other tangible benefits.

But don't look to the successes or failures in your life as a barometer of God's level of approval. If you want to follow him, you'll need to obey what is commanded in Scripture even if short-term benefits are lacking. In the end, you'll find that all your efforts to do right were worthwhile.

[a] 34 Or *move about freely*

his safety; you can hold me personally responsible for him. If I do not bring him back to
you and set him here before you, I will bear the blame before you all my life. 10As it is, if
we had not delayed, we could have gone and returned twice."
11Then their father Israel said to them, "If it must be, then do this: Put some of the best
products of the land in your bags and take them down to the man as a gift—a little balm and
a little honey, some spices and myrrh, some pistachio nuts and almonds. 12Take double the
amount of silver with you, for you must return the silver that was put back into the mouths
of your sacks. Perhaps it was a mistake. 13Take your brother also and go back to the man at
once. 14And may God Almighty[a] grant you mercy before the man so that he will let your oth-
er brother and Benjamin come back with you. As for me, if I am bereaved, I am bereaved."
15So the men took the gifts and double the amount of silver, and Benjamin also. They
hurried down to Egypt and presented themselves to Joseph. 16When Joseph saw Benjamin
with them, he said to the steward of his house, "Take these men to my house, slaughter an
animal and prepare a meal; they are to eat with me at noon."
17The man did as Joseph told him and took the men to Joseph's house. 18Now the men
were frightened when they were taken to his house. They thought, "We were brought here
because of the silver that was put back into our sacks the first time. He wants to attack us
and overpower us and seize us as slaves and take our donkeys."
19So they went up to Joseph's steward and spoke to him at the entrance to the house.
20"We beg your pardon, our lord," they said, "we came down here the first time to buy food.
21But at the place where we stopped for the night we opened our sacks and each of us found
his silver—the exact weight—in the mouth of his sack. So we have brought it back with us.
22We have also brought additional silver with us to buy food. We don't know who put our
silver in our sacks."
23"It's all right," he said. "Don't be afraid. Your God, the God of your father, has given you
treasure in your sacks; I received your silver." Then he brought Simeon out to them.
24The steward took the men into Joseph's house, gave them water to wash their feet and
provided fodder for their donkeys. 25They prepared their gifts for Joseph's arrival at noon,
because they had heard that they were to eat there.
26When Joseph came home, they presented to him the gifts they had brought into the
house, and they bowed down before him to the ground. 27He asked them how they were,
and then he said, "How is your aged father you told me about? Is he still living?"
28They replied, "Your servant our father is still alive and well." And they bowed down,
prostrating themselves before him.
29As he looked about and saw his brother Benjamin, his own mother's son, he asked, "Is
this your youngest brother, the one you told me about?" And he said, "God be gracious to
you, my son." 30Deeply moved at the sight of his brother, Joseph hurried out and looked for
a place to weep. He went into his private room and wept there.
31After he had washed his face, he came out and, controlling himself, said, "Serve the
food."
32They served him by himself, the brothers by themselves, and the Egyptians who ate
with him by themselves, because Egyptians could not eat with Hebrews, for that is detest-
able to Egyptians. 33The men had been seated before him in the order of their ages, from
the firstborn to the youngest; and they looked at each other in astonishment. 34When por-
tions were served to them from Joseph's table, Benjamin's portion was five times as much
as anyone else's. So they feasted and drank freely with him.

A Silver Cup in a Sack

44 Now Joseph gave these instructions to the steward of his house: "Fill the men's
sacks with as much food as they can carry, and put each man's silver in the
mouth of his sack. 2Then put my cup, the silver one, in the mouth of the youn-
gest one's sack, along with the silver for his grain." And he did as Joseph said.
3As morning dawned, the men were sent on their way with their donkeys. 4They had not
gone far from the city when Joseph said to his steward, "Go after those men at once, and

---

[a] 14 Hebrew *El-Shaddai*

when you catch up with them, say to them, 'Why have you repaid good with evil? 5Isn't
this the cup my master drinks from and also uses for divination? This is a wicked thing
you have done.' "
6When he caught up with them, he repeated these words to them. 7But they said to him,
"Why does my lord say such things? Far be it from your servants to do anything like that!
8We even brought back to you from the land of Canaan the silver we found inside the
mouths of our sacks. So why would we steal silver or gold from your master's house? 9If
any of your servants is found to have it, he will die; and the rest of us will become my lord's
slaves."
10"Very well, then," he said, "let it be as you say. Whoever is found to have it will be-
come my slave; the rest of you will be free from blame."
11Each of them quickly lowered his sack to the ground and opened it. 12Then the stew-
ard proceeded to search, beginning with the oldest and ending with the youngest. And the
cup was found in Benjamin's sack. 13At this, they tore their clothes. Then they all loaded
their donkeys and returned to the city.
14Joseph was still in the house when Judah and his brothers came in, and they threw
themselves to the ground before him. 15Joseph said to them, "What is this you have done?
Don't you know that a man like me can find things out by divination?"
16"What can we say to my lord?" Judah replied. "What can we say? How can we prove
our innocence? God has uncovered your servants' guilt. We are now my lord's slaves—we
ourselves and the one who was found to have the cup."
17But Joseph said, "Far be it from me to do such a thing! Only the man who was found
to have the cup will become my slave. The rest of you, go back to your father in peace."
18Then Judah went up to him and said: "Pardon your servant, my lord, let me speak a
word to my lord. Do not be angry with your servant, though you are equal to Pharaoh him-
self. 19My lord asked his servants, 'Do you have a father or a brother?' 20And we answered,
'We have an aged father, and there is a young son born to him in his old age. His brother
is dead, and he is the only one of his mother's sons left, and his father loves him.'
21"Then you said to your servants, 'Bring him down to me so I can see him for myself.'
22And we said to my lord, 'The boy cannot leave his father; if he leaves him, his father will
die.' 23But you told your servants, 'Unless your youngest brother comes down with you,
you will not see my face again.' 24When we went back to your servant my father, we told
him what my lord had said.
25"Then our father said, 'Go back and buy a little more food.' 26But we said, 'We cannot
go down. Only if our youngest brother is with us will we go. We cannot see the man's face
unless our youngest brother is with us.'
27"Your servant my father said to us, 'You know that my wife bore me two sons. 28One
of them went away from me, and I said, "He has surely been torn to pieces." And I have
not seen him since. 29If you take this one from me too and harm comes to him, you will
bring my gray head down to the grave in misery.'
30"So now, if the boy is not with us when I go back to your servant my father, and if my
father, whose life is closely bound up with the boy's life, 31sees that the boy isn't there, he
will die. Your servants will bring the gray head of our father down to the grave in sorrow.
32Your servant guaranteed the boy's safety to my father. I said, 'If I do not bring him back
to you, I will bear the blame before you, my father, all my life!'
33"Now then, please let your servant remain here as my lord's slave in place of the boy,
and let the boy return with his brothers. 34How can I go back to my father if the boy is not
with me? No! Do not let me see the misery that would come on my father."

Joseph Makes Himself Known

45 Then Joseph could no longer control himself before all his attendants, and he
cried out, "Have everyone leave my presence!" So there was no one with Joseph
when he made himself known to his brothers. 2And he wept so loudly that the
Egyptians heard him, and Pharaoh's household heard about it.
3Joseph said to his brothers, "I am Joseph! Is my father still living?" But his brothers
were not able to answer him, because they were terrified at his presence.

[4]Then Joseph said to his brothers, "Come close to me." When they had done so, he said,
"I am your brother Joseph, the one you sold into Egypt! [5]And now, do not be distressed and
do not be angry with yourselves for selling me here, because it was to save lives that God
sent me ahead of you. [6]For two years now there has been famine in the land, and for the
next five years there will be no plowing and reaping. [7]But God sent me ahead of you to pre-
serve for you a remnant on earth and to save your lives by a great deliverance.[a]

[8]"So then, it was not you who sent me here, but God. He made me father to Pharaoh,
lord of his entire household and ruler of all Egypt. [9]Now hurry back to my father and say
to him, 'This is what your son Joseph says: God has made me lord of all Egypt. Come down
to me; don't delay. [10]You shall live in the region of Goshen and be near me—you, your chil-
dren and grandchildren, your flocks and herds, and all you have. [11]I will provide for you
there, because five years of famine are still to come. Otherwise you and your household and
all who belong to you will become destitute.'

[12]"You can see for yourselves, and so can my brother Benjamin, that it is really I who
am speaking to you. [13]Tell my father about all the honor accorded me in Egypt and about
everything you have seen. And bring my father down here quickly."

[14]Then he threw his arms around his brother Benjamin and wept, and Benjamin em-
braced him, weeping. [15]And he kissed all his brothers and wept over them. Afterward his
brothers talked with him.

[16]When the news reached Pharaoh's palace that Joseph's brothers had come, Pharaoh
and all his officials were pleased. [17]Pharaoh said to Joseph, "Tell your brothers, 'Do this:
Load your animals and return to the land of Canaan, [18]and bring your father and your fam-
ilies back to me. I will give you the best of the land of Egypt and you can enjoy the fat of
the land.'

[19]"You are also directed to tell them, 'Do this: Take some carts from Egypt for your chil-
dren and your wives, and get your father and come. [20]Never mind about your belongings,
because the best of all Egypt will be yours.' "

[21]So the sons of Israel did this. Joseph gave them carts, as Pharaoh had commanded,
and he also gave them provisions for their journey. [22]To each of them he gave new cloth-
ing, but to Benjamin he gave three hundred shekels[b] of silver and five sets of clothes. [23]And
this is what he sent to his father: ten donkeys loaded with the best things of Egypt, and
ten female donkeys loaded with grain and bread and other provisions for his journey.
[24]Then he sent his brothers away, and as they were leaving he said to them, "Don't quar-
rel on the way!"

[25]So they went up out of Egypt and came to their father Jacob in the land of Canaan. [26]They
told him, "Joseph is still alive! In fact, he is ruler of all Egypt." Jacob was stunned; he did not
believe them. [27]But when they told him everything Joseph had said to them, and when he
saw the carts Joseph had sent to carry him back, the spirit of their father Jacob revived. [28]And
Israel said, "I'm convinced! My son Joseph is still alive. I will go and see him before I die."

Discovering God

45:8 // The God Who Is There. Joseph saw God at work even in the evil plot of his brothers from years before. While the brothers were responsible for their wrongdoing, God did his work through those events. Through Joseph, God preserved a whole nation and the surrounding regions from a great famine (compare Joseph's words in chapter 50, verses 19–20 [page 66]).

One of the benefits of a relationship with God is that he has promised to work in every circumstance to bring eventual good out of it (see Romans chapter 8, verse 28 [page 210]). That doesn't mean that everything that happens to you will be good (see the note on Genesis chapter 42, verses 21–22 [page 56]), but you can be confident in God's power to reclaim whatever happens for a better purpose.

[a] 7 Or *save you as a great band of survivors* [b] 22 That is, about 7 1/2 pounds or about 3.5 kilograms

Jacob Goes to Egypt

46 So Israel set out with all that was his, and when he reached Beersheba, he of-
fered sacrifices to the God of his father Isaac.
2And God spoke to Israel in a vision at night and said, "Jacob! Jacob!"
"Here I am," he replied.
3"I am God, the God of your father," he said. "Do not be afraid to go down to Egypt, for
I will make you into a great nation there. 4I will go down to Egypt with you, and I will sure-
ly bring you back again. And Joseph's own hand will close your eyes."
5Then Jacob left Beersheba, and Israel's sons took their father Jacob and their children and
their wives in the carts that Pharaoh had sent to transport him. 6So Jacob and all his off-
spring went to Egypt, taking with them their livestock and the possessions they had ac-
quired in Canaan. 7Jacob brought with him to Egypt his sons and grandsons and his
daughters and granddaughters—all his offspring.

8These are the names of the sons of Israel (Jacob and his descendants) who went to Egypt:

Reuben the firstborn of Jacob.
9The sons of Reuben:
Hanok, Pallu, Hezron and Karmi.
10The sons of Simeon:
Jemuel, Jamin, Ohad, Jakin, Zohar and Shaul the son of a Canaanite woman.
11The sons of Levi:
Gershon, Kohath and Merari.
12The sons of Judah:
Er, Onan, Shelah, Perez and Zerah (but Er and Onan had died in the land of Canaan).
The sons of Perez:
Hezron and Hamul.
13The sons of Issachar:
Tola, Puah,[a] Jashub[b] and Shimron.
14The sons of Zebulun:
Sered, Elon and Jahleel.
15These were the sons Leah bore to Jacob in Paddan Aram,[c] besides his daughter Dinah.
These sons and daughters of his were thirty-three in all.

16The sons of Gad:
Zephon,[d] Haggi, Shuni, Ezbon, Eri, Arodi and Areli.
17The sons of Asher:
Imnah, Ishvah, Ishvi and Beriah.
Their sister was Serah.
The sons of Beriah:
Heber and Malkiel.
18These were the children born to Jacob by Zilpah, whom Laban had given to his daugh-
ter Leah—sixteen in all.

19The sons of Jacob's wife Rachel:
Joseph and Benjamin. 20In Egypt, Manasseh and Ephraim were born to Joseph by
Asenath daughter of Potiphera, priest of On.[e]
21The sons of Benjamin:
Bela, Beker, Ashbel, Gera, Naaman, Ehi, Rosh, Muppim, Huppim and Ard.
22These were the sons of Rachel who were born to Jacob—fourteen in all.

---

[a] *13* Samaritan Pentateuch and Syriac (see also 1 Chron. 7:1); Masoretic Text *Puvah*
[b] *13* Samaritan Pentateuch and some Septuagint manuscripts (see also Num. 26:24 and 1 Chron. 7:1); Masoretic Text *Iob* [c] *15* That is, Northwest Mesopotamia [d] *16* Samaritan Pentateuch and Septuagint (see also Num. 26:15); Masoretic Text *Ziphion* [e] *20* That is, Heliopolis

23 The son of Dan:
Hushim.
24 The sons of Naphtali:
Jahziel, Guni, Jezer and Shillem.
25 These were the sons born to Jacob by Bilhah, whom Laban had given to his daughter
Rachel—seven in all.

26 All those who went to Egypt with Jacob—those who were his direct descendants, not
counting his sons' wives—numbered sixty-six persons. 27 With the two sons[a] who had been
born to Joseph in Egypt, the members of Jacob's family, which went to Egypt, were seven-
ty[b] in all.

28 Now Jacob sent Judah ahead of him to Joseph to get directions to Goshen. When they
arrived in the region of Goshen, 29 Joseph had his chariot made ready and went to Goshen
to meet his father Israel. As soon as Joseph appeared before him, he threw his arms around
his father[c] and wept for a long time.
30 Israel said to Joseph, "Now I am ready to die, since I have seen for myself that you are
still alive."
31 Then Joseph said to his brothers and to his father's household, "I will go up and speak
to Pharaoh and will say to him, 'My brothers and my father's household, who were living
in the land of Canaan, have come to me. 32 The men are shepherds; they tend livestock,
and they have brought along their flocks and herds and everything they own.' 33 When Phar-
aoh calls you in and asks, 'What is your occupation?' 34 you should answer, 'Your servants
have tended livestock from our boyhood on, just as our fathers did.' Then you will be al-
lowed to settle in the region of Goshen, for all shepherds are detestable to the Egyptians."

47 Joseph went and told Pharaoh, "My father and brothers, with their flocks and
herds and everything they own, have come from the land of Canaan and are now
in Goshen." 2 He chose five of his brothers and presented them before Pharaoh.
3 Pharaoh asked the brothers, "What is your occupation?"
"Your servants are shepherds," they replied to Pharaoh, "just as our fathers were." 4 They
also said to him, "We have come to live here for a while, because the famine is severe in
Canaan and your servants' flocks have no pasture. So now, please let your servants settle
in Goshen."
5 Pharaoh said to Joseph, "Your father and your brothers have come to you, 6 and the
land of Egypt is before you; settle your father and your brothers in the best part of the
land. Let them live in Goshen. And if you know of any among them with special ability,
put them in charge of my own livestock."
7 Then Joseph brought his father Jacob in and presented him before Pharaoh. After Jacob
blessed[d] Pharaoh, 8 Pharaoh asked him, "How old are you?"
9 And Jacob said to Pharaoh, "The years of my pilgrimage are a hundred and thirty. My
years have been few and difficult, and they do not equal the years of the pilgrimage of my
fathers." 10 Then Jacob blessed[e] Pharaoh and went out from his presence.
11 So Joseph settled his father and his brothers in Egypt and gave them property in the
best part of the land, the district of Rameses, as Pharaoh directed. 12 Joseph also provided
his father and his brothers and all his father's household with food, according to the num-
ber of their children.

Joseph and the Famine

13 There was no food, however, in the whole region because the famine was severe; both
Egypt and Canaan wasted away because of the famine. 14 Joseph collected all the money
that was to be found in Egypt and Canaan in payment for the grain they were buying, and
he brought it to Pharaoh's palace. 15 When the money of the people of Egypt and Canaan
was gone, all Egypt came to Joseph and said, "Give us food. Why should we die before your
eyes? Our money is all gone."

---

[a] 27 Hebrew; Septuagint *the nine children* [b] 27 Hebrew (see also Exodus 1:5 and footnote); Septuagint (see also Acts 7:14) *seventy-five* [c] 29 Hebrew *around him* [d] 7 Or *greeted* [e] 10 Or *said farewell to*

16“Then bring your livestock,” said Joseph. “I will sell you food in exchange for your live-
stock, since your money is gone.” 17So they brought their livestock to Joseph, and he gave
them food in exchange for their horses, their sheep and goats, their cattle and donkeys.
And he brought them through that year with food in exchange for all their livestock.
18When that year was over, they came to him the following year and said, “We cannot
hide from our lord the fact that since our money is gone and our livestock belongs to you,
there is nothing left for our lord except our bodies and our land. 19Why should we perish
before your eyes—we and our land as well? Buy us and our land in exchange for food, and
we with our land will be in bondage to Pharaoh. Give us seed so that we may live and not
die, and that the land may not become desolate.”
20So Joseph bought all the land in Egypt for Pharaoh. The Egyptians, one and all, sold
their fields, because the famine was too severe for them. The land became Pharaoh’s, 21and
Joseph reduced the people to servitude,[a] from one end of Egypt to the other. 22However,
he did not buy the land of the priests, because they received a regular allotment from Phar-
aoh and had food enough from the allotment Pharaoh gave them. That is why they did not
sell their land.
23Joseph said to the people, “Now that I have bought you and your land today for Phar-
aoh, here is seed for you so you can plant the ground. 24But when the crop comes in, give
a fifth of it to Pharaoh. The other four-fifths you may keep as seed for the fields and as food
for yourselves and your households and your children.”
25“You have saved our lives,” they said. “May we find favor in the eyes of our lord; we will
be in bondage to Pharaoh.”
26So Joseph established it as a law concerning land in Egypt—still in force today—that
a fifth of the produce belongs to Pharaoh. It was only the land of the priests that did not
become Pharaoh’s.
27Now the Israelites settled in Egypt in the region of Goshen. They acquired property
there and were fruitful and increased greatly in number.
28Jacob lived in Egypt seventeen years, and the years of his life were a hundred and for-
ty-seven. 29When the time drew near for Israel to die, he called for his son Joseph and said
to him, “If I have found favor in your eyes, put your hand under my thigh and promise that
you will show me kindness and faithfulness. Do not bury me in Egypt, 30but when I rest with
my fathers, carry me out of Egypt and bury me where they are buried.”
“I will do as you say,” he said.
31“Swear to me,” he said. Then Joseph swore to him, and Israel worshiped as he leaned
on the top of his staff.[b]

Manasseh and Ephraim

48 Some time later Joseph was told, “Your father is ill.” So he took his two sons
Manasseh and Ephraim along with him. 2When Jacob was told, “Your son Jo-
seph has come to you,” Israel rallied his strength and sat up on the bed.
3Jacob said to Joseph, “God Almighty[c] appeared to me at Luz in the land of Canaan, and
there he blessed me 4and said to me, ‘I am going to make you fruitful and increase your
numbers. I will make you a community of peoples, and I will give this land as an everlast-
ing possession to your descendants after you.’
5“Now then, your two sons born to you in Egypt before I came to you here will be reck-
oned as mine; Ephraim and Manasseh will be mine, just as Reuben and Simeon are mine.
6Any children born to you after them will be yours; in the territory they inherit they will be
reckoned under the names of their brothers. 7As I was returning from Paddan,[d] to my sor-
row Rachel died in the land of Canaan while we were still on the way, a little distance from
Ephrath. So I buried her there beside the road to Ephrath” (that is, Bethlehem).
8When Israel saw the sons of Joseph, he asked, “Who are these?”
9“They are the sons God has given me here,” Joseph said to his father.
Then Israel said, “Bring them to me so I may bless them.”

---

[a] *21* Samaritan Pentateuch and Septuagint (see also Vulgate); Masoretic Text *and he moved the people into the cities* [b] *31* Or *Israel bowed down at the head of his bed* [c] *3* Hebrew *El-Shaddai*
[d] *7* That is, Northwest Mesopotamia

[10]Now Israel's eyes were failing because of old age, and he could hardly see. So Joseph
brought his sons close to him, and his father kissed them and embraced them.
[11]Israel said to Joseph, "I never expected to see your face again, and now God has al-
lowed me to see your children too."
[12]Then Joseph removed them from Israel's knees and bowed down with his face to the
ground. [13]And Joseph took both of them, Ephraim on his right toward Israel's left hand and
Manasseh on his left toward Israel's right hand, and brought them close to him. [14]But Is-
rael reached out his right hand and put it on Ephraim's head, though he was the younger,
and crossing his arms, he put his left hand on Manasseh's head, even though Manasseh was
the firstborn.
[15]Then he blessed Joseph and said,

"May the God before whom my fathers
Abraham and Isaac walked faithfully,
the God who has been my shepherd
all my life to this day,
[16]the Angel who has delivered me from all harm
—may he bless these boys.
May they be called by my name
and the names of my fathers Abraham and Isaac,
and may they increase greatly
on the earth."

[17]When Joseph saw his father placing his right hand on Ephraim's head he was dis-
pleased; so he took hold of his father's hand to move it from Ephraim's head to Manas-
seh's head. [18]Joseph said to him, "No, my father, this one is the firstborn; put your right
hand on his head."
[19]But his father refused and said, "I know, my son, I know. He too will become a people,
and he too will become great. Nevertheless, his younger brother will be greater than he, and
his descendants will become a group of nations." [20]He blessed them that day and said,

"In your[a] name will Israel pronounce this blessing:
'May God make you like Ephraim and Manasseh.' "

So he put Ephraim ahead of Manasseh.
[21]Then Israel said to Joseph, "I am about to die, but God will be with you[b] and take you[b]
back to the land of your[b] fathers. [22]And to you I give one more ridge of land[c] than to your
brothers, the ridge I took from the Amorites with my sword and my bow."

Jacob Blesses His Sons

49 Then Jacob called for his sons and said: "Gather around so I can tell you what
will happen to you in days to come.

[2]"Assemble and listen, sons of Jacob;
listen to your father Israel.

[3]"Reuben, you are my firstborn,
my might, the first sign of my strength,
excelling in honor, excelling in power.
[4]Turbulent as the waters, you will no longer excel,
for you went up onto your father's bed,
onto my couch and defiled it.

[5]"Simeon and Levi are brothers—
their swords[d] are weapons of violence.
[6]Let me not enter their council,

[a] *20* The Hebrew is singular. [b] *21* The Hebrew is plural. [c] *22* The Hebrew for *ridge of land* is identical with the place name Shechem. [d] *5* The meaning of the Hebrew for this word is uncertain.

let me not join their assembly,
for they have killed men in their anger
and hamstrung oxen as they pleased.
7 Cursed be their anger, so fierce,
and their fury, so cruel!
I will scatter them in Jacob
and disperse them in Israel.

8 "Judah,[a] your brothers will praise you;
your hand will be on the neck of your enemies;
your father's sons will bow down to you.
9 You are a lion's cub, Judah;
you return from the prey, my son.
Like a lion he crouches and lies down,
like a lioness—who dares to rouse him?
10 The scepter will not depart from Judah,
nor the ruler's staff from between his feet,[b]
until he to whom it belongs[c] shall come
and the obedience of the nations be his.
11 He will tether his donkey to a vine,
his colt to the choicest branch;
he will wash his garments in wine,
his robes in the blood of grapes.
12 His eyes will be darker than wine,
his teeth whiter than milk.[d]

13 "Zebulun will live by the seashore
and become a haven for ships;
his border will extend toward Sidon.

14 "Issachar is a rawboned[e] donkey
lying down among the sheep pens.[f]
15 When he sees how good is his resting place
and how pleasant is his land,
he will bend his shoulder to the burden
and submit to forced labor.

16 "Dan[g] will provide justice for his people
as one of the tribes of Israel.
17 Dan will be a snake by the roadside,
a viper along the path,
that bites the horse's heels
so that its rider tumbles backward.

18 "I look for your deliverance, LORD.

19 "Gad[h] will be attacked by a band of raiders,
but he will attack them at their heels.

20 "Asher's food will be rich;
he will provide delicacies fit for a king.

21 "Naphtali is a doe set free
that bears beautiful fawns.[i]

---

[a] 8 *Judah* sounds like and may be derived from the Hebrew for *praise.* [b] 10 Or *from his descendants* [c] 10 Or *to whom tribute belongs*; the meaning of the Hebrew for this phrase is uncertain. [d] 12 Or *will be dull from wine, / his teeth white from milk* [e] 14 Or *strong* [f] 14 Or *the campfires*; or *the saddlebags* [g] 16 *Dan* here means *he provides justice.* [h] 19 *Gad* sounds like the Hebrew for *attack* and also for *band of raiders.* [i] 21 Or *free; / he utters beautiful words*

[22]"Joseph is a fruitful vine,
a fruitful vine near a spring,
whose branches climb over a wall.[a]
[23]With bitterness archers attacked him;
they shot at him with hostility.
[24]But his bow remained steady,
his strong arms stayed[b] limber,
because of the hand of the Mighty One of Jacob,
because of the Shepherd, the Rock of Israel,
[25]because of your father's God, who helps you,
because of the Almighty,[c] who blesses you
with blessings of the heavens above,
blessings of the deep that lies below,
blessings of the breast and womb.
[26]Your father's blessings are greater
than the blessings of the ancient mountains,
than[d] the bounty of the age-old hills.
Let all these rest on the head of Joseph,
on the brow of the prince among[e] his brothers.

[27]"Benjamin is a ravenous wolf;
in the morning he devours the prey,
in the evening he divides the plunder."

[28]All these are the twelve tribes of Israel, and this is what their father said to them when he blessed them, giving each the blessing appropriate to him.

The Death of Jacob

[29]Then he gave them these instructions: "I am about to be gathered to my people. Bury
me with my fathers in the cave in the field of Ephron the Hittite, [30]the cave in the field of
Machpelah, near Mamre in Canaan, which Abraham bought along with the field as a buri-
al place from Ephron the Hittite. [31]There Abraham and his wife Sarah were buried, there
Isaac and his wife Rebekah were buried, and there I buried Leah. [32]The field and the cave
in it were bought from the Hittites.[f]"
[33]When Jacob had finished giving instructions to his sons, he drew his feet up into the
bed, breathed his last and was gathered to his people.

Strengthening Relationships

48:19–20 // Parenting. The parental blessing was very important in Biblical times. It was the means through which a father stated his last will and testament and predicted what he thought would happen in the future.

The blessing summarized the father's observations concerning his children. He didn't just tell them what he would give them—he told them *who they were.* Thus the blessing helped the children understand their place in the world.

It's important in every culture for parents to discover how their children have been uniquely gifted and to affirm their design. One of the sad commentaries on many parents today is that they fail to give their children "the blessing"—the sense that they recognize and approve of their child's unique, God-given identity.

If you're a parent, don't fail to be your children's greatest student. Observe them; learn about them; affirm who they are. The blessing you give—or withhold—will profoundly shape their future.

---

[a] 22 Or *Joseph is a wild colt, / a wild colt near a spring, / a wild donkey on a terraced hill*
[b] 23,24 Or *archers will attack . . . will shoot . . . will remain . . . will stay* [c] 25 Hebrew *Shaddai*
[d] 26 Or *of my progenitors, / as great as* [e] 26 Or *of the one separated from* [f] 32 Or *the descendants of Heth*

50 Joseph threw himself on his father and wept over him and kissed him. 2Then Jo-
seph directed the physicians in his service to embalm his father Israel. So the
physicians embalmed him, 3taking a full forty days, for that was the time re-
quired for embalming. And the Egyptians mourned for him seventy days.
4When the days of mourning had passed, Joseph said to Pharaoh's court, "If I have found
favor in your eyes, speak to Pharaoh for me. Tell him, 5'My father made me swear an oath
and said, "I am about to die; bury me in the tomb I dug for myself in the land of Canaan."
Now let me go up and bury my father; then I will return.' "
6Pharaoh said, "Go up and bury your father, as he made you swear to do."
7So Joseph went up to bury his father. All Pharaoh's officials accompanied him—the
dignitaries of his court and all the dignitaries of Egypt— 8besides all the members of Jo-
seph's household and his brothers and those belonging to his father's household. Only
their children and their flocks and herds were left in Goshen. 9Chariots and horsemen[a]
also went up with him. It was a very large company.
10When they reached the threshing floor of Atad, near the Jordan, they lamented loud-
ly and bitterly; and there Joseph observed a seven-day period of mourning for his father.
11When the Canaanites who lived there saw the mourning at the threshing floor of Atad,
they said, "The Egyptians are holding a solemn ceremony of mourning." That is why that
place near the Jordan is called Abel Mizraim.[b]
12So Jacob's sons did as he had commanded them: 13They carried him to the land of Ca-
naan and buried him in the cave in the field of Machpelah, near Mamre, which Abraham
had bought along with the field as a burial place from Ephron the Hittite. 14After burying
his father, Joseph returned to Egypt, together with his brothers and all the others who had
gone with him to bury his father.

Joseph Reassures His Brothers

15When Joseph's brothers saw that their father was dead, they said, "What if Joseph holds
a grudge against us and pays us back for all the wrongs we did to him?" 16So they sent word
to Joseph, saying, "Your father left these instructions before he died: 17'This is what you are
to say to Joseph: I ask you to forgive your brothers the sins and the wrongs they commit-
ted in treating you so badly.' Now please forgive the sins of the servants of the God of your
father." When their message came to him, Joseph wept.
18His brothers then came and threw themselves down before him. "We are your slaves,"
they said.
19But Joseph said to them, "Don't be afraid. Am I in the place of God? 20You intended to
harm me, but God intended it for good to accomplish what is now being done, the saving
of many lives. 21So then, don't be afraid. I will provide for you and your children." And he
reassured them and spoke kindly to them.

Knowing Yourself

50:19–20 // Sin. You've heard many people say, "Don't get mad; get even." But true God-followers say, "It's okay to get mad, but let God get even." Joseph powerfully exemplifies this higher path in dealing with his brothers.

The Bible never tells us to timidly allow evil to go unchecked. After all, God hates evil because it hurts people. God works through our modern justice system, for example, to control the spread of evil in society. But believers are encouraged to employ a revolutionary method of challenging personal offenses—showing kindness in all circumstances, even to people who have hurt them in some way.

Anger is a justifiable, even healthy, emotion. God is also angry when injustice occurs. But the only way to find freedom from the hurts that have devastated us is by trusting—as Joseph did—that God's justice will prevail in the end.

---

[a] 9 Or *charioteers* [b] 11 *Abel Mizraim* means *mourning of the Egyptians.*

The Death of Joseph

[22]Joseph stayed in Egypt, along with all his father's family. He lived a hundred and ten
years [23]and saw the third generation of Ephraim's children. Also the children of Makir son
of Manasseh were placed at birth on Joseph's knees.[a]
[24]Then Joseph said to his brother Israelites, "I am about to die. But God will surely come
to your aid and take you up out of this land to the land he promised on oath to Abraham,
Isaac and Jacob." [25]And Joseph made the Israelites swear an oath and said, "God will surely
come to your aid, and then you must carry my bones up from this place."
[26]So Joseph died at the age of a hundred and ten. And after they embalmed him, he was
placed in a coffin in Egypt.

Epilogue

This is the first book of the Bible, and it sets the stage for all that follows. *Beginning the Journey* focuses on this book and four others to summarize the central message of the Bible.

In these pages you have read about the God who made everything, the people who ruined that good creation, and the first steps God took to get his wayward human family back.

One of God's most crucial interventions was to identify Abraham as the "seed" of the Hebrew people. Abraham's offspring would eventually grow into a great nation, and that nation would be a light to the whole world.

To read the story of how God established this nation in the land he had promised, turn to the next book, called "Deuteronomy." There you'll meet Moses, the great leader who fulfilled God's promise, spoken through Joseph, to deliver Israel from Egypt (see chapter 50, verses 24–25 above). Notice the theme that is beginning to emerge—God is a deliverer, a rescuer. He fulfills this role throughout the Bible.

People who seek God will find that the barrier between us and him is not just lack of information, but our spiritually self-destructive tendency to sin. To remove that barrier, we need more than just information or education—we need to claim God's promise to free us from our sin and accept the salvation that he offers. God is the only being who can provide that freedom, and he will if we will just ask.

---

[a] *23* That is, were counted as his

Seeker Stories

I couldn't believe it: I had recently left my wife for this woman, and now she wanted me to go to church! It didn't matter what we were doing just before church or just after, or how we lived the rest of the week. She had to be in church every Sunday. Other than this idiosyncrasy, she seemed perfect. So I went with her.

Her church was small and traditional, and the minister preached on why Christians in his particular denomination had a leg up on everyone else. I left telling my girlfriend that the message was baloney. "Fine," she said angrily. "You pick the church next week."

I was stumped. I couldn't go back to her church—that would be admitting I was wrong, and I didn't ever do that. The only church that popped into my mind was one my assistant had been telling me about for four years. "I've heard about this unusual church . . ." I began.

When my girlfriend and I pulled up the following Sunday, I noticed that the grounds were immaculate. "There's somebody around here who cares," I thought. As a middle-management businessman, I paid attention to those kinds of things. I was even more intrigued by the auditorium. It was theater style—there were no stained-glass windows and no statues of the saints. There wasn't even a crucifix. "Is this really a church?" I wondered. Then the music started—I actually liked it! It was the kind of music I listened to, except that the content was different.

The announcements raised my eyebrows even more: The church didn't want my money. "How do they pay for this place?" I wondered. Now they really had my attention.

During the message, the pastor did something I'd never heard a pastor do: He used himself as an example in his message, which was on being patient. He told us about how he had run home from church to catch a football game, scrambled to the local convenience store at half-time to get a newspaper, and then got frustrated when he was caught behind someone who was slowly ordering a sandwich. That was me! Not only was I impatient, but I was also a liar and a thief. I had lost a job because of stealing. I thought that if people really knew me they would run in the opposite direction. God, I had surmised, was the same.

But then I heard the pastor say that I mattered to God. No matter what. No matter where I was in life. A glimmer of hope slipped into my mind: Could this possibly be true? The answer to that question was going to change my family and me forever.

"That was the most sacreligious place I've ever been to," my girlfriend said as we left the church that Sunday. I didn't tell her how I was feeling, but my inner turmoil wouldn't go away. What was that experience all about? Was it a fluke? If there was a God, could I possibly matter to him? In search of an answer, I did something I'd never done before: I decided to go to church by myself. "Impress me again," I half-prayed. "I dare you."

The second Sunday was similar to the first. Again I heard the message that I mattered to God—and to this church. I walked out feeling challenged but encouraged—so much so that I came back the third week. This time the message was on different kinds of faithfulness—marital, relational and spiritual. It didn't take much soul-searching to realize that I had none of the qualities the pastor was speaking about.

What I did next went against everything I had done only months earlier. I broke it off with my girlfriend and called my estranged wife to ask if she would go to church with me the next Sunday. She was shocked and skeptical at my request, but she agreed to go to church with me.

It was a cool ride to the church—and not because of the temperature! We didn't even speak until afterward.

"Well, what did you think?" I asked. She gave me a puzzled look. "I really liked it. It was like coming home."

Several weeks passed. I asked my wife if she was willing to take me back. After some thought she said yes, and we went to counseling. We also met some people who presented the plan of salvation to us. After hearing it we both decided to thoroughly investigate Christianity. People at the church seemed confident we would find the claims of Christ to be true.

Six months later, a weekend message forced me to choose: Was Jesus a liar? Or was he crazy? The only alternative was to accept his claims to be the Son of God and Savior of the world. I had come to the point where I was ready to acknowledge that as the truth. With tears streaming down my face, I asked Jesus to forgive me of my sins and to lead my life. I felt as if a two-ton weight had been removed from my shoulders. My wife accepted Christ a few months later. Now, with God as the center of our lives, our marriage has begun the healing process and is growing stronger and stronger.

Deuteronomy Introduction

THE BOTTOM LINE

All trade agreements, whether as large as a nation's international policy or as small as a contract from the local used car lot, include a series of regulations and stipulations—"We promise this if you do that." In this book, Moses spells out God's agreement (or "covenant") with the people of Israel. The main terms are simple: Israel is to love and obey God, being careful to show his character to the world. In turn, God will establish them in the land he had promised to their ancestor Abraham. God extends a similar offer to us today. He wants us to love him above all else, and to rely on Jesus for forgiveness. To those who do so, God grants pardon from sin (Hebrews chapter 10, verses 10, 16–18).

CENTRAL IDEAS

- God's agreement with Israel: "I will preserve your nation if you obey me."
- We must reject anything that takes away from devotion to God.
- God reaches out to people—not because they're deserving, but because he's gracious.
- Moses restates the Ten Commandments (chapter 5).

OUTLINE

1. **Preamble** (1:1–5)
2. **Historical prologue** (1:6—4:43)
3. **God's agreement with his people** (4:44—26:19)
4. **Results of obedience and disobedience** (chaps. 27–30)
5. **Leadership transferred** (chaps. 31–34)

TITLE

Deuteronomy means "the second law"—Moses gives his final sermon and tells the Israelites God's commandments for the second (and his last) time.

AUTHOR AND READERS

Moses wrote this book as his final words to the people of Israel.

Human love is a powerful force. It can change the course of a person's life, taking someone who seems destined to fail and transforming them into a success story. It can overcome deep-seated prejudices and inspire people to sacrifice themselves for someone else.

Take the true story of Wladyslaw Szpilman (featured in the 2002 movie *The Pianist*). Szpilman was a Polish Jewish musician who took refuge in the rubble of Warsaw during World War II. He watched helplessly as the entire city was emptied, as family and friends were systematically executed by the Nazis. Szpilman himself narrowly escaped death when he was pulled off a train headed for the concentration camp at Treblinka.

As the war drew to a close, Szpilman went into hiding, subsisting on food taken from the ruins of abandoned houses . . . until he was discovered by a Nazi officer. Captain Wilm Hosenfeld turned out to be an unlikely savior. Risking his own life, Hosenfeld hid and fed Szpilman until the German army was finally driven out of Poland. After Hosenfeld's death in a Soviet prison camp, it was discovered that during the war he had protected a number of Jews from the savagery of the Nazi regime. He died an unknown hero.

Love can change the course of a person's life.

As powerful as human love can be, divine love is an even greater power. It takes spiritually dead people and gives them life. God's love causes people to hunger to know him. Once they know him, his love creates within them a desire for his leadership in every facet of life.

As the Israelite people prepared to enter the land God had promised them, God used his spokesman Moses to give them guidance for their new life. In this book, which is actually Moses' farewell speech, Moses reiterates the primary principle upon which the nation will be built—the law of loving God above all else because he loves them. After repeating the famous "Ten Commandments," he teaches them how to apply that law of love and how to pass it on to the next generation. Turn to Deuteronomy chapter 6, verses 4–9 (page 81), to find that guidance.

DEUTERONOMY

The Command to Leave Horeb

1 These are the words Moses spoke to all Israel in the wilderness east of the Jordan—that is, in the Arabah—opposite Suph, between Paran and Tophel, Laban, Hazeroth and Dizahab. 2 (It takes eleven days to go from Horeb to Kadesh Barnea by the Mount Seir road.)

3 In the fortieth year, on the first day of the eleventh month, Moses proclaimed to the Israelites all that the LORD had commanded him concerning them. 4 This was after he had defeated Sihon king of the Amorites, who reigned in Heshbon, and at Edrei had defeated Og king of Bashan, who reigned in Ashtaroth.

5 East of the Jordan in the territory of Moab, Moses began to expound this law, saying:

6 The LORD our God said to us at Horeb, "You have stayed long enough at this mountain. 7 Break camp and advance into the hill country of the Amorites; go to all the neighboring peoples in the Arabah, in the mountains, in the western foothills, in the Negev and along the coast, to the land of the Canaanites and to Lebanon, as far as the great river, the Euphrates. 8 See, I have given you this land. Go in and take possession of the land that the LORD swore he would give to your fathers—to Abraham, Isaac and Jacob—and to their descendants after them."

The Appointment of Leaders

9 At that time I said to you, "You are too heavy a burden for me to carry alone. 10 The LORD your God has increased your numbers so that today you are as many as the stars in the sky. 11 May the LORD, the God of your ancestors, increase you a thousand times and bless you as he has promised! 12 But how can I bear your problems and your burdens and your disputes all by myself? 13 Choose some wise, understanding and respected men from each of your tribes, and I will set them over you."

14 You answered me, "What you propose to do is good."

15 So I took the leading men of your tribes, wise and respected men, and appointed them to have authority over you—as commanders of thousands, of hundreds, of fifties and of tens and as tribal officials. 16 And I charged your judges at that time: Hear the disputes between your people and judge fairly, whether the case is between two Israelites or between an Israelite and a foreigner residing among you. 17 Do not show partiality in judging; hear both small and great alike. Do not be afraid of anyone, for judgment belongs to God. Bring me any case too hard for you, and I will hear it. 18 And at that time I told you everything you were to do.

Spies Sent Out

19 Then, as the LORD our God commanded us, we set out from Horeb and went toward the hill country of the Amorites through all that vast and dreadful wilderness that you have seen, and so we reached Kadesh Barnea. 20 Then I said to you, "You have reached the hill country of the Amorites, which the LORD our God is giving us. 21 See, the LORD your God has

Strengthening Relationships

1:15–17 // Leadership. One function of leaders in Old Testament times was to help settle disagreements. These leaders needed to be wise and discerning as they heard both sides of a story, sorted through details, and determined a fair and impartial solution. Their God-given objective was to give the "little people" in their society the same kind of hearing they gave to the rich and powerful.

What about leaders today? Good leaders in business, government and education must be able to cut to the core of an issue, be open to all points of view until all the evidence is in, and be utterly fair and unbiased.

But notice that the spiritual dimension is lacking in many who wield power in our day. Ultimately, leaders answer to God, not just to those whom they lead. Think of how much better the government and marketplace would function if men and women were to recognize that they were accountable to an all-seeing, impartial God who will someday judge *them!*

given you the land. Go up and take possession of it as the LORD, the God of your ancestors,
told you. Do not be afraid; do not be discouraged."
[22]Then all of you came to me and said, "Let us send men ahead to spy out the land for
us and bring back a report about the route we are to take and the towns we will come to."
[23]The idea seemed good to me; so I selected twelve of you, one man from each tribe.
[24]They left and went up into the hill country, and came to the Valley of Eshkol and explored
it. [25]Taking with them some of the fruit of the land, they brought it down to us and report-
ed, "It is a good land that the LORD our God is giving us."

Rebellion Against the LORD

[26]But you were unwilling to go up; you rebelled against the command of the LORD your
God. [27]You grumbled in your tents and said, "The LORD hates us; so he brought us out of
Egypt to deliver us into the hands of the Amorites to destroy us. [28]Where can we go? Our
brothers have made our hearts melt in fear. They say, 'The people are stronger and taller
than we are; the cities are large, with walls up to the sky. We even saw the Anakites there.' "
[29]Then I said to you, "Do not be terrified; do not be afraid of them. [30]The LORD your God,
who is going before you, will fight for you, as he did for you in Egypt, before your very eyes,
[31]and in the wilderness. There you saw how the LORD your God carried you, as a father car-
ries his son, all the way you went until you reached this place."
[32]In spite of this, you did not trust in the LORD your God, [33]who went ahead of you on your
journey, in fire by night and in a cloud by day, to search out places for you to camp and to
show you the way you should go.
[34]When the LORD heard what you said, he was angry and solemnly swore: [35]"No one from
this evil generation shall see the good land I swore to give your ancestors, [36]except Caleb
son of Jephunneh. He will see it, and I will give him and his descendants the land he set
his feet on, because he followed the LORD wholeheartedly."
[37]Because of you the LORD became angry with me also and said, "You shall not enter it,
either. [38]But your assistant, Joshua son of Nun, will enter it. Encourage him, because he will
lead Israel to inherit it. [39]And the little ones that you said would be taken captive, your chil-
dren who do not yet know good from bad—they will enter the land. I will give it to them
and they will take possession of it. [40]But as for you, turn around and set out toward the
desert along the route to the Red Sea.[a]"
[41]Then you replied, "We have sinned against the LORD. We will go up and fight, as the
LORD our God commanded us." So every one of you put on his weapons, thinking it easy
to go up into the hill country.
[42]But the LORD said to me, "Tell them, 'Do not go up and fight, because I will not be with
you. You will be defeated by your enemies.' "
[43]So I told you, but you would not listen. You rebelled against the LORD's command and
in your arrogance you marched up into the hill country. [44]The Amorites who lived in those
hills came out against you; they chased you like a swarm of bees and beat you down from
Seir all the way to Hormah. [45]You came back and wept before the LORD, but he paid no at-
tention to your weeping and turned a deaf ear to you. [46]And so you stayed in Kadesh many
days—all the time you spent there.

Wanderings in the Wilderness

2 Then we turned back and set out toward the wilderness along the route to the Red
Sea,[a] as the LORD had directed me. For a long time we made our way around the hill
country of Seir.
[2]Then the LORD said to me, [3]"You have made your way around this hill country long
enough; now turn north. [4]Give the people these orders: 'You are about to pass through the
territory of your relatives the descendants of Esau, who live in Seir. They will be afraid of
you, but be very careful. [5]Do not provoke them to war, for I will not give you any of their
land, not even enough to put your foot on. I have given Esau the hill country of Seir as his
own. [6]You are to pay them in silver for the food you eat and the water you drink.' "
[7]The LORD your God has blessed you in all the work of your hands. He has watched over

---

[a] *40,1 Or the Sea of Reeds*

your journey through this vast wilderness. These forty years the LORD your God has been with you, and you have not lacked anything.

[8]So we went on past our relatives the descendants of Esau, who live in Seir. We turned from the Arabah road, which comes up from Elath and Ezion Geber, and traveled along the desert road of Moab.

[9]Then the LORD said to me, "Do not harass the Moabites or provoke them to war, for I will not give you any part of their land. I have given Ar to the descendants of Lot as a possession."

[10](The Emites used to live there—a people strong and numerous, and as tall as the Anakites. [11]Like the Anakites, they too were considered Rephaites, but the Moabites called them Emites. [12]Horites used to live in Seir, but the descendants of Esau drove them out. They destroyed the Horites from before them and settled in their place, just as Israel did in the land the LORD gave them as their possession.)

[13]And the LORD said, "Now get up and cross the Zered Valley." So we crossed the valley.

[14]Thirty-eight years passed from the time we left Kadesh Barnea until we crossed the Zered Valley. By then, that entire generation of fighting men had perished from the camp, as the LORD had sworn to them. [15]The LORD's hand was against them until he had completely eliminated them from the camp.

[16]Now when the last of these fighting men among the people had died, [17]the LORD said to me, [18]"Today you are to pass by the region of Moab at Ar. [19]When you come to the Ammonites, do not harass them or provoke them to war, for I will not give you possession of any land belonging to the Ammonites. I have given it as a possession to the descendants of Lot."

[20](That too was considered a land of the Rephaites, who used to live there; but the Ammonites called them Zamzummites. [21]They were a people strong and numerous, and as tall as the Anakites. The LORD destroyed them from before the Ammonites, who drove them out and settled in their place. [22]The LORD had done the same for the descendants of Esau, who lived in Seir, when he destroyed the Horites from before them. They drove them out and have lived in their place to this day. [23]And as for the Avvites who lived in villages as far as Gaza, the Caphtorites coming out from Caphtor[a] destroyed them and settled in their place.)

Defeat of Sihon King of Heshbon

[24]"Set out now and cross the Arnon Gorge. See, I have given into your hand Sihon the Amorite, king of Heshbon, and his country. Begin to take possession of it and engage him in battle. [25]This very day I will begin to put the terror and fear of you on all the nations under heaven. They will hear reports of you and will tremble and be in anguish because of you."

[26]From the Desert of Kedemoth I sent messengers to Sihon king of Heshbon offering peace and saying, [27]"Let us pass through your country. We will stay on the main road; we will not turn aside to the right or to the left. [28]Sell us food to eat and water to drink for their price in silver. Only let us pass through on foot— [29]as the descendants of Esau, who live in Seir, and the Moabites, who live in Ar, did for us—until we cross the Jordan into the land the LORD our God is giving us." [30]But Sihon king of Heshbon refused to let us pass through. For the LORD your God had made his spirit stubborn and his heart obstinate in order to give him into your hands, as he has now done.

[31]The LORD said to me, "See, I have begun to deliver Sihon and his country over to you. Now begin to conquer and possess his land."

[32]When Sihon and all his army came out to meet us in battle at Jahaz, [33]the LORD our God delivered him over to us and we struck him down, together with his sons and his whole army. [34]At that time we took all his towns and completely destroyed[b] them—men, women and children. We left no survivors. [35]But the livestock and the plunder from the towns we had captured we carried off for ourselves. [36]From Aroer on the rim of the Arnon Gorge,

---

[a] *23* That is, Crete [b] *34* The Hebrew term refers to the irrevocable giving over of things or persons to the LORD, often by totally destroying them.

and from the town in the gorge, even as far as Gilead, not one town was too strong for us. The LORD our God gave us all of them. 37But in accordance with the command of the LORD our God, you did not encroach on any of the land of the Ammonites, neither the land along the course of the Jabbok nor that around the towns in the hills.

Defeat of Og King of Bashan

3 Next we turned and went up along the road toward Bashan, and Og king of Bashan with his whole army marched out to meet us in battle at Edrei. 2The LORD said to me, "Do not be afraid of him, for I have delivered him into your hands, along with his whole army and his land. Do to him what you did to Sihon king of the Amorites, who reigned in Heshbon."

3So the LORD our God also gave into our hands Og king of Bashan and all his army. We struck them down, leaving no survivors. 4At that time we took all his cities. There was not one of the sixty cities that we did not take from them—the whole region of Argob, Og's kingdom in Bashan. 5All these cities were fortified with high walls and with gates and bars, and there were also a great many unwalled villages. 6We completely destroyed[a] them, as we had done with Sihon king of Heshbon, destroying[a] every city—men, women and children. 7But all the livestock and the plunder from their cities we carried off for ourselves.

8So at that time we took from these two kings of the Amorites the territory east of the Jordan, from the Arnon Gorge as far as Mount Hermon. 9(Hermon is called Sirion by the Sidonians; the Amorites call it Senir.) 10We took all the towns on the plateau, and all Gilead, and all Bashan as far as Salekah and Edrei, towns of Og's kingdom in Bashan. 11(Og king of Bashan was the last of the Rephaites. His bed was decorated with iron and was more than nine cubits long and four cubits wide.[b] It is still in Rabbah of the Ammonites.)

Division of the Land

12Of the land that we took over at that time, I gave the Reubenites and the Gadites the territory north of Aroer by the Arnon Gorge, including half the hill country of Gilead, together with its towns. 13The rest of Gilead and also all of Bashan, the kingdom of Og, I gave to the half-tribe of Manasseh. (The whole region of Argob in Bashan used to be known as a land of the Rephaites. 14Jair, a descendant of Manasseh, took the whole region of Argob as far as the border of the Geshurites and the Maakathites; it was named after him, so that to this day Bashan is called Havvoth Jair.[c]) 15And I gave Gilead to Makir. 16But to the Reubenites and the Gadites I gave the territory extending from Gilead down to the Arnon Gorge (the middle of the gorge being the border) and out to the Jabbok River, which is the bor-

Addressing Questions

2:34 // God. Why did God command the Israelites to take such harsh measures when they began to possess the land he had promised them?

God's command to wipe out Canaan's inhabitants was a one-time event that has never been repeated in history. The command was necessary, in part, to establish a nation that would be pivotal in the history of God's dealings with the human race.

Extraordinary evil prompted God to flood the earth and start over with Noah (see Genesis chapters 6–8 [page 11]). Now, prompted by the wretchedness of the Canaanite people, God used the Israelites as instruments of judgment to eradicate their abuses (see Genesis chapter 15, verses 12–16 [page 21] and Deuteronomy chapter 9, verses 4–6 [page 83]). Child sacrifice, prostitution, and sexual perversion typified the Amorite culture (see Deuteronomy chapter 12, verse 31 [page 88]). Any remnant of these people left alive would lure those about to settle there into the same detestable practices—which, unfortunately, did happen later in other regions. The purpose of destroying this culture was to destroy the human suffering that it produced so something better could take its place.

[a] *6* The Hebrew term refers to the irrevocable giving over of things or persons to the LORD, often by totally destroying them. [b] *11* That is, about 13 feet long and 6 feet wide or about 4 meters long and 1.8 meters wide [c] *14* Or *called the settlements of Jair*

der of the Ammonites. [17]Its western border was the Jordan in the Arabah, from Kinnereth
to the Sea of the Arabah (that is, the Dead Sea), below the slopes of Pisgah.
[18]I commanded you at that time: "The LORD your God has given you this land to take pos-
session of it. But all your able-bodied men, armed for battle, must cross over ahead of the
other Israelites. [19]However, your wives, your children and your livestock (I know you have
much livestock) may stay in the towns I have given you, [20]until the LORD gives rest to all
your people as he has to you, and they too have taken over the land that the LORD your God
is giving them across the Jordan. After that, each of you may go back to the possession I
have given you."

Moses Forbidden to Cross the Jordan

[21]At that time I commanded Joshua: "You have seen with your own eyes all that the LORD
your God has done to these two kings. The LORD will do the same to all the kingdoms over
there where you are going. [22]Do not be afraid of them; the LORD your God himself will fight
for you."
[23]At that time I pleaded with the LORD: [24]"Sovereign LORD, you have begun to show to
your servant your greatness and your strong hand. For what god is there in heaven or on
earth who can do the deeds and mighty works you do? [25]Let me go over and see the good
land beyond the Jordan—that fine hill country and Lebanon."
[26]But because of you the LORD was angry with me and would not listen to me. "That is
enough," the LORD said. "Do not speak to me anymore about this matter. [27]Go up to the top
of Pisgah and look west and north and south and east. Look at the land with your own eyes,
since you are not going to cross this Jordan. [28]But commission Joshua, and encourage and
strengthen him, for he will lead this people across and will cause them to inherit the land
that you will see." [29]So we stayed in the valley near Beth Peor.

Obedience Commanded

4 Now, Israel, hear the decrees and laws I am about to teach you. Follow them so that
you may live and may go in and take possession of the land that the LORD, the God of
your ancestors, is giving you. [2]Do not add to what I command you and do not sub-
tract from it, but keep the commands of the LORD your God that I give you.
[3]You saw with your own eyes what the LORD did at Baal Peor. The LORD your God de-
stroyed from among you everyone who followed the Baal of Peor, [4]but all of you who held
fast to the LORD your God are still alive today.
[5]See, I have taught you decrees and laws as the LORD my God commanded me, so that
you may follow them in the land you are entering to take possession of it. [6]Observe them
carefully, for this will show your wisdom and understanding to the nations, who will hear
about all these decrees and say, "Surely this great nation is a wise and understanding peo-
ple." [7]What other nation is so great as to have their gods near them the way the LORD our
God is near us whenever we pray to him? [8]And what other nation is so great as to have
such righteous decrees and laws as this body of laws I am setting before you today?
[9]Only be careful, and watch yourselves closely so that you do not forget the things your
eyes have seen or let them slip from your heart as long as you live. Teach them to your
children and to their children after them. [10]Remember the day you stood before the LORD
your God at Horeb, when he said to me, "Assemble the people before me to hear my words
so that they may learn to revere me as long as they live in the land and may teach them to
their children." [11]You came near and stood at the foot of the mountain while it blazed with

Discovering God

4:2 // Spiritual Fraud. Adding to what God has said in the Bible is just as wrong as taking away from it or ignoring his commandments. Some "religious" people are good at taking God's words and making more out of them than was originally intended. They create rules and regulations for conduct that God never intended for his people. Others tend to minimize God's commands, sometimes even labeling them as irrelevant to today's world.

If you're a seeker, don't assume that everything your "spiritual" friends say is what God commands. Check the source for yourself and see what the Bible *really* says.

fire to the very heavens, with black clouds and deep darkness. 12 Then the LORD spoke to
you out of the fire. You heard the sound of words but saw no form; there was only a voice.
13 He declared to you his covenant, the Ten Commandments, which he commanded you to
follow and then wrote them on two stone tablets. 14 And the LORD directed me at that time
to teach you the decrees and laws you are to follow in the land that you are crossing the
Jordan to possess.

Idolatry Forbidden

15 You saw no form of any kind the day the LORD spoke to you at Horeb out of the fire.
Therefore watch yourselves very carefully, 16 so that you do not become corrupt and make
for yourselves an idol, an image of any shape, whether formed like a man or a woman, 17 or
like any animal on earth or any bird that flies in the air, 18 or like any creature that moves
along the ground or any fish in the waters below. 19 And when you look up to the sky and
see the sun, the moon and the stars—all the heavenly array—do not be enticed into bow-
ing down to them and worshiping things the LORD your God has apportioned to all the na-
tions under heaven. 20 But as for you, the LORD took you and brought you out of the
iron-smelting furnace, out of Egypt, to be the people of his inheritance, as you now are.

21 The LORD was angry with me because of you, and he solemnly swore that I would not
cross the Jordan and enter the good land the LORD your God is giving you as your inheri-
tance. 22 I will die in this land; I will not cross the Jordan; but you are about to cross over
and take possession of that good land. 23 Be careful not to forget the covenant of the LORD
your God that he made with you; do not make for yourselves an idol in the form of any-
thing the LORD your God has forbidden. 24 For the LORD your God is a consuming fire, a
jealous God.

25 After you have had children and grandchildren and have lived in the land a long time—
if you then become corrupt and make any kind of idol, doing evil in the eyes of the LORD
your God and arousing his anger, 26 I call the heavens and the earth as witnesses against you
this day that you will quickly perish from the land that you are crossing the Jordan to pos-
sess. You will not live there long but will certainly be destroyed. 27 The LORD will scatter you
among the peoples, and only a few of you will survive among the nations to which the LORD
will drive you. 28 There you will worship gods of wood and stone made by human hands,
which cannot see or hear or eat or smell. 29 But if from there you seek the LORD your God,
you will find him if you seek him with all your heart and with all your soul. 30 When you are
in distress and all these things have happened to you, then in later days you will return to
the LORD your God and obey him. 31 For the LORD your God is a merciful God; he will not
abandon or destroy you or forget the covenant with your ancestors, which he confirmed to
them by oath.

The LORD Is God

32 Ask now about the former days, long before your time, from the day God creat-
ed human beings on the earth; ask from one end of the heavens to the other. Has any-
thing so great as this ever happened, or has anything like it ever been heard of? 33 Has

Discovering God

4:28–31 // Life with God. Here's a passage every seeker should learn by heart! God promises that people can find him even when they've gone far astray spiritually (in this case, by worshiping other gods).

Although we may not bow down to stone idols today, all of us have allowed things or people in our lives to become more important than God. That's the essence of idolatry. So this passage applies more directly than we might think at first.

But if the bad news applies, so does the good news. Mercy is at the very heart of God's character. He would much rather welcome back a wandering soul than allow that person to live apart from him forever. So on the authority of this passage, consider yourself personally and formally invited to seek God with all your heart and soul. And be comforted by the promise that he is merciful and eager to be in a relationship with you forever.

any other people heard the voice of God[a] speaking out of fire, as you have, and lived?
34 Has any god ever tried to take for himself one nation out of another nation, by test-
ings, by signs and wonders, by war, by a mighty hand and an outstretched arm, or by
great and awesome deeds, like all the things the LORD your God did for you in Egypt
before your very eyes?

35 You were shown these things so that you might know that the LORD is God; besides
him there is no other. 36 From heaven he made you hear his voice to discipline you. On
earth he showed you his great fire, and you heard his words from out of the fire. 37 Because
he loved your ancestors and chose their descendants after them, he brought you out of
Egypt by his Presence and his great strength, 38 to drive out before you nations greater and
stronger than you and to bring you into their land to give it to you for your inheritance, as
it is today.

39 Acknowledge and take to heart this day that the LORD is God in heaven above and on
the earth below. There is no other. 40 Keep his decrees and commands, which I am giving
you today, so that it may go well with you and your children after you and that you may
live long in the land the LORD your God gives you for all time.

Cities of Refuge

41 Then Moses set aside three cities east of the Jordan, 42 to which anyone who had killed
a person could flee if they had unintentionally killed a neighbor without malice afore-
thought. They could flee into one of these cities and save their life. 43 The cities were these:
Bezer in the wilderness plateau, for the Reubenites; Ramoth in Gilead, for the Gadites; and
Golan in Bashan, for the Manassites.

Introduction to the Law

44 This is the law Moses set before the Israelites. 45 These are the stipulations, decrees
and laws Moses gave them when they came out of Egypt 46 and were in the valley near Beth
Peor east of the Jordan, in the land of Sihon king of the Amorites, who reigned in Heshbon
and was defeated by Moses and the Israelites as they came out of Egypt. 47 They took pos-
session of his land and the land of Og king of Bashan, the two Amorite kings east of the
Jordan. 48 This land extended from Aroer on the rim of the Arnon Gorge to Mount Sirion[b]
(that is, Hermon), 49 and included all the Arabah east of the Jordan, as far as the Dead Sea,[c]
below the slopes of Pisgah.

The Ten Commandments

5 Moses summoned all Israel and said:
Hear, Israel, the decrees and laws I declare in your hearing today. Learn them and
be sure to follow them. 2 The LORD our God made a covenant with us at Horeb. 3 It
was not with our ancestors[d] that the LORD made this covenant, but with us, with all of us
who are alive here today. 4 The LORD spoke to you face to face out of the fire on the moun-
tain. 5 (At that time I stood between the LORD and you to declare to you the word of the
LORD, because you were afraid of the fire and did not go up the mountain.) And he said:

6 "I am the LORD your God, who brought you out of Egypt, out of the land of slav-
ery.
7 "You shall have no other gods before[e] me.
8 "You shall not make for yourself an image in the form of anything in heaven above or
on the earth beneath or in the waters below. 9 You shall not bow down to them
or worship them; for I, the LORD your God, am a jealous God, punishing the chil-
dren for the sin of the parents to the third and fourth generation of those who
hate me, 10 but showing love to a thousand generations of those who love me and
keep my commandments.
11 "You shall not misuse the name of the LORD your God, for the LORD will not hold any-
one guiltless who misuses his name.

---

[a] 33 Or *of a god* [b] 48 Syriac (see also Deut. 3:9); Hebrew *Siyon* [c] 49 Hebrew *the Sea of the Arabah* [d] 3 Or *not only with our parents* [e] 7 Or *besides*

Knowing Yourself

5:6–21 // Sin. Of all the "Top 10" lists ever written, these "Ten Commandments" are the most famous. They briefly sum up the essence of everything God wants people to do to live in harmony with him and with every other person on the planet.

So to succeed in life, just follow these precepts, right? Sounds simple enough—that is, until you actually *try*.

Maybe you think you can do better than most. And perhaps you can. But before you get too self-assured, take a closer look at this moral yardstick. How well are you *really* doing? (Warning: This self-examination is not for the faint of heart!)

- Number One—No Other Gods
  Have you ever spent an inappropriate amount of time, energy or money on something less important than God?
- Number Two—No Idols
  Have you ever attributed good luck to some object (such as a crystal, an article of clothing or a rabbit's foot) or considered a religious statue or picture to be of some spiritual benefit to you?
- Number Three—Don't Misuse God's Name
  Have you ever cursed anyone in God's name or said "God" like it was an expletive?
- Number Four—Take A Day Out of Every Seven for God
  Have you ever exhibited workaholic tendencies—unable to "unplug" for days on end—or been so preoccupied with your own activities that you rarely gave a thought to what your soul and God need from you?
- Number Five—Honor Your Parents
  Have you ever lied to, deceived or treated your parents with disrespect?
- Number Six—Don't Murder
  Maybe you haven't actually killed anyone, but have you ever wished that someone were dead? The Bible compares hate to the sin of murder.
- Number Seven—Don't Commit Adultery
  Jesus made it clear that God prohibits not only the physical act of adultery but also the mental act—playing it out in our minds (Matthew chapter 5, verses 27–28).
- Number Eight—Don't Steal
  Have you ever taken something that wasn't yours, cheated on taxes or on an expense account or been inconsiderate of someone else's time?
- Number Nine—Don't Lie
  Have you ever bent the truth in your favor, exaggerated a story "to make it more interesting," or covered up wrongdoing with a lie—even a "little white lie"?
- Number Ten—Don't Covet
  Have you ever wanted something that someone else had so you wouldn't feel inferior, bought something for the sheer sake of what others would think of you or jealously compared your clothing or car to someone else's?

No need to get morbid here, but you have to admit that the picture this paints of your commandment-keeping tendencies is pretty bleak. Interestingly, the Bible is clear that God is not surprised by how you stack up.

Here's the amazing thing. This character yardstick—which shows where you stand and takes away any false hope of innate goodness—actually leads you right where you need to be. By recognizing that consistent goodness isn't just hard, it's impossible, you can now approach God in the right frame of mind. Now you can humbly seek him and his mercy instead of trying to chalk up enough spiritual "brownie points." That attitude of weakness and brokenness is the starting place for every seeker who wants to meet God personally.

[12]"Observe the Sabbath day by keeping it holy, as the LORD your God has commanded
you. [13]Six days you shall labor and do all your work, [14]but the seventh day is a
sabbath to the LORD your God. On it you shall not do any work, neither you, nor
your son or daughter, nor your male or female servant, nor your ox, your donkey
or any of your animals, nor any foreigner residing in your towns, so that your
male and female servants may rest, as you do. [15]Remember that you were slaves
in Egypt and that the LORD your God brought you out of there with a mighty hand
and an outstretched arm. Therefore the LORD your God has commanded you to
observe the Sabbath day.

[16]"Honor your father and your mother, as the LORD your God has commanded you, so
that you may live long and that it may go well with you in the land the LORD your
God is giving you.

[17]"You shall not murder.

[18]"You shall not commit adultery.

[19]"You shall not steal.

[20]"You shall not give false testimony against your neighbor.

[21]"You shall not covet your neighbor's wife. You shall not set your desire on your neigh-
bor's house or land, his male or female servant, his ox or donkey, or anything
that belongs to your neighbor."

[22]These are the commandments the LORD proclaimed in a loud voice to your whole as-
sembly there on the mountain from out of the fire, the cloud and the deep darkness; and he
added nothing more. Then he wrote them on two stone tablets and gave them to me.

[23]When you heard the voice out of the darkness, while the mountain was ablaze with fire,
all the leaders of your tribes and your elders came to me. [24]And you said, "The LORD our God
has shown us his glory and his majesty, and we have heard his voice from the fire. Today we
have seen that people can live even if God speaks with them. [25]But now, why should we die?
This great fire will consume us, and we will die if we hear the voice of the LORD our God any
longer. [26]For what mortal has ever heard the voice of the living God speaking out of fire, as we
have, and survived? [27]Go near and listen to all that the LORD our God says. Then tell us what-
ever the LORD our God tells you. We will listen and obey."

[28]The LORD heard you when you spoke to me, and the LORD said to me, "I have heard
what this people said to you. Everything they said was good. [29]Oh, that their hearts would
be inclined to fear me and keep all my commands always, so that it might go well with
them and their children forever!

[30]"Go, tell them to return to their tents. [31]But you stay here with me so that I may give
you all the commands, decrees and laws you are to teach them to follow in the land I am
giving them to possess."

[32]So be careful to do what the LORD your God has commanded you; do not turn aside to
the right or to the left. [33]Walk in obedience to all that the LORD your God has commanded
you, so that you may live and prosper and prolong your days in the land that you will possess.

Love the LORD Your God

6 These are the commands, decrees and laws the LORD your God directed me to teach you
to observe in the land that you are crossing the Jordan to possess, [2]so that you, your chil-
dren and their children after them may fear the LORD your God as long as you live by
keeping all his decrees and commands that I give you, and so that you may enjoy long life.
[3]Hear, Israel, and be careful to obey so that it may go well with you and that you may increase
greatly in a land flowing with milk and honey, just as the LORD, the God of your ancestors,
promised you.

[4]Hear, O Israel: The LORD our God, the LORD is one.[a] [5]Love the LORD your God with all
your heart and with all your soul and with all your strength. [6]These commandments that
I give you today are to be on your hearts. [7]Impress them on your children. Talk about them
when you sit at home and when you walk along the road, when you lie down and when

---

[a] 4 Or *The LORD our God is one LORD*; or *The LORD is our God, the LORD is one*; or *The LORD is our God, the LORD alone*

you get up. 8Tie them as symbols on your hands and bind them on your foreheads. 9Write
them on the doorframes of your houses and on your gates.
10When the LORD your God brings you into the land he swore to your fathers, to Abraham,
Isaac and Jacob, to give you—a land with large, flourishing cities you did not build, 11houses
filled with all kinds of good things you did not provide, wells you did not dig, and vineyards
and olive groves you did not plant—then when you eat and are satisfied, 12be careful that you
do not forget the LORD, who brought you out of Egypt, out of the land of slavery.
13Fear the LORD your God, serve him only and take your oaths in his name. 14Do not fol-
low other gods, the gods of the peoples around you; 15for the LORD your God, who is among
you, is a jealous God and his anger will burn against you, and he will destroy you from the
face of the land. 16Do not put the LORD your God to the test as you did at Massah. 17Be sure
to keep the commands of the LORD your God and the stipulations and decrees he has giv-
en you. 18Do what is right and good in the LORD's sight, so that it may go well with you and
you may go in and take over the good land that the LORD promised on oath to your ances-
tors, 19thrusting out all your enemies before you, as the LORD said.
20In the future, when your children ask you, "What is the meaning of the stipulations,
decrees and laws the LORD our God has commanded you?" 21tell them: "We were slaves of
Pharaoh in Egypt, but the LORD brought us out of Egypt with a mighty hand. 22Before our
eyes the LORD sent signs and wonders—great and terrible—on Egypt and Pharaoh and his
whole household. 23But he brought us out from there to bring us in and give us the land that
he promised on oath to our ancestors. 24The LORD commanded us to obey all these decrees
and to fear the LORD our God, so that we might always prosper and be kept alive, as is the
case today. 25And if we are careful to obey all this law before the LORD our God, as he has
commanded us, that will be our righteousness."

Driving Out the Nations

7 When the LORD your God brings you into the land you are entering to possess and
drives out before you many nations—the Hittites, Girgashites, Amorites, Canaanites,
Perizzites, Hivites and Jebusites, seven nations larger and stronger than you— 2and
when the LORD your God has delivered them over to you and you have defeated them, then
you must destroy them totally.[a] Make no treaty with them, and show them no mercy. 3Do
not intermarry with them. Do not give your daughters to their sons or take their daughters
for your sons, 4for they will turn your children away from following me to serve other gods,

Strengthening Relationships

6:4–9 // Parenting. When you hear the words "religious education," what images come to mind? Rows of well-scrubbed kids in a church or synagogue? A stern rap on the knuckles with a ruler for not paying attention? A group of adults seated in a circle drinking coffee and politely discussing topics that have no relevance to real life?

Whatever your view, it's a sad commentary on our current spiritual climate that, typically, such recollections are negative. Thankfully, there are notable exceptions. But many adult unbelievers were raised in some sort of religious environment. Did they leave something important behind? What went wrong to change their attitudes?

One of the biggest mistakes religious institutions make is reducing spirituality to mere laws and commandments that children and adults memorize. The God of the Bible has a different perspective. According to this passage, the essence of the spiritual life is a *person* to live *with*, not just *rules* to live *by*.

As parents, it is crucial that we model for our children an authentic relationship with God. The attempt to indoctrinate our children, hoping that they'll somehow embrace beliefs that we obviously don't live out, is an exercise in futility.

That's why this passage emphasizes *lifestyle* teaching rather than academics. There is a need for both. But the place to ground a child's spiritual life is in everyday events. That's where kids sort through what's mere theory and what Mom and Dad really live out.

[a] 2 The Hebrew term refers to the irrevocable giving over of things or persons to the LORD, often by totally destroying them; also in verse 26.

and the LORD's anger will burn against you and will quickly destroy you. 5 This is what you
are to do to them: Break down their altars, smash their sacred stones, cut down their Ashe-
rah poles[a] and burn their idols in the fire. 6 For you are a people holy to the LORD your God.
The LORD your God has chosen you out of all the peoples on the face of the earth to be his
people, his treasured possession.

7 The LORD did not set his affection on you and choose you because you were more nu-
merous than other peoples, for you were the fewest of all peoples. 8 But it was because the
LORD loved you and kept the oath he swore to your ancestors that he brought you out with
a mighty hand and redeemed you from the land of slavery, from the power of Pharaoh king
of Egypt. 9 Know therefore that the LORD your God is God; he is the faithful God, keeping
his covenant of love to a thousand generations of those who love him and keep his com-
mandments. 10 But

> those who hate him he will repay to their face by destruction;
> he will not be slow to repay to their face those who hate him.

11 Therefore, take care to follow the commands, decrees and laws I give you today.

12 If you pay attention to these laws and are careful to follow them, then the LORD your
God will keep his covenant of love with you, as he swore to your ancestors. 13 He will love
you and bless you and increase your numbers. He will bless the fruit of your womb, the
crops of your land—your grain, new wine and olive oil—the calves of your herds and the
lambs of your flocks in the land that he swore to your ancestors to give you. 14 You will be
blessed more than any other people; none of your men or women will be childless, nor any
of your livestock without young. 15 The LORD will keep you free from every disease. He will
not inflict on you the horrible diseases you knew in Egypt, but he will inflict them on all
who hate you. 16 You must destroy all the peoples the LORD your God gives over to you. Do
not look on them with pity and do not serve their gods, for that will be a snare to you.

17 You may say to yourselves, "These nations are stronger than we are. How can we drive
them out?" 18 But do not be afraid of them; remember well what the LORD your God did to
Pharaoh and to all Egypt. 19 You saw with your own eyes the great trials, the signs and won-
ders, the mighty hand and outstretched arm, with which the LORD your God brought you
out. The LORD your God will do the same to all the peoples you now fear. 20 Moreover, the
LORD your God will send the hornet among them until even the survivors who hide from
you have perished. 21 Do not be terrified by them, for the LORD your God, who is among you,
is a great and awesome God. 22 The LORD your God will drive out those nations before you,
little by little. You will not be allowed to eliminate them all at once, or the wild animals will
multiply around you. 23 But the LORD your God will deliver them over to you, throwing them
into great confusion until they are destroyed. 24 He will give their kings into your hand, and
you will wipe out their names from under heaven. No one will be able to stand up against
you; you will destroy them. 25 The images of their gods you are to burn in the fire. Do not
covet the silver and gold on them, and do not take it for yourselves, or you will be ensnared
by it, for it is detestable to the LORD your God. 26 Do not bring a detestable thing into your
house or you, like it, will be set apart for destruction. Regard it as vile and utterly detest it,
for it is set apart for destruction.

Do Not Forget the LORD

8 Be careful to follow every command I am giving you today, so that you may live and
increase and may enter and possess the land that the LORD promised on oath to your
ancestors. 2 Remember how the LORD your God led you all the way in the wilderness
these forty years, to humble and test you in order to know what was in your heart, whether
or not you would keep his commands. 3 He humbled you, causing you to hunger and then
feeding you with manna, which neither you nor your ancestors had known, to teach you
that people do not live on bread alone but on every word that comes from the mouth of the
LORD. 4 Your clothes did not wear out and your feet did not swell during these forty years.

---

[a] 5 That is, wooden symbols of the goddess Asherah; here and elsewhere in Deuteronomy

[5]Know then in your heart that as a man disciplines his son, so the LORD your God disciplines you.

[6]Observe the commands of the LORD your God, walking in obedience to him and revering him. [7]For the LORD your God is bringing you into a good land—a land with streams and pools of water, with springs flowing in the valleys and hills; [8]a land with wheat and barley, vines and fig trees, pomegranates, olive oil and honey; [9]a land where bread will not be scarce and you will lack nothing; a land where the rocks are iron and you can dig copper out of the hills.

[10]When you have eaten and are satisfied, praise the LORD your God for the good land he has given you. [11]Be careful that you do not forget the LORD your God, failing to observe his commands, his laws and his decrees that I am giving you this day. [12]Otherwise, when you eat and are satisfied, when you build fine houses and settle down, [13]and when your herds and flocks grow large and your silver and gold increase and all you have is multiplied, [14]then your heart will become proud and you will forget the LORD your God, who brought you out of Egypt, out of the land of slavery. [15]He led you through the vast and dreadful wilderness, that thirsty and waterless land, with its venomous snakes and scorpions. He brought you water out of hard rock. [16]He gave you manna to eat in the wilderness, something your ancestors had never known, to humble and test you so that in the end it might go well with you. [17]You may say to yourself, "My power and the strength of my hands have produced this wealth for me." [18]But remember the LORD your God, for it is he who gives you the ability to produce wealth, and so confirms his covenant, which he swore to your ancestors, as it is today.

[19]If you ever forget the LORD your God and follow other gods and worship and bow down to them, I testify against you today that you will surely be destroyed. [20]Like the nations the LORD destroyed before you, so you will be destroyed for not obeying the LORD your God.

Not Because of Israel's Righteousness

9 Hear, Israel: You are now about to cross the Jordan to go in and dispossess nations greater and stronger than you, with large cities that have walls up to the sky. [2]The people are strong and tall—Anakites! You know about them and have heard it said: "Who can stand up against the Anakites?" [3]But be assured today that the LORD your God is the one who goes across ahead of you like a devouring fire. He will destroy them; he will subdue them before you. And you will drive them out and annihilate them quickly, as the LORD has promised you.

[4]After the LORD your God has driven them out before you, do not say to yourself, "The LORD has brought me here to take possession of this land because of my righteousness." No, it is on account of the wickedness of these nations that the LORD is going to drive them out before you. [5]It is not because of your righteousness or your integrity that you are go-

Managing Resources

8:17–18 // Position. God created each of us with ambition and a desire for significance, yet it is often that drive that blinds us to our need for him.

The ancient Israelites had this very problem. In this passage Moses reminds the people that they are not self-sufficient. He warns them to guard against allowing their prosperity to become a barrier between them and God.

Like the Israelites, sometimes we allow our successes to give us the impression that our lives are complete without God. But this passage reminds us that *all* of our abilities—our reasoning powers, our talents, our "business sense" and even our physical strength—are gifts from God. We need to be careful to give credit where credit is due. God has given us many opportunities to use our talents for his service, and we need to live out our lives in thanks for his goodness to us.

Even if you are undecided whether to allow God to be the leader of your life, think about the talents that you have. This passage says that these gifts are meant to bring you to an appreciation of God's goodness, and ultimately to the recognition that he has already been very kind to you.

ing in to take possession of their land; but on account of the wickedness of these nations,
the LORD your God will drive them out before you, to accomplish what he swore to your fa-
thers, to Abraham, Isaac and Jacob. 6Understand, then, that it is not because of your righ-
teousness that the LORD your God is giving you this good land to possess, for you are a
stiff-necked people.

The Golden Calf

7Remember this and never forget how you aroused the anger of the LORD your God in
the wilderness. From the day you left Egypt until you arrived here, you have been rebellious
against the LORD. 8At Horeb you aroused the LORD's wrath so that he was angry enough to
destroy you. 9When I went up on the mountain to receive the tablets of stone, the tablets
of the covenant that the LORD had made with you, I stayed on the mountain forty days and
forty nights; I ate no bread and drank no water. 10The LORD gave me two stone tablets in-
scribed by the finger of God. On them were all the commandments the LORD proclaimed
to you on the mountain out of the fire, on the day of the assembly.
11At the end of the forty days and forty nights, the LORD gave me the two stone tablets,
the tablets of the covenant. 12Then the LORD told me, "Go down from here at once, because
your people whom you brought out of Egypt have become corrupt. They have turned away
quickly from what I commanded them and have made an idol for themselves."
13And the LORD said to me, "I have seen this people, and they are a stiff-necked people
indeed! 14Let me alone, so that I may destroy them and blot out their name from under
heaven. And I will make you into a nation stronger and more numerous than they."
15So I turned and went down from the mountain while it was ablaze with fire. And the
two tablets of the covenant were in my hands. 16When I looked, I saw that you had sinned
against the LORD your God; you had made for yourselves an idol cast in the shape of a calf.
You had turned aside quickly from the way that the LORD had commanded you. 17So I took
the two tablets and threw them out of my hands, breaking them to pieces before your eyes.
18Then once again I fell prostrate before the LORD for forty days and forty nights; I ate
no bread and drank no water, because of all the sin you had committed, doing what was
evil in the LORD's sight and so arousing his anger. 19I feared the anger and wrath of the
LORD, for he was angry enough with you to destroy you. But again the LORD listened to me.
20And the LORD was angry enough with Aaron to destroy him, but at that time I prayed for
Aaron too. 21Also I took that sinful thing of yours, the calf you had made, and burned it in
the fire. Then I crushed it and ground it to powder as fine as dust and threw the dust into
a stream that flowed down the mountain.
22You also made the LORD angry at Taberah, at Massah and at Kibroth Hattaavah.
23And when the LORD sent you out from Kadesh Barnea, he said, "Go up and take pos-

Discovering God

10:12–13 // Life with God. Most seekers, if they believe that God exists, assume that he is very concerned that they "do right." But according to these verses, that's only part of the picture.

God didn't create people so he could watch a performance. He made us to be in *relationship* with him. Without the bond of love, our obedience can turn into slavery. Without affection, our worship will become empty ritual. The bottom-line behavior that God requires is a heart-and-soul connection with him, which then naturally affects our attitudes and actions. What's more, the Bible says that God's requirements are rational and make sense—we should follow these directives "for [our] own good" (verse 13).

Can you appreciate how strange this must have sounded to the people of the ancient world? The ancient Egyptians didn't love their god Osiris; the Canaanites had no affection for Baal, their fertility god. Most religion was (and is) based on fear alone, not on the offer of a mutually beneficial relationship.

The God of the Bible, while desiring due respect, invites people into a relationship characterized by tender love. That prospect is amazing, and yet wonderfully true.

session of the land I have given you." But you rebelled against the command of the LORD
your God. You did not trust him or obey him. 24You have been rebellious against the LORD
ever since I have known you.
25I lay prostrate before the LORD those forty days and forty nights because the LORD had said
he would destroy you. 26I prayed to the LORD and said, "Sovereign LORD, do not destroy your
people, your own inheritance that you redeemed by your great power and brought out of
Egypt with a mighty hand. 27Remember your servants Abraham, Isaac and Jacob. Overlook
the stubbornness of this people, their wickedness and their sin. 28Otherwise, the country from
which you brought us will say, 'Because the LORD was not able to take them into the land he
had promised them, and because he hated them, he brought them out to put them to death
in the wilderness.' 29But they are your people, your inheritance that you brought out by your
great power and your outstretched arm."

Tablets Like the First Ones

10 At that time the LORD said to me, "Chisel out two stone tablets like the first ones
and come up to me on the mountain. Also make a wooden ark.[a] 2I will write on
the tablets the words that were on the first tablets, which you broke. Then you
are to put them in the ark."
3So I made the ark out of acacia wood and chiseled out two stone tablets like the first
ones, and I went up on the mountain with the two tablets in my hands. 4The LORD wrote
on these tablets what he had written before, the Ten Commandments he had proclaimed
to you on the mountain, out of the fire, on the day of the assembly. And the LORD gave
them to me. 5Then I came back down the mountain and put the tablets in the ark I had
made, as the LORD commanded me, and they are there now.
6(The Israelites traveled from the wells of Bene Jaakan to Moserah. There Aaron died and
was buried, and Eleazar his son succeeded him as priest. 7From there they traveled to Gud-
godah and on to Jotbathah, a land with streams of water. 8At that time the LORD set apart
the tribe of Levi to carry the ark of the covenant of the LORD, to stand before the LORD to
minister and to pronounce blessings in his name, as they still do today. 9That is why the
Levites have no share or inheritance among their fellow Israelites; the LORD is their inher-
itance, as the LORD your God told them.)
10Now I had stayed on the mountain forty days and nights, as I did the first time, and the
LORD listened to me at this time also. It was not his will to destroy you. 11"Go," the LORD said
to me, "and lead the people on their way, so that they may enter and possess the land that
I swore to their ancestors to give them."

Fear the LORD

12And now, Israel, what does the LORD your God ask of you but to fear the LORD your God,
to walk in obedience to him, to love him, to serve the LORD your God with all your heart and
with all your soul, 13and to observe the LORD's commands and decrees that I am giving you
today for your own good?
14To the LORD your God belong the heavens, even the highest heavens, the earth and ev-
erything in it. 15Yet the LORD set his affection on your ancestors and loved them, and he
chose you, their descendants, above all the nations—as it is today. 16Circumcise your hearts,
therefore, and do not be stiff-necked any longer. 17For the LORD your God is God of gods and
Lord of lords, the great God, mighty and awesome, who shows no partiality and accepts no
bribes. 18He defends the cause of the fatherless and the widow, and loves the foreigners re-
siding among you, giving them food and clothing. 19And you are to love those who are for-
eigners, for you yourselves were foreigners in Egypt. 20Fear the LORD your God and serve
him. Hold fast to him and take your oaths in his name. 21He is your praise; he is your God,
who performed for you those great and awesome wonders you saw with your own eyes.
22Your ancestors who went down into Egypt were seventy in all, and now the LORD your
God has made you as numerous as the stars in the sky.

---

[a] *1* That is, a chest

Love and Obey the LORD

11 Love the LORD your God and keep his requirements, his decrees, his laws and his commands always. 2Remember today that your children were not the ones who saw and experienced the discipline of the LORD your God: his majesty, his mighty hand, his outstretched arm; 3the signs he performed and the things he did in the heart of Egypt, both to Pharaoh king of Egypt and to his whole country; 4what he did to the Egyptian army, to its horses and chariots, how he overwhelmed them with the waters of the Red Sea[a] as they were pursuing you, and how the LORD brought lasting ruin on them. 5It was not your children who saw what he did for you in the wilderness until you arrived at this place, 6and what he did to Dathan and Abiram, sons of Eliab the Reubenite, when the earth opened its mouth right in the middle of all Israel and swallowed them up with their households, their tents and every living thing that belonged to them. 7But it was your own eyes that saw all these great things the LORD has done.

8Observe therefore all the commands I am giving you today, so that you may have the strength to go in and take over the land that you are crossing the Jordan to possess, 9and so that you may live long in the land that the LORD swore to your ancestors to give to them and their descendants, a land flowing with milk and honey. 10The land you are entering to take over is not like the land of Egypt, from which you have come, where you planted your seed and irrigated it by foot as in a vegetable garden. 11But the land you are crossing the Jordan to take possession of is a land of mountains and valleys that drinks rain from heaven. 12It is a land the LORD your God cares for; the eyes of the LORD your God are continually on it from the beginning of the year to its end.

13So if you faithfully obey the commands I am giving you today—to love the LORD your God and to serve him with all your heart and with all your soul— 14then I will send rain on your land in its season, both autumn and spring rains, so that you may gather in your grain, new wine and olive oil. 15I will provide grass in the fields for your cattle, and you will eat and be satisfied.

16Be careful, or you will be enticed to turn away and worship other gods and bow down to them. 17Then the LORD's anger will burn against you, and he will shut the heavens so that it will not rain and the ground will yield no produce, and you will soon perish from the good land the LORD is giving you. 18Fix these words of mine in your hearts and minds; tie them as symbols on your hands and bind them on your foreheads. 19Teach them to your children, talking about them when you sit at home and when you walk along the road, when you lie down and when you get up. 20Write them on the doorframes of your houses and on your gates, 21so that your days and the days of your children may be many in the land that the LORD swore to give your ancestors, as many as the days that the heavens are above the earth.

22If you carefully observe all these commands I am giving you to follow—to love the LORD your God, to walk in obedience to him and to hold fast to him— 23then the LORD will drive out all these nations before you, and you will dispossess nations larger and stronger than you. 24Every place where you set your foot will be yours: Your territory will extend from the desert to Lebanon, and from the Euphrates River to the Mediterranean Sea. 25No one will be able to stand against you. The LORD your God, as he promised you, will put the terror and fear of you on the whole land, wherever you go.

26See, I am setting before you today a blessing and a curse— 27the blessing if you obey the commands of the LORD your God that I am giving you today; 28the curse if you disobey the commands of the LORD your God and turn from the way that I command you today by following other gods, which you have not known. 29When the LORD your God has brought you into the land you are entering to possess, you are to proclaim on Mount Gerizim the blessings, and on Mount Ebal the curses. 30As you know, these mountains are across the Jordan, westward, toward the setting sun, near the great trees of Moreh, in the territory of those Canaanites living in the Arabah in the vicinity of Gilgal. 31You are about to cross the Jordan to enter and take possession of the land the LORD your God is giving you. When you have taken it over and are living there, 32be sure that you obey all the decrees and laws I am setting before you today.

---

[a] 4 Or *the Sea of Reeds*

The One Place of Worship

12 These are the decrees and laws you must be careful to follow in the land that the LORD, the God of your ancestors, has given you to possess—as long as you live in the land. 2Destroy completely all the places on the high mountains, on the hills and under every spreading tree, where the nations you are dispossessing worship their gods. 3Break down their altars, smash their sacred stones and burn their Asherah poles in the fire; cut down the idols of their gods and wipe out their names from those places.

4You must not worship the LORD your God in their way. 5But you are to seek the place the LORD your God will choose from among all your tribes to put his Name there for his dwelling. To that place you must go; 6there bring your burnt offerings and sacrifices, your tithes and special gifts, what you have vowed to give and your freewill offerings, and the firstborn of your herds and flocks. 7There, in the presence of the LORD your God, you and your families shall eat and shall rejoice in everything you have put your hand to, because the LORD your God has blessed you.

8You are not to do as we do here today, everyone doing as they see fit, 9since you have not yet reached the resting place and the inheritance the LORD your God is giving you. 10But you will cross the Jordan and settle in the land the LORD your God is giving you as an inheritance, and he will give you rest from all your enemies around you so that you will live in safety. 11Then to the place the LORD your God will choose as a dwelling for his Name—there you are to bring everything I command you: your burnt offerings and sacrifices, your tithes and special gifts, and all the choice possessions you have vowed to the LORD. 12And there rejoice before the LORD your God—you, your sons and daughters, your male and female servants, and the Levites from your towns who have no allotment or inheritance of their own. 13Be careful not to sacrifice your burnt offerings anywhere you please. 14Offer them only at the place the LORD will choose in one of your tribes, and there observe everything I command you.

15Nevertheless, you may slaughter your animals in any of your towns and eat as much of the meat as you want, as if it were gazelle or deer, according to the blessing the LORD your God gives you. Both the ceremonially unclean and the clean may eat it. 16But you must not eat the blood; pour it out on the ground like water. 17You must not eat in your own towns the tithe of your grain and new wine and olive oil, or the firstborn of your herds and flocks, or whatever you have vowed to give, or your freewill offerings or special gifts. 18Instead, you are to eat them in the presence of the LORD your God at the place the LORD your God will choose—you, your sons and daughters, your male and female servants, and the Levites from your towns—and you are to rejoice before the LORD your God in everything you put your hand to. 19Be careful not to neglect the Levites as long as you live in your land.

20When the LORD your God has enlarged your territory as he promised you, and you crave meat and say, "I would like some meat," then you may eat as much of it as you want. 21If the place where the LORD your God chooses to put his Name is too far away from you, you may slaughter animals from the herds and flocks the LORD has given you, as I have commanded you, and in your own towns you may eat as much of them as you want. 22Eat them as you would gazelle or deer. Both the ceremonially unclean and the clean may eat. 23But be sure you do not eat the blood, because the blood is the life, and you must not eat the life with the meat. 24You must not eat the blood; pour it out on the ground like water. 25Do not eat it, so that it may go well with you and your children after you, because you will be doing what is right in the eyes of the LORD.

26But take your consecrated things and whatever you have vowed to give, and go to the place the LORD will choose. 27Present your burnt offerings on the altar of the LORD your God, both the meat and the blood. The blood of your sacrifices must be poured beside the altar of the LORD your God, but you may eat the meat. 28Be careful to obey all these regulations I am giving you, so that it may always go well with you and your children after you, because you will be doing what is good and right in the eyes of the LORD your God.

29The LORD your God will cut off before you the nations you are about to invade and dispossess. But when you have driven them out and settled in their land, 30and after they have been destroyed before you, be careful not to be ensnared by inquiring about their gods,

saying, "How do these nations serve their gods? We will do the same." [31]You must not wor-
ship the LORD your God in their way, because in worshiping their gods, they do all kinds of
detestable things the LORD hates. They even burn their sons and daughters in the fire as sac-
rifices to their gods.
*[32]See that you do all I command you; do not add to it or take away from it.

Worshiping Other Gods

13 *If a prophet, or one who foretells by dreams, appears among you and announc-
es to you a sign or wonder, [2]and if the sign or wonder spoken of takes place, and
the prophet says, "Let us follow other gods" (gods you have not known) "and let
us worship them," [3]you must not listen to the words of that prophet or dreamer. The LORD
your God is testing you to find out whether you love him with all your heart and with all
your soul. [4]It is the LORD your God you must follow, and him you must revere. Keep his
commands and obey him; serve him and hold fast to him. [5]That prophet or dreamer must
be put to death for inciting rebellion against the LORD your God, who brought you out of
Egypt and redeemed you from the land of slavery. That prophet or dreamer tried to turn
you from the way the LORD your God commanded you to follow. You must purge the evil
from among you.
[6]If your very own brother, or your son or daughter, or the wife you love, or your closest
friend secretly entices you, saying, "Let us go and worship other gods" (gods that neither
you nor your ancestors have known, [7]gods of the peoples around you, whether near or far,
from one end of the land to the other), [8]do not yield to them or listen to them. Show them
no pity. Do not spare them or shield them. [9]You must certainly put them to death. Your
hand must be the first in putting them to death, and then the hands of all the people.
[10]Stone them to death, because they tried to turn you away from the LORD your God, who
brought you out of Egypt, out of the land of slavery. [11]Then all Israel will hear and be afraid,
and no one among you will do such an evil thing again.
[12]If you hear it said about one of the towns the LORD your God is giving you to live in
[13]that wicked persons have arisen among you and have led the people of their town astray,
saying, "Let us go and worship other gods" (gods you have not known), [14]then you must
inquire, probe and investigate it thoroughly. And if it is true and it has been proved that this
detestable thing has been done among you, [15]you must certainly put to the sword all who
live in that town. Destroy it completely,[a] both its people and its livestock. [16]Gather all the
plunder of the town into the middle of the public square and completely burn the town
and all its plunder as a whole burnt offering to the LORD your God. It is to remain a ruin for-

Discovering God

13:1–5 // Spiritual Fraud. *Everything supernatural is not necessarily from God.*

Some people naively assume that if a person has predictive abilities or other supernatural powers, he or she must have some sort of divine enablement. But the Bible emphasizes that, just as there are frauds in other spheres, spiritual deception ensnares unsuspecting people.

If such unusual activity is not a guarantee of God's work, how can a person know what is from God? This passage gives one of the main tests: If the "miracle worker" calls you to follow a god different from the God of the Bible, then reject the message and the messenger.

While that may seem like a strong reaction—perhaps even smacking of closed-mindedness—it makes sense when you realize what's at stake. If someone takes you in with a phony business scam, you lose your money. If someone lures you with false promises, you may suffer a broken heart. But if someone leads you to a false god, you will lose your soul.

---

[a] *15* The Hebrew term refers to the irrevocable giving over of things or persons to the LORD, often by totally destroying them.

*12:32 is numbered 13:1 in Hebrew texts. *13:1-18 is numbered 13:2-19 in Hebrew texts.

ever, never to be rebuilt. 17None of those condemned things[a] shall be found in your hands,
so that the LORD will turn from his fierce anger; he will show you mercy, have compassion
on you, and increase your numbers, as he promised on oath to your ancestors, 18because
you obey the LORD your God, keeping all his commands that I am giving you today and do-
ing what is right in his eyes.

Clean and Unclean Food

14 You are the children of the LORD your God. Do not cut yourselves or shave the
front of your heads for the dead, 2for you are a people holy to the LORD your God.
Out of all the peoples on the face of the earth, the LORD has chosen you to be his
treasured possession.
3Do not eat any detestable thing. 4These are the animals you may eat: the ox, the sheep,
the goat, 5the deer, the gazelle, the roe deer, the wild goat, the ibex, the antelope and the
mountain sheep.[b] 6You may eat any animal that has a divided hoof and that chews the cud.
7However, of those that chew the cud or that have a divided hoof you may not eat the cam-
el, the rabbit or the hyrax. Although they chew the cud, they do not have a divided hoof;
they are ceremonially unclean for you. 8The pig is also unclean; although it has a divided
hoof, it does not chew the cud. You are not to eat their meat or touch their carcasses.
9Of all the creatures living in the water, you may eat any that has fins and scales. 10But
anything that does not have fins and scales you may not eat; for you it is unclean.
11You may eat any clean bird. 12But these you may not eat: the eagle, the vulture, the black
vulture, 13the red kite, the black kite, any kind of falcon, 14any kind of raven, 15the horned owl,
the screech owl, the gull, any kind of hawk, 16the little owl, the great owl, the white owl, 17the
desert owl, the osprey, the cormorant, 18the stork, any kind of heron, the hoopoe and the bat.
19All flying insects that swarm are unclean to you; do not eat them. 20But any winged
creature that is clean you may eat.
21Do not eat anything you find already dead. You may give it to the foreigners residing
in any of your towns, and they may eat it, or you may sell it to any other foreigner. But you
are a people holy to the LORD your God.
Do not cook a young goat in its mother's milk.

Tithes

22Be sure to set aside a tenth of all that your fields produce each year. 23Eat the tithe of
your grain, new wine and olive oil, and the firstborn of your herds and flocks in the pres-
ence of the LORD your God at the place he will choose as a dwelling for his Name, so that
you may learn to revere the LORD your God always. 24But if that place is too distant and
you have been blessed by the LORD your God and cannot carry your tithe (because the place
where the LORD will choose to put his Name is so far away), 25then exchange your tithe for
silver, and take the silver with you and go to the place the LORD your God will choose. 26Use
the silver to buy whatever you like: cattle, sheep, wine or other fermented drink, or anything
you wish. Then you and your household shall eat there in the presence of the LORD your God
and rejoice. 27And do not neglect the Levites living in your towns, for they have no allot-
ment or inheritance of their own.
28At the end of every three years, bring all the tithes of that year's produce and store it in
your towns, 29so that the Levites (who have no allotment or inheritance of their own) and
the foreigners, the fatherless and the widows who live in your towns may come and eat and
be satisfied, and so that the LORD your God may bless you in all the work of your hands.

The Year for Canceling Debts

15 At the end of every seven years you must cancel debts. 2This is how it is to be
done: Every creditor shall cancel any loan they have made to another Israelite.
They shall not require payment from anyone among their own people, because

---

[a] 17 The Hebrew term refers to the irrevocable giving over of things or persons to the LORD, often by totally destroying them. [b] 5 The precise identification of some of the birds and animals in this chapter is uncertain.

the LORD's time for canceling debts has been proclaimed. [3]You may require payment from a foreigner, but you must cancel any debt one of your people owes you. [4]However, there need be no poor people among you, for in the land the LORD your God is giving you to possess as your inheritance, he will richly bless you, [5]if only you fully obey the LORD your God and are careful to follow all these commands I am giving you today. [6]For the LORD your God will bless you as he has promised, and you will lend to many nations but will borrow from none. You will rule over many nations but none will rule over you.

[7]If anyone is poor among your people in any of the towns of the land that the LORD your God is giving you, do not be hardhearted or tightfisted toward them. [8]Rather, be openhanded and freely lend them whatever they need. [9]Be careful not to harbor this wicked thought: "The seventh year, the year for canceling debts, is near," so that you do not show ill will toward the needy among your people and give them nothing. They may then appeal to the LORD against you, and you will be found guilty of sin. [10]Give generously to them and do so without a grudging heart; then because of this the LORD your God will bless you in all your work and in everything you put your hand to. [11]There will always be poor people in the land. Therefore I command you to be openhanded toward those of your people who are poor and needy in your land.

Freeing Servants

[12]If any of your people, men or women, sell themselves to you and serve you six years, in the seventh year you must let them go free. [13]And when you release them, do not send them away empty-handed. [14]Supply them liberally from your flock, your threshing floor and your winepress. Give to them as the LORD your God has blessed you. [15]Remember that you were slaves in Egypt and the LORD your God redeemed you. That is why I give you this command today.

[16]But if your servant says to you, "I do not want to leave you," because he loves you and your family and is well off with you, [17]then take an awl and push it through his ear lobe into the door, and he will become your servant for life. Do the same for your female servant.

[18]Do not consider it a hardship to set your servants free, because their service to you these six years has been worth twice as much as that of a hired hand. And the LORD your God will bless you in everything you do.

The Firstborn Animals

[19]Set apart for the LORD your God every firstborn male of your herds and flocks. Do not put the firstborn of your cows to work, and do not shear the firstborn of your sheep. [20]Each year you and your family are to eat them in the presence of the LORD your God at the place he will choose. [21]If an animal has a defect, is lame or blind, or has any serious flaw, you must not sacrifice it to the LORD your God. [22]You are to eat it in your own towns. Both the

Managing Resources

15:10–11 // Possessions. One of the Biblical principles that goes with acquiring and managing wealth is the willingness to share it. It may seem paradoxical that giving money away would make your business more profitable. But note these two things: First, a society marked by compassion tends to thrive, while a miserly atmosphere breeds discontent that eventually affects the bottom line (remember Ebenezer Scrooge?). Second, God promises his blessing to the person who is concerned about others. God is not a heavenly vending machine, dispensing $100 bills when you give $20 to the church. But when you put God first in your business affairs, you can take seriously these kinds of promises.

These verses also say that, while poverty cannot be completely wiped out, suffering can be lessened by voluntary generosity. We must not depend on the government or on charitable organizations alone to care for disadvantaged individuals.

In short, if you want your business and your society to succeed, don't be tightfisted toward people who need assistance.

ceremonially unclean and the clean may eat it, as if it were gazelle or deer. 23 But you must
not eat the blood; pour it out on the ground like water.

Passover

16 Observe the month of Aviv and celebrate the Passover of the LORD your God, be-
cause in the month of Aviv he brought you out of Egypt by night. 2 Sacrifice as
the Passover to the LORD your God an animal from your flock or herd at the place
the LORD will choose as a dwelling for his Name. 3 Do not eat it with bread made with yeast,
but for seven days eat unleavened bread, the bread of affliction, because you left Egypt in
haste—so that all the days of your life you may remember the time of your departure from
Egypt. 4 Let no yeast be found in your possession in all your land for seven days. Do not let
any of the meat you sacrifice on the evening of the first day remain until morning.
5 You must not sacrifice the Passover in any town the LORD your God gives you 6 except
in the place he will choose as a dwelling for his Name. There you must sacrifice the Pass-
over in the evening, when the sun goes down, on the anniversary[a] of your departure from
Egypt. 7 Roast it and eat it at the place the LORD your God will choose. Then in the morn-
ing return to your tents. 8 For six days eat unleavened bread and on the seventh day hold
an assembly to the LORD your God and do no work.

Festival of Weeks

9 Count off seven weeks from the time you begin to put the sickle to the standing grain.
10 Then celebrate the Festival of Weeks to the LORD your God by giving a freewill offering in
proportion to the blessings the LORD your God has given you. 11 And rejoice before the LORD
your God at the place he will choose as a dwelling for his Name—you, your sons and daugh-
ters, your male and female servants, the Levites in your towns, and the foreigners, the fa-
therless and the widows living among you. 12 Remember that you were slaves in Egypt, and
follow carefully these decrees.

Festival of Tabernacles

13 Celebrate the Festival of Tabernacles for seven days after you have gathered the pro-
duce of your threshing floor and your winepress. 14 Be joyful at your Festival—you, your
sons and daughters, your male and female servants, and the Levites, the foreigners, the
fatherless and the widows who live in your towns. 15 For seven days celebrate the Festival
to the LORD your God at the place the LORD will choose. For the LORD your God will bless
you in all your harvest and in all the work of your hands, and your joy will be complete.
16 Three times a year all your men must appear before the LORD your God at the place he
will choose: at the Festival of Unleavened Bread, the Festival of Weeks and the Festival of
Tabernacles. No one should appear before the LORD empty-handed: 17 Each of you must bring
a gift in proportion to the way the LORD your God has blessed you.

Judges

18 Appoint judges and officials for each of your tribes in every town the LORD your God is
giving you, and they shall judge the people fairly. 19 Do not pervert justice or show partiality.
Do not accept a bribe, for a bribe blinds the eyes of the wise and twists the words of the righ-
teous. 20 Follow justice and justice alone, so that you may live and possess the land the LORD
your God is giving you.

Worshiping Other Gods

21 Do not set up any wooden Asherah pole beside the altar you build to the LORD your
God, 22 and do not erect a sacred stone, for these the LORD your God hates.

17 Do not sacrifice to the LORD your God an ox or a sheep that has any defect or flaw
in it, for that would be detestable to him.
2 If a man or woman living among you in one of the towns the LORD gives you is
found doing evil in the eyes of the LORD your God in violation of his covenant, 3 and con-
trary to my command has worshiped other gods, bowing down to them or to the sun or

---

[a] 6 Or *down, at the time of day*

the moon or the stars in the sky, 4and this has been brought to your attention, then you
must investigate it thoroughly. If it is true and it has been proved that this detestable thing
has been done in Israel, 5take the man or woman who has done this evil deed to your city
gate and stone that person to death. 6On the testimony of two or three witnesses a person
is to be put to death, but no one is to be put to death on the testimony of only one witness.
7The hands of the witnesses must be the first in putting that person to death, and then the
hands of all the people. You must purge the evil from among you.

Law Courts

8If cases come before your courts that are too difficult for you to judge—whether blood-
shed, lawsuits or assaults—take them to the place the LORD your God will choose. 9Go to
the Levitical priests and to the judge who is in office at that time. Inquire of them and they
will give you the verdict. 10You must act according to the decisions they give you at the
place the LORD will choose. Be careful to do everything they instruct you to do. 11Act ac-
cording to whatever they teach you and the decisions they give you. Do not turn aside from
what they tell you, to the right or to the left. 12Anyone who shows contempt for the judge
or for the priest who stands ministering there to the LORD your God is to be put to death.
You must purge the evil from Israel. 13All the people will hear and be afraid, and will not
be contemptuous again.

The King

14When you enter the land the LORD your God is giving you and have taken possession
of it and settled in it, and you say, "Let us set a king over us like all the nations around us,"
15be sure to appoint over you the king the LORD your God chooses. He must be from among
your own people. Do not place a foreigner over you, one who is not an Israelite. 16The king,
moreover, must not acquire great numbers of horses for himself or make the people re-
turn to Egypt to get more of them, for the LORD has told you, "You are not to go back that
way again." 17He must not take many wives, or his heart will be led astray. He must not ac-
cumulate large amounts of silver and gold.

18When he takes the throne of his kingdom, he is to write for himself on a scroll a copy
of this law, taken from that of the Levitical priests. 19It is to be with him, and he is to read
it all the days of his life so that he may learn to revere the LORD his God and follow care-
fully all the words of this law and these decrees 20and not consider himself better than his
fellow Israelites and turn from the law to the right or to the left. Then he and his descen-
dants will reign a long time over his kingdom in Israel.

Offerings for Priests and Levites

18 The Levitical priests—indeed, the whole tribe of Levi—are to have no allotment
or inheritance with Israel. They shall live on the food offerings presented to the
LORD, for that is their inheritance. 2They shall have no inheritance among their
fellow Israelites; the LORD is their inheritance, as he promised them.

3This is the share due the priests from the people who sacrifice a bull or a sheep: the
shoulder, the jowls and the internal organs. 4You are to give them the firstfruits of your
grain, new wine and olive oil, and the first wool from the shearing of your sheep, 5for the

Strengthening Relationships

17:17–20 // Leadership. This passage describes three marks of a good king. They are qualities that leaders in our own day would do well to cultivate.

First, kings were not to have multiple wives. It is very tempting for people in positions of power to multiply their sexual exploits. But men and women who lead should be examples of moral restraint. What people do in the bedroom *does* matter in the boardroom.

Second, kings were not to use their position to become wealthy at the people's expense. The Bible condemns leadership that exploits those who are led.

Finally, kings were to recognize that they came from the same stock as the people they governed and that they too were under God's law. Good leaders share power and know that they are no better than the people they lead.

If you hold a position of leadership, what kind of leader are you?

LORD your God has chosen them and their descendants out of all your tribes to stand and
minister in the LORD's name always.
[6]If a Levite moves from one of your towns anywhere in Israel where he is living, and
comes in all earnestness to the place the LORD will choose, [7]he may minister in the name
of the LORD his God like all other Levites who serve there in the presence of the LORD. [8]He
is to share equally in their benefits, even though he has received money from the sale of
family possessions.

Occult Practices

[9]When you enter the land the LORD your God is giving you, do not learn to imitate the de-
testable ways of the nations there. [10]Let no one be found among you who sacrifices their
son or daughter in the fire, who practices divination or sorcery, interprets omens, engages
in witchcraft, [11]or casts spells, or who is a medium or spiritist or who consults the dead.
[12]Anyone who does these things is detestable to the LORD, and because of these detestable
practices the LORD your God will drive out those nations before you. [13]You must be blame-
less before the LORD your God.

The Prophet

[14]The nations you will dispossess listen to those who practice sorcery or divination. But
as for you, the LORD your God has not permitted you to do so. [15]The LORD your God will
raise up for you a prophet like me from among you, from your own people. You must lis-
ten to him. [16]For this is what you asked of the LORD your God at Horeb on the day of the as-
sembly when you said, "Let us not hear the voice of the LORD our God nor see this great
fire anymore, or we will die."
[17]The LORD said to me: "What they say is good. [18]I will raise up for them a prophet like
you from among their people, and I will put my words in his mouth. He will tell them ev-
erything I command him. [19]I myself will call to account anyone who does not listen to my
words that the prophet speaks in my name. [20]But a prophet who presumes to speak in my
name anything I have not commanded, or a prophet who speaks in the name of other gods,
is to be put to death."

Discovering God

18:10–13 // Spiritual Fraud. God is very concerned that his people not participate in those forms of spiritual experiment commonly known as occult practices. While some occult practices are fake, others actually work because of the evil forces behind them. Such practices are dangerous and are to be avoided.

The Bible gives us plenty of evidence for the existence of unseen evil forces. Jesus encountered a real devil (see Matthew chapter 4, verses 1–11), and the apostle Paul made it clear that there is an invisible spiritual battle going on all around us (Ephesians chapter 6, verses 11–13).

Just as a person doesn't need to experiment with illegal drugs to know that they are harmful, spiritual seekers don't need to dabble in the occult to understand that it is evil. God is not to be found there.

Discovering God

18:21–22 // Spiritual Fraud. Here is another way to discover spiritual counterfeits. The Biblical test for a prophet is 100 percent accuracy. Just one deviation from that standard and the prophet is to be disregarded.

Many so-called prophets predict events in our own day. They seem to think they have a "gift" when they do better than 50 percent. But not one of them has anywhere near 100 percent accuracy. On the other hand, true Biblical prophets *never* made an erroneous prediction. Their information source was the most reliable one in the universe—God himself.

The next time you thumb through the tabloids at the checkout counter, remember this test: Without complete accuracy, any so-called prophet is not from God. Don't waste your time or money on someone who does not have God's endorsement. Rather, invest your

21You may say to yourselves, "How can we know when a message has not been spoken
by the LORD?" 22If what a prophet proclaims in the name of the LORD does not take place
or come true, that is a message the LORD has not spoken. That prophet has spoken pre-
sumptuously. No one should be alarmed.

Cities of Refuge

19 When the LORD your God has destroyed the nations whose land he is giving you,
and when you have driven them out and settled in their towns and houses, 2then
set aside for yourselves three cities in the land the LORD your God is giving you
to possess. 3Build roads to them and divide into three parts the land the LORD your God is
giving you as an inheritance, so that anyone who kills someone else may flee there.
4This is the rule concerning anyone who kills a person and flees there for safety—any-
one who kills a neighbor unintentionally, without malice aforethought. 5For instance, a
man may go into the forest with his neighbor to cut wood, and as he swings his ax to fell
a tree, the head may fly off and hit his neighbor and kill him. That man may flee to one of
these cities and save his life. 6Otherwise, the avenger of blood might pursue him in a rage,
overtake him if the distance is too great, and kill him even though he is not deserving of
death, since he did it to his neighbor without malice aforethought. 7This is why I command
you to set aside for yourselves three cities.
8If the LORD your God enlarges your territory, as he promised on oath to your ancestors,
and gives you the whole land he promised them, 9because you carefully follow all these
laws I command you today—to love the LORD your God and to walk always in obedience
to him—then you are to set aside three more cities. 10Do this so that innocent blood will
not be shed in your land, which the LORD your God is giving you as your inheritance, and
so that you will not be guilty of bloodshed.
11But if out of hate someone lies in wait, assaults and kills a neighbor, and then flees to
one of these cities, 12the killer shall be sent for by the town elders, be brought back from the
city, and be handed over to the avenger of blood to die. 13Show no pity. You must purge from
Israel the guilt of shedding innocent blood, so that it may go well with you.
14Do not move your neighbor's boundary stone set up by your predecessors in the in-
heritance you receive in the land the LORD your God is giving you to possess.

Witnesses

15One witness is not enough to convict anyone accused of any crime or offense they may
have committed. A matter must be established by the testimony of two or three witnesses.
16If a malicious witness takes the stand to accuse someone of a crime, 17the two involved
in the dispute must stand in the presence of the LORD before the priests and the judges
who are in office at the time. 18The judges must make a thorough investigation, and if the
witness proves to be a liar, giving false testimony, 19then do to the false witness as that
witness intended to do to the other party. You must purge the evil from among you. 20The
rest of the people will hear of this and be afraid, and never again will such an evil thing be
done among you. 21Show no pity: life for life, eye for eye, tooth for tooth, hand for hand,
foot for foot.

Going to War

20 When you go to war against your enemies and see horses and chariots and an
army greater than yours, do not be afraid of them, because the LORD your God,
who brought you up out of Egypt, will be with you. 2When you are about to go
into battle, the priest shall come forward and address the army. 3He shall say: "Hear, Isra-
el: Today you are going into battle against your enemies. Do not be fainthearted or afraid;
do not be terrified or give way to panic before them. 4For the LORD your God is the one who
goes with you to fight for you against your enemies to give you victory."
5The officers shall say to the army: "Has anyone built a new house and not yet begun to
live in it? Let him go home, or he may die in battle and someone else may begin to live in it.
6Has anyone planted a vineyard and not begun to enjoy it? Let him go home, or he may die
in battle and someone else enjoy it. 7Has anyone become pledged to a woman and not mar-
ried her? Let him go home, or he may die in battle and someone else marry her." 8Then the

officers shall add, "Is anyone afraid or fainthearted? Let him go home so that the others will not become disheartened too." [9]When the officers have finished speaking to the army, they shall appoint commanders over it.

[10]When you march up to attack a city, make its people an offer of peace. [11]If they accept and open their gates, all the people in it shall be subject to forced labor and shall work for you. [12]If they refuse to make peace and they engage you in battle, lay siege to that city. [13]When the LORD your God delivers it into your hand, put to the sword all the men in it. [14]As for the women, the children, the livestock and everything else in the city, you may take these as plunder for yourselves. And you may use the plunder the LORD your God gives you from your enemies. [15]This is how you are to treat all the cities that are at a distance from you and do not belong to the nations nearby.

[16]However, in the cities of the nations the LORD your God is giving you as an inheritance, do not leave alive anything that breathes. [17]Completely destroy[a] them—the Hittites, Amorites, Canaanites, Perizzites, Hivites and Jebusites—as the LORD your God has commanded you. [18]Otherwise, they will teach you to follow all the detestable things they do in worshiping their gods, and you will sin against the LORD your God.

[19]When you lay siege to a city for a long time, fighting against it to capture it, do not destroy its trees by putting an ax to them, because you can eat their fruit. Do not cut them down. Are the trees people, that you should besiege them?[b] [20]However, you may cut down trees that you know are not fruit trees and use them to build siege works until the city at war with you falls.

Atonement for an Unsolved Murder

21 If someone is found slain, lying in a field in the land the LORD your God is giving you to possess, and it is not known who the killer was, [2]your elders and judges shall go out and measure the distance from the body to the neighboring towns. [3]Then the elders of the town nearest the body shall take a heifer that has never been worked and has never worn a yoke [4]and lead it down to a valley that has not been plowed or planted and where there is a flowing stream. There in the valley they are to break the heifer's neck. [5]The priests, the sons of Levi, shall step forward, for the LORD your God has chosen them to minister and to pronounce blessings in the name of the LORD and to decide all cases of dispute and assault. [6]Then all the elders of the town nearest the body shall wash their hands over the heifer whose neck was broken in the valley, [7]and they shall declare: "Our hands did not shed this blood, nor did our eyes see it done. [8]Accept this atonement for your people Israel, whom you have redeemed, LORD, and do not hold your people guilty of the blood of an innocent person." And the bloodshed will be atoned for. [9]So you will purge from yourselves the guilt of shedding innocent blood, since you have done what is right in the eyes of the LORD.

Marrying a Captive Woman

[10]When you go to war against your enemies and the LORD your God delivers them into your hands and you take captives, [11]if you notice among the captives a beautiful woman and are attracted to her, you may take her as your wife. [12]Bring her into your home and have her shave her head, trim her nails [13]and put aside the clothes she was wearing when captured. After she has lived in your house and mourned her father and mother for a full month, then you may go to her and be her husband and she shall be your wife. [14]If you are

Addressing Questions

20:10–18 // God. Remember, the God of the Bible hates warfare. But at this crucial point in history, these unique, never-to-be-repeated actions served God's justice and gave his nation a foothold in a corner of the world that was filled with abuse and evil (see the note on Deuteronomy chapter 2, verse 34 [page 75]).

[a] 17 The Hebrew term refers to the irrevocable giving over of things or persons to the LORD, often by totally destroying them. [b] 19 Or *down to use in the siege, for the fruit trees are for the benefit of people.*

not pleased with her, let her go wherever she wishes. You must not sell her or treat her as
a slave, since you have dishonored her.

The Right of the Firstborn

[15]If someone has two wives, and he loves one but not the other, and both bear him sons
but the firstborn is the son of the wife he does not love, [16]when he wills his property to his
sons, he must not give the rights of the firstborn to the son of the wife he loves in prefer-
ence to his actual firstborn, the son of the wife he does not love. [17]He must acknowledge
the son of his unloved wife as the firstborn by giving him a double share of all he has. That
son is the first sign of his father's strength. The right of the firstborn belongs to him.

A Rebellious Son

[18]If someone has a stubborn and rebellious son who does not obey his father and moth-
er and will not listen to them when they discipline him, [19]his father and mother shall take
hold of him and bring him to the elders at the gate of his town. [20]They shall say to the el-
ders, "This son of ours is stubborn and rebellious. He will not obey us. He is a profligate
and a drunkard." [21]Then all the men of his town are to stone him to death. You must purge
the evil from among you. All Israel will hear of it and be afraid.

Various Laws

[22]If anyone guilty of a capital offense is put to death and their body is exposed on a pole,
[23]you must not leave the body hanging on the pole overnight. Be sure to bury it that same
day, because anyone who is hung on a pole is under God's curse. You must not desecrate
the land the LORD your God is giving you as an inheritance.

22 If you see someone else's ox or sheep straying, do not ignore it but be sure to take
it back to its owner. [2]If the owner does not live near you or if you do not know who
owns it, take it home with you and keep it until the owner comes looking for it.
Then give it back. [3]Do the same if you find someone's donkey or cloak or anything else they
have lost. Do not ignore it.

[4]If you see someone's donkey or ox fallen on the road, do not ignore it. Help the owner
get it to its feet.

[5]A woman must not wear men's clothing, nor a man wear women's clothing, for the LORD
your God detests anyone who does this.

[6]If you come across a bird's nest beside the road, either in a tree or on the ground, and
the mother is sitting on the young or on the eggs, do not take the mother with the young.
[7]You may take the young, but be sure to let the mother go, so that it may go well with you
and you may have a long life.

[8]When you build a new house, make a parapet around your roof so that you may not
bring the guilt of bloodshed on your house if someone falls from the roof.

[9]Do not plant two kinds of seed in your vineyard; if you do, not only the crops you plant
but also the fruit of the vineyard will be defiled.[a]

[10]Do not plow with an ox and a donkey yoked together.

[11]Do not wear clothes of wool and linen woven together.

[12]Make tassels on the four corners of the cloak you wear.

Marriage Violations

[13]If a man takes a wife and, after sleeping with her, dislikes her [14]and slanders her and
gives her a bad name, saying, "I married this woman, but when I approached her, I did not
find proof of her virginity," [15]then the young woman's father and mother shall bring to the
town elders at the gate proof that she was a virgin. [16]Her father will say to the elders, "I
gave my daughter in marriage to this man, but he dislikes her. [17]Now he has slandered her
and said, 'I did not find your daughter to be a virgin.' But here is the proof of my daugh-
ter's virginity." Then her parents shall display the cloth before the elders of the town, [18]and
the elders shall take the man and punish him. [19]They shall fine him a hundred shekels[b] of

[a] 9 Or *be forfeited to the sanctuary* [b] 19 That is, about 2 1/2 pounds or about 1.2 kilograms

silver and give them to the young woman's father, because this man has given an Israel-
ite virgin a bad name. She shall continue to be his wife; he must not divorce her as long as
he lives.
20 If, however, the charge is true and no proof of the young woman's virginity can be
found, 21 she shall be brought to the door of her father's house and there the men of her
town shall stone her to death. She has done an outrageous thing in Israel by being promis-
cuous while still in her father's house. You must purge the evil from among you.
22 If a man is found sleeping with another man's wife, both the man who slept with her
and the woman must die. You must purge the evil from Israel.
23 If a man happens to meet in a town a virgin pledged to be married and he sleeps with
her, 24 you shall take both of them to the gate of that town and stone them to death—the
young woman because she was in a town and did not scream for help, and the man because
he violated another man's wife. You must purge the evil from among you.
25 But if out in the country a man happens to meet a young woman pledged to be mar-
ried and rapes her, only the man who has done this shall die. 26 Do nothing to the woman;
she has committed no sin deserving death. This case is like that of someone who attacks
and murders a neighbor, 27 for the man found the young woman out in the country, and
though the betrothed woman screamed, there was no one to rescue her.
28 If a man happens to meet a virgin who is not pledged to be married and rapes her and
they are discovered, 29 he shall pay her father fifty shekels[a] of silver. He must marry the
young woman, for he has violated her. He can never divorce her as long as he lives.
*30 A man is not to marry his father's wife; he must not dishonor his father's bed.

Exclusion From the Assembly

23 *No one who has been emasculated by crushing or cutting may enter the assem-
bly of the LORD.
2 No one born of a forbidden marriage[b] nor any offspring from such a marriage
may enter the assembly of the LORD, not even in the tenth generation.
3 No Ammonite or Moabite or any of their descendants may enter the assembly of the
LORD, not even in the tenth generation. 4 For they did not come to meet you with bread and
water on your way when you came out of Egypt, and they hired Balaam son of Beor from

Strengthening Relationships

22:13–20 // Marriage. These strict laws about sexual purity sound harsh in our permissive age. But behind their rigidity lies a timeless principle: God intends that marriage be permanent and that both husband and wife remain faithful to one another.

When people commit adultery, pain spreads out like ripples in a pond. Understand that God doesn't hate sin because he wants to limit our fun or freedom; he hates sin because of the human suffering that results.

Jesus, in the Gospel of John, gives us further instructions for dealing with sin—specifically, the sin of adultery (please turn to John chapter 8, verses 1–11 [page 130]). In that story Jesus clarifies the point of the harsh law that we read in this passage—completely eliminate all traces of this sin from your marriage.

This woman, however, had already committed adultery. Instead of condemning her, Jesus commanded her to "Go now and leave your life of sin." That's a picture of God's willingness to forgive us when we do wrong—a benefit that we can all enjoy when we commit our lives and marriages to him.

Is your marriage a permanent bond? Or are you connected with your spouse only until someone better comes along? Most people see marriage as a positive arrangement as long as two people are in love. But according to God's design, it's a committed marriage that keeps love alive, not the other way around.

---

[a] 29 That is, about 1 1/4 pounds or about 575 grams [b] 2 Or *one of illegitimate birth*

*22:30 is numbered 23:1 in Hebrew texts. *23:1-25 is numbered 23:2-26 in Hebrew texts.

Pethor in Aram Naharaim[a] to pronounce a curse on you. 5 However, the LORD your God would not listen to Balaam but turned the curse into a blessing for you, because the LORD your God loves you. 6 Do not seek a treaty of friendship with them as long as you live.

7 Do not despise an Edomite, for the Edomites are related to you. Do not despise an Egyptian, because you resided as foreigners in their country. 8 The third generation of children born to them may enter the assembly of the LORD.

Uncleanness in the Camp

9 When you are encamped against your enemies, keep away from everything impure. 10 If one of your men is unclean because of a nocturnal emission, he is to go outside the camp and stay there. 11 But as evening approaches he is to wash himself, and at sunset he may return to the camp.

12 Designate a place outside the camp where you can go to relieve yourself. 13 As part of your equipment have something to dig with, and when you relieve yourself, dig a hole and cover up your excrement. 14 For the LORD your God moves about in your camp to protect you and to deliver your enemies to you. Your camp must be holy, so that he will not see among you anything indecent and turn away from you.

Miscellaneous Laws

15 If a slave has taken refuge with you, do not hand them over to their master. 16 Let them live among you wherever they like and in whatever town they choose. Do not oppress them.

17 No Israelite man or woman is to become a shrine prostitute. 18 You must not bring the earnings of a female prostitute or of a male prostitute[b] into the house of the LORD your God to pay any vow, because the LORD your God detests them both.

19 Do not charge an Israelite interest, whether on money or food or anything else that may earn interest. 20 You may charge a foreigner interest, but not another Israelite, so that the LORD your God may bless you in everything you put your hand to in the land you are entering to possess.

21 If you make a vow to the LORD your God, do not be slow to pay it, for the LORD your God will certainly demand it of you and you will be guilty of sin. 22 But if you refrain from making a vow, you will not be guilty. 23 Whatever your lips utter you must be sure to do, because you made your vow freely to the LORD your God with your own mouth.

24 If you enter your neighbor's vineyard, you may eat all the grapes you want, but do not put any in your basket. 25 If you enter your neighbor's grainfield, you may pick kernels with your hands, but you must not put a sickle to the standing grain.

24 If a man marries a woman who becomes displeasing to him because he finds something indecent about her, and he writes her a certificate of divorce, gives it to her and sends her from his house, 2 and if after she leaves his house she becomes the wife of another man, 3 and her second husband dislikes her and writes her a certificate of divorce, gives it to her and sends her from his house, or if he dies, 4 then her first husband, who divorced her, is not allowed to marry her again after she has been defiled. That would be detestable in the eyes of the LORD. Do not bring sin upon the land the LORD your God is giving you as an inheritance.

5 If a man has recently married, he must not be sent to war or have any other duty laid on him. For one year he is to be free to stay at home and bring happiness to the wife he has married.

6 Do not take a pair of millstones—not even the upper one—as security for a debt, because that would be taking a person's livelihood as security.

7 If someone is caught kidnapping another Israelite and treating or selling that Israelite as a slave, the kidnapper must die. You must purge the evil from among you.

8 In cases of defiling skin diseases,[c] be very careful to do exactly as the Levitical priests instruct you. You must follow carefully what I have commanded them. 9 Remember what the LORD your God did to Miriam along the way after you came out of Egypt.

10 When you make a loan of any kind to a neighbor, do not go into the neighbor's house to

---

[a] 4 That is, Northwest Mesopotamia [b] 18 Hebrew *of a dog* [c] 8 The Hebrew word for *defiling skin diseases,* traditionally translated "leprosy," was used for various diseases affecting the skin.

get what is offered to you as a pledge. 11Stay outside and let the neighbor to whom you are making the loan bring the pledge out to you. 12If the neighbor is poor, do not go to sleep with that pledge in your possession. 13Return the cloak by sunset so that your neighbor may sleep in it. Then you will be thanked, and it will be regarded as a righteous act in the sight of the LORD your God.

14Do not take advantage of a hired worker who is poor and needy, whether that worker is an Israelite or is a foreigner residing in one of your towns. 15Pay them their wages each day before sunset, because they are poor and are counting on it. Otherwise they may cry to the LORD against you, and you will be guilty of sin.

16Parents are not to be put to death for their children, nor children put to death for their parents; each of you will die for your own sin.

17Do not deprive the foreigner or the fatherless of justice, or take the cloak of the widow as a pledge. 18Remember that you were slaves in Egypt and the LORD your God redeemed you from there. That is why I command you to do this.

19When you are harvesting in your field and you overlook a sheaf, do not go back to get it. Leave it for the foreigner, the fatherless and the widow, so that the LORD your God may bless you in all the work of your hands. 20When you beat the olives from your trees, do not go over the branches a second time. Leave what remains for the foreigner, the fatherless and the widow. 21When you harvest the grapes in your vineyard, do not go over the vines again. Leave what remains for the foreigner, the fatherless and the widow. 22Remember that you were slaves in Egypt. That is why I command you to do this.

25 When people have a dispute, they are to take it to court and the judges will decide the case, acquitting the innocent and condemning the guilty. 2If the one who is guilty deserves to be beaten, the judge shall make them lie down and have them flogged in his presence with the number of lashes the crime deserves, 3but the judge must not impose more than forty lashes. If the guilty party is flogged more than that, your Israelite neighbor will be degraded in your eyes.

4Do not muzzle an ox while it is treading out the grain.

5If brothers are living together and one of them dies without a son, his widow must not marry outside the family. Her husband's brother shall take her and marry her and fulfill the duty of a brother-in-law to her. 6The first son she bears shall carry on the name of the dead brother so that his name will not be blotted out from Israel.

7However, if a man does not want to marry his brother's wife, she shall go to the elders at the town gate and say, "My husband's brother refuses to carry on his brother's name in Israel. He will not fulfill the duty of a brother-in-law to me." 8Then the elders of his town shall summon him and talk to him. If he persists in saying, "I do not want to marry her," 9his brother's widow shall go up to him in the presence of the elders, take off one of his sandals, spit in his face and say, "This is what is done to the man who will not build up his brother's family line." 10That man's line shall be known in Israel as The Family of the Unsandaled.

11If two men are fighting and the wife of one of them comes to rescue her husband from his assailant, and she reaches out and seizes him by his private parts, 12you shall cut off her hand. Show her no pity.

13Do not have two differing weights in your bag—one heavy, one light. 14Do not have two differing measures in your house—one large, one small. 15You must have accurate and honest weights and measures, so that you may live long in the land the LORD your God is giving you. 16For the LORD your God detests anyone who does these things, anyone who deals dishonestly.

Managing Resources

24:14–15 // Business. If you are an employer, God is concerned that you are not only fair, but also compassionate. The practice of paying wages each day ensured that poor individuals who lived literally hand-to-mouth would not be stuck waiting for their pay. Such a delay might have been permissible, but cold-hearted.

What a wonderful reputation you would make for yourself if your business treated all employees with dignity and—don't fall down here—paid all its bills on time!

[17]Remember what the Amalekites did to you along the way when you came out of Egypt.
[18]When you were weary and worn out, they met you on your journey and attacked all who
were lagging behind; they had no fear of God. [19]When the LORD your God gives you rest
from all the enemies around you in the land he is giving you to possess as an inheritance,
you shall blot out the name of Amalek from under heaven. Do not forget!

Firstfruits and Tithes

26 When you have entered the land the LORD your God is giving you as an inheri-
tance and have taken possession of it and settled in it, [2]take some of the first-
fruits of all that you produce from the soil of the land the LORD your God is giving
you and put them in a basket. Then go to the place the LORD your God will choose as a
dwelling for his Name [3]and say to the priest in office at the time, "I declare today to the
LORD your God that I have come to the land the LORD swore to our ancestors to give us."
[4]The priest shall take the basket from your hands and set it down in front of the altar of the
LORD your God. [5]Then you shall declare before the LORD your God: "My father was a wan-
dering Aramean, and he went down into Egypt with a few people and lived there and be-
came a great nation, powerful and numerous. [6]But the Egyptians mistreated us and made
us suffer, subjecting us to harsh labor. [7]Then we cried out to the LORD, the God of our an-
cestors, and the LORD heard our voice and saw our misery, toil and oppression. [8]So the LORD
brought us out of Egypt with a mighty hand and an outstretched arm, with great terror and
with signs and wonders. [9]He brought us to this place and gave us this land, a land flowing
with milk and honey; [10]and now I bring the firstfruits of the soil that you, LORD, have giv-
en me." Place the basket before the LORD your God and bow down before him. [11]Then you
and the Levites and the foreigners residing among you shall rejoice in all the good things
the LORD your God has given to you and your household.

[12]When you have finished setting aside a tenth of all your produce in the third year, the
year of the tithe, you shall give it to the Levite, the foreigner, the fatherless and the wid-
ow, so that they may eat in your towns and be satisfied. [13]Then say to the LORD your God:
"I have removed from my house the sacred portion and have given it to the Levite, the for-
eigner, the fatherless and the widow, according to all you commanded. I have not turned
aside from your commands nor have I forgotten any of them. [14]I have not eaten any of the
sacred portion while I was in mourning, nor have I removed any of it while I was unclean,
nor have I offered any of it to the dead. I have obeyed the LORD my God; I have done every-
thing you commanded me. [15]Look down from heaven, your holy dwelling place, and bless
your people Israel and the land you have given us as you promised on oath to our ances-
tors, a land flowing with milk and honey."

Follow the LORD's Commands

[16]The LORD your God commands you this day to follow these decrees and laws; careful-
ly observe them with all your heart and with all your soul. [17]You have declared this day that
the LORD is your God and that you will walk in obedience to him, that you will keep his de-
crees, commands and laws—that you will listen to him. [18]And the LORD has declared this
day that you are his people, his treasured possession as he promised, and that you are to
keep all his commands. [19]He has declared that he will set you in praise, fame and honor
high above all the nations he has made and that you will be a people holy to the LORD your
God, as he promised.

The Altar on Mount Ebal

27 Moses and the elders of Israel commanded the people: "Keep all these com-
mands that I give you today. [2]When you have crossed the Jordan into the land
the LORD your God is giving you, set up some large stones and coat them with
plaster. [3]Write on them all the words of this law when you have crossed over to enter the
land the LORD your God is giving you, a land flowing with milk and honey, just as the LORD,
the God of your ancestors, promised you. [4]And when you have crossed the Jordan, set up
these stones on Mount Ebal, as I command you today, and coat them with plaster. [5]Build
there an altar to the LORD your God, an altar of stones. Do not use any iron tool on them.

[6]Build the altar of the LORD your God with fieldstones and offer burnt offerings on it to the LORD your God. [7]Sacrifice fellowship offerings there, eating them and rejoicing in the presence of the LORD your God. [8]And you shall write very clearly all the words of this law on these stones you have set up."

Curses From Mount Ebal

[9]Then Moses and the Levitical priests said to all Israel, "Be silent, Israel, and listen! You have now become the people of the LORD your God. [10]Obey the LORD your God and follow his commands and decrees that I give you today."

[11]On the same day Moses commanded the people:

[12]When you have crossed the Jordan, these tribes shall stand on Mount Gerizim to bless the people: Simeon, Levi, Judah, Issachar, Joseph and Benjamin. [13]And these tribes shall stand on Mount Ebal to pronounce curses: Reuben, Gad, Asher, Zebulun, Dan and Naphtali.

[14]The Levites shall recite to all the people of Israel in a loud voice:

> [15]"Cursed is anyone who makes an idol—a thing detestable to the LORD, the work of skilled hands—and sets it up in secret."
> Then all the people shall say, "Amen!"
>
> [16]"Cursed is anyone who dishonors their father or mother."
> Then all the people shall say, "Amen!"
>
> [17]"Cursed is anyone who moves their neighbor's boundary stone."
> Then all the people shall say, "Amen!"
>
> [18]"Cursed is anyone who leads the blind astray on the road."
> Then all the people shall say, "Amen!"
>
> [19]"Cursed is anyone who withholds justice from the foreigner, the fatherless or the widow."
> Then all the people shall say, "Amen!"
>
> [20]"Cursed is anyone who sleeps with his father's wife, for he dishonors his father's bed."
> Then all the people shall say, "Amen!"
>
> [21]"Cursed is anyone who has sexual relations with any animal."
> Then all the people shall say, "Amen!"
>
> [22]"Cursed is anyone who sleeps with his sister, the daughter of his father or the daughter of his mother."
> Then all the people shall say, "Amen!"
>
> [23]"Cursed is anyone who sleeps with his mother-in-law."
> Then all the people shall say, "Amen!"
>
> [24]"Cursed is anyone who kills their neighbor secretly."
> Then all the people shall say, "Amen!"
>
> [25]"Cursed is anyone who accepts a bribe to kill an innocent person."
> Then all the people shall say, "Amen!"

Discovering God

27:7 // Life with God. As a seeker, you need to know that God is not down on pleasure. Here he actually commands Israel to enjoy a steak dinner as an act of worship!

If you perceive church as being dull and boring, realize that it's not supposed to be that way. God wants people to see time with him as something enjoyable and desirable. This verse shows us that a whole range of human emotions can be expressed during worship, including excitement, awe, joy, and wonder.

The challenge of accepting God is one of the most exciting and dangerous propositions humans can ever face. It calls for a radical, revolutionary life-change, and forces people to consider living for a cause outside of themselves. It involves tapping into the power of the very God who created the universe and all that is in it. People who devote their lives to the cause of Christ find thrills and chills that last—not just for a moment, but for eternity. What better reason could there be for celebration?

Are you ready for the thrill of a lifetime?

26“Cursed is anyone who does not uphold the words of this law by carrying them out.”
Then all the people shall say, “Amen!”

Blessings for Obedience

28 If you fully obey the LORD your God and carefully follow all his commands I give
you today, the LORD your God will set you high above all the nations on earth.
2All these blessings will come on you and accompany you if you obey the LORD
your God:

3You will be blessed in the city and blessed in the country.
4The fruit of your womb will be blessed, and the crops of your land and the young
of your livestock—the calves of your herds and the lambs of your flocks.
5Your basket and your kneading trough will be blessed.
6You will be blessed when you come in and blessed when you go out.

7The LORD will grant that the enemies who rise up against you will be defeated before
you. They will come at you from one direction but flee from you in seven.
8The LORD will send a blessing on your barns and on everything you put your hand to.
The LORD your God will bless you in the land he is giving you.
9The LORD will establish you as his holy people, as he promised you on oath, if you keep
the commands of the LORD your God and walk in obedience to him. 10Then all the peoples
on earth will see that you are called by the name of the LORD, and they will fear you. 11The
LORD will grant you abundant prosperity—in the fruit of your womb, the young of your live-
stock and the crops of your ground—in the land he swore to your ancestors to give you.
12The LORD will open the heavens, the storehouse of his bounty, to send rain on your
land in season and to bless all the work of your hands. You will lend to many nations but
will borrow from none. 13The LORD will make you the head, not the tail. If you pay atten-
tion to the commands of the LORD your God that I give you this day and carefully follow
them, you will always be at the top, never at the bottom. 14Do not turn aside from any of
the commands I give you today, to the right or to the left, following other gods and serv-
ing them.

Curses for Disobedience

15However, if you do not obey the LORD your God and do not carefully follow all his
commands and decrees I am giving you today, all these curses will come on you and over-
take you:

16You will be cursed in the city and cursed in the country.
17Your basket and your kneading trough will be cursed.
18The fruit of your womb will be cursed, and the crops of your land, and the calves
of your herds and the lambs of your flocks.
19You will be cursed when you come in and cursed when you go out.

20The LORD will send on you curses, confusion and rebuke in everything you put your
hand to, until you are destroyed and come to sudden ruin because of the evil you have
done in forsaking him.[a] 21The LORD will plague you with diseases until he has destroyed
you from the land you are entering to possess. 22The LORD will strike you with wasting dis-
ease, with fever and inflammation, with scorching heat and drought, with blight and mil-
dew, which will plague you until you perish. 23The sky over your head will be bronze, the
ground beneath you iron. 24The LORD will turn the rain of your country into dust and pow-
der; it will come down from the skies until you are destroyed.
25The LORD will cause you to be defeated before your enemies. You will come at them
from one direction but flee from them in seven, and you will become a thing of horror to
all the kingdoms on earth. 26Your carcasses will be food for all the birds and the wild ani-
mals, and there will be no one to frighten them away. 27The LORD will afflict you with the
boils of Egypt and with tumors, festering sores and the itch, from which you cannot be

[a] *20* Hebrew *me*

cured. 28The LORD will afflict you with madness, blindness and confusion of mind. 29At mid-
day you will grope about like a blind person in the dark. You will be unsuccessful in every-
thing you do; day after day you will be oppressed and robbed, with no one to rescue you.

30You will be pledged to be married to a woman, but another will take her and ravish
her. You will build a house, but you will not live in it. You will plant a vineyard, but you will
not even begin to enjoy its fruit. 31Your ox will be slaughtered before your eyes, but you will
eat none of it. Your donkey will be forcibly taken from you and will not be returned. Your
sheep will be given to your enemies, and no one will rescue them. 32Your sons and daugh-
ters will be given to another nation, and you will wear out your eyes watching for them
day after day, powerless to lift a hand. 33A people that you do not know will eat what your
land and labor produce, and you will have nothing but cruel oppression all your days. 34The
sights you see will drive you mad. 35The LORD will afflict your knees and legs with painful
boils that cannot be cured, spreading from the soles of your feet to the top of your head.

36The LORD will drive you and the king you set over you to a nation unknown to you or
your ancestors. There you will worship other gods, gods of wood and stone. 37You will be-
come a thing of horror, a byword and an object of ridicule among all the peoples where
the LORD will drive you.

38You will sow much seed in the field but you will harvest little, because locusts will de-
vour it. 39You will plant vineyards and cultivate them but you will not drink the wine or
gather the grapes, because worms will eat them. 40You will have olive trees throughout
your country but you will not use the oil, because the olives will drop off. 41You will have
sons and daughters but you will not keep them, because they will go into captivity.
42Swarms of locusts will take over all your trees and the crops of your land.

43The foreigners who reside among you will rise above you higher and higher, but you
will sink lower and lower. 44They will lend to you, but you will not lend to them. They will
be the head, but you will be the tail.

45All these curses will come on you. They will pursue you and overtake you until you are
destroyed, because you did not obey the LORD your God and observe the commands and
decrees he gave you. 46They will be a sign and a wonder to you and your descendants for-
ever. 47Because you did not serve the LORD your God joyfully and gladly in the time of pros-
perity, 48therefore in hunger and thirst, in nakedness and dire poverty, you will serve the
enemies the LORD sends against you. He will put an iron yoke on your neck until he has de-
stroyed you.

49The LORD will bring a nation against you from far away, from the ends of the earth,
like an eagle swooping down, a nation whose language you will not understand, 50a fierce-
looking nation without respect for the old or pity for the young. 51They will devour the
young of your livestock and the crops of your land until you are destroyed. They will leave
you no grain, new wine or olive oil, nor any calves of your herds or lambs of your flocks un-
til you are ruined. 52They will lay siege to all the cities throughout your land until the high
fortified walls in which you trust fall down. They will besiege all the cities throughout the
land the LORD your God is giving you.

53Because of the suffering that your enemy will inflict on you during the siege, you will
eat the fruit of the womb, the flesh of the sons and daughters the LORD your God has giv-
en you. 54Even the most gentle and sensitive man among you will have no compassion on
his own brother or the wife he loves or his surviving children, 55and he will not give to one
of them any of the flesh of his children that he is eating. It will be all he has left because
of the suffering your enemy will inflict on you during the siege of all your cities. 56The most
gentle and sensitive woman among you—so sensitive and gentle that she would not ven-
ture to touch the ground with the sole of her foot—will begrudge the husband she loves
and her own son or daughter 57the afterbirth from her womb and the children she bears.
For in her dire need she intends to eat them secretly because of the suffering your enemy
will inflict on you during the siege of your cities.

58If you do not carefully follow all the words of this law, which are written in this book,
and do not revere this glorious and awesome name—the LORD your God— 59the LORD will
send fearful plagues on you and your descendants, harsh and prolonged disasters, and se-
vere and lingering illnesses. 60He will bring on you all the diseases of Egypt that you dread-

ed, and they will cling to you. 61The LORD will also bring on you every kind of sickness and
disaster not recorded in this Book of the Law, until you are destroyed. 62You who were as
numerous as the stars in the sky will be left but few in number, because you did not obey
the LORD your God. 63Just as it pleased the LORD to make you prosper and increase in num-
ber, so it will please him to ruin and destroy you. You will be uprooted from the land you
are entering to possess.
64Then the LORD will scatter you among all nations, from one end of the earth to the
other. There you will worship other gods—gods of wood and stone, which neither you nor
your ancestors have known. 65Among those nations you will find no repose, no resting place
for the sole of your foot. There the LORD will give you an anxious mind, eyes weary with
longing, and a despairing heart. 66You will live in constant suspense, filled with dread both
night and day, never sure of your life. 67In the morning you will say, "If only it were eve-
ning!" and in the evening, "If only it were morning!"—because of the terror that will fill your
hearts and the sights that your eyes will see. 68The LORD will send you back in ships to Egypt
on a journey I said you should never make again. There you will offer yourselves for sale
to your enemies as male and female slaves, but no one will buy you.

Renewal of the Covenant

29 *These are the terms of the covenant the LORD commanded Moses to make with
the Israelites in Moab, in addition to the covenant he had made with them at
Horeb.
*2Moses summoned all the Israelites and said to them:

Your eyes have seen all that the LORD did in Egypt to Pharaoh, to all his officials and to
all his land. 3With your own eyes you saw those great trials, those signs and great wonders.
4But to this day the LORD has not given you a mind that understands or eyes that see or ears
that hear. 5During the forty years that I led you through the wilderness, your clothes did not
wear out, nor did the sandals on your feet. 6You ate no bread and drank no wine or other
fermented drink. I did this so that you might know that I am the LORD your God.
7When you reached this place, Sihon king of Heshbon and Og king of Bashan came out
to fight against us, but we defeated them. 8We took their land and gave it as an inheritance
to the Reubenites, the Gadites and the half-tribe of Manasseh.
9Carefully follow the terms of this covenant, so that you may prosper in everything you
do. 10All of you are standing today in the presence of the LORD your God—your leaders and
chief men, your elders and officials, and all the other men of Israel, 11together with your chil-
dren and your wives, and the foreigners living in your camps who chop your wood and car-
ry your water. 12You are standing here in order to enter into a covenant with the LORD your
God, a covenant the LORD is making with you this day and sealing with an oath, 13to con-
firm you this day as his people, that he may be your God as he promised you and as he
swore to your fathers, Abraham, Isaac and Jacob. 14I am making this covenant, with its
oath, not only with you 15who are standing here with us today in the presence of the LORD
our God but also with those who are not here today.
16You yourselves know how we lived in Egypt and how we passed through the countries
on the way here. 17You saw among them their detestable images and idols of wood and
stone, of silver and gold. 18Make sure there is no man or woman, clan or tribe among you
today whose heart turns away from the LORD our God to go and worship the gods of those
nations; make sure there is no root among you that produces such bitter poison.
19When such persons hear the words of this oath and invoke a blessing on themselves,
thinking, "I will be safe, even though I persist in going my own way," they will bring disas-
ter on the watered land as well as the dry. 20The LORD will never be willing to forgive them;
his wrath and zeal will burn against them. All the curses written in this book will fall on
them, and the LORD will blot out their names from under heaven. 21The LORD will single
them out from all the tribes of Israel for disaster, according to all the curses of the cov-
enant written in this Book of the Law.
22Your children who follow you in later generations and foreigners who come from dis-
tant lands will see the calamities that have fallen on the land and the diseases with which

*29:1 is numbered 28:69 in Hebrew texts. *29:2-29 is numbered 29:1-28 in Hebrew texts.

the LORD has afflicted it. 23 The whole land will be a burning waste of salt and sulfur—noth-
ing planted, nothing sprouting, no vegetation growing on it. It will be like the destruction
of Sodom and Gomorrah, Admah and Zeboyim, which the LORD overthrew in fierce anger.
24 All the nations will ask: "Why has the LORD done this to this land? Why this fierce, burn-
ing anger?"

25 And the answer will be: "It is because this people abandoned the covenant of the LORD,
the God of their ancestors, the covenant he made with them when he brought them out of
Egypt. 26 They went off and worshiped other gods and bowed down to them, gods they did
not know, gods he had not given them. 27 Therefore the LORD's anger burned against this
land, so that he brought on it all the curses written in this book. 28 In furious anger and in
great wrath the LORD uprooted them from their land and thrust them into another land, as
it is now."

29 The secret things belong to the LORD our God, but the things revealed belong to us and
to our children forever, that we may follow all the words of this law.

Prosperity After Turning to the LORD

30 When all these blessings and curses I have set before you come on you and you
take them to heart wherever the LORD your God disperses you among the na-
tions, 2 and when you and your children return to the LORD your God and obey
him with all your heart and with all your soul according to everything I command you to-
day, 3 then the LORD your God will restore your fortunes[a] and have compassion on you and
gather you again from all the nations where he scattered you. 4 Even if you have been ban-
ished to the most distant land under the heavens, from there the LORD your God will gath-
er you and bring you back. 5 He will bring you to the land that belonged to your ancestors,
and you will take possession of it. He will make you more prosperous and numerous than
your ancestors. 6 The LORD your God will circumcise your hearts and the hearts of your de-
scendants, so that you may love him with all your heart and with all your soul, and live.
7 The LORD your God will put all these curses on your enemies who hate and persecute you.
8 You will again obey the LORD and follow all his commands I am giving you today. 9 Then
the LORD your God will make you most prosperous in all the work of your hands and in the
fruit of your womb, the young of your livestock and the crops of your land. The LORD will
again delight in you and make you prosperous, just as he delighted in your ancestors, 10 if
you obey the LORD your God and keep his commands and decrees that are written in this
Book of the Law and turn to the LORD your God with all your heart and with all your soul.

The Offer of Life or Death

11 Now what I am commanding you today is not too difficult for you or beyond your reach.
12 It is not up in heaven, so that you have to ask, "Who will ascend into heaven to get it and
proclaim it to us so we may obey it?" 13 Nor is it beyond the sea, so that you have to ask,
"Who will cross the sea to get it and proclaim it to us so we may obey it?" 14 No, the word
is very near you; it is in your mouth and in your heart so you may obey it.

15 See, I set before you today life and prosperity, death and destruction. 16 For I command
you today to love the LORD your God, to walk in obedience to him, and to keep his commands,

Addressing Questions

29:29 // God. Every question you'll ever ask about God has an answer—but not necessarily one you'll find in your lifetime!

Because we have finite minds, the spiritual realm holds many mysteries that we'll never comprehend as long as we live on earth. However, we can know enough about God to find meaning in life and relate to him.

The study you've done up to this point has given you some good information about God. And, as you keep seeking, you'll learn more. The God you're seeking has revealed much about himself through nature, through the Bible, and most clearly through Jesus Christ.

As best you can, why not breathe a quick prayer to say "thanks" for the book you're holding and for the people who've helped you during your spiritual search?

[a] 3 Or *will bring you back from captivity*

decrees and laws; then you will live and increase, and the LORD your God will bless you in
the land you are entering to possess.
[17]But if your heart turns away and you are not obedient, and if you are drawn away to
bow down to other gods and worship them, [18]I declare to you this day that you will certain-
ly be destroyed. You will not live long in the land you are crossing the Jordan to enter and
possess.
[19]This day I call the heavens and the earth as witnesses against you that I have set be-
fore you life and death, blessings and curses. Now choose life, so that you and your chil-
dren may live [20]and that you may love the LORD your God, listen to his voice, and hold fast
to him. For the LORD is your life, and he will give you many years in the land he swore to
give to your fathers, Abraham, Isaac and Jacob.

Joshua to Succeed Moses

31 Then Moses went out and spoke these words to all Israel: [2]"I am now a hundred
and twenty years old and I am no longer able to lead you. The LORD has said to
me, 'You shall not cross the Jordan.' [3]The LORD your God himself will cross over
ahead of you. He will destroy these nations before you, and you will take possession of
their land. Joshua also will cross over ahead of you, as the LORD said. [4]And the LORD will do
to them what he did to Sihon and Og, the kings of the Amorites, whom he destroyed along
with their land. [5]The LORD will deliver them to you, and you must do to them all that I have
commanded you. [6]Be strong and courageous. Do not be afraid or terrified because of them,
for the LORD your God goes with you; he will never leave you nor forsake you."
[7]Then Moses summoned Joshua and said to him in the presence of all Israel, "Be strong
and courageous, for you must go with this people into the land that the LORD swore to their
ancestors to give them, and you must divide it among them as their inheritance. [8]The LORD
himself goes before you and will be with you; he will never leave you nor forsake you. Do
not be afraid; do not be discouraged."

The Reading of the Law

[9]So Moses wrote down this law and gave it to the priests, the sons of Levi, who carried
the ark of the covenant of the LORD, and to all the elders of Israel. [10]Then Moses command-
ed them: "At the end of every seven years, in the year for canceling debts, during the Fes-
tival of Tabernacles, [11]when all Israel comes to appear before the LORD your God at the place
he will choose, you shall read this law before them in their hearing. [12]Assemble the peo-
ple—men, women and children, and the foreigners residing in your towns—so they can lis-
ten and learn to fear the LORD your God and follow carefully all the words of this law. [13]Their
children, who do not know this law, must hear it and learn to fear the LORD your God as long
as you live in the land you are crossing the Jordan to possess."

Israel's Rebellion Predicted

[14]The LORD said to Moses, "Now the day of your death is near. Call Joshua and present
yourselves at the tent of meeting, where I will commission him." So Moses and Joshua
came and presented themselves at the tent of meeting.

Reasons to Believe

30:19–20 // The Christian Experience. According to this passage, God does not force anyone to follow him. He offers people the choice of accepting his love—and with it, eternal life.

God gave that choice to the people of ancient Israel. In the verses preceding this passage, God spoke forthrightly to these people, warning them that hard times would come if they disobeyed. He also promised wonderful blessings if they would remain faithful to him.

This challenge was uttered more than three millennia ago to a rag-tag band of ex-slaves. But a timeless principle remains: God has set before you today—even as you read this—life or death, a blessing or a curse.

Choose life, so that you may really live!

15Then the LORD appeared at the tent in a pillar of cloud, and the cloud stood over the
entrance to the tent. 16And the LORD said to Moses: "You are going to rest with your ances-
tors, and these people will soon prostitute themselves to the foreign gods of the land they
are entering. They will forsake me and break the covenant I made with them. 17And in that
day I will become angry with them and forsake them; I will hide my face from them, and
they will be destroyed. Many disasters and calamities will come on them, and in that day
they will ask, 'Have not these disasters come on us because our God is not with us?' 18And
I will certainly hide my face in that day because of all their wickedness in turning to oth-
er gods.

19"Now write down this song and teach it to the Israelites and have them sing it, so that
it may be a witness for me against them. 20When I have brought them into the land flow-
ing with milk and honey, the land I promised on oath to their ancestors, and when they eat
their fill and thrive, they will turn to other gods and worship them, rejecting me and break-
ing my covenant. 21And when many disasters and calamities come on them, this song will
testify against them, because it will not be forgotten by their descendants. I know what
they are disposed to do, even before I bring them into the land I promised them on oath."
22So Moses wrote down this song that day and taught it to the Israelites.

23The LORD gave this command to Joshua son of Nun: "Be strong and courageous, for you
will bring the Israelites into the land I promised them on oath, and I myself will be with
you."

24After Moses finished writing in a book the words of this law from beginning to end, 25he
gave this command to the Levites who carried the ark of the covenant of the LORD: 26"Take
this Book of the Law and place it beside the ark of the covenant of the LORD your God.
There it will remain as a witness against you. 27For I know how rebellious and stiff-necked
you are. If you have been rebellious against the LORD while I am still alive and with you,
how much more will you rebel after I die! 28Assemble before me all the elders of your tribes
and all your officials, so that I can speak these words in their hearing and call the heavens
and the earth to testify against them. 29For I know that after my death you are sure to be-
come utterly corrupt and to turn from the way I have commanded you. In days to come,
disaster will fall on you because you will do evil in the sight of the LORD and arouse his an-
ger by what your hands have made."

The Song of Moses

30And Moses recited the words of this song from beginning to end in the hearing of the
whole assembly of Israel:

32

Listen, you heavens, and I will speak;
    hear, you earth, the words of my mouth.
2 Let my teaching fall like rain
    and my words descend like dew,
like showers on new grass,
    like abundant rain on tender plants.

3 I will proclaim the name of the LORD.
    Oh, praise the greatness of our God!
4 He is the Rock, his works are perfect,
    and all his ways are just.
A faithful God who does no wrong,
    upright and just is he.

5 They are corrupt and not his children;
    to their shame they are a warped and crooked generation.
6 Is this the way you repay the LORD,
    you foolish and unwise people?
Is he not your Father, your Creator,[a]
    who made you and formed you?

---

[a] 6 Or *Father, who bought you*

[7]Remember the days of old;
consider the generations long past.
Ask your father and he will tell you,
your elders, and they will explain to you.
[8]When the Most High gave the nations their inheritance,
when he divided all the human race,
he set up boundaries for the peoples
according to the number of the sons of Israel.[a]
[9]For the LORD's portion is his people,
Jacob his allotted inheritance.

[10]In a desert land he found him,
in a barren and howling waste.
He shielded him and cared for him;
he guarded him as the apple of his eye,
[11]like an eagle that stirs up its nest
and hovers over its young,
that spreads its wings to catch them
and carries them aloft.
[12]The LORD alone led him;
no foreign god was with him.

[13]He made him ride on the heights of the land
and fed him with the fruit of the fields.
He nourished him with honey from the rock,
and with oil from the flinty crag,
[14]with curds and milk from herd and flock
and with fattened lambs and goats,
with choice rams of Bashan
and the finest kernels of wheat.
You drank the foaming blood of the grape.

[15]Jeshurun[b] grew fat and kicked;
filled with food, he became heavy and sleek.
He abandoned the God who made him
and rejected the Rock his Savior.
[16]They made him jealous with their foreign gods
and angered him with their detestable idols.
[17]They sacrificed to demons, which are not God—
gods they had not known,
gods that recently appeared,
gods your ancestors did not fear.
[18]You deserted the Rock, who bore you;
you forgot the God who gave you birth.

[19]The LORD saw this and rejected them
because he was angered by his sons and daughters.
[20]"I will hide my face from them," he said,
"and see what their end will be;
for they are a perverse generation,
children who are unfaithful.
[21]They made me jealous by what is no god
and angered me with their worthless idols.
I will make them envious by those who are not a people;
I will make them angry by a nation that has no understanding.

[a] 8 Masoretic Text; Dead Sea Scrolls (see also Septuagint) *sons of God* [b] 15 *Jeshurun* means *the upright one*, that is, Israel.

22 For a fire will be kindled by my wrath,
 one that burns down to the realm of the dead below.
It will devour the earth and its harvests
 and set afire the foundations of the mountains.

23 "I will heap calamities on them
 and spend my arrows against them.
24 I will send wasting famine against them,
 consuming pestilence and deadly plague;
I will send against them the fangs of wild beasts,
 the venom of vipers that glide in the dust.
25 In the street the sword will make them childless;
 in their homes terror will reign.
The young men and young women will perish,
 the infants and those with gray hair.
26 I said I would scatter them
 and erase their name from human memory,
27 but I dreaded the taunt of the enemy,
 lest the adversary misunderstand
and say, 'Our hand has triumphed;
 the LORD has not done all this.' "

28 They are a nation without sense,
 there is no discernment in them.
29 If only they were wise and would understand this
 and discern what their end will be!
30 How could one man chase a thousand,
 or two put ten thousand to flight,
unless their Rock had sold them,
 unless the LORD had given them up?
31 For their rock is not like our Rock,
 as even our enemies concede.
32 Their vine comes from the vine of Sodom
 and from the fields of Gomorrah.
Their grapes are filled with poison,
 and their clusters with bitterness.
33 Their wine is the venom of serpents,
 the deadly poison of cobras.

34 "Have I not kept this in reserve
 and sealed it in my vaults?
35 It is mine to avenge; I will repay.
 In due time their foot will slip;
their day of disaster is near
 and their doom rushes upon them."

36 The LORD will vindicate his people
 and relent concerning his servants
when he sees their strength is gone
 and no one is left, slave or free.[a]
37 He will say: "Now where are their gods,
 the rock they took refuge in,
38 the gods who ate the fat of their sacrifices
 and drank the wine of their drink offerings?
Let them rise up to help you!
 Let them give you shelter!

---

[a] 36 Or *and they are without a ruler or leader*

39 "See now that I myself am He!
There is no god besides me.
I put to death and I bring to life,
I have wounded and I will heal,
and no one can deliver out of my hand.
40 I lift my hand to heaven and declare:
As surely as I live forever,
41 when I sharpen my flashing sword
and my hand grasps it in judgment,
I will take vengeance on my adversaries
and repay those who hate me.
42 I will make my arrows drunk with blood,
while my sword devours flesh:
the blood of the slain and the captives,
the heads of the enemy leaders."

43 Rejoice, you nations, with his people,[a,b]
for he will avenge the blood of his servants;
he will take vengeance on his enemies
and make atonement for his land and people.

44 Moses came with Joshua[c] son of Nun and spoke all the words of this song in the hearing of the people. 45 When Moses finished reciting all these words to all Israel, 46 he said to them, "Take to heart all the words I have solemnly declared to you this day, so that you may command your children to obey carefully all the words of this law. 47 They are not just idle words for you—they are your life. By them you will live long in the land you are crossing the Jordan to possess."

Moses to Die on Mount Nebo

48 On that same day the LORD told Moses, 49 "Go up into the Abarim Range to Mount Nebo in Moab, across from Jericho, and view Canaan, the land I am giving the Israelites as their own possession. 50 There on the mountain that you have climbed you will die and

Knowing Yourself

32:52 // Emotions. Great leaders often have one or more serious character flaws. In Moses' case, it was his temper.

When Moses was a young man, he committed murder in an outburst of anger, killing an Egyptian who was beating a Hebrew slave. When he came down from the mountain with the original Ten Commandments, he was so angry at Israel's disobedience that he smashed the stone tablets that had God's very words on them. And in one of his most costly outbursts, he struck a rock with the symbol of his leadership authority—the staff he carried—in direct disobedience to God's command.

The result of that last action was especially painful for Moses. At the end of Moses' life, after decades of faithful service, he was not allowed to see the land he had led his people to possess. God made it clear why this was so (verse 51): Moses' temper had cost him the privilege.

Is there any underlying rage in your soul that leaks out at inopportune times? Anger is not necessarily sin, but if your anger has led you to actions you regret, maybe it's time to take a closer look at what's going on deep inside of you.

Learn from this sad picture of Moses, seeing his dream at a distance but never living to experience it. Don't let the anger boiling inside you scald those you care about. Find help so you can get to the root of your rage—and root it out.

---

[a] 43 Or *Make his people rejoice, you nations* [b] 43 Masoretic Text; Dead Sea Scrolls (see also Septuagint) *people, / and let all the angels worship him /* [c] 44 Hebrew *Hoshea,* a variant of *Joshua*

be gathered to your people, just as your brother Aaron died on Mount Hor and was gath-
ered to his people. 51 This is because both of you broke faith with me in the presence of the
Israelites at the waters of Meribah Kadesh in the Desert of Zin and because you did not
uphold my holiness among the Israelites. 52 Therefore, you will see the land only from a
distance; you will not enter the land I am giving to the people of Israel."

Moses Blesses the Tribes

33 This is the blessing that Moses the man of God pronounced on the Israelites before his death. 2 He said:

"The LORD came from Sinai
and dawned over them from Seir;
he shone forth from Mount Paran.
He came with[a] myriads of holy ones
from the south, from his mountain slopes.[b]
3 Surely it is you who love the people;
all the holy ones are in your hand.
At your feet they all bow down,
and from you receive instruction,
4 the law that Moses gave us,
the possession of the assembly of Jacob.
5 He was king over Jeshurun[c]
when the leaders of the people assembled,
along with the tribes of Israel.

6 "Let Reuben live and not die,
nor[d] his people be few."

7 And this he said about Judah:

"Hear, LORD, the cry of Judah;
bring him to his people.
With his own hands he defends his cause.
Oh, be his help against his foes!"

8 About Levi he said:

"Your Thummim and Urim belong
to your faithful servant.
You tested him at Massah;
you contended with him at the waters of Meribah.
9 He said of his father and mother,
'I have no regard for them.'
He did not recognize his brothers
or acknowledge his own children,
but he watched over your word
and guarded your covenant.
10 He teaches your precepts to Jacob
and your law to Israel.
He offers incense before you
and whole burnt offerings on your altar.
11 Bless all his skills, LORD,
and be pleased with the work of his hands.
Strike down those who rise against him,
his foes till they rise no more."

---

[a] 2 Or *from* [b] 2 The meaning of the Hebrew for this phrase is uncertain. [c] 5 *Jeshurun* means *the upright one,* that is, Israel; also in verse 26. [d] 6 Or *but let*

12About Benjamin he said:

"Let the beloved of the LORD rest secure in him,
for he shields him all day long,
and the one the LORD loves rests between his shoulders."

13About Joseph he said:

"May the LORD bless his land
with the precious dew from heaven above
and with the deep waters that lie below;
14with the best the sun brings forth
and the finest the moon can yield;
15with the choicest gifts of the ancient mountains
and the fruitfulness of the everlasting hills;
16with the best gifts of the earth and its fullness
and the favor of him who dwelt in the burning bush.
Let all these rest on the head of Joseph,
on the brow of the prince among[a] his brothers.
17In majesty he is like a firstborn bull;
his horns are the horns of a wild ox.
With them he will gore the nations,
even those at the ends of the earth.
Such are the ten thousands of Ephraim;
such are the thousands of Manasseh."

18About Zebulun he said:

"Rejoice, Zebulun, in your going out,
and you, Issachar, in your tents.
19They will summon peoples to the mountain
and there offer the sacrifices of the righteous;
they will feast on the abundance of the seas,
on the treasures hidden in the sand."

20About Gad he said:

"Blessed is he who enlarges Gad's domain!
Gad lives there like a lion,
tearing at arm or head.
21He chose the best land for himself;
the leader's portion was kept for him.
When the heads of the people assembled,
he carried out the LORD's righteous will,
and his judgments concerning Israel."

22About Dan he said:

"Dan is a lion's cub,
springing out of Bashan."

23About Naphtali he said:

"Naphtali is abounding with the favor of the LORD
and is full of his blessing;
he will inherit southward to the lake."

24About Asher he said:

"Most blessed of sons is Asher;
let him be favored by his brothers,

---

[a] 16 Or *of the one separated from*

and let him bathe his feet in oil.
25 The bolts of your gates will be iron and bronze,
and your strength will equal your days.

26 "There is no one like the God of Jeshurun,
who rides on the heavens to help you
and on the clouds in his majesty.
27 The eternal God is your refuge,
and underneath are the everlasting arms.
He will drive out your enemies before you,
saying, 'Destroy them!'
28 So Israel will live in safety;
Jacob will dwell[a] secure
in a land of grain and new wine,
where the heavens drop dew.
29 Blessed are you, Israel!
Who is like you,
a people saved by the LORD?
He is your shield and helper
and your glorious sword.
Your enemies will cower before you,
and you will tread on their heights."

The Death of Moses

34 Then Moses climbed Mount Nebo from the plains of Moab to the top of Pisgah,
across from Jericho. There the LORD showed him the whole land—from Gilead
to Dan, 2 all of Naphtali, the territory of Ephraim and Manasseh, all the land of
Judah as far as the Mediterranean Sea, 3 the Negev and the whole region from the Valley of
Jericho, the City of Palms, as far as Zoar. 4 Then the LORD said to him, "This is the land I
promised on oath to Abraham, Isaac and Jacob when I said, 'I will give it to your descen-
dants.' I have let you see it with your eyes, but you will not cross over into it."
5 And Moses the servant of the LORD died there in Moab, as the LORD had said. 6 He bur-
ied him[b] in Moab, in the valley opposite Beth Peor, but to this day no one knows where his
grave is. 7 Moses was a hundred and twenty years old when he died, yet his eyes were not
weak nor his strength gone. 8 The Israelites grieved for Moses in the plains of Moab thirty
days, until the time of weeping and mourning was over.
9 Now Joshua son of Nun was filled with the spirit[c] of wisdom because Moses had laid
his hands on him. So the Israelites listened to him and did what the LORD had command-
ed Moses.
10 Since then, no prophet has risen in Israel like Moses, whom the LORD knew face to
face, 11 who did all those signs and wonders the LORD sent him to do in Egypt—to Pharaoh
and to all his officials and to his whole land. 12 For no one has ever shown the mighty pow-
er or performed the awesome deeds that Moses did in the sight of all Israel.

Discovering God

34:10–12 // Life with God. This last chapter of Deuteronomy was probably written by Joshua, Moses' successor. He used several key phrases to sum up Moses' life's work: "signs and wonders," "mighty power" and "awesome deeds."

All those phrases make for an impressive tombstone inscription. But notice the most important phrase of all, the one that tops the list of accomplishments. Joshua said of Moses, "The LORD knew [him] face to face."

When all is said and done, the most significant human experience is to live in a relationship with the God who created us. To know God and enjoy him forever is the reason we were created. To a large extent, we can have what Moses had if we will seek it with all our hearts.

---

[a] 28 Septuagint; Hebrew *Jacob's spring is* [b] 6 Or *He was buried* [c] 9 Or *Spirit*

Epilogue

As a seeker, no more important goal exists for you than to be able to say, "I have found what I was looking for."

You were made to know God. Your sin, like everybody else's, is the main barrier between you and God. But God has graciously offered to take it away and to give you a new start.

Through this book—the second of five books that summarize the whole Bible's message—pictures of a great God, a great leader (Moses), and a great nation (Israel) come into focus. God didn't set this nation aside simply because he wanted to encourage a small earthly population to be totally devoted to him. God chose this nation as his instrument—the people who would eventually reach out to the world and invite them to know God.

In time one particular Israelite would embody everything God wanted to say to the world. You can read about this ultimate manifestation of God in the next book, the Gospel of John. Some 1,400 years after Moses, Jesus of Nazareth showed the world what God was like. He followed every one of God's commandments perfectly. He did miraculous deeds, as Moses had. And then he did what no one else had done: After his execution he rose from the dead, never to die again.

You can read more about Jesus' life and teachings in the book of John (page 116). There you'll meet the most famous person in all of history. Jesus' influence has changed the lives of millions of individuals over the centuries. He is still alive today, and he invites you to know him and to experience the new life he offers.

Seeker Stories

I became a sexaholic at a very early age and developed a secret life. As the years went by, my addiction because worse and worse until evil was almost totally in command of my life. Pornography ruled me. I knew its power and recognized its hold on me, but I could not act; I was powerless over the evil that gripped me. I could see that my marriage was fast coming to an end. Still, I could not change my course.

Then one day, at the urging of my daughter and wife, I went to a "seeker service" at my wife's church. This experience ignited a spark—the beginning of my salvation. Although my secret was still hidden at the time, God began to slowly and gently open my heart. Finally my secret became known.

My coming to know Christ has been slow. After three-and-a-half years of Christian counseling, 12-step programs, and church involvement, I began praying directly to Jesus to take my hand and lead me out of my despair and hopelessness. That was when my life really started to change.

Today I am beginning to feel like a human being again. God has worked miracles; my lifestyle and attitudes have changed. The power of prayer is real. I asked God to hold my marriage together and he did. It's on the mend. Can you believe it? Yea God! Yea God!

I am very grateful now for the opportunity God has given me through Jesus Christ to be born again. What a tremendous gift to a guy who for such a long time traveled down some very dark roads.

John Introduction

THE BOTTOM LINE

This book will help you see Jesus as the divine Son of God. He may have been an ordinary man in appearance, but no other religious leader ever did the things he did, or claimed to be God in human form as he did. After he died, he did what was only possible for God to do—he came back to life and appeared to many witnesses. If you want to know God personally, only Jesus can "introduce" you to him (see chapter 14, verse 6 [page 141]).

CENTRAL IDEAS

- Jesus was at the same time both totally human and totally divine.
- Jesus showed his power through miracles.
- Most of the disagreements people had with Jesus were not about his teaching, but about his claims to be God.
- We must get to know the real Jesus because only he has the power to forgive us and lead us to God.

OUTLINE

1. **Prologue** (1:1–18)
2. **Beginnings of Jesus' ministry** (1:19–51)
3. **Jesus' public ministry: signs and discourses** (chaps. 2–11)
4. **Jesus' final week** (chaps. 12–19)
5. **Jesus' resurrection** (20:1–29)
6. **Statement of purpose** (20:30–31)
7. **Epilogue** (chap. 21)

TITLE

This book is named after John, the disciple of Jesus who wrote this Gospel.

AUTHOR AND READERS

John was one of Jesus' youngest followers; he lived the longest of any of Jesus' close associates after Jesus ascended to heaven. The original readers of John's book were mostly non-Jewish people who were being confused by Greek philosophies that contradicted the fact of Christ's divine and human nature. John tells us exactly why he wrote this book in chapter 20, verse 31 (page 152): "These are written that you may believe that Jesus is the Messiah, the Son of God, and that by believing you may have life in his name."

A lot of us wrestle with disillusionment in our quest for spiritual truth. We see Christians whose actions don't line up with what they say they believe about God. A prominent religious figure who falls from grace, caught in an embarrassing scandal. Next door neighbors who talk incessantly about God's love, yet they verbally abuse their own children.

We sense the disconnect and we wonder, *Does faith make any difference?*

In the search for something to believe in, it's normal to struggle with questions and doubts. It's all right if part of you resonates with the honest, searching cry of the U2 lyrics, "You speak of signs and wonders / I need something other / I would believe if I was able / But I'm waiting on the crumbs from your table."*

The question is, once you find whatever it is you're looking for, will you risk everything for it? What does it mean to go from *saying* you believe in Jesus to putting your life in his hands?

When some people say they believe in God, what they mean is that they intellectually acknowledge his existence, yet their belief makes little or no difference in how they live. That kind of "faith" is easy. But when it comes down to the wire, they watch others step out in faith while they remain on the sidelines.

If such people acknowledge the reality of God but go on living without relating to him, they actually have more in common with someone who denies his existence than with a true Christ-follower. As a matter of fact, that kind of "belief" is exactly what the devil himself has (James chapter 2, verse 19)!

Fortunately, many people go beyond mere intellectual assent when they say they believe. Their belief involves trust. Yes, such belief includes an element of risk, and many true believers still wrestle with doubt. *But they experience the benefit because the one they trust in has time and again proven himself trustworthy.*

God wants this kind of faith from us. He asks us to consider the extraordinary claims of Jesus and, after we've examined his credentials, to cast ourselves unreservedly on the back of Christ, trusting in his merits to bring us across the chasm of sin so that we can know God.

The Gospel of John is a great book for seekers because it was written to help people trust Christ with their lives. Within its pages Jesus invites those he meets to consider his claim to be "God with us"—all the while providing solid reasons to trust in and follow him. As you weigh out your decision whether to do just that, understand that questions and doubts will naturally arise. The same was true in Jesus' day. To read about a famous encounter between Jesus and a doubter, turn to John chapter 20, verses 24-31 (page 152).

* U2, "Crumbs From Your Table," *How to Dismantle an Atomic Bomb*

JOHN

The Word Became Flesh

1 In the beginning was the Word, and the Word was with God, and the Word was God. 2He was with God in the beginning. 3Through him all things were made; without him nothing was made that has been made. 4In him was life, and that life was the light of all people. 5The light shines in the darkness, and the darkness has not overcome[a] it.

6There was a man sent from God whose name was John. 7He came as a witness to testify concerning that light, so that through him all might believe. 8He himself was not the light; he came only as a witness to the light.

9The true light that gives light to everyone was coming into the world. 10He was in the world, and though the world was made through him, the world did not recognize him. 11He came to that which was his own, but his own did not receive him. 12Yet to all who did receive him, to those who believed in his name, he gave the right to become children of God— 13children born not of natural descent, nor of human decision or a husband's will, but born of God.

14The Word became flesh and made his dwelling among us. We have seen his glory, the glory of the one and only ⌞Son⌟, who came from the Father, full of grace and truth.

15(John testified concerning him. He cried out, saying, "This is he of whom I said, 'He who comes after me has surpassed me because he was before me.' ") 16Out of his fullness we have all received grace in place of grace already given. 17For the law was given through Moses; grace and truth came through Jesus Christ. 18No one has ever seen God, but the one and only ⌞Son⌟, who is himself God and[b] is in closest relationship with the Father, has made him known.

John the Baptist Denies Being the Messiah

19Now this was John's testimony when the Jewish leaders in Jerusalem sent priests and Levites to ask him who he was. 20He did not fail to confess, but confessed freely, "I am not the Messiah."

21They asked him, "Then who are you? Are you Elijah?"

He said, "I am not."

"Are you the Prophet?"

He answered, "No."

22Finally they said, "Who are you? Give us an answer to take back to those who sent us. What do you say about yourself?"

23John replied in the words of Isaiah the prophet, "I am the voice of one calling in the wilderness, 'Make straight the way for the Lord.' "[c]

Discovering God

1:1–3 // Jesus, the God-Man. John wrote this book to help his readers understand that Jesus is more than just a good man—he's the "God-Man."

John begins his collection of stories about Jesus by echoing the first sentence of the Bible. Genesis reads, "In the beginning, *God . . .*" John writes, "In the beginning was the Word." This phrase, combined with the images of creation in verse 3, make John's identification of Jesus as God unmistakable (see also verse 14). Jesus is the sum total of all God wants to say to us. He is the "flesh and bones" of the message of God—in short, God's *Word* to the world.

The basis of Christianity is not the moral teachings of Jesus, as important as those are. The true basis of Christianity is Jesus himself. As a seeker, you can dismiss Christianity if you can discredit the person of Jesus Christ. If he isn't who he said he was—namely, the eternal God (the second person of the trinity) who became one of us—then you're correct in saying that Christians are tragically deluded and that Christianity is just another human-made religion.

As you read this book, carefully consider the evidence about Jesus' identity. A seeker can answer no question more important than the one Jesus himself asked: *"Who do you say I am?"* (Matthew chapter 16, verse 15; see also John chapter 8, verses 23–24 [page 131], where Jesus further clarified his identity).

[a] *5* Or *understood* [b] *18* Some manuscripts *but the only Son, who* [c] *23* Isaiah 40:3

[24]Now the Pharisees who had been sent [25]questioned him, "Why then do you baptize if
you are not the Messiah, nor Elijah, nor the Prophet?"
[26]"I baptize with[a] water," John replied, "but among you stands one you do not know.
[27]He is the one who comes after me, the thongs of whose sandals I am not worthy to untie."
[28]This all happened at Bethany on the other side of the Jordan, where John was baptizing.

John's Testimony About Jesus

[29]The next day John saw Jesus coming toward him and said, "Look, the Lamb of God, who
takes away the sin of the world! [30]This is the one I meant when I said, 'A man who comes after me has surpassed me because he was before me.' [31]I myself did not know him, but the reason I came baptizing with water was that he might be revealed to Israel."
[32]Then John gave this testimony: "I saw the Spirit come down from heaven as a dove and
remain on him. [33]And I myself did not know him, but the one who sent me to baptize with
water told me, 'The man on whom you see the Spirit come down and remain is the one who
will baptize with the Holy Spirit.' [34]I have seen and I testify that this is God's Chosen One."[b]

John's Disciples Follow Jesus

[35]The next day John was there again with two of his disciples. [36]When he saw Jesus passing by, he said, "Look, the Lamb of God!"
[37]When the two disciples heard him say this, they followed Jesus. [38]Turning around, Jesus
saw them following and asked, "What do you want?"
They said, "Rabbi" (which means "Teacher"), "where are you staying?"
[39]"Come," he replied, "and you will see."
So they went and saw where he was staying, and they spent that day with him. It was
about four in the afternoon.
[40]Andrew, Simon Peter's brother, was one of the two who heard what John had said
and who had followed Jesus. [41]The first thing Andrew did was to find his brother Simon
and tell him, "We have found the Messiah" (that is, the Christ). [42]And he brought him
to Jesus.
Jesus looked at him and said, "You are Simon son of John. You will be called Cephas"
(which, when translated, is Peter[c]).

Jesus Calls Philip and Nathanael

[43]The next day Jesus decided to leave for Galilee. Finding Philip, he said to him, "Follow me."
[44]Philip, like Andrew and Peter, was from the town of Bethsaida. [45]Philip found Nathanael and told him, "We have found the one Moses wrote about in the Law, and about whom
the prophets also wrote—Jesus of Nazareth, the son of Joseph."
[46]"Nazareth! Can anything good come from there?" Nathanael asked.
"Come and see," said Philip.
[47]When Jesus saw Nathanael approaching, he said of him, "Here truly is an Israelite in
whom there is no deceit."
[48]"How do you know me?" Nathanael asked.
Jesus answered, "I saw you while you were still under the fig tree before Philip called
you."

Discovering God

1:12–13 // Life with God. Though we're all God's creatures, we don't become his children until we receive the forgiveness and leadership of Christ. This new beginning is described here as being "born of God" (in contrast to being born naturally from human parents). Jesus expands on this concept in his conversation with a man named Nicodemus in chapter 3 (page 121).

[a] 26 Or *in*; also in verses 31 and 33 (twice) [b] 34 See Isaiah 42:1; many manuscripts *is the Son of God.* [c] 42 *Cephas* (Aramaic) and *Peter* (Greek) both mean *rock*.

49Then Nathanael declared, "Rabbi, you are the Son of God; you are the king of Israel."
50Jesus said, "You believe[a] because I told you I saw you under the fig tree. You will see
greater things than that." 51He then added, "Very truly I tell you,[b] you[b] will see 'heaven
open, and the angels of God ascending and descending on'[c] the Son of Man."

Jesus Changes Water into Wine

2 On the third day a wedding took place at Cana in Galilee. Jesus' mother was there,
2and Jesus and his disciples had also been invited to the wedding. 3When the wine
was gone, Jesus' mother said to him, "They have no more wine."
4"Woman,[d] why do you involve me?" Jesus replied. "My hour has not yet come."
5His mother said to the servants, "Do whatever he tells you."
6Nearby stood six stone water jars, the kind used by the Jews for ceremonial washing,
each holding from twenty to thirty gallons.[e]
7Jesus said to the servants, "Fill the jars with water"; so they filled them to the brim.
8Then he told them, "Now draw some out and take it to the master of the banquet."
They did so, 9and the master of the banquet tasted the water that had been turned into
wine. He did not realize where it had come from, though the servants who had drawn the
water knew. Then he called the bridegroom aside 10and said, "Everyone brings out the
choice wine first and then the cheaper wine after the guests have had too much to drink;
but you have saved the best till now."
11What Jesus did here in Cana of Galilee was the first of the signs through which he re-
vealed his glory; and his disciples put their faith in him.
12After this he went down to Capernaum with his mother and brothers and his disciples.
There they stayed for a few days.

Jesus Clears the Temple Courts

13When it was almost time for the Jewish Passover, Jesus went up to Jerusalem. 14In the
temple courts he found people selling cattle, sheep and doves, and others sitting at tables
exchanging money. 15So he made a whip out of cords, and drove all from the temple courts,
both sheep and cattle; he scattered the coins of the money changers and overturned their
tables. 16To those who sold doves he said, "Get these out of here! Stop turning my Father's
house into a market!" 17His disciples remembered that it is written: "Zeal for your house
will consume me."[f]
18The Jews then responded to him, "What sign can you show us to prove your authority
to do all this?"
19Jesus answered them, "Destroy this temple, and I will raise it again in three days."
20They replied, "It has taken forty-six years to build this temple, and you are going to
raise it in three days?" 21But the temple he had spoken of was his body. 22After he was raised
from the dead, his disciples recalled what he had said. Then they believed the scripture
and the words that Jesus had spoken.
23Now while he was in Jerusalem at the Passover Festival, many people saw the signs he
was performing and believed in his name.[g] 24But Jesus would not entrust himself to them,
for he knew all people. 25He did not need human testimony about them, for he knew what
was in them.

Reasons to Believe

2:1–11 // The Incomparable Jesus. Like all of Jesus' supernatural activities, this first miracle had obvious practical benefits—in this case, providing for this wedding's festivities and protecting the host from embarrassment.

But the main reason Jesus did miracles—and the primary reason John records them—is because of their value as "signposts" that point to Jesus as the Son of God. Jesus used his supernatural abilities to draw people to his person, not to his power. He desires that we do what the disciples did—put our faith (trust) in him.

---

[a] 50 Or *Do you believe . . . ?* [b] 51 The Greek is plural. [c] 51 Gen. 28:12 [d] 4 The Greek for *Woman* does not denote any disrespect. [e] 6 Or from about 75 to about 115 liters [f] 17 Psalm 69:9 [g] 23 Or *in him*

Jesus Teaches Nicodemus

3 Now there was a Pharisee, a man named Nicodemus who was a member of the Jew-
ish ruling council. [2]He came to Jesus at night and said, "Rabbi, we know that you are
a teacher who has come from God. For no one could perform the signs you are do-
ing if God were not with him."
[3]Jesus replied, "Very truly I tell you, no one can see the kingdom of God without being
born again.[a]"
[4]"How can anyone be born when they are old?" Nicodemus asked. "Surely they cannot
enter a second time into their mother's womb to be born!"
[5]Jesus answered, "Very truly I tell you, no one can enter the kingdom of God without
being born of water and the Spirit. [6]Flesh gives birth to flesh, but the Spirit[b] gives birth to
spirit. [7]You should not be surprised at my saying, 'You[c] must be born again.' [8]The wind
blows wherever it pleases. You hear its sound, but you cannot tell where it comes from or
where it is going. So it is with everyone born of the Spirit."[d]
[9]"How can this be?" Nicodemus asked.
[10]"You are Israel's teacher," said Jesus, "and do you not understand these things? [11]Very
truly I tell you, we speak of what we know, and we testify to what we have seen, but still
you people do not accept our testimony. [12]I have spoken to you of earthly things and you
do not believe; how then will you believe if I speak of heavenly things? [13]No one has ever
gone into heaven except the one who came from heaven—the Son of Man.[e] [14]Just as Mo-
ses lifted up the snake in the wilderness, so the Son of Man must be lifted up,[f] [15]that ev-
eryone who believes may have eternal life in him."[g]
[16]For God so loved the world that he gave his one and only Son, that whoever believes in
him shall not perish but have eternal life. [17]For God did not send his Son into the world to
condemn the world, but to save the world through him. [18]Whoever believes in him is not
condemned, but whoever does not believe stands condemned already because they have
not believed in the name of God's one and only Son. [19]This is the verdict: Light has come
into the world, but people loved darkness instead of light because their deeds were evil. [20]All
those who do evil hate the light, and will not come into the light for fear that their deeds will
be exposed. [21]But those who live by the truth come into the light, so that it may be seen
plainly that what they have done has been done in the sight of God.

John Testifies Again About Jesus

[22]After this, Jesus and his disciples went out into the Judean countryside, where he spent
some time with them, and baptized. [23]Now John also was baptizing at Aenon near Salim,
because there was plenty of water, and people were coming and being baptized. [24](This was
before John was put in prison.) [25]An argument developed between some of John's disci-
ples and a certain Jew over the matter of ceremonial washing. [26]They came to John and
said to him, "Rabbi, that man who was with you on the other side of the Jordan—the one
you testified about—look, he is baptizing, and everyone is going to him."
[27]To this John replied, "A person can receive only what is given from heaven. [28]You your-
selves can testify that I said, 'I am not the Messiah but am sent ahead of him.' [29]The bride
belongs to the bridegroom. The friend who attends the bridegroom waits and listens for
him, and is full of joy when he hears the bridegroom's voice. That joy is mine, and it is now
complete. [30]He must become greater; I must become less."[h]

Knowing Yourself

2:23–25 // Sin. We all have secrets—private thoughts and actions that, if uncovered, would embarrass us. But Jesus sees every hidden corner of our hearts. And because he knows us better than we know ourselves—even our dark sides—we're assured that his invitation to forgive us is real. He has seen the skeletons in our inner closets. By not abandoning us, he demonstrates his readiness to help us face and remove them.

[a] *3* The Greek for *again* also means *from above*; also in verse 7. [b] *6* Or *but spirit*
[c] *7* The Greek is plural. [d] *8* The Greek for *Spirit* is the same as that for *wind*. [e] *13* Some manuscripts *Man, who is in heaven* [f] *14* The Greek for *lifted up* also means *exalted*.
[g] *15* Some interpreters end the quotation with verse 21. [h] *30* Some interpreters end the quotation with verse 36.

Knowing Yourself

3:1–21 // A New Identity. Jesus had an uncanny knack for cutting through "small talk."

Nicodemus, an important member of the religious ruling class, came to Jesus late one night. Was he afraid to be seen with Jesus? Did he want to avoid the crowds? We don't know for sure. But when he began his conversation with a few polite remarks, Jesus cut right to the chase. His statement in verse 3 can be loosely paraphrased, "Nicodemus, you're right about my spiritual position, but you're dead wrong about yours."

Jesus knew that Nicodemus didn't need a lot of tact—he needed the truth.

Nicodemus's robes, his title, and his degrees impressed everyone in his religious circle. But Jesus saw right through those outer trappings. He knew that a human heart beat under all that finery—a struggling heart that was tired of carrying the weight, the responsibilities and the endless need to appear "in control" of his religious condition. So before Nicodemus could even formulate his question, Jesus gave the answer, telling him in effect, "What you need is a new start, Nicodemus. It's not too late."

If you, like Nicodemus, are counting on your accomplishments to lead to some sort of ultimate fulfillment or spiritual security, Jesus says the same thing to you.

Accomplishments can't be happy. Titles have no feelings. Degrees don't laugh. Even religion can get in the way of knowing God, because religion is mostly what *we* do. That's what was happening to Nicodemus, and what Jesus tried to address in their conversation. Life with God means becoming a "faith-follower," not trying to be a "do-gooder." Jesus knew that Nicodemus, a religious leader and teacher, didn't understand this basic truth.

Nicodemus needed to make a break with his religiously legalistic past, and to make a new spiritual start in his life, one that centered on a relationship with God. Jesus called this new start being "born again."

Then Jesus made mention of something that happened centuries before, in Moses' day (verse 14; Numbers chapter 21, verses 4–9). When a plague of poisonous snakes killed many Israelites, Moses followed God's command to make a bronze snake and attach it to a pole. People who had been bitten didn't have to pray, go to the temple, try to drain the poison, or do any kind of "religious" act. They were simply told to take God at his word, look at the snake, and believe. Those who did were miraculously healed. Those who didn't died. (By the way, this Biblical event is the origin of the snake on the pole in medical insignias.) By using this well-known story as a metaphor for his own crucifixion, Jesus knew that Nicodemus would get the point—God sent Jesus to earth so that people could believe in him, trust him, and have eternal life.

He further explained this principle in verse 16, one of the most famous verses in the Bible. This one sentence contains the greatest message, from the greatest source, describing the greatest love, demonstrated by the greatest sacrifice ever given. It contains important news for everyone, especially those who think they have to "be religious" to get God's approval.

The bad news is that we can't *do* enough to gain God's approval. The good news is that God has already *done* it on our behalf.

What would prevent you from accepting Jesus' invitation to Nicodemus (verse 3)? Being born again isn't complicated. Simply agree with Jesus that you have a spiritual need that you'll never be able to fill through your own efforts. Then recognize that Jesus didn't come to condemn you, but to pay for your sins, forgive you, and to begin to remake you from the inside. Finally, come to him as your rescuer and leader and ask him to do what he said he was dying to do—give you eternal life. This is not a cheap gift; Jesus gave his very lifeblood to obtain it. But it is a *free* gift. And it's yours for the asking.

Note: Later in Jesus' ministry, Nicodemus defended Jesus when the religious leaders of his day condemned him unfairly (see chapter 7, verses 50–51 [page 130]). Nicodemus also showed up at Jesus' death, where he and another influential leader, Joseph of Arimathea, prepared Jesus' body for burial (chapter 19, verses 38–42 [page 150]). Beyond that, we don't know anything about Nicodemus or his response to Jesus' invitation.

31 The one who comes from above is above all; the one who is from the earth belongs to
the earth, and speaks as one from the earth. The one who comes from heaven is above all.
32 He testifies to what he has seen and heard, but no one accepts his testimony. 33 The per-
son who has accepted it has certified that God is truthful. 34 For the one whom God has
sent speaks the words of God, for God[a] gives the Spirit without limit. 35 The Father loves the
Son and has placed everything in his hands. 36 Whoever believes in the Son has eternal life,
but whoever rejects the Son will not see life, for God's wrath remains on them.

Jesus Talks With a Samaritan Woman

4 Now Jesus learned that the Pharisees had heard that he was gaining and baptizing
more disciples than John— 2 although in fact it was not Jesus who baptized, but his
disciples. 3 So he left Judea and went back once more to Galilee.
4 Now he had to go through Samaria. 5 So he came to a town in Samaria called Sychar,
near the plot of ground Jacob had given to his son Joseph. 6 Jacob's well was there, and
Jesus, tired as he was from the journey, sat down by the well. It was about noon.
7 When a Samaritan woman came to draw water, Jesus said to her, "Will you give me a
drink?" 8 (His disciples had gone into the town to buy food.)
9 The Samaritan woman said to him, "You are a Jew and I am a Samaritan woman. How
can you ask me for a drink?" (For Jews do not associate with Samaritans.[b])
10 Jesus answered her, "If you knew the gift of God and who it is that asks you for a drink,
you would have asked him and he would have given you living water."
11 "Sir," the woman said, "you have nothing to draw with and the well is deep. Where
can you get this living water? 12 Are you greater than our father Jacob, who gave us the well
and drank from it himself, as did also his sons and his flocks and herds?"
13 Jesus answered, "Everyone who drinks this water will be thirsty again, 14 but those who
drink the water I give them will never thirst. Indeed, the water I give them will become in
them a spring of water welling up to eternal life."
15 The woman said to him, "Sir, give me this water so that I won't get thirsty and have to
keep coming here to draw water."
16 He told her, "Go, call your husband and come back."
17 "I have no husband," she replied.
Jesus said to her, "You are right when you say you have no husband. 18 The fact is, you
have had five husbands, and the man you now have is not your husband. What you have
just said is quite true."
19 "Sir," the woman said, "I can see that you are a prophet. 20 Our ancestors worshiped on
this mountain, but you Jews claim that the place where we must worship is in Jerusalem."
21 "Woman,"[c] Jesus replied, "believe me, a time is coming when you will worship the Fa-
ther neither on this mountain nor in Jerusalem. 22 You Samaritans worship what you do not

Discovering God

4:4–42 // Jesus, the God-Man. Here is a classic encounter between Jesus and a seeker—in this case, an admittedly sinful woman who thought for sure that God would never bother with her.

This woman was an outcast, as evidenced by her coming to the well in the heat of the day to avoid others. Yet there she met a man who told her "everything [she] ever did." At first, she could hardly believe Jesus would take the time to speak to her. Then Jesus amazed her further by outlining the details of her lifestyle!

Here Jesus demonstrated both tender compassion and supernatural insight. He overcame huge racial, gender, and positional barriers to reach into this woman's world. In reality, Jesus was a "seeker" in this situation too. And he still seeks out those who need him today.

The woman brought almost the whole town out to see Jesus, and they too discovered that he was unlike any person they had ever met. The townspeople said what people down through the ages have said after they have investigated the claims of Christ—"We have heard for ourselves, and we know that this man really is the Savior of the world" (verse 42).

[a] 34 Greek *he* [b] 9 Or *do not use dishes Samaritans have used* [c] 21 The Greek for *Woman* does not denote any disrespect.

know; we worship what we do know, for salvation is from the Jews. [23]Yet a time is coming
and has now come when the true worshipers will worship the Father in the Spirit and in
truth, for they are the kind of worshipers the Father seeks. [24]God is spirit, and his worship-
ers must worship in the Spirit and in truth."
[25]The woman said, "I know that Messiah" (called Christ) "is coming. When he comes,
he will explain everything to us."
[26]Then Jesus declared, "I, the one speaking to you—I am he."

The Disciples Rejoin Jesus

[27]Just then his disciples returned and were surprised to find him talking with a woman.
But no one asked, "What do you want?" or "Why are you talking with her?"
[28]Then, leaving her water jar, the woman went back to the town and said to the people,
[29]"Come, see a man who told me everything I ever did. Could this be the Messiah?" [30]They
came out of the town and made their way toward him.
[31]Meanwhile his disciples urged him, "Rabbi, eat something."
[32]But he said to them, "I have food to eat that you know nothing about."
[33]Then his disciples said to each other, "Could someone have brought him food?"
[34]"My food," said Jesus, "is to do the will of him who sent me and to finish his work.
[35]Don't you have a saying, 'It's still four months until harvest'? I tell you, open your eyes
and look at the fields! They are ripe for harvest. [36]Even now those who reap draw their wag-
es, even now they harvest the crop for eternal life, so that the sower and the reaper may
be glad together. [37]Thus the saying 'One sows and another reaps' is true. [38]I sent you to
reap what you have not worked for. Others have done the hard work, and you have reaped
the benefits of their labor."

Many Samaritans Believe

[39]Many of the Samaritans from that town believed in him because of the woman's tes-
timony, "He told me everything I ever did." [40]So when the Samaritans came to him, they
urged him to stay with them, and he stayed two days. [41]And because of his words many
more became believers.
[42]They said to the woman, "We no longer believe just because of what you said; now we
have heard for ourselves, and we know that this man really is the Savior of the world."

Jesus Heals the Official's Son

[43]After the two days he left for Galilee. [44](Now Jesus himself had pointed out that proph-
ets have no honor in their own country.) [45]When he arrived in Galilee, the Galileans wel-
comed him. They had seen all that he had done in Jerusalem at the Passover Festival, for
they also had been there.
[46]Once more he visited Cana in Galilee, where he had turned the water into wine. And there
was a certain royal official whose son lay sick at Capernaum. [47]When this man heard that Jesus
had arrived in Galilee from Judea, he went to him and begged him to come and heal his son,
who was close to death.
[48]"Unless you people see signs and wonders," Jesus told him, "you will never believe."
[49]The royal official said, "Sir, come down before my child dies."
[50]"Go," Jesus replied, "your son will live."
The man took Jesus at his word and departed. [51]While he was still on the way, his ser-
vants met him with the news that his boy was living. [52]When he inquired as to the time
when his son got better, they said to him, "Yesterday, at one in the afternoon, the fever left
him."
[53]Then the father realized that this was the exact time at which Jesus had said to him,
"Your son will live." So he and his whole household believed.
[54]This was the second sign Jesus performed after coming from Judea to Galilee.

The Healing at the Pool

5 Some time later, Jesus went up to Jerusalem for one of the Jewish festivals. [2]Now
there is in Jerusalem near the Sheep Gate a pool, which in Aramaic is called Bethes-
da[a] and which is surrounded by five covered colonnades. [3[4]]Here a great number of
disabled people used to lie—the blind, the lame, the paralyzed.[b] [5]One who was there had
been an invalid for thirty-eight years. [6]When Jesus saw him lying there and learned that he
had been in this condition for a long time, he asked him, "Do you want to get well?"
[7]"Sir," the invalid replied, "I have no one to help me into the pool when the water is
stirred. While I am trying to get in, someone else goes down ahead of me."
[8]Then Jesus said to him, "Get up! Pick up your mat and walk." [9]At once the man was
cured; he picked up his mat and walked.
The day on which this took place was a Sabbath, [10]and so the Jewish leaders said to the
man who had been healed, "It is the Sabbath; the law forbids you to carry your mat."
[11]But he replied, "The man who made me well said to me, 'Pick up your mat and walk.' "
[12]So they asked him, "Who is this fellow who told you to pick it up and walk?"
[13]The man who was healed had no idea who it was, for Jesus had slipped away into the
crowd that was there.
[14]Later Jesus found him at the temple and said to him, "See, you are well again. Stop sin-
ning or something worse may happen to you." [15]The man went away and told the Jewish
leaders that it was Jesus who had made him well.

The Authority of the Son

[16]So, because Jesus was doing these things on the Sabbath, the Jewish leaders began to
persecute him. [17]In his defense Jesus said to them, "My Father is always at his work to this
very day, and I too am working." [18]For this reason they tried all the more to kill him; not
only was he breaking the Sabbath, but he was even calling God his own Father, making
himself equal with God.
[19]Jesus gave them this answer: "Very truly I tell you, the Son can do nothing by himself;
he can do only what he sees his Father doing, because whatever the Father does the Son
also does. [20]For the Father loves the Son and shows him all he does. Yes, and he will show
him even greater works than these, so that you will be amazed. [21]For just as the Father rais-
es the dead and gives them life, even so the Son gives life to whom he is pleased to give it.
[22]Moreover, the Father judges no one, but has entrusted all judgment to the Son, [23]that all
may honor the Son just as they honor the Father. Whoever does not honor the Son does not
honor the Father, who sent him.
[24]"Very truly I tell you, whoever hears my word and believes him who sent me has eter-
nal life and will not be judged but has crossed over from death to life. [25]Very truly I tell
you, a time is coming and has now come when the dead will hear the voice of the Son of
God and those who hear will live. [26]For as the Father has life in himself, so he has granted
the Son also to have life in himself. [27]And he has given him authority to judge because he
is the Son of Man.
[28]"Do not be amazed at this, for a time is coming when all who are in their graves will
hear his voice [29]and come out—those who have done what is good will rise to live, and

Discovering God

5:18 // Jesus, the God-Man. Jesus' enemies clearly understood his claim to be God. They connected Jesus' miraculous activities, his disdain for their man-made rules, and his direct statements about existing on a par with God. Scandalized by these outrageous assertions, they were determined to shut him up. The one option Jesus' enemies failed to consider was the most obvious one—the one every honest seeker should agree is possible: *Jesus may have been right.*

[a] 2 Some manuscripts *Bethzatha*; other manuscripts *Bethsaida* [b] 3 Some later manuscripts and some ancient witnesses, wholly or in part, *paralyzed—and they waited for the moving of the waters.* [4]*From time to time an angel of the Lord would come down and stir up the waters. The first person into the pool after each such disturbance would be cured of whatever disease they had.*

those who have done what is evil will rise to be condemned. 30By myself I can do nothing;
I judge only as I hear, and my judgment is just, for I seek not to please myself but him who
sent me.

Testimonies About Jesus

31"If I testify about myself, my testimony is not true. 32There is another who testifies in
my favor, and I know that his testimony about me is true.
33"You have sent to John and he has testified to the truth. 34Not that I accept human tes-
timony; but I mention it that you may be saved. 35John was a lamp that burned and gave
light, and you chose for a time to enjoy his light.
36"I have testimony weightier than that of John. For the works that the Father has given
me to finish—the very works that I am doing—testify that the Father has sent me. 37And
the Father who sent me has himself testified concerning me. You have never heard his
voice nor seen his form, 38nor does his word dwell in you, for you do not believe the one
he sent. 39You study[a] the Scriptures diligently because you think that in them you possess
eternal life. These are the very Scriptures that testify about me, 40yet you refuse to come
to me to have life.
41"I do not accept glory from human beings, 42but I know you. I know that you do not
have the love of God in your hearts. 43I have come in my Father's name, and you do not ac-
cept me; but if someone else comes in his own name, you will accept him. 44How can you
believe since you accept glory from one another but do not seek the glory that comes from
the only God[b]?
45"But do not think I will accuse you before the Father. Your accuser is Moses, on whom
your hopes are set. 46If you believed Moses, you would believe me, for he wrote about me.
47But since you do not believe what he wrote, how are you going to believe what I say?"

Jesus Feeds the Five Thousand

6 Some time after this, Jesus crossed to the far shore of the Sea of Galilee (that is, the
Sea of Tiberias), 2and a great crowd of people followed him because they saw the
signs he had performed by healing the sick. 3Then Jesus went up on a mountainside
and sat down with his disciples. 4The Jewish Passover Festival was near.
5When Jesus looked up and saw a great crowd coming toward him, he said to Philip,
"Where shall we buy bread for these people to eat?" 6He asked this only to test him, for he
already had in mind what he was going to do.

Reasons to Believe

6:5–15 // The Incomparable Jesus. When Jesus gave a picnic, it was an event to remember!

This passage shows how Jesus' miraculous power convinced a crowd that someone great was in their midst. You may wonder why God doesn't do more miracles today—surely that would convince all doubters, right?

Not necessarily. And this story illustrates the problem with human belief that is based on miracles, as was the case with this crowd. These people were impressed with Jesus' power, but they wanted to use it for their own ends. After benefiting directly from Jesus' miracle, they wanted to make him king so he could use his miraculous power to defeat the oppression of their Roman rulers. But Jesus had no intention of ruling over an earthly kingdom. He wanted their loyalty for reasons other than his ability to influence the elements.

Notice how these fickle fans cheered Jesus at first, but gave up on him after the razzle-dazzle stopped (see verse 66). That's why Jesus used miracles sparingly, and why on many occasions he told people who had benefited directly from his power to keep it to themselves (for example, Mark chapter 5, verses 35–43).

Ultimately, people need a relationship with Jesus that is based on love, forgiveness and trust. When the crowds left, Jesus' person and his words—not his wonders—secured his followers' lasting devotion (see verses 67–69).

---

[a] 39 Or 39*Study*   [b] 44 Some early manuscripts *the Only One*

[7]Philip answered him, "It would take almost a year's wages[a] to buy enough bread for each one to have a bite!"

[8]Another of his disciples, Andrew, Simon Peter's brother, spoke up, [9]"Here is a boy with five small barley loaves and two small fish, but how far will they go among so many?"

[10]Jesus said, "Have the people sit down." There was plenty of grass in that place, and they sat down (about five thousand men were there). [11]Jesus then took the loaves, gave thanks, and distributed to those who were seated as much as they wanted. He did the same with the fish.

[12]When they had all had enough to eat, he said to his disciples, "Gather the pieces that are left over. Let nothing be wasted." [13]So they gathered them and filled twelve baskets with the pieces of the five barley loaves left over by those who had eaten.

[14]After the people saw the sign Jesus performed, they began to say, "Surely this is the Prophet who is to come into the world." [15]Jesus, knowing that they intended to come and make him king by force, withdrew again to a mountain by himself.

Jesus Walks on the Water

[16]When evening came, his disciples went down to the lake, [17]where they got into a boat and set off across the lake for Capernaum. By now it was dark, and Jesus had not yet joined them. [18]A strong wind was blowing and the waters grew rough. [19]When they had rowed about three or three and a half miles,[b] they saw Jesus approaching the boat, walking on the water; and they were frightened. [20]But he said to them, "It is I; don't be afraid." [21]Then they were willing to take him into the boat, and immediately the boat reached the shore where they were heading.

[22]The next day the crowd that had stayed on the opposite shore of the lake realized that only one boat had been there, and that Jesus had not entered it with his disciples, but that they had gone away alone. [23]Then some boats from Tiberias landed near the place where the people had eaten the bread after the Lord had given thanks. [24]Once the crowd realized that neither Jesus nor his disciples were there, they got into the boats and went to Capernaum in search of Jesus.

Jesus the Bread of Life

[25]When they found him on the other side of the lake, they asked him, "Rabbi, when did you get here?"

[26]Jesus answered, "Very truly I tell you, you are looking for me, not because you saw the signs I performed but because you ate the loaves and had your fill. [27]Do not work for food that spoils, but for food that endures to eternal life, which the Son of Man will give you. On him God the Father has placed his seal of approval."

[28]Then they asked him, "What must we do to do the works God requires?"

[29]Jesus answered, "The work of God is this: to believe in the one he has sent."

[30]So they asked him, "What sign then will you give that we may see it and believe you? What will you do? [31]Our ancestors ate the manna in the wilderness; as it is written: 'He gave them bread from heaven to eat.'[c]"

[32]Jesus said to them, "Very truly I tell you, it is not Moses who has given you the bread from heaven, but it is my Father who gives you the true bread from heaven. [33]For the bread of God is the bread that comes down from heaven and gives life to the world."

[34]"Sir," they said, "always give us this bread."

[35]Then Jesus declared, "I am the bread of life. Whoever comes to me will never go hungry, and whoever believes in me will never be thirsty. [36]But as I told you, you have seen me and still you do not believe. [37]All whom the Father gives me will come to me, and whoever comes to me I will never drive away. [38]For I have come down from heaven not to do my will but to do the will of him who sent me. [39]And this is the will of him who sent me, that I shall lose none of all those he has given me, but raise them up at the last day. [40]For my Father's will is that everyone who looks to the Son and believes in him shall have eternal life, and I will raise them up at the last day."

---

[a] *7* Greek *take two hundred denarii* [b] *19* Or about 5 or 6 kilometers [c] *31* Exodus 16:4; Neh. 9:15; Psalm 78:24,25

41At this the Jews there began to grumble about him because he said, "I am the bread
that came down from heaven." 42They said, "Is this not Jesus, the son of Joseph, whose fa-
ther and mother we know? How can he now say, 'I came down from heaven'?"
43"Stop grumbling among yourselves," Jesus answered. 44"No one can come to me un-
less the Father who sent me draws them, and I will raise them up at the last day. 45It is
written in the Prophets: 'They will all be taught by God.'[a] Everyone who has heard the Fa-
ther and learned from him comes to me. 46No one has seen the Father except the one who
is from God; only he has seen the Father. 47Very truly I tell you, whoever believes has eter-
nal life. 48I am the bread of life. 49Your ancestors ate the manna in the wilderness, yet they
died. 50But here is the bread that comes down from heaven, which people may eat and not
die. 51I am the living bread that came down from heaven. Whoever eats of this bread will
live forever. This bread is my flesh, which I will give for the life of the world."
52Then the Jews began to argue sharply among themselves, "How can this man give us
his flesh to eat?"
53Jesus said to them, "Very truly I tell you, unless you eat the flesh of the Son of Man and
drink his blood, you have no life in you. 54Whoever eats my flesh and drinks my blood has
eternal life, and I will raise them up at the last day. 55For my flesh is real food and my blood
is real drink. 56Whoever eats my flesh and drinks my blood remains in me, and I in them.
57Just as the living Father sent me and I live because of the Father, so the one who feeds
on me will live because of me. 58This is the bread that came down from heaven. Your an-
cestors ate manna and died, but whoever feeds on this bread will live forever." 59He said
this while teaching in the synagogue in Capernaum.

Many Disciples Desert Jesus

60On hearing it, many of his disciples said, "This is a hard teaching. Who can accept it?"
61Aware that his disciples were grumbling about this, Jesus said to them, "Does this offend
you? 62Then what if you see the Son of Man ascend to where he was before! 63The Spirit gives
life; the flesh counts for nothing. The words I have spoken to you—they are full of the Spir-
it[b] and life. 64Yet there are some of you who do not believe." For Jesus had known from the
beginning which of them did not believe and who would betray him. 65He went on to say,
"This is why I told you that no one can come to me unless the Father has enabled them."
66From this time many of his disciples turned back and no longer followed him.
67"You do not want to leave too, do you?" Jesus asked the Twelve.
68Simon Peter answered him, "Lord, to whom shall we go? You have the words of eter-
nal life. 69We have come to believe and to know that you are the Holy One of God."
70Then Jesus replied, "Have I not chosen you, the Twelve? Yet one of you is a devil!"
71(He meant Judas, the son of Simon Iscariot, who, though one of the Twelve, was later to
betray him.)

Jesus Goes to the Festival of Tabernacles

7 After this, Jesus went around in Galilee. He did not want[c] to go about in Judea because
the Jewish leaders there were looking for a way to kill him. 2But when the Jewish Fes-
tival of Tabernacles was near, 3Jesus' brothers said to him, "Leave Galilee and go to Ju-
dea, so that your disciples there may see the works you do. 4No one who wants to become
a public figure acts in secret. Since you are doing these things, show yourself to the world."
5For even his own brothers did not believe in him.
6Therefore Jesus told them, "My time is not yet here; for you any time will do. 7The world
cannot hate you, but it hates me because I testify that its works are evil. 8You go to the Fes-
tival. I am not[d] going up to this Festival, because my time has not yet fully come." 9Hav-
ing said this, he stayed in Galilee.
10However, after his brothers had left for the Festival, he went also, not publicly, but in
secret. 11Now at the Festival the Jewish leaders were watching for Jesus and asking, "Where
is he?"

---

[a] *45* Isaiah 54:13 [b] *63* Or *are Spirit*; or *are spirit* [c] *1* Some manuscripts *not have authority*
[d] *8* Some manuscripts *not yet*

[12]Among the crowds there was widespread whispering about him. Some said, "He is a
good man."
Others replied, "No, he deceives the people." [13]But no one would say anything publicly
about him for fear of the leaders.

Jesus Teaches at the Festival

[14]Not until halfway through the Festival did Jesus go up to the temple courts and begin
to teach. [15]The Jews there were amazed and asked, "How did this man get such learning
without having been taught?"
[16]Jesus answered, "My teaching is not my own. It comes from the one who sent me.
[17]Anyone who chooses to do the will of God will find out whether my teaching comes from
God or whether I speak on my own. [18]Whoever speaks on their own does so to gain person-
al glory, but he who seeks the glory of the one who sent him is a man of truth; there is
nothing false about him. [19]Has not Moses given you the law? Yet not one of you keeps the
law. Why are you trying to kill me?"
[20]"You are demon-possessed," the crowd answered. "Who is trying to kill you?"
[21]Jesus said to them, "I did one miracle, and you are all amazed. [22]Yet, because Moses gave
you circumcision (though actually it did not come from Moses, but from the patriarchs), you
circumcise a boy on the Sabbath. [23]Now if a boy can be circumcised on the Sabbath so that
the law of Moses may not be broken, why are you angry with me for healing a man's whole
body on the Sabbath? [24]Stop judging by mere appearances, but instead judge correctly."

Division Over Who Jesus Is

[25]At that point some of the people of Jerusalem began to ask, "Isn't this the man they
are trying to kill? [26]Here he is, speaking publicly, and they are not saying a word to him.
Have the authorities really concluded that he is the Messiah? [27]But we know where this
man is from; when the Messiah comes, no one will know where he is from."
[28]Then Jesus, still teaching in the temple courts, cried out, "Yes, you know me, and you
know where I am from. I am not here on my own authority, but he who sent me is true. You
do not know him, [29]but I know him because I am from him and he sent me."
[30]At this they tried to seize him, but no one laid a hand on him, because his hour had
not yet come. [31]Still, many in the crowd put their faith in him. They said, "When the Mes-
siah comes, will he perform more signs than this man?"
[32]The Pharisees heard the crowd whispering such things about him. Then the chief
priests and the Pharisees sent temple guards to arrest him.
[33]Jesus said, "I am with you for only a short time, and then I go to the one who sent me.
[34]You will look for me, but you will not find me; and where I am, you cannot come."
[35]The Jews said to one another, "Where does this man intend to go that we cannot find
him? Will he go where our people live scattered among the Greeks, and teach the Greeks?
[36]What did he mean when he said, 'You will look for me, but you will not find me,' and
'Where I am, you cannot come'?"
[37]On the last and greatest day of the Festival, Jesus stood and said in a loud voice, "Let
anyone who is thirsty come to me and drink. [38]Whoever believes in me, as Scripture has
said, rivers of living water will flow from within them."[a] [39]By this he meant the Spirit, whom
those who believed in him were later to receive. Up to that time the Spirit had not been
given, since Jesus had not yet been glorified.
[40]On hearing his words, some of the people said, "Surely this man is the Prophet."
[41]Others said, "He is the Messiah."
Still others asked, "How can the Messiah come from Galilee? [42]Does not Scripture say
that the Messiah will come from David's descendants and from Bethlehem, the town where
David lived?" [43]Thus the people were divided because of Jesus. [44]Some wanted to seize
him, but no one laid a hand on him.

---

[a] 37,38 *Or me. And let anyone drink* [38]*who believes in me." As Scripture has said, "Out of him* (or
them) *will flow rivers of living water."*

Unbelief of the Jewish Leaders

45Finally the temple guards went back to the chief priests and the Pharisees, who asked
them, "Why didn't you bring him in?"
46"No one ever spoke the way this man does," the guards replied.
47"You mean he has deceived you also?" the Pharisees retorted. 48"Have any of the rul-
ers or of the Pharisees believed in him? 49No! But this mob that knows nothing of the law—
there is a curse on them."
50Nicodemus, who had gone to Jesus earlier and who was one of their own number,
asked, 51"Does our law condemn a man without first hearing him to find out what he has
been doing?"
52They replied, "Are you from Galilee, too? Look into it, and you will find that a proph-
et does not come out of Galilee."

[The earliest manuscripts and many other ancient witnesses do not have John 7:53–8:11.]

8 *53Then they all went home, 1but Jesus went to the Mount of Olives.*
2At dawn he appeared again in the temple courts, where all the people gathered around him, and
he sat down to teach them. 3The teachers of the law and the Pharisees brought in a woman caught
in adultery. They made her stand before the group 4and said to Jesus, "Teacher, this woman was caught
in the act of adultery. 5In the Law Moses commanded us to stone such women. Now what do you say?"
6They were using this question as a trap, in order to have a basis for accusing him.
But Jesus bent down and started to write on the ground with his finger. 7When they kept on question-
ing him, he straightened up and said to them, "Let any one of you who is without sin be the first to throw
a stone at her." 8Again he stooped down and wrote on the ground.
9At this, those who heard began to go away one at a time, the older ones first, until only Jesus was left,
with the woman still standing there. 10Jesus straightened up and asked her, "Woman,[a] where are they?
Has no one condemned you?"
11"No one, sir," she said.
"Then neither do I condemn you," Jesus declared. "Go now and leave your life of sin."

Dispute Over Jesus' Testimony

12When Jesus spoke again to the people, he said, "I am the light of the world. Whoever
follows me will never walk in darkness, but will have the light of life."
13The Pharisees challenged him, "Here you are, appearing as your own witness; your
testimony is not valid."

Discovering God

7:37–39 // The Holy Spirit. Friends of Jesus not only enjoy a close relationship with God, they also have the assurance that God's Spirit will come to dwell inside them. With Jesus' earthly appearance, something new happened in the ongoing saga of God's relationship to humankind (see also Genesis chapter 3 [page 8] and chapter 12, verses 1–3 [page 18]). God has always been available to people relationally, but through Jesus he has established the way to reside in his followers permanently. This individual indwelling of God is accomplished through the divine person here called "the Spirit" (elsewhere, the "Holy Spirit").

Jesus promised that after his resurrection from the dead, God would unite with his people in this new way. The result would be an internal, inexhaustible fountain of "living water"—a refreshing, spiritual power that would continually sustain believers in their relationship with him. (For more on the Holy Spirit, see chapters 14 and 16 [pages 141 and 144].)

That same Spirit and his power is available to you today!

---

[a] *10* The Greek for *Woman* does not denote any disrespect.

14 Jesus answered, "Even if I testify on my own behalf, my testimony is valid, for I know where I came from and where I am going. But you have no idea where I come from or where I am going. 15 You judge by human standards; I pass judgment on no one. 16 But if I do judge, my decisions are true, because I am not alone. I stand with the Father, who sent me. 17 In your own Law it is written that the testimony of two witnesses is true. 18 I am one who testifies for myself; my other witness is the Father, who sent me."

19 Then they asked him, "Where is your father?"

"You do not know me or my Father," Jesus replied. "If you knew me, you would know my Father also." 20 He spoke these words while teaching in the temple courts near the place where the offerings were put. Yet no one seized him, because his hour had not yet come.

Dispute Over Who Jesus Is

21 Once more Jesus said to them, "I am going away, and you will look for me, and you will die in your sin. Where I go, you cannot come."

22 This made the Jews ask, "Will he kill himself? Is that why he says, 'Where I go, you cannot come'?"

23 But he continued, "You are from below; I am from above. You are of this world; I am not of this world. 24 I told you that you would die in your sins; if you do not believe that I am he, you will indeed die in your sins."

25 "Who are you?" they asked.

"Just what I have been telling you from the beginning," Jesus replied. 26 "I have much to say in judgment of you. But he who sent me is trustworthy, and what I have heard from him I tell the world."

27 They did not understand that he was telling them about his Father. 28 So Jesus said, "When you have lifted up[a] the Son of Man, then you will know that I am he and that I do nothing on my own but speak just what the Father has taught me. 29 The one who sent me is with me; he has not left me alone, for I always do what pleases him." 30 Even as he spoke, many put their faith in him.

Dispute Over Whose Children Jesus' Opponents Are

31 To the Jews who had believed him, Jesus said, "If you hold to my teaching, you are really my disciples. 32 Then you will know the truth, and the truth will set you free."

33 They answered him, "We are Abraham's descendants and have never been slaves of anyone. How can you say that we shall be set free?"

34 Jesus replied, "Very truly I tell you, everyone who sins is a slave to sin. 35 Now a slave has no permanent place in the family, but a son belongs to it forever. 36 So if the Son sets you free, you will be free indeed. 37 I know you are Abraham's descendants. Yet you are looking for a way to kill me, because you have no room for my word. 38 I am telling you what I have seen in the Father's presence, and you are doing what you have heard from your father.[b]"

39 "Abraham is our father," they answered.

"If you were Abraham's children," said Jesus, "then you would[c] do what Abraham did. 40 As it is, you are looking for a way to kill me, a man who has told you the truth that I heard from God. Abraham did not do such things. 41 You are doing the works of your own father."

Discovering God

8:21–24 // Jesus, the God-Man. Clearly, Jesus wanted his listeners to understand that his identity was no cause for mere speculation. He had told them who he was—the Son of God—and would tell them repeatedly. Their eternal destiny (as well as ours) depended on agreeing with Jesus about his divine origin.

[a] 28 The Greek for *lifted up* also means *exalted.* [b] 38 Or *presence. Therefore do what you have heard from the Father.* [c] 39 Some early manuscripts *"If you are Abraham's children," said Jesus, "then*

"We are not illegitimate children," they protested. "The only Father we have is God himself."

42Jesus said to them, "If God were your Father, you would love me, for I came from God and now am here. I have not come on my own; but he sent me. 43Why is my language not clear to you? Because you are unable to hear what I say. 44You belong to your father, the devil, and you want to carry out your father's desires. He was a murderer from the beginning, not holding to the truth, for there is no truth in him. When he lies, he speaks his native language, for he is a liar and the father of lies. 45Yet because I tell the truth, you do not believe me! 46Can any of you prove me guilty of sin? If I am telling the truth, why don't you believe me? 47Whoever belongs to God hears what God says. The reason you do not hear is that you do not belong to God."

Jesus' Claims About Himself

48The Jews answered him, "Aren't we right in saying that you are a Samaritan and demon-possessed?"

49"I am not possessed by a demon," said Jesus, "but I honor my Father and you dishonor me. 50I am not seeking glory for myself; but there is one who seeks it, and he is the judge. 51Very truly I tell you, whoever obeys my word will never see death."

52At this they exclaimed, "Now we know that you are demon-possessed! Abraham died and so did the prophets, yet you say that whoever obeys your word will never taste death. 53Are you greater than our father Abraham? He died, and so did the prophets. Who do you think you are?"

54Jesus replied, "If I glorify myself, my glory means nothing. My Father, whom you claim as your God, is the one who glorifies me. 55Though you do not know him, I know him. If I said I did not, I would be a liar like you, but I do know him and obey his word. 56Your father Abraham rejoiced at the thought of seeing my day; he saw it and was glad."

57"You are not yet fifty years old," they said to him, "and you have seen Abraham!"

58"Very truly I tell you," Jesus answered, "before Abraham was born, I am!" 59At this, they picked up stones to stone him, but Jesus hid himself, slipping away from the temple grounds.

Jesus Heals a Man Born Blind

9 As he went along, he saw a man blind from birth. 2His disciples asked him, "Rabbi, who sinned, this man or his parents, that he was born blind?"

3"Neither this man nor his parents sinned," said Jesus, "but this happened so that the works of God might be displayed in him. 4As long as it is day, we must do the works of him who sent me. Night is coming, when no one can work. 5While I am in the world, I am the light of the world."

6Having said this, he spit on the ground, made some mud with the saliva, and put it on the man's eyes. 7"Go," he told him, "wash in the Pool of Siloam" (this word means "Sent"). So the man went and washed, and came home seeing.

Discovering God

8:42–59 // Jesus, the God-Man. This argument between Jesus and a group of religious leaders known as Pharisees is one of the clearest examples in the New Testament of Jesus' claim to be God. Here Jesus asserts that he was alive in Abraham's day (some 1800 years earlier) by using the present tense—"I am," not the expected "I was." With that turn of a phrase, he takes on the very title of the one true God.

When God first appeared to Moses he called himself, "I AM WHO I AM" (Exodus chapter 3, verse 14). God also referred to himself similarly in the book of Isaiah with the phrase "I am he" (chapter 41, verse 4, and chapter 48, verse 12). In this discussion, Jesus leaves absolutely no doubt about what he is claiming.

The crowd he is speaking to gets the point. In the face of such a statement, there are only two options: bow down and worship, or try to destroy this impostor who is pretending to be God. They chose the latter.

What will be your response?

[8]His neighbors and those who had formerly seen him begging asked, "Isn't this the same man who used to sit and beg?" [9]Some claimed that he was.

Others said, "No, he only looks like him."

But he himself insisted, "I am the man."

[10]"How then were your eyes opened?" they asked.

[11]He replied, "The man they call Jesus made some mud and put it on my eyes. He told me to go to Siloam and wash. So I went and washed, and then I could see."

[12]"Where is this man?" they asked him.

"I don't know," he said.

The Pharisees Investigate the Healing

[13]They brought to the Pharisees the man who had been blind. [14]Now the day on which Jesus had made the mud and opened the man's eyes was a Sabbath. [15]Therefore the Pharisees also asked him how he had received his sight. "He put mud on my eyes," the man replied, "and I washed, and now I see."

[16]Some of the Pharisees said, "This man is not from God, for he does not keep the Sabbath."

But others asked, "How can a sinner perform such signs?" So they were divided.

[17]Then they turned again to the blind man, "What have you to say about him? It was your eyes he opened."

The man replied, "He is a prophet."

[18]They still did not believe that he had been blind and had received his sight until they sent for the man's parents. [19]"Is this your son?" they asked. "Is this the one you say was born blind? How is it that now he can see?"

[20]"We know he is our son," the parents answered, "and we know he was born blind. [21]But how he can see now, or who opened his eyes, we don't know. Ask him. He is of age; he will speak for himself." [22]His parents said this because they were afraid of the Jewish leaders, who already had decided that anyone who acknowledged that Jesus was the Messiah would be put out of the synagogue. [23]That was why his parents said, "He is of age; ask him."

[24]A second time they summoned the man who had been blind. "Give glory to God and tell the truth," they said. "We know this man is a sinner."

[25]He replied, "Whether he is a sinner or not, I don't know. One thing I do know. I was blind but now I see!"

[26]Then they asked him, "What did he do to you? How did he open your eyes?"

[27]He answered, "I have told you already and you did not listen. Why do you want to hear it again? Do you want to become his disciples too?"

Addressing Questions

9:1–3 // Human Experience. In making his point in this passage, Jesus obliterates the notion of "karma," the Eastern belief that everything happens to us because of some action we've taken—either in this life or in an alleged previous one. Jesus teaches that we can't assume a one-to-one correlation between today's personal problems and the amount of sin we've committed in the past. Sometimes bad people get away with—at least for the time being—things they shouldn't, and sometimes good people suffer unjustly.

In the opening chapters of the Bible, God shows us the reason why human existence is full of heartbreak—sin. Like random gunfire, sin wounds innocent bystanders. This damaging, nonspecific effect of evil is one reason why God is so opposed to it in any form. He knows that too often the wrong people suffer.

In this passage, Jesus does not assign blame to the family. His words liberate this man from decades of shame and self-hatred, and release the man's parents from wondering what they might have done wrong to bring about their son's blindness. The Jesus mercifully notes that even this blind man's situation can bring glory to God. And by healing him, Jesus shows his compassion and power.

Does this story mean that God will heal all of our wounds? Not necessarily—not on earth, anyway. But although we experience hardship in this life, followers of Christ can hang on to what Jesus has done in anticipation of what he promises to do (Revelation chapter 21, verses 3–4).

28 Then they hurled insults at him and said, "You are this fellow's disciple! We are disci-
ples of Moses! 29 We know that God spoke to Moses, but as for this fellow, we don't even
know where he comes from."

30 The man answered, "Now that is remarkable! You don't know where he comes from,
yet he opened my eyes. 31 We know that God does not listen to sinners. He listens to the god-
ly person who does his will. 32 Nobody has ever heard of opening the eyes of a man born
blind. 33 If this man were not from God, he could do nothing."

34 To this they replied, "You were steeped in sin at birth; how dare you lecture us!" And
they threw him out.

Spiritual Blindness

35 Jesus heard that they had thrown him out, and when he found him, he said, "Do you
believe in the Son of Man?"

36 "Who is he, sir?" the man asked. "Tell me so that I may believe in him."

37 Jesus said, "You have now seen him; in fact, he is the one speaking with you."

38 Then the man said, "Lord, I believe," and he worshiped him.

39 Jesus said,[a] "For judgment I have come into this world, so that the blind will see and
those who see will become blind."

40 Some Pharisees who were with him heard him say this and asked, "What? Are we blind
too?"

41 Jesus said, "If you were blind, you would not be guilty of sin; but now that you claim
you can see, your guilt remains.

The Good Shepherd and His Sheep

10 "Very truly I tell you Pharisees, anyone who does not enter the sheep pen by the
gate, but climbs in by some other way, is a thief and a robber. 2 The one who en-
ters by the gate is the shepherd of the sheep. 3 The gatekeeper opens the gate for
him, and the sheep listen to his voice. He calls his own sheep by name and leads them
out. 4 When he has brought out all his own, he goes on ahead of them, and his sheep fol-
low him because they know his voice. 5 But they will never follow a stranger; in fact, they
will run away from him because they do not recognize a stranger's voice." 6 Jesus used this
figure of speech, but the Pharisees did not understand what he was telling them.

7 Therefore Jesus said again, "Very truly I tell you, I am the gate for the sheep. 8 All who
have come before me are thieves and robbers, but the sheep have not listened to them. 9 I
am the gate; whoever enters through me will be saved.[b] They will come in and go out, and

Reasons to Believe

9:34–41 // The Incomparable Jesus. The man whom Jesus heals in this chapter faces harsh treatment by the religious leaders for his unwillingness to renounce Jesus. Alone and rejected, this man ponders how he could have received such a wonderful gift, yet be so misunderstood by people who are supposed to know God. Jesus speaks to the confused man, asking him the most important question a seeker can hear: "Do you believe in [trust and rely on] the Son of Man?" (verse 35). In other words, do you believe in the One who came from God and who healed you? The man responds with belief and worship.

Notice the two-way seeking here. Jesus is the original seeker. He finds people in need even before they can do any looking themselves. His activity precedes any human effort to reach out.

Is it too much to think that, as you read this story, God is attempting to let you know that he desires to reach you? Is he, right now, "touching your eyes" and opening them to see in new ways? If so, do as this man did—just say thanks for how he has brought you this far (in spite of how others around you may misunderstand what is happening). And don't shy away from putting your complete trust in Jesus for all of what life—and death—may hold. He has proven himself trustworthy.

[a] *38,39* Some early manuscripts do not have verses 38 and 39a. [b] *9* Or *kept safe*

find pasture. [10]The thief comes only to steal and kill and destroy; I have come that they
may have life, and have it to the full.
[11]"I am the good shepherd. The good shepherd lays down his life for the sheep. [12]The
hired hand is not the shepherd and does not own the sheep. So when he sees the wolf com-
ing, he abandons the sheep and runs away. Then the wolf attacks the flock and scatters it.
[13]The man runs away because he is a hired hand and cares nothing for the sheep.
[14]"I am the good shepherd; I know my sheep and my sheep know me— [15]just as the Fa-
ther knows me and I know the Father—and I lay down my life for the sheep. [16]I have oth-
er sheep that are not of this sheep pen. I must bring them also. They too will listen to my
voice, and there shall be one flock and one shepherd. [17]The reason my Father loves me is
that I lay down my life—only to take it up again. [18]No one takes it from me, but I lay it
down of my own accord. I have authority to lay it down and authority to take it up again.
This command I received from my Father."
[19]The Jews who heard these words were again divided. [20]Many of them said, "He is de-
mon-possessed and raving mad. Why listen to him?"
[21]But others said, "These are not the sayings of someone possessed by a demon. Can a
demon open the eyes of the blind?"

Further Conflict Over Jesus' Claims

[22]Then came the Festival of Dedication[a] at Jerusalem. It was winter, [23]and Jesus was in
the temple courts walking in Solomon's Colonnade. [24]The Jews who were there gathered
around him, saying, "How long will you keep us in suspense? If you are the Messiah, tell
us plainly."
[25]Jesus answered, "I did tell you, but you do not believe. The works I do in my Father's
name testify about me, [26]but you do not believe because you are not my sheep. [27]My sheep
listen to my voice; I know them, and they follow me. [28]I give them eternal life, and they
shall never perish; no one will snatch them out of my hand. [29]My Father, who has given
them to me, is greater than all[b]; no one can snatch them out of my Father's hand. [30]I and
the Father are one."
[31]Again the Jews picked up stones to stone him, [32]but Jesus said to them, "I have shown
you many good works from the Father. For which of these do you stone me?"

Reasons to Believe

10:14–16 // The Incomparable Jesus. In comparing himself to a shepherd, Jesus evoked an image that those who listened to him clearly understood. But as our shepherd, he goes much farther than what even the best shepherd of the day would have done. Not only does he know each member of his "flock" by name, but he was also willing to die for them—an act he literally carried out by allowing himself to be nailed to the cross. The "other sheep" Jesus mentions are his followers from every race and nation down through the ages. Maybe even you!

Discovering God

10:30 // Jesus, the God-Man. In this verse, Jesus again asserts his equality with God the Father.

Some interpreters have tried to soften the impact of these words by suggesting that maybe Jesus only claimed a "unity of purpose" with God. But Jesus' enemies knew exactly what he was claiming—and they were furious. They didn't even bother to deny his miracles; they just decided, based on an irrational bias, that he was a blasphemer who was worthy of death (verses 31–33).

Jesus' presence doesn't quell all doubts. Spectators who are determined to contradict him will be allowed to do so. Of course, they will have to discount important facts and react emotionally instead of rationally. But turning away—even from the miracle-working power of God—can be done. All it takes is a closed mind and a hard heart.

---

[a] 22 That is, Hanukkah [b] 29 Many early manuscripts *What my Father has given me is greater than all*

33“We are not stoning you for any good work,” they replied, “but for blasphemy, because
you, a mere man, claim to be God.”
34Jesus answered them, “Is it not written in your Law, ‘I have said you are “gods” ’[a]? 35If
he called them ‘gods,’ to whom the word of God came—and Scripture cannot be broken—
36what about the one whom the Father set apart as his very own and sent into the world?
Why then do you accuse me of blasphemy because I said, ‘I am God’s Son’? 37Do not be-
lieve me unless I do the works of my Father. 38But if I do them, even though you do not be-
lieve me, believe the works, that you may know and understand that the Father is in me,
and I in the Father.” 39Again they tried to seize him, but he escaped their grasp.
40Then Jesus went back across the Jordan to the place where John had been baptizing
in the early days. Here he stayed 41and many people came to him. They said, “Though John
never performed a sign, all that John said about this man was true.” 42And in that place
many believed in Jesus.

The Death of Lazarus

11 Now a man named Lazarus was sick. He was from Bethany, the village of Mary
and her sister Martha. 2(This Mary, whose brother Lazarus now lay sick, was the
same one who poured perfume on the Lord and wiped his feet with her hair.) 3So
the sisters sent word to Jesus, “Lord, the one you love is sick.”
4When he heard this, Jesus said, “This sickness will not end in death. No, it is for God’s
glory so that God’s Son may be glorified through it.” 5Now Jesus loved Martha and her sis-
ter and Lazarus. 6So when he heard that Lazarus was sick, he stayed where he was two more
days, 7and then he said to his disciples, “Let us go back to Judea.”
8“But Rabbi,” they said, “a short while ago the Jews there tried to stone you, and yet you
are going back?”
9Jesus answered, “Are there not twelve hours of daylight? Those who walk in the daytime
will not stumble, for they see by this world’s light. 10It is when people walk at night that they
stumble, for they have no light.”
11After he had said this, he went on to tell them, “Our friend Lazarus has fallen asleep;
but I am going there to wake him up.”
12His disciples replied, “Lord, if he sleeps, he will get better.” 13Jesus had been speaking
of his death, but his disciples thought he meant natural sleep.
14So then he told them plainly, “Lazarus is dead, 15and for your sake I am glad I was not
there, so that you may believe. But let us go to him.”
16Then Thomas (also known as Didymus[b]) said to the rest of the disciples, “Let us also
go, that we may die with him.”

Jesus Comforts the Sisters of Lazarus

17On his arrival, Jesus found that Lazarus had already been in the tomb for four days.
18Now Bethany was less than two miles[c] from Jerusalem, 19and many Jews had come to
Martha and Mary to comfort them in the loss of their brother. 20When Martha heard that
Jesus was coming, she went out to meet him, but Mary stayed at home.
21“Lord,” Martha said to Jesus, “if you had been here, my brother would not have died.
22But I know that even now God will give you whatever you ask.”
23Jesus said to her, “Your brother will rise again.”
24Martha answered, “I know he will rise again in the resurrection at the last day.”
25Jesus said to her, “I am the resurrection and the life. Anyone who believes in me will
live, even though they die; 26and whoever lives by believing in me will never die. Do you
believe this?”
27“Yes, Lord,” she told him, “I believe that you are the Messiah, the Son of God, who was
to come into the world.”
28After she had said this, she went back and called her sister Mary aside. “The Teacher
is here,” she said, “and is asking for you.” 29When Mary heard this, she got up quickly and
went to him. 30Now Jesus had not yet entered the village, but was still at the place where

---

[a] *34* Psalm 82:6 [b] *16* *Thomas* (Aramaic) and *Didymus* (Greek) both mean *twin*. [c] *18* Or about 3 kilometers

Martha had met him. [31]When the Jews who had been with Mary in the house, comforting
her, noticed how quickly she got up and went out, they followed her, supposing she was
going to the tomb to mourn there.
[32]When Mary reached the place where Jesus was and saw him, she fell at his feet and
said, "Lord, if you had been here, my brother would not have died."
[33]When Jesus saw her weeping, and the Jews who had come along with her also weep-
ing, he was deeply moved in spirit and troubled. [34]"Where have you laid him?" he asked.
"Come and see, Lord," they replied.
[35]Jesus wept.
[36]Then the Jews said, "See how he loved him!"
[37]But some of them said, "Could not he who opened the eyes of the blind man have kept
this man from dying?"

Jesus Raises Lazarus From the Dead

[38]Jesus, once more deeply moved, came to the tomb. It was a cave with a stone laid
across the entrance. [39]"Take away the stone," he said.
"But, Lord," said Martha, the sister of the dead man, "by this time there is a bad odor,
for he has been there four days."
[40]Then Jesus said, "Did I not tell you that if you believe, you will see the glory of God?"
[41]So they took away the stone. Then Jesus looked up and said, "Father, I thank you that
you have heard me. [42]I knew that you always hear me, but I said this for the benefit of the
people standing here, that they may believe that you sent me."
[43]When he had said this, Jesus called in a loud voice, "Lazarus, come out!" [44]The dead
man came out, his hands and feet wrapped with strips of linen, and a cloth around his face.
Jesus said to them, "Take off the grave clothes and let him go."

The Plot to Kill Jesus

[45]Therefore many of the Jews who had come to visit Mary, and had seen what Jesus did,
put their faith in him. [46]But some of them went to the Pharisees and told them what Jesus
had done. [47]Then the chief priests and the Pharisees called a meeting of the Sanhedrin.
"What are we accomplishing?" they asked. "Here is this man performing many signs.
[48]If we let him go on like this, everyone will believe in him, and then the Romans will come
and take away both our temple and our nation."
[49]Then one of them, named Caiaphas, who was high priest that year, spoke up, "You
know nothing at all! [50]You do not realize that it is better for you that one man die for the
people than that the whole nation perish."
[51]He did not say this on his own, but as high priest that year he prophesied that Jesus
would die for the Jewish nation, [52]and not only for that nation but also for the scattered chil-
dren of God, to bring them together and make them one. [53]So from that day on they plot-
ted to take his life.
[54]Therefore Jesus no longer moved about publicly among the Jews. Instead he withdrew
to a region near the wilderness, to a village called Ephraim, where he stayed with his dis-
ciples.

Knowing Yourself

11:47–50—Sin. Sometimes people keep their distance from Jesus because they don't want him meddling in their lives.

Many of Jesus' contemporaries opposed him for that reason. Their security was wrapped up in a fragile political alliance with the Roman government that protected their land rights and place of worship. Jesus' appeal to the masses threatened that source of security. These Jewish leaders weren't willing to risk losing what they had—at best, a temporary security—for the promise of new life and eternal safe-keeping that Jesus had to offer.

Jesus knows that anything that takes the place of God in our lives will lead to disappointment. Humans simply aren't wired to function without a vital connection to our Creator. If we "hot wire" our lives to some other source of security, we'll self-destruct—as these religious leaders would soon learn.

55When it was almost time for the Jewish Passover, many went up from the country to
Jerusalem for their ceremonial cleansing before the Passover. 56They kept looking for Jesus,
and as they stood in the temple courts they asked one another, "What do you think? Isn't
he coming to the Festival at all?" 57But the chief priests and the Pharisees had given orders
that anyone who found out where Jesus was should report it so that they might arrest him.

Jesus Anointed at Bethany

12 Six days before the Passover, Jesus came to Bethany, where Lazarus lived, whom
Jesus had raised from the dead. 2Here a dinner was given in Jesus' honor. Martha
served, while Lazarus was among those reclining at the table with him. 3Then
Mary took about a pint[a] of pure nard, an expensive perfume; she poured it on Jesus' feet
and wiped his feet with her hair. And the house was filled with the fragrance of the per-
fume.

4But one of his disciples, Judas Iscariot, who was later to betray him, objected, 5"Why
wasn't this perfume sold and the money given to the poor? It was worth a year's wages.[b]"
6He did not say this because he cared about the poor but because he was a thief; as keep-
er of the money bag, he used to help himself to what was put into it.

7"Leave her alone," Jesus replied. "⌞It was intended⌟ that she should save this perfume
for the day of my burial. 8You will always have the poor among you,[c] but you will not al-
ways have me."

9Meanwhile a large crowd of Jews found out that Jesus was there and came, not only be-
cause of him but also to see Lazarus, whom he had raised from the dead. 10So the chief
priests made plans to kill Lazarus as well, 11for on account of him many of the Jews were
going over to Jesus and putting their faith in him.

Jesus Comes to Jerusalem as King

12The next day the great crowd that had come for the Festival heard that Jesus was
on his way to Jerusalem. 13They took palm branches and went out to meet him, shouting,

"Hosanna![d]"

"Blessed is he who comes in the name of the Lord!"[e]

"Blessed is the king of Israel!"

14Jesus found a young donkey and sat on it, as it is written:

15"Do not be afraid, Daughter Zion;
see, your king is coming,
seated on a donkey's colt."[f]

16At first his disciples did not understand all this. Only after Jesus was glorified did they
realize that these things had been written about him and that these things had been done
to him.

Addressing Questions

12:9–11 // Human Experience. Have you ever thought that if you witnessed an indisputable miracle, you'd have no trouble believing in God? Astonishingly, Jesus' act of raising Lazarus from the dead (see chapter 11, verses 38–44) didn't convince the skeptical religious leaders of Jesus' claims. They didn't deny that something miraculous had happened. They just ignored it and plotted to kill Jesus. They even plotted to *re*kill Lazarus to complete the cover-up!

What people strongly believe often has little to do with sound reasoning. In our stubborn opposition, we can go to great lengths to suppress evidence if the facts contradict our made-up minds.

As you learn more about God, be careful not to make the same mistake. Determine that you'll keep an open mind as you consider the validity of Jesus' claims.

[a] *3* Or about half a liter [b] *5* Greek *three hundred denarii* [c] *8* See Deut. 15:11. [d] *13* A Hebrew expression meaning "Save!" which became an exclamation of praise [e] *13* Psalm 118:25,26
[f] *15* Zech. 9:9

17Now the crowd that was with him when he called Lazarus from the tomb and raised
him from the dead continued to spread the word. 18Many people, because they had heard
that he had performed this sign, went out to meet him. 19So the Pharisees said to one an-
other, "See, this is getting us nowhere. Look how the whole world has gone after him!"

Jesus Predicts His Death

20Now there were some Greeks among those who went up to worship at the Festival. 21They
came to Philip, who was from Bethsaida in Galilee, with a request. "Sir," they said, "we would
like to see Jesus." 22Philip went to tell Andrew; Andrew and Philip in turn told Jesus.
23Jesus replied, "The hour has come for the Son of Man to be glorified. 24Very truly I tell
you, unless a kernel of wheat falls to the ground and dies, it remains only a single seed. But
if it dies, it produces many seeds. 25Those who love their life will lose it, while those who
hate their life in this world will keep it for eternal life. 26Whoever serves me must follow
me; and where I am, my servant also will be. My Father will honor the one who serves me.
27"Now my soul is troubled, and what shall I say? 'Father, save me from this hour'? No,
it was for this very reason I came to this hour. 28Father, glorify your name!"
Then a voice came from heaven, "I have glorified it, and will glorify it again." 29The
crowd that was there and heard it said it had thundered; others said an angel had spoken
to him.
30Jesus said, "This voice was for your benefit, not mine. 31Now is the time for judgment
on this world; now the prince of this world will be driven out. 32And I, when I am lifted up[a]
from the earth, will draw all people to myself." 33He said this to show the kind of death he
was going to die.
34The crowd spoke up, "We have heard from the Law that the Messiah will remain for-
ever, so how can you say, 'The Son of Man must be lifted up'? Who is this 'Son of Man'?"
35Then Jesus told them, "You are going to have the light just a little while longer. Walk
while you have the light, before darkness overtakes you. Those who walk in the dark do
not know where they are going. 36Put your trust in the light while you have the light, so
that you may become children of light." When he had finished speaking, Jesus left and hid
himself from them.

Belief and Unbelief Among the Jews

37Even after Jesus had performed so many signs in their presence, they still would not
believe in him. 38This was to fulfill the word of Isaiah the prophet:

> "Lord, who has believed our message
> and to whom has the arm of the Lord been revealed?"[b]

39For this reason they could not believe, because, as Isaiah says elsewhere:

> 40"He has blinded their eyes
> and hardened their hearts,
> so they can neither see with their eyes,
> nor understand with their hearts,
> nor turn—and I would heal them."[c]

41Isaiah said this because he saw Jesus' glory and spoke about him.
42Yet at the same time many even among the leaders believed in him. But because of
the Pharisees they would not openly acknowledge their faith for fear they would be put
out of the synagogue; 43for they loved human glory more than the glory of God.
44Then Jesus cried out, "Those who believe in me do not believe in me only, but in the
one who sent me. 45When they look at me, they see the one who sent me. 46I have come
into the world as a light, so that no one who believes in me should stay in darkness.
47"As for those who hear my words but do not keep them, I do not judge them. For I did
not come to judge the world, but to save the world. 48There is a judge for those who reject
me and do not accept my words; the very words I have spoken will condemn them at the
last day. 49For I did not speak on my own, but the Father who sent me commanded me to

---

[a] *32* The Greek for *lifted up* also means *exalted.* [b] *38* Isaiah 53:1 [c] *40* Isaiah 6:10

say all that I have spoken. [50]I know that his command leads to eternal life. So whatever I say is just what the Father has told me to say."

Jesus Washes His Disciples' Feet

13 It was just before the Passover Festival. Jesus knew that the hour had come for him to leave this world and go to the Father. Having loved his own who were in the world, he loved them to the end.

[2]The evening meal was in progress, and the devil had already prompted Judas, the son of Simon Iscariot, to betray Jesus. [3]Jesus knew that the Father had put all things under his power, and that he had come from God and was returning to God; [4]so he got up from the meal, took off his outer clothing, and wrapped a towel around his waist. [5]After that, he poured water into a basin and began to wash his disciples' feet, drying them with the towel that was wrapped around him.

[6]He came to Simon Peter, who said to him, "Lord, are you going to wash my feet?"

[7]Jesus replied, "You do not realize now what I am doing, but later you will understand."

[8]"No," said Peter, "you shall never wash my feet."

Jesus answered, "Unless I wash you, you have no part with me."

[9]"Then, Lord," Simon Peter replied, "not just my feet but my hands and my head as well!"

[10]Jesus answered, "Those who have had a bath need only to wash their feet; their whole body is clean. And you are clean, though not every one of you." [11]For he knew who was going to betray him, and that was why he said not every one was clean.

[12]When he had finished washing their feet, he put on his clothes and returned to his place. "Do you understand what I have done for you?" he asked them. [13]"You call me 'Teacher' and 'Lord,' and rightly so, for that is what I am. [14]Now that I, your Lord and Teacher, have washed your feet, you also should wash one another's feet. [15]I have set you an example that you should do as I have done for you. [16]Very truly I tell you, servants are not greater than their master, nor are messengers greater than the one who sent them. [17]Now that you know these things, you will be blessed if you do them.

Jesus Predicts His Betrayal

[18]"I am not referring to all of you; I know those I have chosen. But this is to fulfill this passage of Scripture: 'He who shared my bread has lifted up his heel against me.'[a]

[19]"I am telling you now before it happens, so that when it does happen you will believe that I am who I am. [20]Very truly I tell you, whoever accepts anyone I send accepts me; and whoever accepts me accepts the one who sent me."

[21]After he had said this, Jesus was troubled in spirit and testified, "Very truly I tell you, one of you is going to betray me."

[22]His disciples stared at one another, at a loss to know which of them he meant. [23]One of them, the disciple whom Jesus loved, was reclining next to him. [24]Simon Peter motioned to this disciple and said, "Ask him which one he means."

Strengthening Relationships

13:1–17 // Social. In Jesus' time, a foot-washing slave was at the very lowest rung of society's ladder. Yet that is exactly the role Jesus took on in this passage. His followers had seen Jesus display his power. They had heard him speak with authority. They knew he could do the miraculous. But wash their dirty feet? Never!

Jesus insisted that in the new world he envisioned, the most important people would serve and care for others. This upside-down ethic—treating all people with honor and respect—is a distinguishing feature of Christianity. Were it more widely practiced in our day, the impact on government, business, schools, and every other sphere of life would be revolutionary.

Many individuals spend time voluntarily serving other people. Those who do so in the name of God, in whose image we are all created, show the world not only that Jesus is who he says he is, but that his followers are who they say they are.

[a] *18* Psalm 41:9

25Leaning back against Jesus, he asked him, "Lord, who is it?"
26Jesus answered, "It is the one to whom I will give this piece of bread when I have
dipped it in the dish." Then, dipping the piece of bread, he gave it to Judas, the son of Si-
mon Iscariot. 27As soon as Judas took the bread, Satan entered into him.
So Jesus told him, "What you are about to do, do quickly." 28But no one at the meal un-
derstood why Jesus said this to him. 29Since Judas had charge of the money, some thought
Jesus was telling him to buy what was needed for the Festival, or to give something to the
poor. 30As soon as Judas had taken the bread, he went out. And it was night.

Jesus Predicts Peter's Denial

31When he was gone, Jesus said, "Now is the Son of Man glorified and God is glorified
in him. 32If God is glorified in him,[a] God will glorify the Son in himself, and will glorify him
at once.
33"My children, I will be with you only a little longer. You will look for me, and just as I
told the Jews, so I tell you now: Where I am going, you cannot come.
34"A new command I give you: Love one another. As I have loved you, so you must love
one another. 35By this everyone will know that you are my disciples, if you love one an-
other."
36Simon Peter asked him, "Lord, where are you going?"
Jesus replied, "Where I am going, you cannot follow now, but you will follow later."
37Peter asked, "Lord, why can't I follow you now? I will lay down my life for you."
38Then Jesus answered, "Will you really lay down your life for me? Very truly I tell you,
before the rooster crows, you will disown me three times!

Jesus Comforts His Disciples

14 "Do not let your hearts be troubled. Trust in God[b]; trust also in me. 2My Father's
house has plenty of room; if that were not so, would I have told you that I am go-
ing there to prepare a place for you? 3And if I go and prepare a place for you, I will
come back and take you to be with me that you also may be where I am. 4You know the way
to the place where I am going."

Jesus the Way to the Father

5Thomas said to him, "Lord, we don't know where you are going, so how can we know
the way?"
6Jesus answered, "I am the way and the truth and the life. No one comes to the Father ex-
cept through me. 7If you really know me, you will know[c] my Father as well. From now on, you
do know him and have seen him."
8Philip said, "Lord, show us the Father and that will be enough for us."

Addressing Questions

13:21–27 // Unseen Realities. No one knows for sure exactly why Judas handed Jesus over to the authorities. Whatever the reason, he received supernatural assistance from an evil angel called Satan (or the devil) to carry out his plan.

Notice that the devil did not force Judas to do anything. The devil's tools were (and still are today) human desires and decisions—he merely amplified and empowered the direction that Judas had already chosen. Judas later realized what he had done, and took his own life as a result (Matthew chapter 27, verses 3–5).

Dabbling in anything satanic leads a person into powerful spiritual bondage. Satan is like a caged lion. Get in the cage with him, and you will be in grave danger. Pretend he doesn't exist, and you leave the door of the cage open—he will get out and do harm. Only if you stay close to God are you safe (James chapter 4, verses 7–10). The devil may "roar" and try to scare you, but he is no match for God.

Jesus *always* won when he and the devil went toe-to-toe. That victory is still available to those who live in union with Jesus today.

[a] 32 Many early manuscripts do not have *If God is glorified in him.* [b] 1 Or *You trust in God*
[c] 7 Some manuscripts *If you really knew me, you would know*

[9]Jesus answered: "Don't you know me, Philip, even after I have been among you such a
long time? Anyone who has seen me has seen the Father. How can you say, 'Show us the
Father'? [10]Don't you believe that I am in the Father, and that the Father is in me? The words
I say to you I do not speak on my own authority. Rather, it is the Father, living in me, who
is doing his work. [11]Believe me when I say that I am in the Father and the Father is in me;
or at least believe on the evidence of the works themselves. [12]Very truly I tell you, all who
have faith in me will do the works I have been doing, and they will do even greater things
than these, because I am going to the Father. [13]And I will do whatever you ask in my name,
so that the Father may be glorified in the Son. [14]You may ask me for anything in my name,
and I will do it.

Jesus Promises the Holy Spirit

[15]"If you love me, keep my commands. [16]And I will ask the Father, and he will give you
another advocate to help you and be with you forever— [17]the Spirit of truth. The world can-
not accept him, because it neither sees him nor knows him. But you know him, for he lives
with you and will be[a] in you. [18]I will not leave you as orphans; I will come to you. [19]Before
long, the world will not see me anymore, but you will see me. Because I live, you also will
live. [20]On that day you will realize that I am in my Father, and you are in me, and I am in
you. [21]Whoever has my commands and keeps them is the one who loves me. Anyone who
loves me will be loved by my Father, and I too will love them and show myself to them."

[22]Then Judas (not Judas Iscariot) said, "But, Lord, why do you intend to show yourself
to us and not to the world?"

[23]Jesus replied, "Anyone who loves me will obey my teaching. My Father will love them,
and we will come to them and make our home with them. [24]Anyone who does not love me
will not obey my teaching. These words you hear are not my own; they belong to the Fa-
ther who sent me.

Addressing Questions

14:6 // God. Is belief in Jesus Christ the *one and only* way to find salvation?

Jesus' answer is clear from this passage. Many Christians have been accused of being narrow-minded (sometimes with good reason!); but when it comes to the claim that Jesus is the only way to God, Christians are narrow-minded because *Jesus* is. And every seeker must reckon with Jesus' claim. As British theologian and writer C. S. Lewis once pointed out, if Jesus isn't a liar or a lunatic, then he must be *Lord*.

Perhaps an illustration will shed some light on this idea. From the air an airport runway looks "narrow." A pilot who insists on landing there may well be considered narrow-minded. But a runway is the only safe place for a jet to land. Say, for example, that a well-intentioned passenger recommends that the pilot land on a local expressway instead of the runway. It looks safe, after all, and would be much more convenient than circling the city waiting for the runway to clear. The pilot, resisting the appeals of the uninformed passenger who proposes an unsafe alternative, will be credited with courage for saving the life of every passenger—even the one who complained about the inconvenience of it all.

Jesus is like that pilot, trying to tell us that it's not safe to put down anywhere else. He's not limiting our options—he's protecting us from a crash.

If this concept troubles you, you're not alone. It's a common criticism of Christianity in our pluralistic, relativistic culture. But realize that, as a seeker, you're ultimately going to have to take up this claim—not with Christians, but with Jesus Christ himself. Pit your arguments, your credentials, your character and your insight against his. But don't enter the debate unless you're willing to yield to the winner.

Discovering God

14:14 // Jesus, the God-Man. Jesus is the only person in the Bible who invites prayer *to* him, in *his* name, and who then says that *he* will grant those requests. Jesus clearly affirms his divine identity by claiming prerogatives belonging to God alone.

[a] *17* Some early manuscripts *and is*

25“All this I have spoken while still with you. 26But the Advocate, the Holy Spirit, whom
the Father will send in my name, will teach you all things and will remind you of everything
I have said to you. 27Peace I leave with you; my peace I give you. I do not give to you as the
world gives. Do not let your hearts be troubled and do not be afraid.
28“You heard me say, ‘I am going away and I am coming back to you.’ If you loved me,
you would be glad that I am going to the Father, for the Father is greater than I. 29I have
told you now before it happens, so that when it does happen you will believe. 30I will not
say much more to you, for the prince of this world is coming. He has no hold over me, 31but
he comes so that the world may learn that I love the Father and do exactly what my Father
has commanded me.
“Come now; let us leave.

The Vine and the Branches

15 “I am the true vine, and my Father is the gardener. 2He cuts off every branch in
me that bears no fruit, while every branch that does bear fruit he prunes[a] so that
it will be even more fruitful. 3You are already clean because of the word I have
spoken to you. 4Remain in me, as I also remain in you. No branch can bear fruit by itself;
it must remain in the vine. Neither can you bear fruit unless you remain in me.
5“I am the vine; you are the branches. If you remain in me and I in you, you will bear
much fruit; apart from me you can do nothing. 6If you do not remain in me, you are like a
branch that is thrown away and withers; such branches are picked up, thrown into the fire
and burned. 7If you remain in me and my words remain in you, ask whatever you wish,
and it will be done for you. 8This is to my Father’s glory, that you bear much fruit, show-
ing yourselves to be my disciples.
9“As the Father has loved me, so have I loved you. Now remain in my love. 10If you keep
my commands, you will remain in my love, just as I have kept my Father’s commands and
remain in his love. 11I have told you this so that my joy may be in you and that your joy
may be complete. 12My command is this: Love each other as I have loved you. 13Greater
love has no one than this: to lay down one’s life for one’s friends. 14You are my friends if
you do what I command. 15I no longer call you servants, because servants do not know their
master’s business. Instead, I have called you friends, for everything that I learned from my
Father I have made known to you. 16You did not choose me, but I chose you and appoint-
ed you so that you might go and bear fruit—fruit that will last—and so that whatever you
ask in my name the Father will give you. 17This is my command: Love each other.

The World Hates the Disciples

18“If the world hates you, keep in mind that it hated me first. 19If you belonged to the
world, it would love you as its own. As it is, you do not belong to the world, but I have

Discovering God

15:5 // Life with God. Have you ever been concerned that if you became a serious follower of Jesus, you wouldn’t be able to live the Christian life—that it’s out of reach for someone like you?

The Christian life is a paradox, because living like Jesus *is* impossible, at least on our own. What makes it work is that Jesus gives us his power so we can live beyond our natural limits and abilities. Our responsibility is to *abide*—to stay connected to him, like a grafted-in branch that draws nutrients and support from the main vine.

In verse 7 Jesus describes a practical way his power comes to us: through his words “remaining” in us. The best way to accomplish this is through consistently reading those words in the Bible.

Another way we connect to Christ is through prayer. Formal prayers have their place (usually in the worship setting), but our personal connection with Christ is strengthened most when we approach prayer as a simple conversation between two friends. Unpretentious, authentic prayer helps us to stay closely connected—in other words, to *abide*—with Jesus.

---

[a] 2 The Greek for *he prunes* also means *he cleans*.

chosen you out of the world. That is why the world hates you. [20]Remember what I told you:
'Servants are not greater than their master.'[a] If they persecuted me, they will persecute
you also. If they obeyed my teaching, they will obey yours also. [21]They will treat you this
way because of my name, for they do not know the one who sent me. [22]If I had not come
and spoken to them, they would not be guilty of sin; but now they have no excuse for their
sin. [23]Those who hate me hate my Father as well. [24]If I had not done among them the
works no one else did, they would not be guilty of sin. As it is, they have seen, and yet
they have hated both me and my Father. [25]But this is to fulfill what is written in their Law:
'They hated me without reason.'[b]

The Work of the Holy Spirit

[26]"When the Advocate comes, whom I will send to you from the Father—the Spirit of
truth who goes out from the Father—he will testify about me. [27]And you also must testify,
for you have been with me from the beginning.

16 "All this I have told you so that you will not fall away. [2]They will put you out of
the synagogue; in fact, the hour is coming when those who kill you will think they
are offering a service to God. [3]They will do such things because they have not
known the Father or me. [4]I have told you this, so that when their hour comes you will re-
member that I warned you about them. I did not tell you this from the beginning because
I was with you, [5]but now I am going to him who sent me. None of you asks me, 'Where are
you going?' [6]Rather, you are filled with grief because I have said these things. [7]But very
truly I tell you, it is for your good that I am going away. Unless I go away, the Advocate
will not come to you; but if I go, I will send him to you. [8]When he comes, he will prove the
world to be in the wrong about sin and righteousness and judgment: [9]about sin, because
people do not believe in me; [10]about righteousness, because I am going to the Father, where
you can see me no longer; [11]and about judgment, because the prince of this world now
stands condemned.

[12]"I have much more to say to you, more than you can now bear. [13]But when he, the Spir-
it of truth, comes, he will guide you into all the truth. He will not speak on his own; he will
speak only what he hears, and he will tell you what is yet to come. [14]He will glorify me be-
cause it is from me that he will receive what he will make known to you. [15]All that belongs
to the Father is mine. That is why I said the Spirit will receive from me what he will make
known to you."

The Disciples' Grief Will Turn to Joy

[16]Jesus went on to say, "In a little while you will see me no more, and then after a little
while you will see me."

[17]At this, some of his disciples said to one another, "What does he mean by saying, 'In
a little while you will see me no more, and then after a little while you will see me,' and
'Because I am going to the Father'?" [18]They kept asking, "What does he mean by 'a little
while'? We don't understand what he is saying."

[19]Jesus saw that they wanted to ask him about this, so he said to them, "Are you asking
one another what I meant when I said, 'In a little while you will see me no more, and then
after a little while you will see me'? [20]Very truly I tell you, you will weep and mourn while

Discovering God

15:26–27 // The Holy Spirit. Jesus refers to the Holy Spirit here as "the Advocate." The term literally means "one called alongside to help."

Perhaps you've felt the Spirit's ministry while reading this book or when a Christian friend or co-worker was talking to you. Have you ever experienced a breakthrough during such times—a point at which "a light turned on" and the discussion began to make sense? That might well have been God working in you to help you grasp his message and apply it to your life. During such moments "the Advocate" does his work, just as Jesus promised he would 2000 years ago.

---

[a] *20* John 13:16 [b] *25* Psalms 35:19; 69:4

the world rejoices. You will grieve, but your grief will turn to joy. 21A woman giving birth to
a child has pain because her time has come; but when her baby is born she forgets the an-
guish because of her joy that a child is born into the world. 22So with you: Now is your time
of grief, but I will see you again and you will rejoice, and no one will take away your joy.
23In that day you will no longer ask me anything. Very truly I tell you, my Father will give
you whatever you ask in my name. 24Until now you have not asked for anything in my
name. Ask and you will receive, and your joy will be complete.

25"Though I have been speaking figuratively, a time is coming when I will no longer use
this kind of language but will tell you plainly about my Father. 26In that day you will ask in
my name. I am not saying that I will ask the Father on your behalf. 27No, the Father himself
loves you because you have loved me and have believed that I came from God. 28I came from
the Father and entered the world; now I am leaving the world and going back to the Father."

29Then Jesus' disciples said, "Now you are speaking clearly and without figures of
speech. 30Now we can see that you know all things and that you do not even need to have
anyone ask you questions. This makes us believe that you came from God."

31"Do you now believe?" Jesus replied. 32"A time is coming and in fact has come when
you will be scattered, each to your own home. You will leave me all alone. Yet I am not
alone, for my Father is with me.

33"I have told you these things, so that in me you may have peace. In this world you will
have trouble. But take heart! I have overcome the world."

Jesus Prays to Be Glorified

17 After Jesus said this, he looked toward heaven and prayed:

"Father, the hour has come. Glorify your Son, that your Son may glorify you.
2For you granted him authority over all people that he might give eternal life to all those
you have given him. 3Now this is eternal life: that they know you, the only true God, and
Jesus Christ, whom you have sent. 4I have brought you glory on earth by finishing the

Discovering God

16:33 // Life with God. Jesus never promised his followers that their lives would be trouble-free. In fact, he promised just the opposite. But what did he mean when he said that he had "overcome the world"?

Jesus was talking here about the final victory he would claim when God would raise him from the dead (you'll read more about this as you continue reading through this book). Jesus submitted to death on the cross out of his own will. After three days, as he predicted (Mark chapter 8, verse 31). God brought him back to life. In breaking the power of death, Jesus demolished the power of sin in this world. Individuals who place their trust in Jesus are personally connected to him and his victory.

So, while life as a Christian may have its bleak periods, Jesus' resurrection gives believers hope that no defeat on earth is permanent. Jesus' troops may lose some battles, but his victory assures them that they'll win the war.

Knowing Yourself

17:3 // A New Identity. What does it mean to have "eternal life"?

According to Jesus, eternal life begins *right here on earth*—the very moment we invite Christ to be our forgiver and leader. We have a choice whether to live with him now or apart from him now. After physical death we continue experiencing the kind of spiritual life we had here: Either we live in paradise with Christ or in hell without him. But we continue to exist somewhere eternally.

So how do we receive eternal life with him? By doing the right rituals? Living a clean life? Appearing to be religious? None of these options open the way to eternal life. Jesus gives this simple answer: *We need to know him.* This goes beyond mere knowledge, however, because even the devil "knows him" in the sense of having accurate theology. Jesus calls us into a *relationship* with him. We have the chance to "know him" now and to be with him after we die.

That's the meaning of eternal life. It's a *quality* of life—both now and later—not just a *quantity* of life.

work you gave me to do. 5And now, Father, glorify me in your presence with the glory I had with you before the world began.

Jesus Prays for His Disciples

6"I have revealed you[a] to those whom you gave me out of the world. They were yours; you gave them to me and they have obeyed your word. 7Now they know that everything you have given me comes from you. 8For I gave them the words you gave me and they accepted them. They knew with certainty that I came from you, and they believed that you sent me. 9I pray for them. I am not praying for the world, but for those you have given me, for they are yours. 10All I have is yours, and all you have is mine. And glory has come to me through them. 11I will remain in the world no longer, but they are still in the world, and I am coming to you. Holy Father, protect them by the power of[b] your name, the name you gave me, so that they may be one as we are one. 12While I was with them, I protected them and kept them safe by[c] that name you gave me. None has been lost except the one doomed to destruction so that Scripture would be fulfilled.

13"I am coming to you now, but I say these things while I am still in the world, so that they may have the full measure of my joy within them. 14I have given them your word and the world has hated them, for they are not of the world any more than I am of the world. 15My prayer is not that you take them out of the world but that you protect them from the evil one. 16They are not of the world, even as I am not of it. 17Sanctify them by[d] the truth; your word is truth. 18As you sent me into the world, I have sent them into the world. 19For them I sanctify myself, that they too may be truly sanctified.

Jesus Prays for All Believers

20"My prayer is not for them alone. I pray also for those who will believe in me through their message, 21that all of them may be one, Father, just as you are in me and I am in you. May they also be in us so that the world may believe that you have sent me. 22I have given them the glory that you gave me, that they may be one as we are one— 23I in them and you in me—so that they may be brought to complete unity. Then the world will know that you sent me and have loved them even as you have loved me.

24"Father, I want those you have given me to be with me where I am, and to see my glory, the glory you have given me because you loved me before the creation of the world.

25"Righteous Father, though the world does not know you, I know you, and they know that you have sent me. 26I have made you known to them, and will continue to make you known in order that the love you have for me may be in them and that I myself may be in them."

Jesus Arrested

18 When he had finished praying, Jesus left with his disciples and crossed the Kidron Valley. On the other side there was a garden, and he and his disciples went into it.

2Now Judas, who betrayed him, knew the place, because Jesus had often met there with his disciples. 3So Judas came to the garden, guiding a detachment of soldiers and some officials from the chief priests and the Pharisees. They were carrying torches, lanterns and weapons.

4Jesus, knowing all that was going to happen to him, went out and asked them, "Who is it you want?"

5"Jesus of Nazareth," they replied.

"I am he," Jesus said. (And Judas the traitor was standing there with them.) 6When Jesus said, "I am he," they drew back and fell to the ground.

---

[a] 6 Greek *your name*; also in verse 26 [b] 11 Or *Father, keep them faithful to* [c] 12 Or *kept them faithful to* [d] 17 Or *them to live in accordance with*

[7]Again he asked them, "Who is it you want?"
"Jesus of Nazareth," they said.
[8]Jesus answered, "I told you that I am he. If you are looking for me, then let these men go." [9]This happened so that the words he had spoken would be fulfilled: "I have not lost one of those you gave me."[a]
[10]Then Simon Peter, who had a sword, drew it and struck the high priest's servant, cutting off his right ear. (The servant's name was Malchus.)
[11]Jesus commanded Peter, "Put your sword away! Shall I not drink the cup the Father has given me?"
[12]Then the detachment of soldiers with its commander and the Jewish officials arrested Jesus. They bound him [13]and brought him first to Annas, who was the father-in-law of Caiaphas, the high priest that year. [14]Caiaphas was the one who had advised the Jewish leaders that it would be good if one man died for the people.

Peter's First Denial

[15]Simon Peter and another disciple were following Jesus. Because this disciple was known to the high priest, he went with Jesus into the high priest's courtyard, [16]but Peter had to wait outside at the door. The other disciple, who was known to the high priest, came back, spoke to the servant girl on duty there and brought Peter in.
[17]"You aren't one of this man's disciples too, are you?" she asked Peter.
He replied, "I am not."
[18]It was cold, and the servants and officials stood around a fire they had made to keep warm. Peter also was standing with them, warming himself.

The High Priest Questions Jesus

[19]Meanwhile, the high priest questioned Jesus about his disciples and his teaching.
[20]"I have spoken openly to the world," Jesus replied. "I always taught in synagogues or at the temple, where all the Jews come together. I said nothing in secret. [21]Why question me? Ask those who heard me. Surely they know what I said."
[22]When Jesus said this, one of the officials nearby slapped him in the face. "Is this the way you answer the high priest?" he demanded.
[23]"If I said something wrong," Jesus replied, "testify as to what is wrong. But if I spoke the truth, why did you strike me?" [24]Then Annas sent him bound to Caiaphas the high priest.

Peter's Second and Third Denials

[25]Meanwhile, Simon Peter was still standing there warming himself. So they asked him, "You aren't one of his disciples too, are you?"
He denied it, saying, "I am not."
[26]One of the high priest's servants, a relative of the man whose ear Peter had cut off, challenged him, "Didn't I see you with him in the garden?" [27]Again Peter denied it, and at that moment a rooster began to crow.

Jesus Before Pilate

[28]Then the Jewish leaders took Jesus from Caiaphas to the palace of the Roman governor. By now it was early morning, and to avoid ceremonial uncleanness they did not enter the palace, because they wanted to be able to eat the Passover. [29]So Pilate came out to them and asked, "What charges are you bringing against this man?"
[30]"If he were not a criminal," they replied, "we would not have handed him over to you."
[31]Pilate said, "Take him yourselves and judge him by your own law."
"But we have no right to execute anyone," they objected. [32]This took place to fulfill what Jesus had said about the kind of death he was going to die.
[33]Pilate then went back inside the palace, summoned Jesus and asked him, "Are you the king of the Jews?"

---

[a] 9 John 6:39

34“Is that your own idea,” Jesus asked, “or did others talk to you about me?”
35“Am I a Jew?” Pilate replied. “Your own people and chief priests handed you over to me.
What is it you have done?”
36Jesus said, “My kingdom is not of this world. If it were, my servants would fight to pre-
vent my arrest by the Jewish leaders. But now my kingdom is from another place.”
37“You are a king, then!” said Pilate.
Jesus answered, “You say that I am a king. In fact, the reason I was born and came into
the world is to testify to the truth. Everyone on the side of truth listens to me.”
38“What is truth?” retorted Pilate. With this he went out again to the Jews gathered there
and said, “I find no basis for a charge against him. 39But it is your custom for me to release
to you one prisoner at the time of the Passover. Do you want me to release ‘the king of the
Jews’?”
40They shouted back, “No, not him! Give us Barabbas!” Now Barabbas had taken part in
an uprising.

Jesus Sentenced to Be Crucified

19 Then Pilate took Jesus and had him flogged. 2The soldiers twisted together a
crown of thorns and put it on his head. They clothed him in a purple robe 3and
went up to him again and again, saying, “Hail, king of the Jews!” And they slapped
him in the face.
4Once more Pilate came out and said to the Jews, “Look, I am bringing him out to you
to let you know that I find no basis for a charge against him.” 5When Jesus came out wear-
ing the crown of thorns and the purple robe, Pilate said to them, “Here is the man!”
6As soon as the chief priests and their officials saw him, they shouted, “Crucify! Cru-
cify!”
But Pilate answered, “You take him and crucify him. As for me, I find no basis for a
charge against him.”
7The Jews insisted, “We have a law, and according to that law he must die, because he
claimed to be the Son of God.”
8When Pilate heard this, he was even more afraid, 9and he went back inside the palace.
“Where do you come from?” he asked Jesus, but Jesus gave him no answer. 10“Do you refuse
to speak to me?” Pilate said. “Don’t you realize I have power either to free you or to cruci-
fy you?”
11Jesus answered, “You would have no power over me if it were not given to you from
above. Therefore the one who handed me over to you is guilty of a greater sin.”
12From then on, Pilate tried to set Jesus free, but the Jews kept shouting, “If you let this
man go, you are no friend of Caesar. Anyone who claims to be a king opposes Caesar.”
13When Pilate heard this, he brought Jesus out and sat down on the judge’s seat at a
place known as the Stone Pavement (which in Aramaic is Gabbatha). 14It was the day of
Preparation of the Passover; it was about noon.
“Here is your king,” Pilate said to the Jews.
15But they shouted, “Take him away! Take him away! Crucify him!”
“Shall I crucify your king?” Pilate asked.
“We have no king but Caesar,” the chief priests answered.
16Finally Pilate handed him over to them to be crucified.

Addressing Questions

18:39–40 // Unseen Realities. Barabbas was guilty of a crime and deserving of death. Jesus was innocent and should have been released. But Jesus ended up dying—literally in Barabbas’s place.

This exchange parallels a powerful spiritual transaction that occurred on the day Christ died. While hanging on the cross, Jesus took upon himself the sins of the world. God gave to his own Son the death sentence we owed for our rebellion. In that sense, Jesus died in our place that day. Because of his sacrifice, we, like Barabbas, can walk right out of our spiritual prison—if we simply receive the forgiveness and leadership of Christ.

The Crucifixion of Jesus

So the soldiers took charge of Jesus. 17Carrying his own cross, he went out to the place
of the Skull (which in Aramaic is called Golgotha). 18Here they crucified him, and with him
two others—one on each side and Jesus in the middle.
19Pilate had a notice prepared and fastened to the cross. It read: JESUS OF NAZARETH, THE
KING OF THE JEWS. 20Many of the Jews read this sign, for the place where Jesus was crucified
was near the city, and the sign was written in Aramaic, Latin and Greek. 21The chief priests
of the Jews protested to Pilate, "Do not write 'The King of the Jews,' but that this man
claimed to be king of the Jews."
22Pilate answered, "What I have written, I have written."
23When the soldiers crucified Jesus, they took his clothes, dividing them into four shares,
one for each of them, with the undergarment remaining. This garment was seamless, wo-
ven in one piece from top to bottom.
24"Let's not tear it," they said to one another. "Let's decide by lot who will get it."
This happened that the scripture might be fulfilled that said,

> "They divided my clothes among them
> and cast lots for my garment."[a]

Reasons to Believe

19:23–24 // The Amazing Bible. One of the distinguishing features of the Bible is its prophetic element. Centuries before Jesus' birth, a prophet named Isaiah penned several songs about a coming Servant. Though chosen by God, this Servant would be rejected by the very people he came to reach. Isaiah included incredible detail in his writings that is strikingly fulfilled in the life, death and resurrection of Jesus.

Other Old Testament writers also made predictions about this coming Messiah. The events in this passage, for example, fulfill a prophecy written down some 1000 years earlier by Israel's King David (Psalm chapter 22, verses 16–18).

The following chart shows some other amazing predictions that were fulfilled in Jesus' life. If Jesus had been a mere man, he couldn't have controlled many of these occurrences. The fact that they happened exactly as predicted proves that he is the fulfillment of these prophecies.

Event in Jesus' Life	Prophetic Passage
• Born in Bethlehem	Micah 5:2; fulfilled in Luke 2:4–7
• Sold for 30 pieces of silver	Zechariah 11:13; fulfilled in Matthew 26:15
• Betrayal money given to buy a potter's field	Zechariah 11:13; fulfilled in Matthew 27:6
• Forsaken at the end of his life	Psalm 22:1; fulfilled in Matthew 26:56
• Silent when accused	Isaiah 53:7; fulfilled in Matthew 27:12–14
• Condemned with criminals	Isaiah 53:12; fulfilled in Luke 23:32–33
• Crucified (hands and feet pierced)	Psalm 22:16; fulfilled in John 19:18
• Mocked while he died	Psalm 22:7–8; fulfilled in Luke 23:39
• Raging thirst when dying	Psalm 22:15; fulfilled in John 19:28
• Died for our sins	Isaiah 53:4–6; fulfilled in John 19:30
• Pierced after death	Isaiah 53:5, Zechariah 12:10; fulfilled in Luke 23:46
• Buried by a rich man	Isaiah 53:9; fulfilled in Matthew 27:57–60
• Suffering not the end (resurrection)	Isaiah 53:11, Psalm 16:9–11; fulfilled in Luke 24:1–8

No other major world religion has prophetic writings that describe its leader in this kind of detail centuries before the leader appeared. Such prophecies give readers good reason to trust the Bible and recognize its divine origin.

Reasons to Believe

19:34–35 // The Incomparable Jesus. John wants us to be clear—Jesus was *dead.* By piercing his body with a spear, the unnamed soldier established that fact beyond any shadow of a doubt. Any theory that Jesus' resurrection appearances came about because he hadn't really died ignores this important eyewitness testimony.

---

[a] *24* Psalm 22:18

So this is what the soldiers did.

[25]Near the cross of Jesus stood his mother, his mother's sister, Mary the wife of Clopas, and Mary Magdalene. [26]When Jesus saw his mother there, and the disciple whom he loved standing nearby, he said to her, "Woman,[a] here is your son," [27]and to the disciple, "Here is your mother." From that time on, this disciple took her into his home.

The Death of Jesus

[28]Later, knowing that everything had now been finished, and so that Scripture would be fulfilled, Jesus said, "I am thirsty." [29]A jar of wine vinegar was there, so they soaked a sponge in it, put the sponge on a stalk of the hyssop plant, and lifted it to Jesus' lips. [30]When he had received the drink, Jesus said, "It is finished." With that, he bowed his head and gave up his spirit.

[31]Now it was the day of Preparation, and the next day was to be a special Sabbath. Because the Jewish leaders did not want the bodies left on the crosses during the Sabbath, they asked Pilate to have the legs broken and the bodies taken down. [32]The soldiers therefore came and broke the legs of the first man who had been crucified with Jesus, and then those of the other. [33]But when they came to Jesus and found that he was already dead, they did not break his legs. [34]Instead, one of the soldiers pierced Jesus' side with a spear, bringing a sudden flow of blood and water. [35]The man who saw it has given testimony, and his testimony is true. He knows that he tells the truth, and he testifies so that you also may believe. [36]These things happened so that the scripture would be fulfilled: "Not one of his bones will be broken,"[b] [37]and, as another scripture says, "They will look on the one they have pierced."[c]

The Burial of Jesus

[38]Later, Joseph of Arimathea asked Pilate for the body of Jesus. Now Joseph was a disciple of Jesus, but secretly because he feared the Jewish leaders. With Pilate's permission, he came and took the body away. [39]He was accompanied by Nicodemus, the man who earlier had visited Jesus at night. Nicodemus brought a mixture of myrrh and aloes, about seventy-five pounds.[d] [40]Taking Jesus' body, the two of them wrapped it, with the spices, in strips of linen. This was in accordance with Jewish burial customs. [41]At the place where Jesus was crucified, there was a garden, and in the garden a new tomb, in which no one had ever been laid. [42]Because it was the Jewish day of Preparation and since the tomb was nearby, they laid Jesus there.

The Empty Tomb

20 Early on the first day of the week, while it was still dark, Mary Magdalene went to the tomb and saw that the stone had been removed from the entrance. [2]So she came running to Simon Peter and the other disciple, the one Jesus loved, and said, "They have taken the Lord out of the tomb, and we don't know where they have put him!"

[3]So Peter and the other disciple started for the tomb. [4]Both were running, but the other disciple outran Peter and reached the tomb first. [5]He bent over and looked in at the strips of linen lying there but did not go in. [6]Then Simon Peter came along behind him and went straight into the tomb. He saw the strips of linen lying there, [7]as well as the cloth that had been wrapped around Jesus' head. The cloth was still lying in its place, separate from the linen. [8]Finally the other disciple, who had reached the tomb first, also went inside. He saw and believed. [9](They still did not understand from Scripture that Jesus had to rise from the dead.) [10]Then the disciples went back to where they were staying.

Jesus Appears to Mary Magdalene

[11]Now Mary stood outside the tomb crying. As she wept, she bent over to look into the tomb [12]and saw two angels in white, seated where Jesus' body had been, one at the head and the other at the foot.

---

[a] *26* The Greek for *Woman* does not denote any disrespect. [b] *36* Exodus 12:46; Num. 9:12; Psalm 34:20 [c] *37* Zech. 12:10 [d] *39* Or about 34 kilograms

Resons to Believe

20:1–31 // The Incomparable Jesus. The resurrection of Jesus is the most fantastic event Christianity has ever asked the world to take seriously. If it isn't true, all of the claims of Jesus are irrelevant. If it is true, it substantiates all of Jesus' claims, and no other event in history has more significance. Establish the authenticity of the resurrection, and no other "son of God" need apply—the human race has its Savior.

As you read the account of the resurrection, notice that skeptics were everywhere. Jesus' disciples—especially Thomas—didn't expect to see him. Jesus' enemies didn't want to see him, and offered alternate—though easily refuted—explanations for the empty tomb. Let's look at two of those explanations.

Jesus' resurrection was just wishful thinking on the part of his disciples. They developed this myth to substantiate their claims.

Some modern critics speculate that the resurrection appearances were the disciples' hallucinations, which occurred because they worked themselves into a hysteria hoping that Jesus would come back from the dead. But that explanation doesn't take into account the disciples' overall misunderstanding of Jesus' resurrection predictions (see John chapter 16, verses 17–18 [page 144]).

After Jesus' death, the disciples didn't sit in anticipation of the resurrection. When Jesus appeared to most of them, they were hiding out in fear of the authorities (verses 19–20), not boldly proclaiming that their leader would return from the dead. Basically, the disciples didn't "get it" until after the fact. So lack of belief—not hysterical fantasizing—emerges as their state of mind before the resurrection.

But, for the sake of argument, let's say the disciples hallucinated. To refute their claim, their critics would only have had to go to the tomb and show everyone the body. The tomb, however, was empty. (*Note:* All of the world's religions have places of honor commemorating their dead founders. Only Christianity has an empty tomb.) Given the uncontested fact of a bodiless grave, another explanation surfaced.

Jesus' resurrection is an elaborate hoax. While the guards slept, the disciples came and stole the body, then told everyone that their leader was alive. (See Matthew chapter 28, verses 11–15.)

Many problems arise with this theory. For starters, the Jewish leaders of the day had taken great pains to ensure that the tomb could not be robbed (see Matthew chapter 27, verses 62–66). Pilate himself placed these guards on special duty. And even if they had dozed off, how could the guards have known who robbed the tomb? They were supposedly sleeping!

This argument also ignores the disciples' fear of being caught and prosecuted by the Jewish leaders of the day. Verse 19 shows them all locked in a room together, hidden away in fear. These men weren't about to leave the building, let alone go up against armed guards to steal a body.

And what else but Jesus' resurrection could have transformed these disciples from timid cowards to bold advocates, preaching that Jesus was alive in the very city in which his murderers still held power? (See Acts chapter 2, verses 22–47 [page 160]). Eventually, almost all of these men died martyrs' deaths. If this had been a hoax, wouldn't they have admitted to that fact when faced with the prospect of dying for it?

As a seeker trying to understand the most controversial claim of Christianity—that Jesus Christ, the Son of God, rose bodily from the grave—be sure to recognize its crucial importance in the context of world events. Explore all the theories you want; many more than these two have been posited over the centuries. But realize that in the 2000 years since Jesus' death, not one person has convincingly refuted the claims of the Bible on this score. Also realize that this event, the basis of Christianity, has changed millions upon millions of lives throughout the centuries.

Thomas, the disciple whose reputation as "the doubter" has dogged him for centuries, saw Jesus and believed. As you seek out the truth behind Christ's claims, remember his promise: "Blessed are those who have not seen and yet have believed" (verse 29).

13 They asked her, "Woman,[a] why are you crying?"
"They have taken my Lord away," she said, "and I don't know where they have put him."
14 At this, she turned around and saw Jesus standing there, but she did not realize that it was
Jesus.
15 He asked her, "Woman, why are you crying? Who is it you are looking for?"
Thinking he was the gardener, she said, "Sir, if you have carried him away, tell me where
you have put him, and I will get him."
16 Jesus said to her, "Mary."
She turned toward him and cried out in Aramaic, "Rabboni!" (which means "Teacher").
17 Jesus said, "Do not hold on to me, for I have not yet ascended to the Father. Go in-
stead to my brothers and tell them, 'I am ascending to my Father and your Father, to my
God and your God.' "
18 Mary Magdalene went to the disciples with the news: "I have seen the Lord!" And she
told them that he had said these things to her.

Jesus Appears to His Disciples

19 On the evening of that first day of the week, when the disciples were together, with the
doors locked for fear of the Jewish leaders, Jesus came and stood among them and said,
"Peace be with you!" 20 After he said this, he showed them his hands and side. The disciples
were overjoyed when they saw the Lord.
21 Again Jesus said, "Peace be with you! As the Father has sent me, I am sending you."
22 And with that he breathed on them and said, "Receive the Holy Spirit. 23 If you forgive the
sins of anyone, their sins are forgiven; if you do not forgive them, they are not forgiven."

Jesus Appears to Thomas

24 Now Thomas (also known as Didymus[b]), one of the Twelve, was not with the disci-
ples when Jesus came. 25 So the other disciples told him, "We have seen the Lord!"
But he said to them, "Unless I see the nail marks in his hands and put my finger where
the nails were, and put my hand into his side, I will not believe."
26 A week later his disciples were in the house again, and Thomas was with them. Though
the doors were locked, Jesus came and stood among them and said, "Peace be with you!"
27 Then he said to Thomas, "Put your finger here; see my hands. Reach out your hand and
put it into my side. Stop doubting and believe."
28 Thomas said to him, "My Lord and my God!"
29 Then Jesus told him, "Because you have seen me, you have believed; blessed are those
who have not seen and yet have believed."

The Purpose of John's Gospel

30 Jesus performed many other signs in the presence of his disciples, which are not re-
corded in this book. 31 But these are written that you may believe[c] that Jesus is the Messi-
ah, the Son of God, and that by believing you may have life in his name.

Jesus and the Miraculous Catch of Fish

21 Afterward Jesus appeared again to his disciples, by the Sea of Galilee.[d] It hap-
pened this way: 2 Simon Peter, Thomas (also known as Didymus[e]), Nathanael
from Cana in Galilee, the sons of Zebedee, and two other disciples were togeth-
er. 3 "I'm going out to fish," Simon Peter told them, and they said, "We'll go with you." So
they went out and got into the boat, but that night they caught nothing.
4 Early in the morning, Jesus stood on the shore, but the disciples did not realize that it
was Jesus.
5 He called out to them, "Friends, haven't you any fish?"
"No," they answered.

---

[a] *13* The Greek for *Woman* does not denote any disrespect; also in verse 15. [b] *24 Thomas* (Aramaic) and *Didymus* (Greek) both mean *twin.* [c] *31* Or *may continue to believe.* [d] *1* Greek *Tiberias* [e] *2 Thomas* (Aramaic) and *Didymus* (Greek) both mean *twin.*

6He said, "Throw your net on the right side of the boat and you will find some." When they did, they were unable to haul the net in because of the large number of fish.

7Then the disciple whom Jesus loved said to Peter, "It is the Lord!" As soon as Simon Peter heard him say, "It is the Lord," he wrapped his outer garment around him (for he had taken it off) and jumped into the water. 8The other disciples followed in the boat, towing the net full of fish, for they were not far from shore, about a hundred yards.[a] 9When they landed, they saw a fire of burning coals there with fish on it, and some bread.

10Jesus said to them, "Bring some of the fish you have just caught."

11Simon Peter climbed aboard and dragged the net ashore. It was full of large fish, 153, but even with so many the net was not torn. 12Jesus said to them, "Come and have breakfast." None of the disciples dared ask him, "Who are you?" They knew it was the Lord. 13Jesus came, took the bread and gave it to them, and did the same with the fish. 14This was now the third time Jesus appeared to his disciples after he was raised from the dead.

Jesus Reinstates Peter

15When they had finished eating, Jesus said to Simon Peter, "Simon son of John, do you love me more than these?"

"Yes, Lord," he said, "you know that I love you."

Jesus said, "Feed my lambs."

16Again Jesus said, "Simon son of John, do you love me?"

He answered, "Yes, Lord, you know that I love you."

Jesus said, "Take care of my sheep."

17The third time he said to him, "Simon son of John, do you love me?"

Peter was hurt because Jesus asked him the third time, "Do you love me?" He said, "Lord, you know all things; you know that I love you."

Jesus said, "Feed my sheep. 18Very truly I tell you, when you were younger you dressed yourself and went where you wanted; but when you are old you will stretch out your hands, and someone else will dress you and lead you where you do not want to go." 19Jesus said this to indicate the kind of death by which Peter would glorify God. Then he said to him, "Follow me!"

20Peter turned and saw that the disciple whom Jesus loved was following them. (This was the one who had leaned back against Jesus at the supper and had said, "Lord, who is going to betray you?") 21When Peter saw him, he asked, "Lord, what about him?"

Reasons to Believe

21:12–19 // The Incomparable Jesus. Ever wonder if you might push Jesus' patience to the limit and never get another chance? Peter's experience is instructive for those of us who are frightened that we've committed too great a sin to warrant Jesus' forgiveness.

Jesus—the champion of the second chance—sets the stage for Peter's restoration by preparing a breakfast of fish and bread. Perhaps the meal reminded Peter of Jesus' feeding the masses, and maybe the smell of the coals reminded him of the night he denied he knew Jesus while warming himself by a fire. Jesus reminds Peter not only of his failure, but also of their long and well-established relationship—one that has been sorely strained, but not destroyed.

Three times Jesus asks Peter to affirm his love, and three times Peter does so. Then Jesus give Peter the charge to get back into the ministry. Jesus, the good shepherd, has finally turned Peter the fisherman into a shepherd himself. Peter's restoration is complete.

Jesus will do the same for you if you'll let him. He wants to make you his lifetime follower—his disciple. He'll even *remake* you as many times as is necessary.

Jesus is unlike any other person you'll ever meet. He will not—he *cannot*—let you down. He is, as John described him in the introduction of this book, "full of grace and truth" (chapter 1, verse 14 [page 118]). If you put your trust in him, you will not be disappointed.

[a] *8* Or about 90 meters

22Jesus answered, "If I want him to remain alive until I return, what is that to you? You
must follow me." 23Because of this, the rumor spread among the believers that this disci-
ple would not die. But Jesus did not say that he would not die; he only said, "If I want him
to remain alive until I return, what is that to you?"
24This is the disciple who testifies to these things and who wrote them down. We know
that his testimony is true.
25Jesus did many other things as well. If every one of them were written down, I suppose
that even the whole world would not have room for the books that would be written.

Epilogue

The book you've just read is probably the most important book in the Bible. The most important person in the Bible is the one you've just read about. And the person God wants to affect through all this is the one reading these words right now—you!

Take a moment to turn back to chapter 3, verse 16 (page 121). After reading through this book you should know a lot more about Jesus, the Son of God. Will you accept his forgiveness and leadership in your life?

Seeker Stories

Whoever said "Your school years are the best years of your life" certainly didn't know me.

By the time I was in seventh grade, I was drinking heavily. Looking back I can see the beginnings of alcoholism in my life, even though I never would have admitted it. During my freshman year of high school I started smoking pot. I became involved in an unhealthy relationship with a fellow alcoholic who also had a drug problem. And before my sophomore year began, my parents' relationship ended in divorce. Between the substance abuse and the relationship problems I experienced, life was difficult. Shortly after my eighteenth birthday, I left a good job and began working in the adult entertainment industry.

My only philosophy on life and death was to do as much as I could of whatever I wanted and get the most out of life. I see now that those two statements contradict each other. As is the case with many people, I didn't realize that what I did had a direct effect on other people around me. By doing whatever I wanted, I was definitely not getting the most out of life.

By the end of my eighteenth year my best friend—my mom—had become seriously ill. Within the course of one month she was misdiagnosed with multiple sclerosis, mistreated, and was lying in a coma. After further testing the doctors determined that she had cancer, which had originated in her lungs (even though she was not a smoker) and spread throughout her body. She died about a month before my nineteenth birthday.

When Mom became ill, the seriousness of life and death finally dawned on me. The night before she died I asked Christ to come into my life and forgive me of all of my sins. It was amazing! The very next day my sister, her husband and I were able to comfort each other with God's love.

Unfortunately, I didn't give up any of my old ways. It wasn't long before I put God up on a shelf—a convenient distance away from the rest of my life.

It's incredible the way God works. One night after work, the girls and I went out drinking as usual. I was my normal self—swearing and drunk and looking for beautiful men. When I saw one, I went up to him and demanded his number. He gave it to me and added some Scripture at the bottom, along with a note saying "I am a Christian." Little did I know that God would use that stranger to get to me. I ran back to God and took him off that shelf.

I've been a devoted follower of Christ for about eight months now. I know I'm not where I want to be in my relationship with God, but I'm sure it's better than where I was. With God's help, I've been able to give up many of my former ways, including drinking, drugs and unhealthy relationships. I've also traded my career in adult entertainment for a management position in a retail store.

My life has never been better! I've never know security or love like this. I have so much to be thankful for. I can't believe God has forgiven me for all that I've done, but he has. He walks with me day by day, providing me with everything I need to survive and picking me up when I fall along the way.

"Father, I'm so grateful I have you. Thank you so much, and please know that I love you!"

Acts Introduction

THE BOTTOM LINE

The movie is over. As the credits roll and the lights slowly come up, you sit almost motionless, still captivated by the story. What happens next? Is there a sequel in the works? People who read the story of Jesus have the same reaction. *And this book is the sequel!*

Acts follows the trail of Jesus' disciples as they perform amazing miracles and preach to multitudes of people. It introduces you to Paul, a missionary who once viciously persecuted Jesus' followers. The story of Paul's conversion—including a flash of light from the sky and Jesus' own voice—is one of the most dramatic stories in the whole Bible. In the Gospels, Jesus promised his disciples that he would never leave them, even though he would no longer be with them physically. In this book, that promise is fulfilled. The Holy Spirit comes to dwell inside the disciples, as he does all of Jesus' followers today.

CENTRAL IDEAS

- The Holy Spirit has amazing power to change people's lives
- The church spread as incredible numbers of new converts responded to the challenge of the gospel.
- The disciples faithfully followed Jesus' directives, even though doing so brought suffering.
- The gospel of Christ is for all people.

OUTLINE

1. **Peter and the beginnings of the Jerusalem church** (chaps. 1–12)
2. **Paul and the expansion of the church** (chaps. 13–28)

TITLE

The title of this book is short for "The Acts of the Apostles," the events that this book describes.

AUTHOR AND READERS

Luke, who also wrote one of the four accounts of Jesus' life contained in the Bible, penned these words to chronicle the events of the early church.

While walking along a deserted beach one morning, a man spotted a little boy off in the distance throwing objects into the ocean. As the hiker got closer, he noticed that the boy was picking up starfish. The waves had washed up literally hundreds of thousands of them the night before.

Puzzled, he approached the boy. "Hello there. I was wondering what you're doing."

"I'm throwing starfish back into the ocean," answered the lad. "Otherwise, they'll die."

"Yes that's true," the hiker replied, "but look around you. There are so many of them on this beach. You can't help even a tiny fraction of them. What difference will it make?"

The boy smiled, bent down, and picked up another starfish. As he threw it back into the sea, he replied, "I bet it'll make a difference to that one!"

"I bet it'll make a difference to that one!"

Making a difference—one person at a time. That's a picture of what God wants to do for all of us, and it's also a picture of what he wants all of us to do.

After his resurrection, Jesus appeared to his disciples and gave them a mission that every Christ-follower must accept: to tell every human being on earth—one at a time—that he or she matters to God and that he or she can be forgiven and come to know him personally.

At first, such a mission seems unachievable. *How could I possibly make any difference when it comes to reaching the whole world with the message of Jesus?* It's like trying to . . . well, like trying to rescue thousands of starfish washed up on a beach.

But remember this: You wouldn't even be in a position to consider your part in fulfilling God's purposes if someone hadn't talked to you. And if someone hadn't told that person. And if someone else hadn't told the person before, and so on. An unbroken chain of people sharing this message stretches from the first century right up to *you.*

Want a better picture of how Jesus set in motion a force that has gathered enough steam to propel the truth across the ages straight to you? Turn to Acts chapter 1, verse 8 (page 158). Jesus' words might even inspire you to get in on the action and help spread his message to a whole new generation of seekers.

ACTS

Jesus Taken Up Into Heaven

1 In my former book, Theophilus, I wrote about all that Jesus began to do and to teach
2until the day he was taken up to heaven, after giving instructions through the Holy Spir-
it to the apostles he had chosen. 3After his suffering, he presented himself to them and
gave many convincing proofs that he was alive. He appeared to them over a period of forty
days and spoke about the kingdom of God. 4On one occasion, while he was eating with them,
he gave them this command: "Do not leave Jerusalem, but wait for the gift my Father prom-
ised, which you have heard me speak about. 5For John baptized with[a] water, but in a few
days you will be baptized with[a] the Holy Spirit."
6So when they met together, they asked him, "Lord, are you at this time going to restore
the kingdom to Israel?"
7He said to them: "It is not for you to know the times or dates the Father has set by his
own authority. 8But you will receive power when the Holy Spirit comes on you; and you will
be my witnesses in Jerusalem, and in all Judea and Samaria, and to the ends of the earth."
9After he said this, he was taken up before their very eyes, and a cloud hid him from
their sight.

Addressing Questions

1:8 // Human Experience. "Why am I here?"

The answer to that question—even if a person says "I don't know"—leads to the creation of a powerful mental map that his or her life's journey will inevitably follow.

After Jesus' resurrection his followers must have asked this same question. They probably wondered what was going to happen next. It's not hard to imagine them thinking, *If you're leaving, Jesus, why are we staying? What is our purpose here on earth?*

Jesus had a plan for his disciples—a plan to take over the world. But instead of overthrowing the Roman Empire militarily, he would conquer the hearts of men and women—one by one. His "army" would be those who knew him. Their "weapon" would be the message of forgiveness and new life offered by Christ himself. These "commandos" would relay God's commands and take captives with God's compassion—first their neighbors, then individuals across town, and finally people in other countries. Eventually they would tell the whole world about Jesus.

The words of verse 8, a variation on what is often called Jesus' "Great Commission," provide a purpose and direction for all of Jesus' followers. In light of the value that God's followers place on knowing him, what could be more important than helping others know him? Introducing someone else to God would bring that person into a relationship that would have eternal benefits.

And what about you? Consider for a moment the book you're now holding. Perhaps someone gave it to you, or perhaps you bought it out of your own spiritual curiosity. Either way, people who care about you and value Jesus' message passed it on to you in this written form. Yet before they could tell you about Jesus, someone else explained his story to them. And before those people became believers, there were others who in turn were taught by Jesus' followers before them. *An unbroken line of people relaying Jesus' truth goes all the way back to Jesus standing with his disciples on that hillside two thousand years ago—and it continues right up to this moment, with you reading these words!*

If you accept this message as truth to trust, you'll begin an extraordinary adventure. You will fulfill your main purpose for living by experiencing all that Jesus has in mind for you—especially by sharing that reality with others. You'll be joining a continuous succession of believers who are serious about taking their leader's message "to the ends of the earth." That's why Jesus left those early followers on earth, and that's why he's eager to begin his work through you.

---

[a] 5 Or *in*

10They were looking intently up into the sky as he was going, when suddenly two men
dressed in white stood beside them. 11"Men of Galilee," they said, "why do you stand here
looking into the sky? This same Jesus, who has been taken from you into heaven, will come
back in the same way you have seen him go into heaven."

Matthias Chosen to Replace Judas

12Then the apostles returned to Jerusalem from the hill called the Mount of Olives, a
Sabbath day's walk[a] from the city. 13When they arrived, they went upstairs to the room
where they were staying. Those present were Peter, John, James and Andrew; Philip and
Thomas, Bartholomew and Matthew; James son of Alphaeus and Simon the Zealot, and
Judas son of James. 14They all joined together constantly in prayer, along with the women
and Mary the mother of Jesus, and with his brothers.

15In those days Peter stood up among the believers (a group numbering about a hun-
dred and twenty) 16and said, "Brothers and sisters, the Scripture had to be fulfilled in which
the Holy Spirit spoke long ago through David concerning Judas, who served as guide for
those who arrested Jesus. 17He was one of our number and shared in our ministry."

18(With the reward he got for his wickedness, Judas bought a field; there he fell headlong,
his body burst open and all his intestines spilled out. 19Everyone in Jerusalem heard about
this, so they called that field in their language Akeldama, that is, Field of Blood.)

20"For," said Peter, "it is written in the Book of Psalms:

> " 'May his place be deserted;
> let there be no one to dwell in it,'[b]

and,

> " 'May another take his place of leadership.'[c]

21Therefore it is necessary to choose one of the men who have been with us the whole time
the Lord Jesus went in and out among us, 22beginning from John's baptism to the time
when Jesus was taken up from us. For one of these must become a witness with us of his
resurrection."

23So they proposed the names of two men: Joseph called Barsabbas (also known as Jus-
tus) and Matthias. 24Then they prayed, "Lord, you know everyone's heart. Show us which
of these two you have chosen 25to take over this apostolic ministry, which Judas left to go
where he belongs." 26Then they cast lots, and the lot fell to Matthias; so he was added to
the eleven apostles.

The Holy Spirit Comes at Pentecost

2 When the day of Pentecost came, they were all together in one place. 2Suddenly a
sound like the blowing of a violent wind came from heaven and filled the whole house
where they were sitting. 3They saw what seemed to be tongues of fire that separat-
ed and came to rest on each of them. 4All of them were filled with the Holy Spirit and be-
gan to speak in other tongues[d] as the Spirit enabled them.

5Now there were staying in Jerusalem God-fearing Jews from every nation under heav-
en. 6When they heard this sound, a crowd came together in bewilderment, because each
one heard their own language being spoken. 7Utterly amazed, they asked: "Aren't all these
who are speaking Galileans? 8Then how is it that each of us hears them in our native lan-
guage? 9Parthians, Medes and Elamites; residents of Mesopotamia, Judea and Cappadocia,
Pontus and Asia,[e] 10Phrygia and Pamphylia, Egypt and the parts of Libya near Cyrene; vis-
itors from Rome 11(both Jews and converts to Judaism); Cretans and Arabs—we hear them
declaring the wonders of God in our own tongues!" 12Amazed and perplexed, they asked one
another, "What does this mean?"

13Some, however, made fun of them and said, "They have had too much wine."

---

[a] *12* That is, about 5/8 mile or about 1 kilometer [b] *20* Psalm 69:25 [c] *20* Psalm 109:8
[d] *4* Or *languages*; also in verse 11 [e] *9* That is, the Roman province by that name

Peter Addresses the Crowd

14Then Peter stood up with the Eleven, raised his voice and addressed the crowd: "Fel-
low Jews and all of you who live in Jerusalem, let me explain this to you; listen carefully to
what I say. 15These people are not drunk, as you suppose. It's only nine in the morning!
16No, this is what was spoken by the prophet Joel:

17" 'In the last days, God says,
I will pour out my Spirit on all people.
Your sons and daughters will prophesy,
your young men will see visions,
your old men will dream dreams.
18Even on my servants, both men and women,
I will pour out my Spirit in those days,
and they will prophesy.
19I will show wonders in the heaven above
and signs on the earth below,
blood and fire and billows of smoke.
20The sun will be turned to darkness
and the moon to blood
before the coming of the great and glorious day of the Lord.
21And everyone who calls
on the name of the Lord will be saved.'[a]

22"People of Israel, listen to this: Jesus of Nazareth was a man accredited by God to you
by miracles, wonders and signs, which God did among you through him, as you yourselves
know. 23This man was handed over to you by God's deliberate plan and foreknowledge;
and you, with the help of wicked men,[b] put him to death by nailing him to the cross. 24But
God raised him from the dead, freeing him from the agony of death, because it was impos-
sible for death to keep its hold on him. 25David said about him:

" 'I saw the Lord always before me.
Because he is at my right hand,
I will not be shaken.

Discovering God

2:14–40 // Jesus, the God-Man. This "sermon" is the first by one of Jesus' followers to be recorded in the Bible. It is of particular interest to seekers because in it, Peter succinctly touches on virtually every important aspect of Christianity. Grasp this message, and you'll have a good handle on what the Christian faith is all about. Among the points Peter mentions:

- Jesus did miracles and was unlike any other person who has ever lived (verse 22).
- Jesus was a real, historical person. He suffered, died, and was raised from death (verses 23–24). As such, the Christian message fulfills the plan that God began long before Jesus' life on earth.
- The Jewish prophets made specific prophecies about Jesus before he was born, giving proof that the Bible is God's Word (verses 16–21 and 25–28).
- Jesus is Lord (Ruler of all, God in a human body) and Messiah (the promised Deliverer of Israel [verse 36]).
- Trust in Jesus—not yourself—for salvation (verse 38).
- God wants to dwell in you through the Holy Spirit (verses 38–39).
- The rest of the world is headed for disaster apart from God. Don't get entangled by its corruption (verse 40).

[a] *21* Joel 2:28-32 [b] *23* Or *of those not having the law* (that is, Gentiles)

26 Therefore my heart is glad and my tongue rejoices;
my body also will rest in hope,
27 because you will not abandon me to the realm of the dead,
you will not let your holy one see decay.
28 You have made known to me the paths of life;
you will fill me with joy in your presence.’[a]

29 “Brothers and sisters, we all know that the patriarch David died and was buried, and
his tomb is here to this day. 30 But he was a prophet and knew that God had promised him
on oath that he would place one of his descendants on his throne. 31 Seeing what was to
come, he spoke of the resurrection of the Messiah, that he was not abandoned to the realm
of the dead, nor did his body see decay. 32 God has raised this Jesus to life, and we are all
witnesses of the fact. 33 Exalted to the right hand of God, he has received from the Father
the promised Holy Spirit and has poured out what you now see and hear. 34 For David did
not ascend to heaven, and yet he said,

“ ‘The Lord said to my Lord:
“Sit at my right hand
35 until I make your enemies
a footstool for your feet.” ’[b]

36 “Therefore let all Israel be assured of this: God has made this Jesus, whom you cruci-
fied, both Lord and Messiah.”
37 When the people heard this, they were cut to the heart and said to Peter and the oth-
er apostles, “Brothers, what shall we do?”
38 Peter replied, “Repent and be baptized, every one of you, in the name of Jesus Christ
for the forgiveness of your sins. And you will receive the gift of the Holy Spirit. 39 The prom-
ise is for you and your children and for all who are far off—for all whom the Lord our God
will call.”
40 With many other words he warned them; and he pleaded with them, “Save yourselves
from this corrupt generation.” 41 Those who accepted his message were baptized, and about
three thousand were added to their number that day.

The Fellowship of the Believers

42 They devoted themselves to the apostles’ teaching and to fellowship, to the breaking
of bread and to prayer. 43 Everyone was filled with awe at the many wonders and signs per-
formed by the apostles. 44 All the believers were together and had everything in common.
45 They sold property and possessions to give to anyone who had need. 46 Every day they
continued to meet together in the temple courts. They broke bread in their homes and ate
together with glad and sincere hearts, 47 praising God and enjoying the favor of all the peo-
ple. And the Lord added to their number daily those who were being saved.

Peter Heals a Lame Beggar

3 One day Peter and John were going up to the temple at the time of prayer—at three
in the afternoon. 2 Now a man who was lame from birth was being carried to the
temple gate called Beautiful, where he was put every day to beg from those going
into the temple courts. 3 When he saw Peter and John about to enter, he asked them for
money. 4 Peter looked straight at him, as did John. Then Peter said, “Look at us!” 5 So the
man gave them his attention, expecting to get something from them.
6 Then Peter said, “Silver or gold I do not have, but what I do have I give you. In the name
of Jesus Christ of Nazareth, walk.” 7 Taking him by the right hand, he helped him up, and in-
stantly the man’s feet and ankles became strong. 8 He jumped to his feet and began to walk.
Then he went with them into the temple courts, walking and jumping, and praising God.
9 When all the people saw him walking and praising God, 10 they recognized him as the same
man who used to sit begging at the temple gate called Beautiful, and they were filled with
wonder and amazement at what had happened to him.

[a] *28* Psalm 16:8-11 (see Septuagint) [b] *35* Psalm 110:1

Peter Speaks to the Onlookers

[11]While the man held on to Peter and John, all the people were astonished and came run-
ning to them in the place called Solomon's Colonnade. [12]When Peter saw this, he said to
them: "People of Israel, why does this surprise you? Why do you stare at us as if by our own
power or godliness we had made this man walk? [13]The God of Abraham, Isaac and Jacob, the
God of our fathers, has glorified his servant Jesus. You handed him over to be killed, and
you disowned him before Pilate, though he had decided to let him go. [14]You disowned the
Holy and Righteous One and asked that a murderer be released to you. [15]You killed the au-
thor of life, but God raised him from the dead. We are witnesses of this. [16]By faith in the
name of Jesus, this man whom you see and know was made strong. It is Jesus' name and
the faith that comes through him that has completely healed him, as you can all see.

[17]"Now, brothers and sisters, I know that you acted in ignorance, as did your leaders.
[18]But this is how God fulfilled what he had foretold through all the prophets, saying that
his Messiah would suffer. [19]Repent, then, and turn to God, so that your sins may be wiped
out, that times of refreshing may come from the Lord, [20]and that he may send the Messi-
ah, who has been appointed for you—even Jesus. [21]Heaven must receive him until the time
comes for God to restore everything, as he promised long ago through his holy prophets.
[22]For Moses said, 'The Lord your God will raise up for you a prophet like me from among
your own people; you must listen to everything he tells you. [23]Anyone who does not listen
to him will be completely cut off from their people.'[a]

[24]"Indeed, beginning with Samuel, all the prophets who have spoken have foretold these
days. [25]And you are heirs of the prophets and of the covenant God made with your fathers.
He said to Abraham, 'Through your offspring all peoples on earth will be blessed.'[b] [26]When
God raised up his servant, he sent him first to you to bless you by turning each of you from
your wicked ways."

Peter and John Before the Sanhedrin

4 The priests and the captain of the temple guard and the Sadducees came up to Pe-
ter and John while they were speaking to the people. [2]They were greatly disturbed
because the apostles were teaching the people, proclaiming in Jesus the resurrec-
tion of the dead. [3]They seized Peter and John, and because it was evening, they put them
in jail until the next day. [4]But many who heard the message believed; so the number of
men who believed grew to about five thousand.

[5]The next day the rulers, the elders and the teachers of the law met in Jerusalem. [6]An-
nas the high priest was there, and so were Caiaphas, John, Alexander and others of the
high priest's family. [7]They had Peter and John brought before them and began to question
them: "By what power or what name did you do this?"

[8]Then Peter, filled with the Holy Spirit, said to them: "Rulers and elders of the people!
[9]If we are being called to account today for an act of kindness shown to a man who was
lame and are being asked how he was healed, [10]then know this, you and all the people of
Israel: It is by the name of Jesus Christ of Nazareth, whom you crucified but whom God
raised from the dead, that this man stands before you healed. [11]Jesus is

> " 'the stone you builders rejected,
> which has become the cornerstone.'[c]

[12]Salvation is found in no one else, for there is no other name given under heaven by which
we must be saved."

[13]When they saw the courage of Peter and John and realized that they were unschooled,
ordinary men, they were astonished and they took note that these men had been with
Jesus. [14]But since they could see the man who had been healed standing there with them,
there was nothing they could say. [15]So they ordered them to withdraw from the Sanhedrin
and then conferred together. [16]"What are we going to do with these men?" they asked. "Ev-
eryone living in Jerusalem knows they have performed a notable sign, and we cannot deny
it. [17]But to stop this thing from spreading any further among the people, we must warn
them to speak no longer to anyone in this name."

---

[a] *23* Deut. 18:15,18,19 [b] *25* Gen. 22:18; 26:4 [c] *11* Psalm 118:22

18 Then they called them in again and commanded them not to speak or teach at all in
the name of Jesus. 19 But Peter and John replied, "Which is right in God's eyes: to listen to
you, or to him? You be the judges! 20 As for us, we cannot help speaking about what we
have seen and heard."
21 After further threats they let them go. They could not decide how to punish them, be-
cause all the people were praising God for what had happened. 22 For the man who was mi-
raculously healed was over forty years old.

The Believers' Prayer

23 On their release, Peter and John went back to their own people and reported all that
the chief priests and the elders had said to them. 24 When they heard this, they raised their
voices together in prayer to God. "Sovereign Lord," they said, "you made the heaven and
the earth and the sea, and everything in them. 25 You spoke by the Holy Spirit through the
mouth of your servant, our father David:

> " 'Why do the nations rage
> and the peoples plot in vain?
> 26 The kings of the earth rise up
> and the rulers band together
> against the Lord
> and against his anointed one.'[a,b]

27 Indeed Herod and Pontius Pilate met together with the Gentiles and the people of Isra-
el in this city to conspire against your holy servant Jesus, whom you anointed. 28 They did
what your power and will had decided beforehand should happen. 29 Now, Lord, consider
their threats and enable your servants to speak your word with great boldness. 30 Stretch out
your hand to heal and perform signs and wonders through the name of your holy servant
Jesus."
31 After they prayed, the place where they were meeting was shaken. And they were all
filled with the Holy Spirit and spoke the word of God boldly.

The Believers Share Their Possessions

32 All the believers were one in heart and mind. No one claimed that any of their posses-
sions was their own, but they shared everything they had. 33 With great power the apostles
continued to testify to the resurrection of the Lord Jesus. And God's grace was so power-
fully at work in them all 34 that there were no needy persons among them. For from time
to time those who owned land or houses sold them, brought the money from the sales
35 and put it at the apostles' feet, and it was distributed to anyone who had need.

Reasons to Believe

4:12–13 // The Christian Experience. What transformed these "unschooled, ordinary men" into such bold, powerful speakers? They "had been with Jesus." According to Peter's words in verse 12, Jesus is the only way to salvation, and his name is the *only* one with power to transform ordinary people into sons and daughters of God.

Such thinking seems terribly narrow. Didn't Peter and John know that the world is full of "sincere" people who don't buy into Jesus' deity—who follow "other paths to God"? Were these men really that prejudiced against other religions, or were they just ignorant?

Actually, this dispute should be directed toward Jesus. These men were merely relaying what Jesus himself had clearly said on several occasions (for example, in John chapter 14, verse 6 [page 141]). It was a shocking claim, backed up by Jesus' life, death and resurrection. And his power in his disciples' lives confirmed this claim—even as it does today!

[a] 26 That is, Messiah or Christ [b] 26 Psalm 2:1,2

36 Joseph, a Levite from Cyprus, whom the apostles called Barnabas (which means "son of encouragement"), 37 sold a field he owned and brought the money and put it at the apostles' feet.

Ananias and Sapphira

5 Now a man named Ananias, together with his wife Sapphira, also sold a piece of property. 2 With his wife's full knowledge he kept back part of the money for himself, but brought the rest and put it at the apostles' feet.

3 Then Peter said, "Ananias, how is it that Satan has so filled your heart that you have lied to the Holy Spirit and have kept for yourself some of the money you received for the land? 4 Didn't it belong to you before it was sold? And after it was sold, wasn't the money at your disposal? What made you think of doing such a thing? You have not lied just to human beings but to God."

5 When Ananias heard this, he fell down and died. And great fear seized all who heard what had happened. 6 Then some young men came forward, wrapped up his body, and carried him out and buried him.

7 About three hours later his wife came in, not knowing what had happened. 8 Peter asked her, "Tell me, is this the price you and Ananias got for the land?"

"Yes," she said, "that is the price."

9 Peter said to her, "How could you conspire to test the Spirit of the Lord? Listen! The feet of those who buried your husband are at the door, and they will carry you out also."

10 At that moment she fell down at his feet and died. Then the young men came in and, finding her dead, carried her out and buried her beside her husband. 11 Great fear seized the whole church and all who heard about these events.

The Apostles Heal Many

12 The apostles performed many signs and wonders among the people. And all the believers used to meet together in Solomon's Colonnade. 13 No one else dared join them, even though they were highly regarded by the people. 14 Nevertheless, more and more men and women believed in the Lord and were added to their number. 15 As a result, people brought the sick into the streets and laid them on beds and mats so that at least Peter's shadow might fall on some of them as he passed by. 16 Crowds gathered also from the towns around Jerusalem, bringing their sick and those tormented by evil[a] spirits, and all of them were healed.

The Apostles Persecuted

17 Then the high priest and all his associates, who were members of the party of the Sadducees, were filled with jealousy. 18 They arrested the apostles and put them in the public jail. 19 But during the night an angel of the Lord opened the doors of the jail and brought them out. 20 "Go, stand in the temple courts," he said, "and tell the people all about this new life."

21 At daybreak they entered the temple courts, as they had been told, and began to teach the people.

When the high priest and his associates arrived, they called together the Sanhedrin—the full assembly of the elders of Israel—and sent to the jail for the apostles. 22 But on arriving at the jail, the officers did not find them there. So they went back and reported, 23 "We found the jail securely locked, with the guards standing at the doors; but when we opened them, we found no one inside." 24 On hearing this report, the captain of the temple guard and the chief priests were puzzled, wondering what this might lead to.

25 Then someone came and said, "Look! The men you put in jail are standing in the temple courts teaching the people." 26 At that, the captain went with his officers and brought the apostles. They did not use force, because they feared that the people would stone them.

27 The apostles were brought in and made to appear before the Sanhedrin to be questioned by the high priest. 28 "We gave you strict orders not to teach in this name," he said.

---

[a] 16 Greek *unclean*

"Yet you have filled Jerusalem with your teaching and are determined to make us guilty of
this man's blood."
[29]Peter and the other apostles replied: "We must obey God rather than human beings!
[30]The God of our ancestors raised Jesus from the dead—whom you killed by hanging him
on a cross. [31]God exalted him to his own right hand as Prince and Savior that he might
bring Israel to repentance and forgive their sins. [32]We are witnesses of these things, and so
is the Holy Spirit, whom God has given to those who obey him."
[33]When they heard this, they were furious and wanted to put them to death. [34]But a
Pharisee named Gamaliel, a teacher of the law, who was honored by all the people, stood
up in the Sanhedrin and ordered that the men be put outside for a little while. [35]Then he
addressed the Sanhedrin: "Men of Israel, consider carefully what you intend to do to these
men. [36]Some time ago Theudas appeared, claiming to be somebody, and about four hun-
dred men rallied to him. He was killed, all his followers were dispersed, and it all came to
nothing. [37]After him, Judas the Galilean appeared in the days of the census and led a band
of people in revolt. He too was killed, and all his followers were scattered. [38]Therefore, in
the present case I advise you: Leave these men alone! Let them go! For if their purpose or
activity is of human origin, it will fail. [39]But if it is from God, you will not be able to stop
these men; you will only find yourselves fighting against God."
[40]His speech persuaded them. They called the apostles in and had them flogged. Then
they ordered them not to speak in the name of Jesus, and let them go.
[41]The apostles left the Sanhedrin, rejoicing because they had been counted worthy of suf-
fering disgrace for the Name. [42]Day after day, in the temple courts and from house to house,
they never stopped teaching and proclaiming the good news that Jesus is the Messiah.

The Choosing of the Seven

6 In those days when the number of disciples was increasing, the Hellenistic Jews[a] among
them complained against the Hebraic Jews because their widows were being over-
looked in the daily distribution of food. [2]So the Twelve gathered all the disciples to-
gether and said, "It would not be right for us to neglect the ministry of the word of God in
order to wait on tables. [3]Brothers and sisters, choose seven men from among you who are
known to be full of the Spirit and wisdom. We will turn this responsibility over to them [4]and
will give our attention to prayer and the ministry of the word."
[5]This proposal pleased the whole group. They chose Stephen, a man full of faith and of
the Holy Spirit; also Philip, Procorus, Nicanor, Timon, Parmenas, and Nicolas from Antioch,

Reasons to Believe

5:41–42 // The Christian Experience. If the original purpose of Christianity had been to make life easier, Peter and the other apostles would probably have been checking the "fine print" for an escape clause! But they knew, after following Jesus and watching his example, that suffering is part of our human experience. They also knew that following Christ could at times make life more difficult.

So why did they go on? Because there is no one like Jesus and there is no adventure like following him. Jesus' followers take the bad with the good, much as a loving spouse stays faithful "for better or for worse."

The early Christians frequently faced severe persecution. This book and other early records abound with moving accounts of people who preferred to be punished or even killed rather than deny Jesus (see chapter 7, verses 54–60 [page 168], for a story of a man forgiving his murderers even as they stone him to death).

In our own day, when some people are embarrassed to even mention spiritual matters among peers, such stories of courage serve as powerful evidence that Christianity is true. Jesus' message has radically transformed lives for thousands of years. Those who have accepted his message and have lived in the hope that it provides find that it is worth much more than anything this world has to offer—even life itself.

[a] *1* That is, Jews who had adopted the Greek language and culture

a convert to Judaism. 6They presented them to the apostles, who prayed and laid their hands
on them.
7So the word of God spread. The number of disciples in Jerusalem increased rapidly,
and a large number of priests became obedient to the faith.

Stephen Seized

8Now Stephen, a man full of God's grace and power, performed great wonders and signs
among the people. 9Opposition arose, however, from members of the Synagogue of the
Freedmen (as it was called)—Jews of Cyrene and Alexandria as well as the provinces of
Cilicia and Asia—who began to argue with Stephen. 10But they could not stand up against
the wisdom the Spirit gave him as he spoke.
11Then they secretly persuaded some men to say, "We have heard Stephen speak blas-
phemous words against Moses and against God."
12So they stirred up the people and the elders and the teachers of the law. They seized
Stephen and brought him before the Sanhedrin. 13They produced false witnesses, who tes-
tified, "This fellow never stops speaking against this holy place and against the law. 14For
we have heard him say that this Jesus of Nazareth will destroy this place and change the
customs Moses handed down to us."
15All who were sitting in the Sanhedrin looked intently at Stephen, and they saw that
his face was like the face of an angel.

Stephen's Speech to the Sanhedrin

7 Then the high priest asked Stephen, "Are these charges true?"
2To this he replied: "Brothers and fathers, listen to me! The God of glory appeared to
our father Abraham while he was still in Mesopotamia, before he lived in Harran.
3'Leave your country and your people,' God said, 'and go to the land I will show you.'[a]
4"So he left the land of the Chaldeans and settled in Harran. After the death of his fa-
ther, God sent him to this land where you are now living. 5He gave him no inheritance
here, not even enough ground to set his foot on. But God promised him that he and his
descendants after him would possess the land, even though at that time Abraham had no
child. 6God spoke to him in this way: 'For four hundred years your descendants will be
strangers in a country not their own, and they will be enslaved and mistreated. 7But I will
punish the nation they serve as slaves,' God said, 'and afterward they will come out of that
country and worship me in this place.'[b] 8Then he gave Abraham the covenant of circum-
cision. And Abraham became the father of Isaac and circumcised him eight days after his
birth. Later Isaac became the father of Jacob, and Jacob became the father of the twelve
patriarchs.
9"Because the patriarchs were jealous of Joseph, they sold him as a slave into Egypt.
But God was with him 10and rescued him from all his troubles. He gave Joseph wisdom
and enabled him to gain the goodwill of Pharaoh king of Egypt. So Pharaoh made him rul-
er over Egypt and all his palace.
11"Then a famine struck all Egypt and Canaan, bringing great suffering, and our people
could not find food. 12When Jacob heard that there was grain in Egypt, he sent our ances-
tors on their first visit. 13On their second visit, Joseph told his brothers who he was, and
Pharaoh learned about Joseph's family. 14After this, Joseph sent for his father Jacob and his
whole family, seventy-five in all. 15Then Jacob went down to Egypt, where he and our an-
cestors died. 16Their bodies were brought back to Shechem and placed in the tomb that
Abraham had bought from the sons of Hamor at Shechem for a certain sum of money.
17"As the time drew near for God to fulfill his promise to Abraham, the number of our
people in Egypt had greatly increased. 18Then 'a new king, to whom Joseph meant nothing,
came to power in Egypt.'[c] 19He dealt treacherously with our people and oppressed our an-
cestors by forcing them to throw out their newborn babies so that they would die.
20"At that time Moses was born, and he was no ordinary child.[d] For three months he was
cared for in his parents' home. 21When he was placed outside, Pharaoh's daughter took

[a] *3* Gen. 12:1 [b] *7* Gen. 15:13,14 [c] *18* Exodus 1:8 [d] *20* Or *was fair in the sight of God*

him and brought him up as her own son. 22 Moses was educated in all the wisdom of the
Egyptians and was powerful in speech and action.
23 "When Moses was forty years old, he decided to visit his own people, the Israelites.
24 He saw one of them being mistreated by an Egyptian, so he went to his defense and
avenged him by killing the Egyptian. 25 Moses thought that his own people would realize
that God was using him to rescue them, but they did not. 26 The next day Moses came upon
two Israelites who were fighting. He tried to reconcile them by saying, 'Men, you are broth-
ers; why do you want to hurt each other?'
27 "But the man who was mistreating the other pushed Moses aside and said, 'Who made
you ruler and judge over us? 28 Are you thinking of killing me as you killed the Egyptian
yesterday?'[a] 29 When Moses heard this, he fled to Midian, where he settled as a foreigner
and had two sons.
30 "After forty years had passed, an angel appeared to Moses in the flames of a burning
bush in the desert near Mount Sinai. 31 When he saw this, he was amazed at the sight. As
he went over to get a closer look, he heard the Lord say: 32 'I am the God of your fathers, the
God of Abraham, Isaac and Jacob.'[b] Moses trembled with fear and did not dare to look.
33 "Then the Lord said to him, 'Take off your sandals, for the place where you are stand-
ing is holy ground. 34 I have indeed seen the oppression of my people in Egypt. I have heard
their groaning and have come down to set them free. Now come, I will send you back to
Egypt.'[c]
35 "This is the same Moses they had rejected with the words, 'Who made you ruler and
judge?' He was sent to be their ruler and deliverer by God himself, through the angel who
appeared to him in the bush. 36 He led them out of Egypt and performed wonders and signs
in Egypt, at the Red Sea and for forty years in the wilderness.
37 "This is the Moses who told the Israelites, 'God will send you a prophet like me from
your own people.'[d] 38 He was in the assembly in the wilderness, with the angel who spoke to
him on Mount Sinai, and with our ancestors; and he received living words to pass on to us.
39 "But our ancestors refused to obey him. Instead, they rejected him and in their hearts
turned back to Egypt. 40 They told Aaron, 'Make us gods who will go before us. As for this
fellow Moses who led us out of Egypt—we don't know what has happened to him!'[e] 41 That
was the time they made an idol in the form of a calf. They brought sacrifices to it and rev-
eled in what their own hands had made. 42 But God turned away from them and gave them
over to the worship of the sun, moon and stars. This agrees with what is written in the
book of the prophets:

> " 'Did you bring me sacrifices and offerings
> forty years in the wilderness, house of Israel?
> 43 You have taken up the tabernacle of Molek
> and the star of your god Rephan,
> the idols you made to worship.
> Therefore I will send you into exile'[f] beyond Babylon.

44 "Our ancestors had the tabernacle of the covenant law with them in the wilderness.
It had been made as God directed Moses, according to the pattern he had seen. 45 Having
received the tabernacle, our ancestors under Joshua brought it with them when they took
the land from the nations God drove out before them. It remained in the land until the
time of David, 46 who enjoyed God's favor and asked that he might provide a dwelling place
for the God of Jacob.[g] 47 But it was Solomon who built a house for him.
48 "However, the Most High does not live in houses made by human hands. As the proph-
et says:

> 49 " 'Heaven is my throne,
> and the earth is my footstool.
> What kind of house will you build for me?
> says the Lord.

---

[a] *28* Exodus 2:14 [b] *32* Exodus 3:6 [c] *34* Exodus 3:5,7,8,10 [d] *37* Deut. 18:15 [e] *40* Exodus 32:1
[f] *43* Amos 5:25-27 (see Septuagint) [g] *46* Some early manuscripts *the house of Jacob*

Or where will my resting place be?
50 Has not my hand made all these things?'[a]

51 "You stiff-necked people! Your hearts and ears are still uncircumcised. You are just like
your ancestors: You always resist the Holy Spirit! 52 Was there ever a prophet your ances-
tors did not persecute? They even killed those who predicted the coming of the Righteous
One. And now you have betrayed and murdered him— 53 you who have received the law
that was given through angels but have not obeyed it."

The Stoning of Stephen

54 When the members of the Sanhedrin heard this, they were furious and gnashed their
teeth at him. 55 But Stephen, full of the Holy Spirit, looked up to heaven and saw the glory
of God, and Jesus standing at the right hand of God. 56 "Look," he said, "I see heaven open
and the Son of Man standing at the right hand of God."
57 At this they covered their ears and, yelling at the top of their voices, they all rushed at
him, 58 dragged him out of the city and began to stone him. Meanwhile, the witnesses laid
their coats at the feet of a young man named Saul.
59 While they were stoning him, Stephen prayed, "Lord Jesus, receive my spirit." 60 Then
he fell on his knees and cried out, "Lord, do not hold this sin against them." When he had
said this, he fell asleep.
8 And Saul approved of their killing him.

The Church Persecuted and Scattered

On that day a great persecution broke out against the church in Jerusalem, and all ex-
cept the apostles were scattered throughout Judea and Samaria. 2 Godly men buried Ste-
phen and mourned deeply for him. 3 But Saul began to destroy the church. Going from
house to house, he dragged off both men and women and put them in prison.

Philip in Samaria

4 Those who had been scattered preached the word wherever they went. 5 Philip went
down to a city in Samaria and proclaimed the Messiah there. 6 When the crowds heard Phil-
ip and saw the signs he performed, they all paid close attention to what he said. 7 With
shrieks, evil[b] spirits came out of many, and many who were paralyzed or lame were healed.
8 So there was great joy in that city.

Simon the Sorcerer

9 Now for some time a man named Simon had practiced sorcery in the city and amazed
all the people of Samaria. He boasted that he was someone great, 10 and all the people, both
high and low, gave him their attention and exclaimed, "This man is rightly called the Great
Power of God." 11 They followed him because he had amazed them for a long time with his
sorcery. 12 But when they believed Philip as he proclaimed the good news of the kingdom
of God and the name of Jesus Christ, they were baptized, both men and women. 13 Simon
himself believed and was baptized. And he followed Philip everywhere, astonished by the
great signs and miracles he saw.
14 When the apostles in Jerusalem heard that Samaria had accepted the word of God,
they sent Peter and John to Samaria. 15 When they arrived, they prayed for the new believ-
ers there that they might receive the Holy Spirit, 16 because the Holy Spirit had not yet come
on any of them; they had simply been baptized into[c] the name of the Lord Jesus. 17 Then
Peter and John placed their hands on them, and they received the Holy Spirit.
18 When Simon saw that the Spirit was given at the laying on of the apostles' hands, he
offered them money 19 and said, "Give me also this ability so that everyone on whom I lay
my hands may receive the Holy Spirit."
20 Peter answered: "May your money perish with you, because you thought you could
buy the gift of God with money! 21 You have no part or share in this ministry, because your

---

[a] *50* Isaiah 66:1,2 [b] *7* Greek *unclean* [c] *16* Or *in*

heart is not right before God. [22]Repent of this wickedness and pray to the Lord in the hope
that he may forgive you for having such a thought in your heart. [23]For I see that you are full
of bitterness and captive to sin."
[24]Then Simon answered, "Pray to the Lord for me so that nothing you have said may
happen to me."
[25]After they had further proclaimed the word of the Lord and testified about Jesus, Pe-
ter and John returned to Jerusalem, preaching the gospel in many Samaritan villages.

Philip and the Ethiopian

[26]Now an angel of the Lord said to Philip, "Go south to the road—the desert road—that
goes down from Jerusalem to Gaza." [27]So he started out, and on his way he met an Ethio-
pian[a] eunuch, an important official in charge of all the treasury of the Kandake (which
means "queen of the Ethiopians"). This man had gone to Jerusalem to worship, [28]and on
his way home was sitting in his chariot reading the Book of Isaiah the prophet. [29]The Spir-
it told Philip, "Go to that chariot and stay near it."
[30]Then Philip ran up to the chariot and heard the man reading Isaiah the prophet. "Do
you understand what you are reading?" Philip asked.
[31]"How can I," he said, "unless someone explains it to me?" So he invited Philip to come
up and sit with him.
[32]This is the passage of Scripture the eunuch was reading:

> "He was led like a sheep to the slaughter,
> and as a lamb before its shearer is silent,
> so he did not open his mouth.
> [33]In his humiliation he was deprived of justice.
> Who can speak of his descendants?
> For his life was taken from the earth."[b]

[34]The eunuch asked Philip, "Tell me, please, who is the prophet talking about, himself
or someone else?" [35]Then Philip began with that very passage of Scripture and told him the
good news about Jesus.
[36][37]As they traveled along the road, they came to some water and the eunuch said,
"Look, here is water. What can stand in the way of my being baptized?"[c] [38]And he gave or-
ders to stop the chariot. Then both Philip and the eunuch went down into the water and
Philip baptized him. [39]When they came up out of the water, the Spirit of the Lord sudden-
ly took Philip away, and the eunuch did not see him again, but went on his way rejoicing.

Discovering God

8:18–19 // Spiritual Fraud. Counterfeit spiritual experience existed in the days of the early church even as it does in our own day. Attracted by its power and prestige, Simon had been involved in sorcery, impressing people with his use of what was, oddly enough, similar to "The Force" of *Star Wars* fame (see verse 10). To him, the Christian experience was just another way to gain power over people, so he actually asked to *buy* the ability to dispense the Holy Spirit.

Fundamental to all occult practices (astrology, divination, fortune-telling, channeling, Wicca, etc.) is the belief that one can manipulate the physical and spiritual environment by using the correct ritual, practice, knowledge or incantation. In contrast, Christianity says that we must *yield* our lives to be in a relationship with God. Christians don't control God, and certainly don't "use" him, but rather submit to and follow him.

Occult practices will never be compatible with Christianity, because they are fundamentally at odds with how God wants us to relate to him and our world. (See chapter 13, verses 6–12 [page 175] for another confrontation between the Christian message and the occult. Also see Deuteronomy chapter 18, verses 9–13 [page 93], for further warnings from God concerning these practices.)

---

[a] *27* That is, from the southern Nile region [b] *33* Isaiah 53:7,8 (see Septuagint) [c] *36* Some late manuscripts *baptized?" [37]Philip said, "If you believe with all your heart, you may." The eunuch answered, "I believe that Jesus Christ is the Son of God."*

40 Philip, however, appeared at Azotus and traveled about, preaching the gospel in all the
towns until he reached Caesarea.

Saul's Conversion

9 Meanwhile, Saul was still breathing out murderous threats against the Lord's disci-
ples. He went to the high priest 2 and asked him for letters to the synagogues in Da-
mascus, so that if he found any there who belonged to the Way, whether men or
women, he might take them as prisoners to Jerusalem. 3 As he neared Damascus on his
journey, suddenly a light from heaven flashed around him. 4 He fell to the ground and heard
a voice say to him, "Saul, Saul, why do you persecute me?"
5 "Who are you, Lord?" Saul asked.
"I am Jesus, whom you are persecuting," he replied. 6 "Now get up and go into the city,
and you will be told what you must do."
7 The men traveling with Saul stood there speechless; they heard the sound but did not
see anyone. 8 Saul got up from the ground, but when he opened his eyes he could see noth-
ing. So they led him by the hand into Damascus. 9 For three days he was blind, and did not
eat or drink anything.
10 In Damascus there was a disciple named Ananias. The Lord called to him in a vision,
"Ananias!"
"Yes, Lord," he answered.
11 The Lord told him, "Go to the house of Judas on Straight Street and ask for a man from
Tarsus named Saul, for he is praying. 12 In a vision he has seen a man named Ananias come
and place his hands on him to restore his sight."
13 "Lord," Ananias answered, "I have heard many reports about this man and all the harm
he has done to your people in Jerusalem. 14 And he has come here with authority from the
chief priests to arrest all who call on your name."
15 But the Lord said to Ananias, "Go! This man is my chosen instrument to proclaim my
name to the Gentiles and their kings and to the people of Israel. 16 I will show him how
much he must suffer for my name."
17 Then Ananias went to the house and entered it. Placing his hands on Saul, he said,
"Brother Saul, the Lord—Jesus, who appeared to you on the road as you were coming
here—has sent me so that you may see again and be filled with the Holy Spirit." 18 Imme-
diately, something like scales fell from Saul's eyes, and he could see again. He got up and
was baptized, 19 and after taking some food, he regained his strength.

Saul in Damascus and Jerusalem

Saul spent several days with the disciples in Damascus. 20 At once he began to preach
in the synagogues that Jesus is the Son of God. 21 All those who heard him were astonished
and asked, "Isn't he the man who raised havoc in Jerusalem among those who call on this
name? And hasn't he come here to take them as prisoners to the chief priests?" 22 Yet Saul
grew more and more powerful and baffled the Jews living in Damascus by proving that
Jesus is the Messiah.

Knowing Yourself

9:1–20 // A New Identity. After Saul's dramatic conversion, he spoke out about his new beliefs. As was the case throughout the book of Acts, the crux of his message concerned Jesus' true identity. The kernel of Saul's first message to the outside world was simple: *Jesus is the Son of God.*

As a seeker, note the significance of this transformation. Saul became a new person, and his encounter with Jesus was at the heart of that change. Saul had known about Jesus and was convinced that he existed. What was at issue—and what radically changed—was Saul's belief about who Jesus is.

A personal encounter with Jesus will also be at the heart of any change that occurs in your life. Merely knowing about Jesus won't save you. But when you look to him for salvation and make the same confession as Saul did, you will most certainly find eternal life (see John chapter 3, verse 18 [page 121]).

[23]After many days had gone by, there was a conspiracy among the Jews to kill him, [24]but Saul learned of their plan. Day and night they kept close watch on the city gates in order to kill him. [25]But his followers took him by night and lowered him in a basket through an opening in the wall.

[26]When he came to Jerusalem, he tried to join the disciples, but they were all afraid of him, not believing that he really was a disciple. [27]But Barnabas took him and brought him to the apostles. He told them how Saul on his journey had seen the Lord and that the Lord had spoken to him, and how in Damascus he had preached fearlessly in the name of Jesus. [28]So Saul stayed with them and moved about freely in Jerusalem, speaking boldly in the name of the Lord. [29]He talked and debated with the Hellenistic Jews,[a] but they tried to kill him. [30]When the believers learned of this, they took him down to Caesarea and sent him off to Tarsus.

[31]Then the church throughout Judea, Galilee and Samaria enjoyed a time of peace and was strengthened. Living in the fear of the Lord and encouraged by the Holy Spirit, it increased in numbers.

Aeneas and Dorcas

[32]As Peter traveled about the country, he went to visit the Lord's people who lived in Lydda. [33]There he found a man named Aeneas, who was paralyzed and had been bedridden for eight years. [34]"Aeneas," Peter said to him, "Jesus Christ heals you. Get up and roll up your mat." Immediately Aeneas got up. [35]All those who lived in Lydda and Sharon saw him and turned to the Lord.

[36]In Joppa there was a disciple named Tabitha (in Greek her name is Dorcas); she was always doing good and helping the poor. [37]About that time she became sick and died, and her body was washed and placed in an upstairs room. [38]Lydda was near Joppa; so when the disciples heard that Peter was in Lydda, they sent two men to him and urged him, "Please come at once!"

[39]Peter went with them, and when he arrived he was taken upstairs to the room. All the widows stood around him, crying and showing him the robes and other clothing that Dorcas had made while she was still with them.

[40]Peter sent them all out of the room; then he got down on his knees and prayed. Turning toward the dead woman, he said, "Tabitha, get up." She opened her eyes, and seeing Peter she sat up. [41]He took her by the hand and helped her to her feet. Then he called for the believers, especially the widows, and presented her to them alive. [42]This became known all over Joppa, and many people believed in the Lord. [43]Peter stayed in Joppa for some time with a tanner named Simon.

Cornelius Calls for Peter

10 At Caesarea there was a man named Cornelius, a centurion in what was known as the Italian Regiment. [2]He and all his family were devout and God-fearing; he gave generously to those in need and prayed to God regularly. [3]One day at about three in the afternoon he had a vision. He distinctly saw an angel of God, who came to him and said, "Cornelius!"

[4]Cornelius stared at him in fear. "What is it, Lord?" he asked.

The angel answered, "Your prayers and gifts to the poor have come up as a memorial offering before God. [5]Now send men to Joppa to bring back a man named Simon who is called Peter. [6]He is staying with Simon the tanner, whose house is by the sea."

[7]When the angel who spoke to him had gone, Cornelius called two of his servants and a devout soldier who was one of his attendants. [8]He told them everything that had happened and sent them to Joppa.

Peter's Vision

[9]About noon the following day as they were on their journey and approaching the city, Peter went up on the roof to pray. [10]He became hungry and wanted something to eat, and

---

[a] 29 That is, Jews who had adopted the Greek language and culture

while the meal was being prepared, he fell into a trance. [11]He saw heaven opened and something like a large sheet being let down to earth by its four corners. [12]It contained all kinds of four-footed animals, as well as reptiles and birds. [13]Then a voice told him, "Get up, Peter. Kill and eat."

[14]"Surely not, Lord!" Peter replied. "I have never eaten anything impure or unclean."

[15]The voice spoke to him a second time, "Do not call anything impure that God has made clean."

[16]This happened three times, and immediately the sheet was taken back to heaven.

[17]While Peter was wondering about the meaning of the vision, the men sent by Cornelius found out where Simon's house was and stopped at the gate. [18]They called out, asking if Simon who was known as Peter was staying there.

[19]While Peter was still thinking about the vision, the Spirit said to him, "Simon, three[a] men are looking for you. [20]So get up and go downstairs. Do not hesitate to go with them, for I have sent them."

[21]Peter went down and said to the men, "I'm the one you're looking for. Why have you come?"

[22]The men replied, "We have come from Cornelius the centurion. He is a righteous and God-fearing man, who is respected by all the Jewish people. A holy angel told him to ask you to come to his house so that he could hear what you have to say." [23]Then Peter invited the men into the house to be his guests.

Peter at Cornelius's House

The next day Peter started out with them, and some of the believers from Joppa went along. [24]The following day he arrived in Caesarea. Cornelius was expecting them and had called together his relatives and close friends. [25]As Peter entered the house, Cornelius met him and fell at his feet in reverence. [26]But Peter made him get up. "Stand up," he said, "I am only human myself."

[27]While talking with him, Peter went inside and found a large gathering of people. [28]He said to them: "You are well aware that it is against our law for a Jew to associate with Gentiles or visit them. But God has shown me that I should not call anyone impure or unclean. [29]So when I was sent for, I came without raising any objection. May I ask why you sent for me?"

[30]Cornelius answered: "Three days ago I was in my house praying at this hour, at three in the afternoon. Suddenly a man in shining clothes stood before me [31]and said, 'Cornelius, God has heard your prayer and remembered your gifts to the poor. [32]Send to Joppa for Simon who is called Peter. He is a guest in the home of Simon the tanner, who lives by the sea.' [33]So I sent for you immediately, and it was good of you to come. Now we are all here in the presence of God to listen to everything the Lord has commanded you to tell us."

[34]Then Peter began to speak: "I now realize how true it is that God does not show favoritism [35]but accepts those from every nation who fear him and do what is right. [36]You know the message God sent to the people of Israel, announcing the good news of peace through Jesus Christ, who is Lord of all. [37]You know what has happened throughout the province of Judea, beginning in Galilee after the baptism that John preached— [38]how God anointed Jesus of Nazareth with the Holy Spirit and power, and how he went around doing good and healing all who were under the power of the devil, because God was with him.

[39]"We are witnesses of everything he did in the country of the Jews and in Jerusalem. They killed him by hanging him on a cross, [40]but God raised him from the dead on the

Discovering God

10:1–48 // The God Who Is There. The story of how this Roman seeker, Cornelius, found what he was looking for is a dramatic example of the lengths God will go to reach those who are open to him.

God may not send an angel to you, but rest assured that if you seek God, you will find him—as this story so aptly demonstrates.

[a] 19 One early manuscript *two*; other manuscripts do not have the number.

third day and caused him to be seen. 41He was not seen by all the people, but by witnesses whom God had already chosen—by us who ate and drank with him after he rose from the dead. 42He commanded us to preach to the people and to testify that he is the one whom God appointed as judge of the living and the dead. 43All the prophets testify about him that everyone who believes in him receives forgiveness of sins through his name."

44While Peter was still speaking these words, the Holy Spirit came on all who heard the message. 45The circumcised believers who had come with Peter were astonished that the gift of the Holy Spirit had been poured out even on Gentiles. 46For they heard them speaking in tongues[a] and praising God.

Then Peter said, 47"Surely no one can stand in the way of their being baptized with water. They have received the Holy Spirit just as we have." 48So he ordered that they be baptized in the name of Jesus Christ. Then they asked Peter to stay with them for a few days.

Peter Explains His Actions

11 The apostles and the believers throughout Judea heard that the Gentiles also had received the word of God. 2So when Peter went up to Jerusalem, the circumcised believers criticized him 3and said, "You went into the house of the uncircumcised and ate with them."

4Starting from the beginning, Peter told them the whole story: 5"I was in the city of Joppa praying, and in a trance I saw a vision. I saw something like a large sheet being let down from heaven by its four corners, and it came down to where I was. 6I looked into it and saw four-footed animals of the earth, wild beasts, reptiles and birds. 7Then I heard a voice telling me, 'Get up, Peter. Kill and eat.'

8"I replied, 'Surely not, Lord! Nothing impure or unclean has ever entered my mouth.'

9"The voice spoke from heaven a second time, 'Do not call anything impure that God has made clean.' 10This happened three times, and then it was all pulled up to heaven again.

11"Right then three men who had been sent to me from Caesarea stopped at the house where I was staying. 12The Spirit told me to have no hesitation about going with them. These six brothers also went with me, and we entered the man's house. 13He told us how he had seen an angel appear in his house and say, 'Send to Joppa for Simon who is called Peter. 14He will bring you a message through which you and all your household will be saved.'

15"As I began to speak, the Holy Spirit came on them as he had come on us at the beginning. 16Then I remembered what the Lord had said: 'John baptized with[b] water, but you will be baptized with[b] the Holy Spirit.' 17So if God gave them the same gift he gave us who believed in the Lord Jesus Christ, who was I to think that I could stand in God's way?"

18When they heard this, they had no further objections and praised God, saying, "So then, even to Gentiles God has granted repentance that leads to life."

The Church in Antioch

19Now those who had been scattered by the persecution that broke out when Stephen was killed traveled as far as Phoenicia, Cyprus and Antioch, spreading the word only among

Discovering God

11:18 // Life with God. The first Christians were almost all Jews who believed that Jesus was their Messiah. But God's plan has always been to include *all* nations in his family (see Genesis chapter 12, verse 3 [page 18]). This verse demonstrates how the members of the early church accepted, even celebrated, that God's message is for all people.

Throughout the book of Acts there is a gradual shift from Christianity as a subset of Judaism to a faith that increasingly draws in people from non-Jewish backgrounds. Twenty centuries later, Jesus is still the promised Messiah to the Jews. But he is much more than that—he is truly the Savior of the *world*.

---

[a] 46 Or *other languages*   [b] 16 Or *in*

Jews. [20]Some of them, however, men from Cyprus and Cyrene, went to Antioch and began to speak to Greeks also, telling them the good news about the Lord Jesus. [21]The Lord's hand was with them, and a great number of people believed and turned to the Lord.

[22]News of this reached the ears of the church in Jerusalem, and they sent Barnabas to Antioch. [23]When he arrived and saw what the grace of God had done, he was glad and encouraged them all to remain true to the Lord with all their hearts. [24]He was a good man, full of the Holy Spirit and faith, and a great number of people were brought to the Lord.

[25]Then Barnabas went to Tarsus to look for Saul, [26]and when he found him, he brought him to Antioch. So for a whole year Barnabas and Saul met with the church and taught great numbers of people. The disciples were called Christians first at Antioch.

[27]During this time some prophets came down from Jerusalem to Antioch. [28]One of them, named Agabus, stood up and through the Spirit predicted that a severe famine would spread over the entire Roman world. (This happened during the reign of Claudius.) [29]The disciples, as each one was able, decided to provide help for the believers living in Judea. [30]This they did, sending their gift to the elders by Barnabas and Saul.

Peter's Miraculous Escape From Prison

12 It was about this time that King Herod arrested some who belonged to the church, intending to persecute them. [2]He had James, the brother of John, put to death with the sword. [3]When he saw that this met with approval among the Jews, he proceeded to seize Peter also. This happened during the Festival of Unleavened Bread. [4]After arresting him, he put him in prison, handing him over to be guarded by four squads of four soldiers each. Herod intended to bring him out for public trial after the Passover.

[5]So Peter was kept in prison, but the church was earnestly praying to God for him.

[6]The night before Herod was to bring him to trial, Peter was sleeping between two soldiers, bound with two chains, and sentries stood guard at the entrance. [7]Suddenly an angel of the Lord appeared and a light shone in the cell. He struck Peter on the side and woke him up. "Quick, get up!" he said, and the chains fell off Peter's wrists.

[8]Then the angel said to him, "Put on your clothes and sandals." And Peter did so. "Wrap your cloak around you and follow me," the angel told him. [9]Peter followed him out of the prison, but he had no idea that what the angel was doing was really happening; he thought he was seeing a vision. [10]They passed the first and second guards and came to the iron gate leading to the city. It opened for them by itself, and they went through it. When they had walked the length of one street, suddenly the angel left him.

[11]Then Peter came to himself and said, "Now I know without a doubt that the Lord has sent his angel and rescued me from Herod's clutches and from everything the Jewish people were hoping would happen."

[12]When this had dawned on him, he went to the house of Mary the mother of John, also called Mark, where many people had gathered and were praying. [13]Peter knocked at the outer entrance, and a servant named Rhoda came to answer the door. [14]When she recognized Peter's voice, she was so overjoyed she ran back without opening it and exclaimed, "Peter is at the door!"

[15]"You're out of your mind," they told her. When she kept insisting that it was so, they said, "It must be his angel."

[16]But Peter kept on knocking, and when they opened the door and saw him, they were astonished. [17]Peter motioned with his hand for them to be quiet and described how the Lord had brought him out of prison. "Tell James and the other brothers and sisters about this," he said, and then he left for another place.

[18]In the morning, there was no small commotion among the soldiers as to what had become of Peter. [19]After Herod had a thorough search made for him and did not find him, he cross-examined the guards and ordered that they be executed.

Herod's Death

Then Herod went from Judea to Caesarea and stayed there. [20]He had been quarreling with the people of Tyre and Sidon; they now joined together and sought an audience with him. Having secured the support of Blastus, a trusted personal servant of the king, they asked for peace, because they depended on the king's country for their food supply.

21On the appointed day Herod, wearing his royal robes, sat on his throne and delivered
a public address to the people. 22They shouted, "This is the voice of a god, not of a mere
mortal." 23Immediately, because Herod did not give praise to God, an angel of the Lord
struck him down, and he was eaten by worms and died.
24But the word of God continued to increase and spread.

Barnabas and Saul Sent Off

25When Barnabas and Saul had finished their mission, they returned from [a] Jerusalem,
13 taking with them John, also called Mark. 1Now in the church at Antioch
there were prophets and teachers: Barnabas, Simeon called Niger, Lucius
of Cyrene, Manaen (who had been brought up with Herod the tetrarch) and
Saul. 2While they were worshiping the Lord and fasting, the Holy Spirit said, "Set apart
for me Barnabas and Saul for the work to which I have called them." 3So after they had
fasted and prayed, they placed their hands on them and sent them off.

On Cyprus

4The two of them, sent on their way by the Holy Spirit, went down to Seleucia and sailed
from there to Cyprus. 5When they arrived at Salamis, they proclaimed the word of God in
the Jewish synagogues. John was with them as their helper.
6They traveled through the whole island until they came to Paphos. There they met a Jew-
ish sorcerer and false prophet named Bar-Jesus, 7who was an attendant of the proconsul, Ser-
gius Paulus. The proconsul, an intelligent man, sent for Barnabas and Saul because he wanted
to hear the word of God. 8But Elymas the sorcerer (for that is what his name means) opposed
them and tried to turn the proconsul from the faith. 9Then Saul, who was also called Paul,
filled with the Holy Spirit, looked straight at Elymas and said, 10"You are a child of the devil
and an enemy of everything that is right! You are full of all kinds of deceit and trickery. Will
you never stop perverting the right ways of the Lord? 11Now the hand of the Lord is against
you. You are going to be blind for a time, not even able to see the light of the sun."
Immediately mist and darkness came over him, and he groped about, seeking someone
to lead him by the hand. 12When the proconsul saw what had happened, he believed, for
he was amazed at the teaching about the Lord.

In Pisidian Antioch

13From Paphos, Paul and his companions sailed to Perga in Pamphylia, where John left
them to return to Jerusalem. 14From Perga they went on to Pisidian Antioch. On the Sab-
bath they entered the synagogue and sat down. 15After the reading from the Law and the
Prophets, the leaders of the synagogue sent word to them, saying, "Brothers, if you have a
word of exhortation for the people, please speak."
16Standing up, Paul motioned with his hand and said: "People of Israel and you Gentiles
who worship God, listen to me! 17The God of the people of Israel chose our ancestors; he
made the people prosper during their stay in Egypt; with mighty power he led them out of
that country; 18for about forty years he endured their conduct [b] in the wilderness; 19and he
overthrew seven nations in Canaan, giving their land to his people as their inheritance.
20All this took about 450 years.
"After this, God gave them judges until the time of Samuel the prophet. 21Then the peo-
ple asked for a king, and he gave them Saul son of Kish, of the tribe of Benjamin, who ruled
forty years. 22After removing Saul, he made David their king. God testified concerning him:
'I have found David son of Jesse, a man after my own heart; he will do everything I want
him to do.'
23"From this man's descendants God has brought to Israel the Savior Jesus, as he prom-
ised. 24Before the coming of Jesus, John preached repentance and baptism to all the peo-
ple of Israel. 25As John was completing his work, he said: 'Who do you suppose I am? I am
not the one you are looking for. But there is someone coming after me whose sandals I am
not worthy to untie.'

---

[a] *25* Some manuscripts *to* [b] *18* Some manuscripts *he cared for them*

26“Brothers and sisters from the children of Abraham and you God-fearing Gentiles, it
is to us that this message of salvation has been sent. 27The people of Jerusalem and their
rulers did not recognize Jesus, yet in condemning him they fulfilled the words of the proph-
ets that are read every Sabbath. 28Though they found no proper ground for a death sen-
tence, they asked Pilate to have him executed. 29When they had carried out all that was
written about him, they took him down from the cross and laid him in a tomb. 30But God
raised him from the dead, 31and for many days he was seen by those who had traveled with
him from Galilee to Jerusalem. They are now his witnesses to our people.
32“We tell you the good news: What God promised our ancestors 33he has fulfilled for us,
their children, by raising up Jesus. As it is written in the second Psalm:

> “ ‘You are my son;
> today I have become your father.’[a]

34God raised him from the dead so that he will never be subject to decay. As God has said,

> “ ‘I will give you the holy and sure blessings promised to David.’[b]

35So it is also stated elsewhere:

> “ ‘You will not let your holy one see decay.’[c]

36“Now when David had served God’s purpose in his own generation, he fell asleep; he
was buried with his ancestors and his body decayed. 37But the one whom God raised from
the dead did not see decay.
38“Therefore, my brothers and sisters, I want you to know that through Jesus the for-
giveness of sins is proclaimed to you. 39Through him everyone who believes is set free from
every sin, a justification you were not able to obtain under the law of Moses. 40Take care
that what the prophets have said does not happen to you:

> 41“ ‘Look, you scoffers,
> wonder and perish,
> for I am going to do something in your days
> that you would never believe,
> even if someone told you.’[d]”

42As Paul and Barnabas were leaving the synagogue, the people invited them to speak
further about these things on the next Sabbath. 43When the congregation was dismissed,
many of the Jews and devout converts to Judaism followed Paul and Barnabas, who talked
with them and urged them to continue in the grace of God.
44On the next Sabbath almost the whole city gathered to hear the word of the Lord.
45When the Jews saw the crowds, they were filled with jealousy. They began to contradict
what Paul was saying and heaped abuse on him.

Reasons to Believe

13:38–41 // The Incomparable Jesus. Notice how Paul sums up his message: Jesus is the source of God’s forgiveness. Jesus can give us what no amount of religious rule-keeping can—forgiveness and relief from sin.

As a seeker, you may be looking for a way to salve your troubled conscience. You may regret past actions that have hurt other people. You may have even adopted religious rules and regulations to try to change your behavior. But real change begins when you accept God’s forgiveness first.

God’s plan is hard to accept because it goes against our human inclination to try to earn our way back to God. But here’s the good news: Jesus has come and is prepared to give you what you can’t gain for yourself. If you are ready to respond, why not ask Jesus, even right now, to be your forgiver and leader? And when you do, tell someone about your decision and do what Paul advised in verse 43: “Continue in the grace of God” for the rest of your life. It’s a decision you’ll never regret!

[a] *33* Psalm 2:7 [b] *34* Isaiah 55:3 [c] *35* Psalm 16:10 (see Septuagint) [d] *41* Hab. 1:5

46 Then Paul and Barnabas answered them boldly: "We had to speak the word of God to
you first. Since you reject it and do not consider yourselves worthy of eternal life, we now
turn to the Gentiles. 47 For this is what the Lord has commanded us:

> " 'I have made you[a] a light for the Gentiles,
> that you[a] may bring salvation to the ends of the earth.'[b]"

48 When the Gentiles heard this, they were glad and honored the word of the Lord; and
all who were appointed for eternal life believed.
49 The word of the Lord spread through the whole region. 50 But the Jewish leaders incit-
ed the God-fearing women of high standing and the leading men of the city. They stirred
up persecution against Paul and Barnabas, and expelled them from their region. 51 So they
shook the dust off their feet as a warning to them and went to Iconium. 52 And the disciples
were filled with joy and with the Holy Spirit.

In Iconium

14 At Iconium Paul and Barnabas went as usual into the Jewish synagogue. There
they spoke so effectively that a great number of Jews and Greeks believed. 2 But
the Jews who refused to believe stirred up the other Gentiles and poisoned their
minds against the brothers. 3 So Paul and Barnabas spent considerable time there, speak-
ing boldly for the Lord, who confirmed the message of his grace by enabling them to per-
form signs and wonders. 4 The people of the city were divided; some sided with the Jews,
others with the apostles. 5 There was a plot afoot among both Gentiles and Jews, together
with their leaders, to mistreat them and stone them. 6 But they found out about it and fled
to the Lycaonian cities of Lystra and Derbe and to the surrounding country, 7 where they
continued to preach the gospel.

In Lystra and Derbe

8 In Lystra there sat a man who was lame. He had been that way from birth and had nev-
er walked. 9 He listened to Paul as he was speaking. Paul looked directly at him, saw that
he had faith to be healed 10 and called out, "Stand up on your feet!" At that, the man jumped
up and began to walk.
11 When the crowd saw what Paul had done, they shouted in the Lycaonian language,
"The gods have come down to us in human form!" 12 Barnabas they called Zeus, and Paul
they called Hermes because he was the chief speaker. 13 The priest of Zeus, whose temple
was just outside the city, brought bulls and wreaths to the city gates because he and the
crowd wanted to offer sacrifices to them.
14 But when the apostles Barnabas and Paul heard of this, they tore their clothes and
rushed out into the crowd, shouting: 15 "Friends, why are you doing this? We too are only
human, like you. We are bringing you good news, telling you to turn from these worthless
things to the living God, who made heaven and earth and sea and everything in them. 16 In

Discovering God

14:15 // Spiritual Fraud. People are incurably religious. The problem is, they tend to worship the wrong things. Here the crowd, after witnessing a healing miracle, wanted to worship Paul and Barnabas instead of God. These two missionaries sternly rebuked the crowd for their misdirected praise. True believers direct glory and attention to God, not themselves.

It's not enough to be "religious." Paul said that we must turn from "worthless things" (here Zeus; in our own day—well, you fill in the blank!) and instead put our trust in the living God who made everything. Christianity is incompatible with other religions—it claims that we must leave them behind as a false hope and instead put all our faith in Christ.

Christianity is also incompatible with a lifestyle that makes anything more important than God. Someone once lamented, "We worship our work, work at our play, and play at our worship." Only through embracing true Christianity can we rearrange our scrambled priorities!

---

[a] *47* The Greek is singular. [b] *47* Isaiah 49:6

the past, he let all nations go their own way. 17Yet he has not left himself without testimo-
ny: He has shown kindness by giving you rain from heaven and crops in their seasons; he
provides you with plenty of food and fills your hearts with joy." 18Even with these words,
they had difficulty keeping the crowd from sacrificing to them.
19Then some Jews came from Antioch and Iconium and won the crowd over. They stoned
Paul and dragged him outside the city, thinking he was dead. 20But after the disciples had
gathered around him, he got up and went back into the city. The next day he and Barna-
bas left for Derbe.

The Return to Antioch in Syria

21They preached the gospel in that city and won a large number of disciples. Then they
returned to Lystra, Iconium and Antioch, 22strengthening the disciples and encouraging
them to remain true to the faith. "We must go through many hardships to enter the king-
dom of God," they said. 23Paul and Barnabas appointed elders[a] for them in each church
and, with prayer and fasting, committed them to the Lord, in whom they had put their
trust. 24After going through Pisidia, they came into Pamphylia, 25and when they had
preached the word in Perga, they went down to Attalia.
26From Attalia they sailed back to Antioch, where they had been committed to the grace
of God for the work they had now completed. 27On arriving there, they gathered the church
together and reported all that God had done through them and how he had opened a door
of faith to the Gentiles. 28And they stayed there a long time with the disciples.

The Council at Jerusalem

15
Certain individuals came down from Judea to Antioch and were teaching the be-
lievers: "Unless you are circumcised, according to the custom taught by Moses,
you cannot be saved." 2This brought Paul and Barnabas into sharp dispute and
debate with them. So Paul and Barnabas were appointed, along with some other believers,
to go up to Jerusalem to see the apostles and elders about this question. 3The church sent
them on their way, and as they traveled through Phoenicia and Samaria, they told how the
Gentiles had been converted. This news made all the believers very glad. 4When they came
to Jerusalem, they were welcomed by the church and the apostles and elders, to whom
they reported everything God had done through them.
5Then some of the believers who belonged to the party of the Pharisees stood up and
said, "The Gentiles must be circumcised and required to keep the law of Moses."
6The apostles and elders met to consider this question. 7After much discussion, Peter got
up and addressed them: "Brothers, you know that some time ago God made a choice
among you that the Gentiles might hear from my lips the message of the gospel and be-
lieve. 8God, who knows the heart, showed that he accepted them by giving the Holy Spir-
it to them, just as he did to us. 9He did not discriminate between us and them, for he
purified their hearts by faith. 10Now then, why do you try to test God by putting on the
necks of Gentiles a yoke that neither we nor our ancestors have been able to bear? 11No!
We believe it is through the grace of our Lord Jesus that we are saved, just as they are."
12The whole assembly became silent as they listened to Barnabas and Paul telling about
the signs and wonders God had done among the Gentiles through them. 13When they fin-
ished, James spoke up. "Brothers," he said, "listen to me. 14Simon[b] has described to us how
God first intervened to choose a people for his name from the Gentiles. 15The words of the
prophets are in agreement with this, as it is written:

16" 'After this I will return
  and rebuild David's fallen tent.
Its ruins I will rebuild,
  and I will restore it,
17that the rest of humanity may seek the Lord,
  even all the Gentiles who bear my name,

---

[a] 23 Or *Barnabas ordained elders*; or *Barnabas had elders elected*
[b] 14 Greek *Simeon*, a variant of *Simon*; that is, Peter

says the Lord, who does these things’[a]—
18 things known from long ago.[b]

19“It is my judgment, therefore, that we should not make it difficult for the Gentiles who
are turning to God. 20Instead we should write to them, telling them to abstain from food
polluted by idols, from sexual immorality, from the meat of strangled animals and from
blood. 21For the law of Moses has been preached in every city from the earliest times and
is read in the synagogues on every Sabbath.”

The Council’s Letter to Gentile Believers

22Then the apostles and elders, with the whole church, decided to choose some of their
own men and send them to Antioch with Paul and Barnabas. They chose Judas (called Bar-
sabbas) and Silas, who were leaders among the believers. 23With them they sent the fol-
lowing letter:

The apostles and elders, your brothers,

To the Gentile believers in Antioch, Syria and Cilicia:

Greetings.

24We have heard that some went out from us without our authorization and dis-
turbed you, troubling your minds by what they said. 25So we all agreed to choose some
men and send them to you with our dear friends Barnabas and Paul— 26men who
have risked their lives for the name of our Lord Jesus Christ. 27Therefore we are send-
ing Judas and Silas to confirm by word of mouth what we are writing. 28It seemed
good to the Holy Spirit and to us not to burden you with anything beyond the follow-
ing requirements: 29You are to abstain from food sacrificed to idols, from blood, from
the meat of strangled animals and from sexual immorality. You will do well to avoid
these things.

Farewell.

30So they were sent off and went down to Antioch, where they gathered the church to-
gether and delivered the letter. 31The people read it and were glad for its encouraging mes-
sage. 32Judas and Silas, who themselves were prophets, said much to encourage and
strengthen the believers. 33[34]After spending some time there, they were sent off by the
believers with the blessing of peace to return to those who had sent them. 35But Paul and
Barnabas remained in Antioch, where they and many others taught and preached the word
of the Lord.

Disagreement Between Paul and Barnabas

36Some time later Paul said to Barnabas, “Let us go back and visit the believers in all
the towns where we preached the word of the Lord and see how they are doing.” 37Barna-
bas wanted to take John, also called Mark, with them, 38but Paul did not think it wise to take
him, because he had deserted them in Pamphylia and had not continued with them in the
work. 39They had such a sharp disagreement that they parted company. Barnabas took
Mark and sailed for Cyprus, 40but Paul chose Silas and left, commended by the believers
to the grace of the Lord. 41He went through Syria and Cilicia, strengthening the churches.

Timothy Joins Paul and Silas

16 Paul came to Derbe and then to Lystra, where a disciple named Timothy lived,
whose mother was Jewish and a believer but whose father was a Greek. 2The
believers at Lystra and Iconium spoke well of him. 3Paul wanted to take him
along on the journey, so he circumcised him because of the Jews who lived in that area,
for they all knew that his father was a Greek. 4As they traveled from town to town, they

---

[a] 17 Amos 9:11,12 (see Septuagint) [b] 17,18 Some manuscripts *things’— / 18the Lord’s work is known to him from long ago*

delivered the decisions reached by the apostles and elders in Jerusalem for the people to
obey. 5So the churches were strengthened in the faith and grew daily in numbers.

Paul's Vision of the Man of Macedonia

6Paul and his companions traveled throughout the region of Phrygia and Galatia, hav-
ing been kept by the Holy Spirit from preaching the word in the province of Asia. 7When
they came to the border of Mysia, they tried to enter Bithynia, but the Spirit of Jesus would
not allow them to. 8So they passed by Mysia and went down to Troas. 9During the night Paul
had a vision of a man of Macedonia standing and begging him, "Come over to Macedonia
and help us." 10After Paul had seen the vision, we got ready at once to leave for Macedo-
nia, concluding that God had called us to preach the gospel to them.

Lydia's Conversion in Philippi

11From Troas we put out to sea and sailed straight for Samothrace, and the next day we
went on to Neapolis. 12From there we traveled to Philippi, a Roman colony and the leading
city of that district[a] of Macedonia. And we stayed there several days.

13On the Sabbath we went outside the city gate to the river, where we expected to find
a place of prayer. We sat down and began to speak to the women who had gathered there.
14One of those listening was a woman from the city of Thyatira named Lydia, a dealer in
purple cloth. She was a worshiper of God. The Lord opened her heart to respond to Paul's
message. 15When she and the members of her household were baptized, she invited us to
her home. "If you consider me a believer in the Lord," she said, "come and stay at my
house." And she persuaded us.

Paul and Silas in Prison

16Once when we were going to the place of prayer, we were met by a female slave who
had a spirit by which she predicted the future. She earned a great deal of money for her
owners by fortune-telling. 17She followed Paul and the rest of us, shouting, "These men are
servants of the Most High God, who are telling you the way to be saved." 18She kept this
up for many days. Finally Paul became so annoyed that he turned around and said to the
spirit, "In the name of Jesus Christ I command you to come out of her!" At that moment
the spirit left her.

19When her owners realized that their hope of making money was gone, they seized Paul
and Silas and dragged them into the marketplace to face the authorities. 20They brought
them before the magistrates and said, "These men are Jews, and are throwing our city into
an uproar 21by advocating customs unlawful for us Romans to accept or practice."

22The crowd joined in the attack against Paul and Silas, and the magistrates ordered
them to be stripped and beaten with rods. 23After they had been severely flogged, they were
thrown into prison, and the jailer was commanded to guard them carefully. 24When he re-
ceived these orders, he put them in the inner cell and fastened their feet in the stocks.

25About midnight Paul and Silas were praying and singing hymns to God, and the oth-
er prisoners were listening to them. 26Suddenly there was such a violent earthquake that
the foundations of the prison were shaken. At once all the prison doors flew open, and ev-
eryone's chains came loose. 27The jailer woke up, and when he saw the prison doors open,
he drew his sword and was about to kill himself because he thought the prisoners had es-
caped. 28But Paul shouted, "Don't harm yourself! We are all here!"

29The jailer called for lights, rushed in and fell trembling before Paul and Silas. 30He
then brought them out and asked, "Sirs, what must I do to be saved?"

31They replied, "Believe in the Lord Jesus, and you will be saved—you and your house-
hold." 32Then they spoke the word of the Lord to him and to all the others in his house.
33At that hour of the night the jailer took them and washed their wounds; then immediate-
ly he and all his household were baptized. 34The jailer brought them into his house and set
a meal before them; he was filled with joy because he had come to believe in God—he and
his whole household.

---

[a] *12* The text and meaning of the Greek for *the leading city of that district* are uncertain.

35When it was daylight, the magistrates sent their officers to the jailer with the order:
"Release those men." 36The jailer told Paul, "The magistrates have ordered that you and Si-
las be released. Now you can leave. Go in peace."
37But Paul said to the officers: "They beat us publicly without a trial, even though we are
Roman citizens, and threw us into prison. And now do they want to get rid of us quietly?
No! Let them come themselves and escort us out."
38The officers reported this to the magistrates, and when they heard that Paul and Silas
were Roman citizens, they were alarmed. 39They came to appease them and escorted them
from the prison, requesting them to leave the city. 40After Paul and Silas came out of the
prison, they went to Lydia's house, where they met with the believers and encouraged
them. Then they left.

In Thessalonica

17 When Paul and his companions had passed through Amphipolis and Apollonia,
they came to Thessalonica, where there was a Jewish synagogue. 2As was his cus-
tom, Paul went into the synagogue, and on three Sabbath days he reasoned with
them from the Scriptures, 3explaining and proving that the Messiah had to suffer and rise
from the dead. "This Jesus I am proclaiming to you is the Messiah," he said. 4Some of the
Jews were persuaded and joined Paul and Silas, as did a large number of God-fearing Greeks
and not a few prominent women.
5But other Jews were jealous; so they rounded up some bad characters from the market-
place, formed a mob and started a riot in the city. They rushed to Jason's house in search
of Paul and Silas in order to bring them out to the crowd.[a] 6But when they did not find
them, they dragged Jason and some other believers before the city officials, shouting:
"These men who have caused trouble all over the world have now come here, 7and Jason
has welcomed them into his house. They are all defying Caesar's decrees, saying that there
is another king, one called Jesus." 8When they heard this, the crowd and the city officials
were thrown into turmoil. 9Then they made Jason and the others post bond and let them go.

In Berea

10As soon as it was night, the believers sent Paul and Silas away to Berea. On arriving
there, they went to the Jewish synagogue. 11Now the Berean Jews were of more noble char-
acter than those in Thessalonica, for they received the message with great eagerness and
examined the Scriptures every day to see if what Paul said was true. 12Many of them be-
lieved, as did also a number of prominent Greek women and many Greek men.
13But when the Jews in Thessalonica learned that Paul was preaching the word of God
at Berea, some of them went there too, agitating the crowds and stirring them up. 14The be-
lievers immediately sent Paul to the coast, but Silas and Timothy stayed at Berea. 15Those

Discovering God

16:25–31 // The God Who Is There. This man, who had just moments before nearly committed suicide, fell before Paul and Silas. His brush with death shook him out of his complacency—he was ready to start life all over again. Earnestly—desperately—he begged: "What must I do to be saved?"

What would you have told him? Paul had a ready answer, saying in effect: "Go to Jesus. Believe in him; trust him; depend on him. He will give you a new start. And not just you—your family can have it too."

The Christian message is simple. God may use a crisis to help you get to the point where you just want the bottom line, and want it *now,* as this jailer did. When that happens, the answer will be the same today as back then: "Believe in the Lord Jesus, and you will be saved."

Why wait for a crisis, when you can know and experience him now?

---

[a] 5 Or *the assembly of the people*

who escorted Paul brought him to Athens and then left with instructions for Silas and Timothy to join him as soon as possible.

In Athens

16While Paul was waiting for them in Athens, he was greatly distressed to see that the city was full of idols. 17So he reasoned in the synagogue with both Jews and God-fearing Greeks, as well as in the marketplace day by day with those who happened to be there. 18A group of Epicurean and Stoic philosophers began to debate with him. Some of them asked, "What is this babbler trying to say?" Others remarked, "He seems to be advocating foreign gods." They said this because Paul was preaching the good news about Jesus and the resurrection. 19Then they took him and brought him to a meeting of the Areopagus, where they said to him, "May we know what this new teaching is that you are presenting? 20You are bringing some strange ideas to our ears, and we would like to know what they mean." 21(All the Athenians and the foreigners who lived there spent their time doing nothing but talking about and listening to the latest ideas.)

22Paul then stood up in the meeting of the Areopagus and said: "People of Athens! I see that in every way you are very religious. 23For as I walked around and looked carefully at your objects of worship, I even found an altar with this inscription: TO AN UNKNOWN GOD. So you are ignorant of the very thing you worship—and this is what I am going to proclaim to you.

24"The God who made the world and everything in it is the Lord of heaven and earth and does not live in temples built by hands. 25And he is not served by human hands, as if he needed anything. Rather, he himself gives everyone life and breath and everything else. 26From one man he made all the nations, that they should inhabit the whole earth; and he marked out their appointed times in history and the boundaries of their lands. 27God did this so that they would seek him and perhaps reach out for him and find him, though he is not far from any one of us. 28'For in him we live and move and have our being.'[a] As some of your own poets have said, 'We are his offspring.'[b]

29"Therefore since we are God's offspring, we should not think that the divine being is like gold or silver or stone—an image made by human design and skill. 30In the past God overlooked such ignorance, but now he commands all people everywhere to repent. 31For he has set a day when he will judge the world with justice by the man he has appointed. He has given proof of this to everyone by raising him from the dead."

32When they heard about the resurrection of the dead, some of them sneered, but others said, "We want to hear you again on this subject." 33At that, Paul left the Council. 34Some of the people became followers of Paul and believed. Among them was Dionysius, a member of the Areopagus, also a woman named Damaris, and a number of others.

In Corinth

18 After this, Paul left Athens and went to Corinth. 2There he met a Jew named Aquila, a native of Pontus, who had recently come from Italy with his wife Priscilla, because Claudius had ordered all Jews to leave Rome. Paul went to see them, 3and because he was a tentmaker as they were, he stayed and worked with them. 4Every Sabbath he reasoned in the synagogue, trying to persuade Jews and Greeks.

5When Silas and Timothy came from Macedonia, Paul devoted himself exclusively to preaching, testifying to the Jews that Jesus was the Messiah. 6But when they opposed Paul and became abusive, he shook out his clothes in protest and said to them, "Your blood be on your own heads! I am innocent of it. From now on I will go to the Gentiles."

7Then Paul left the synagogue and went next door to the house of Titius Justus, a worshiper of God. 8Crispus, the synagogue leader, and his entire household believed in the Lord; and many of the Corinthians who heard Paul believed and were baptized.

9One night the Lord spoke to Paul in a vision: "Do not be afraid; keep on speaking, do not be silent. 10For I am with you, and no one is going to attack and harm you, because I have many people in this city." 11So Paul stayed in Corinth for a year and a half, teaching them the word of God.

---

[a] *28* From the Cretan philosopher Epimenides [b] *28* From the Cilician Stoic philosopher Aratus

12While Gallio was proconsul of Achaia, the Jews of Corinth made a united attack on
Paul and brought him to the place of judgment. 13"This man," they charged, "is persuad-
ing the people to worship God in ways contrary to the law."
14Just as Paul was about to speak, Gallio said to them, "If you Jews were making a com-
plaint about some misdemeanor or serious crime, it would be reasonable for me to listen
to you. 15But since it involves questions about words and names and your own law—settle
the matter yourselves. I will not be a judge of such things." 16So he drove them off. 17Then
the crowd there turned on Sosthenes the synagogue leader and beat him in front of the
proconsul; and Gallio showed no concern whatever.

Priscilla, Aquila and Apollos

18Paul stayed on in Corinth for some time. Then he left the believers and sailed for Syr-
ia, accompanied by Priscilla and Aquila. Before he sailed, he had his hair cut off at Cen-
chreae because of a vow he had taken. 19They arrived at Ephesus, where Paul left Priscilla
and Aquila. He himself went into the synagogue and reasoned with the Jews. 20When they
asked him to spend more time with them, he declined. 21But as he left, he promised, "I will
come back if it is God's will." Then he set sail from Ephesus. 22When he landed at Caesa-
rea, he went up to Jerusalem and greeted the church and then went down to Antioch.
23After spending some time in Antioch, Paul set out from there and traveled from place
to place throughout the region of Galatia and Phrygia, strengthening all the disciples.
24Meanwhile a Jew named Apollos, a native of Alexandria, came to Ephesus. He was a
learned man, with a thorough knowledge of the Scriptures. 25He had been instructed in the
way of the Lord, and he spoke with great fervor[a] and taught about Jesus accurately, though
he knew only the baptism of John. 26He began to speak boldly in the synagogue. When Pris-
cilla and Aquila heard him, they invited him to their home and explained to him the way of
God more adequately.
27When Apollos wanted to go to Achaia, the believers encouraged him and wrote to the
disciples there to welcome him. When he arrived, he was a great help to those who by grace
had believed. 28For he vigorously refuted the Jews in public debate, proving from the Scrip-
tures that Jesus was the Messiah.

Paul in Ephesus

19 While Apollos was at Corinth, Paul took the road through the interior and arrived
at Ephesus. There he found some disciples 2and asked them, "Did you receive
the Holy Spirit when[b] you believed?"
They answered, "No, we have not even heard that there is a Holy Spirit."
3So Paul asked, "Then what baptism did you receive?"
"John's baptism," they replied.
4Paul said, "John's baptism was a baptism of repentance. He told the people to believe
in the one coming after him, that is, in Jesus." 5On hearing this, they were baptized into[c] the

Reasons to Believe

18:27–28 // The Christian Experience. The practice of giving evidence to support the claims of the gospel message has a long history in the Christian tradition.

Apollos was a powerful public spokesman for Jesus. He didn't promise favors from God in exchange for financial support, as some shady televangelists do today. Rather, he "vigorously" debated Christ's claims with thoughtful opponents and effectively showed how Scripture verified Jesus' role as the Messiah. Paul did the same thing in chapter 19, verse 8.

If you're a seeker, it's okay to ask questions about the validity of Christianity. There are plenty of reference materials and Christian people who can help you find the answers you need. The evidence is there, and you will find it if you keep seeking.

[a] 25 Or *with fervor in the Spirit* [b] 2 Or *after* [c] 5 Or *in*

name of the Lord Jesus. 6When Paul placed his hands on them, the Holy Spirit came on
them, and they spoke in tongues[a] and prophesied. 7There were about twelve men in all.
8Paul entered the synagogue and spoke boldly there for three months, arguing persua-
sively about the kingdom of God. 9But some of them became obstinate; they refused to
believe and publicly maligned the Way. So Paul left them. He took the disciples with him
and had discussions daily in the lecture hall of Tyrannus. 10This went on for two years, so
that all the Jews and Greeks who lived in the province of Asia heard the word of the Lord.
11God did extraordinary miracles through Paul, 12so that even handkerchiefs and aprons
that had touched him were taken to the sick, and their illnesses were cured and the evil
spirits left them.
13Some Jews who went around driving out evil spirits tried to invoke the name of the
Lord Jesus over those who were demon-possessed. They would say, "In the name of the
Jesus whom Paul preaches, I command you to come out." 14Seven sons of Sceva, a Jewish
chief priest, were doing this. 15⌊One day⌋ the evil spirit answered them, "Jesus I know, and
I know about Paul, but who are you?" 16Then the man who had the evil spirit jumped on
them and overpowered them all. He gave them such a beating that they ran out of the
house naked and bleeding.
17When this became known to the Jews and Greeks living in Ephesus, they were all seized
with fear, and the name of the Lord Jesus was held in high honor. 18Many of those who be-
lieved now came and openly confessed what they had done. 19A number who had practiced
sorcery brought their scrolls together and burned them publicly. When they calculated the
value of the scrolls, the total came to fifty thousand drachmas.[b] 20In this way the word of
the Lord spread widely and grew in power.
21After all this had happened, Paul decided[c] to go to Jerusalem, passing through Mace-
donia and Achaia. "After I have been there," he said, "I must visit Rome also." 22He sent two
of his helpers, Timothy and Erastus, to Macedonia, while he stayed in the province of Asia
a little longer.

The Riot in Ephesus

23About that time there arose a great disturbance about the Way. 24A silversmith named
Demetrius, who made silver shrines of Artemis, brought in no little business for the skilled
workers there. 25He called them together, along with the workers in related trades, and
said: "You know, my friends, that we receive a good income from this business. 26And you
see and hear how this fellow Paul has convinced and led astray large numbers of people
here in Ephesus and in practically the whole province of Asia. He says that gods made by
human hands are no gods at all. 27There is danger not only that our trade will lose its good
name, but also that the temple of the great goddess Artemis will be discredited; and the
goddess herself, who is worshiped throughout the province of Asia and the world, will be
robbed of her divine majesty."
28When they heard this, they were furious and began shouting: "Great is Artemis of the
Ephesians!" 29Soon the whole city was in an uproar. The people seized Gaius and Aristar-
chus, Paul's traveling companions from Macedonia, and all of them rushed together into
the theater. 30Paul wanted to appear before the crowd, but the disciples would not let him.
31Even some of the officials of the province, friends of Paul, sent him a message begging
him not to venture into the theater.
32The assembly was in confusion: Some were shouting one thing, some another. Most of
the people did not even know why they were there. 33The Jews in the crowd pushed Alexan-
der to the front, and they shouted instructions to him. He motioned for silence in order to
make a defense before the people. 34But when they realized he was a Jew, they all shouted
in unison for about two hours: "Great is Artemis of the Ephesians!"
35The city clerk quieted the crowd and said: "People of Ephesus, doesn't all the world
know that the city of Ephesus is the guardian of the temple of the great Artemis and of her
image, which fell from heaven? 36Therefore, since these facts are undeniable, you ought to

[a] 6 Or *other languages* [b] 19 A drachma was a silver coin worth about a day's wages.
[c] 21 Or *decided in the Spirit*

calm down and not do anything rash. [37]You have brought these men here, though they have
neither robbed temples nor blasphemed our goddess. [38]If, then, Demetrius and his associ-
ates have a grievance against anybody, the courts are open and there are proconsuls. They
can press charges. [39]If there is anything further you want to bring up, it must be settled in
a legal assembly. [40]As it is, we are in danger of being charged with rioting because of what
happened today. In that case we would not be able to account for this commotion, since
there is no reason for it." [41]After he had said this, he dismissed the assembly.

Through Macedonia and Greece

20 When the uproar had ended, Paul sent for the disciples and, after encouraging
them, said good-by and set out for Macedonia. [2]He traveled through that area,
speaking many words of encouragement to the people, and finally arrived in
Greece, [3]where he stayed three months. Because some Jews had plotted against him just
as he was about to sail for Syria, he decided to go back through Macedonia. [4]He was ac-
companied by Sopater son of Pyrrhus from Berea, Aristarchus and Secundus from Thessa-
lonica, Gaius from Derbe, Timothy also, and Tychicus and Trophimus from the province of
Asia. [5]These men went on ahead and waited for us at Troas. [6]But we sailed from Philippi
after the Festival of Unleavened Bread, and five days later joined the others at Troas, where
we stayed seven days.

Eutychus Raised From the Dead at Troas

[7]On the first day of the week we came together to break bread. Paul spoke to the people and,
because he intended to leave the next day, kept on talking until midnight. [8]There were many
lamps in the upstairs room where we were meeting. [9]Seated in a window was a young man
named Eutychus, who was sinking into a deep sleep as Paul talked on and on. When he was
sound asleep, he fell to the ground from the third story and was picked up dead. [10]Paul went
down, threw himself on the young man and put his arms around him. "Don't be alarmed," he
said. "He's alive!" [11]Then he went upstairs again and broke bread and ate. After talking until
daylight, he left. [12]The people took the young man home alive and were greatly comforted.

Paul's Farewell to the Ephesian Elders

[13]We went on ahead to the ship and sailed for Assos, where we were going to take Paul
aboard. He had made this arrangement because he was going there on foot. [14]When he
met us at Assos, we took him aboard and went on to Mitylene. [15]The next day we set sail
from there and arrived off Chios. The day after that we crossed over to Samos, and on the
following day arrived at Miletus. [16]Paul had decided to sail past Ephesus to avoid spending
time in the province of Asia, for he was in a hurry to reach Jerusalem, if possible, by the day
of Pentecost.

[17]From Miletus, Paul sent to Ephesus for the elders of the church. [18]When they arrived,
he said to them: "You know how I lived the whole time I was with you, from the first day I
came into the province of Asia. [19]I served the Lord with great humility and with tears and
in the midst of severe testing by the plots of the Jews. [20]You know that I have not hesitat-
ed to preach anything that would be helpful to you but have taught you publicly and from
house to house. [21]I have declared to both Jews and Greeks that they must turn to God in
repentance and have faith in our Lord Jesus.

[22]"And now, compelled by the Spirit, I am going to Jerusalem, not knowing what will hap-
pen to me there. [23]I only know that in every city the Holy Spirit warns me that prison and hard-
ships are facing me. [24]However, I consider my life worth nothing to me; my only aim is to
finish the race and complete the task the Lord Jesus has given me—the task of testifying to
the good news of God's grace.

[25]"Now I know that none of you among whom I have gone about preaching the king-
dom will ever see me again. [26]Therefore, I declare to you today that I am innocent of the
blood of everyone. [27]For I have not hesitated to proclaim to you the whole will of God.
[28]Keep watch over yourselves and all the flock of which the Holy Spirit has made you over-
seers. Be shepherds of the church of God,[a] which he bought with his own blood. [29]I know

---

[a] *28* Many manuscripts *of the Lord*

that after I leave, savage wolves will come in among you and will not spare the flock. 30Even
from your own number some will arise and distort the truth in order to draw away disci-
ples after them. 31So be on your guard! Remember that for three years I never stopped warn-
ing each of you night and day with tears.
32"Now I commit you to God and to the word of his grace, which can build you up and
give you an inheritance among all those who are sanctified. 33I have not coveted anyone's
silver or gold or clothing. 34You yourselves know that these hands of mine have supplied
my own needs and the needs of my companions. 35In everything I did, I showed you that
by this kind of hard work we must help the weak, remembering the words the Lord Jesus
himself said: 'It is more blessed to give than to receive.' "
36When Paul had finished speaking, he knelt down with all of them and prayed. 37They
all wept as they embraced him and kissed him. 38What grieved them most was his state-
ment that they would never see his face again. Then they accompanied him to the ship.

On to Jerusalem

21 After we had torn ourselves away from them, we put out to sea and sailed straight
to Kos. The next day we went to Rhodes and from there to Patara. 2We found a
ship crossing over to Phoenicia, went on board and set sail. 3After sighting Cy-
prus and passing to the south of it, we sailed on to Syria. We landed at Tyre, where our ship
was to unload its cargo. 4We sought out the disciples there and stayed with them seven
days. Through the Spirit they urged Paul not to go on to Jerusalem. 5When it was time to
leave, we left and continued on our way. All of them, including wives and children, accom-
panied us out of the city, and there on the beach we knelt to pray. 6After saying good-by to
each other, we went aboard the ship, and they returned home.
7We continued our voyage from Tyre and landed at Ptolemais, where we greeted the be-
lievers and stayed with them for a day. 8Leaving the next day, we reached Caesarea and
stayed at the house of Philip the evangelist, one of the Seven. 9He had four unmarried
daughters who prophesied.
10After we had been there a number of days, a prophet named Agabus came down from
Judea. 11Coming over to us, he took Paul's belt, tied his own hands and feet with it and said,
"The Holy Spirit says, 'In this way the Jewish leaders in Jerusalem will bind the owner of
this belt and will hand him over to the Gentiles.' "
12When we heard this, we and the people there pleaded with Paul not to go up to Jeru-
salem. 13Then Paul answered, "Why are you weeping and breaking my heart? I am ready
not only to be bound, but also to die in Jerusalem for the name of the Lord Jesus." 14When
he would not be dissuaded, we gave up and said, "The Lord's will be done."
15After this, we started on our way up to Jerusalem. 16Some of the disciples from Caesa-
rea accompanied us and brought us to the home of Mnason, where we were to stay. He was
a man from Cyprus and one of the early disciples.

Paul's Arrival at Jerusalem

17When we arrived at Jerusalem, the believers received us warmly. 18The next day Paul
and the rest of us went to see James, and all the elders were present. 19Paul greeted them
and reported in detail what God had done among the Gentiles through his ministry.
20When they heard this, they praised God. Then they said to Paul: "You see, brother, how
many thousands of Jews have believed, and all of them are zealous for the law. 21They have
been informed that you teach all the Jews who live among the Gentiles to turn away from
Moses, telling them not to circumcise their children or live according to our customs. 22What
shall we do? They will certainly hear that you have come, 23so do what we tell you. There
are four men with us who have made a vow. 24Take these men, join in their purification rites

Discovering God

20:35 // Jesus, the God-Man. Paul's quote from Jesus in this verse is the only one in the New Testament that is not found in the four Gospels (Matthew, Mark, Luke and John). This shows that Jesus' teachings were widely circulated and well known, even though every word wasn't written down (see the very last verse in John's Gospel [page 154]).

and pay their expenses, so that they can have their heads shaved. Then everyone will know there is no truth in these reports about you, but that you yourself are living in obedience to the law. [25]As for the Gentile believers, we have written to them our decision that they should abstain from food sacrificed to idols, from blood, from the meat of strangled animals and from sexual immorality."

[26]The next day Paul took the men and purified himself along with them. Then he went to the temple to give notice of the date when the days of purification would end and the offering would be made for each of them.

Paul Arrested

[27]When the seven days were nearly over, some Jews from the province of Asia saw Paul at the temple. They stirred up the whole crowd and seized him, [28]shouting, "People of Israel, help us! This is the man who teaches everyone everywhere against our people and our law and this place. And besides, he has brought Greeks into the temple and defiled this holy place." [29](They had previously seen Trophimus the Ephesian in the city with Paul and assumed that Paul had brought him into the temple.)

[30]The whole city was aroused, and the people came running from all directions. Seizing Paul, they dragged him from the temple, and immediately the gates were shut. [31]While they were trying to kill him, news reached the commander of the Roman troops that the whole city of Jerusalem was in an uproar. [32]He at once took some officers and soldiers and ran down to the crowd. When the rioters saw the commander and his soldiers, they stopped beating Paul.

[33]The commander came up and arrested him and ordered him to be bound with two chains. Then he asked who he was and what he had done. [34]Some in the crowd shouted one thing and some another, and since the commander could not get at the truth because of the uproar, he ordered that Paul be taken into the barracks. [35]When Paul reached the steps, the violence of the mob was so great he had to be carried by the soldiers. [36]The crowd that followed kept shouting, "Get rid of him!"

Paul Speaks to the Crowd

[37]As the soldiers were about to take Paul into the barracks, he asked the commander, "May I say something to you?"

"Do you speak Greek?" he replied. [38]"Aren't you the Egyptian who started a revolt and led four thousand terrorists out into the wilderness some time ago?"

[39]Paul answered, "I am a Jew, from Tarsus in Cilicia, a citizen of no ordinary city. Please let me speak to the people."

[40]Having received the commander's permission, Paul stood on the steps and motioned

22 to the crowd. When they were all silent, he said to them in Aramaic[a]: [1]"Brothers and fathers, listen now to my defense."

[2]When they heard him speak to them in Aramaic, they became very quiet.

Then Paul said: [3]"I am a Jew, born in Tarsus of Cilicia, but brought up in this city. I studied under Gamaliel and was thoroughly trained in the law of our ancestors. I was just as zealous for God as any of you are today. [4]I persecuted the followers of this Way to their death, arresting both men and women and throwing them into prison, [5]as the high priest and all the Council can themselves testify. I even obtained letters from them to their associates in Damascus, and went there to bring these people as prisoners to Jerusalem to be punished.

[6]"About noon as I came near Damascus, suddenly a bright light from heaven flashed around me. [7]I fell to the ground and heard a voice say to me, 'Saul! Saul! Why do you persecute me?'

[8]" 'Who are you, Lord?' I asked.

" 'I am Jesus of Nazareth, whom you are persecuting,' he replied. [9]My companions saw the light, but they did not understand the voice of him who was speaking to me.

[10]" 'What shall I do, Lord?' I asked.

---

[a] *40* Or possibly *Hebrew*; also in 22:2

" 'Get up,' the Lord said, 'and go into Damascus. There you will be told all that you have
been assigned to do.' [11]My companions led me by the hand into Damascus, because the
brilliance of the light had blinded me.
[12]"A man named Ananias came to see me. He was a devout observer of the law and high-
ly respected by all the Jews living there. [13]He stood beside me and said, 'Brother Saul, re-
ceive your sight!' And at that very moment I was able to see him.
[14]"Then he said: 'The God of our ancestors has chosen you to know his will and to see
the Righteous One and to hear words from his mouth. [15]You will be his witness to all peo-
ple of what you have seen and heard. [16]And now what are you waiting for? Get up, be bap-
tized and wash your sins away, calling on his name.'
[17]"When I returned to Jerusalem and was praying at the temple, I fell into a trance [18]and
saw the Lord speaking to me. 'Quick!' he said. 'Leave Jerusalem immediately, because the
people here will not accept your testimony about me.'
[19]" 'Lord,' I replied, 'these people know that I went from one synagogue to another to im-
prison and beat those who believe in you. [20]And when the blood of your martyr[a] Stephen
was shed, I stood there giving my approval and guarding the clothes of those who were
killing him.'
[21]"Then the Lord said to me, 'Go; I will send you far away to the Gentiles.' "

Paul the Roman Citizen

[22]The crowd listened to Paul until he said this. Then they raised their voices and shout-
ed, "Rid the earth of him! He's not fit to live!"
[23]As they were shouting and throwing off their cloaks and flinging dust into the air, [24]the
commander ordered that Paul be taken into the barracks. He directed that he be flogged
and interrogated in order to find out why the people were shouting at him like this. [25]As
they stretched him out to flog him, Paul said to the centurion standing there, "Is it legal
for you to flog a Roman citizen who hasn't even been found guilty?"
[26]When the centurion heard this, he went to the commander and reported it. "What are
you going to do?" he asked. "This man is a Roman citizen."
[27]The commander went to Paul and asked, "Tell me, are you a Roman citizen?"
"Yes, I am," he answered.
[28]Then the commander said, "I had to pay a lot of money for my citizenship."
"But I was born a citizen," Paul replied.
[29]Those who were about to interrogate him withdrew immediately. The commander him-
self was alarmed when he realized that he had put Paul, a Roman citizen, in chains.

Addressing Questions

22:21–22 // Human Experience. Paul's testimony about his conversion in this chapter highlights a central theme that made Christianity controversial in the first century—its claim that it was the one religion for all the people of the world. The Jewish people who heard Paul speak felt that taking Jesus' story to non-Jews diluted the faith and compromised their practices. But reaching spiritual outsiders was Jesus' priority; he never intended that his message be strictly for the Jews. People who were distressed that Christ's message was also for those who were not like them were putting faith in the wrong thing.

Oddly enough, sometimes people who are most familiar with Jesus' teaching act like the Jews of Paul's day—they have a hard time reaching out to nonbelievers. But to be a consistent follower of Jesus is to value what he valued, and Jesus said he "came to seek and to save what was lost" (Luke chapter 19, verse 10).

Perhaps you've run into some Christians in your spiritual journey that haven't been too enthused about your questions. If so, realize that God is seeking you out even though his earthly followers might fail from time to time. Keep looking and asking questions—you'll find what you're after!

[a] 20 Or *witness*

Paul Before the Sanhedrin

30The commander wanted to find out exactly why Paul was being accused by the Jews.
So the next day he released him and ordered the chief priests and all the members of the
Sanhedrin to assemble. Then he brought Paul and had him stand before them.

23 Paul looked straight at the Sanhedrin and said, "My brothers, I have fulfilled my
duty to God in all good conscience to this day." 2At this the high priest Ananias
ordered those standing near Paul to strike him on the mouth. 3Then Paul said
to him, "God will strike you, you whitewashed wall! You sit there to judge me according to
the law, yet you yourself violate the law by commanding that I be struck!"
4Those who were standing near Paul said, "How dare you insult God's high priest!"
5Paul replied, "Brothers, I did not realize that he was the high priest; for it is written: 'Do
not speak evil about the ruler of your people.'[a]"
6Then Paul, knowing that some of them were Sadducees and the others Pharisees, called
out in the Sanhedrin, "My brothers, I am a Pharisee, descended from Pharisees. I stand on
trial because of the hope of the resurrection of the dead." 7When he said this, a dispute
broke out between the Pharisees and the Sadducees, and the assembly was divided. 8(The
Sadducees say that there is no resurrection, and that there are neither angels nor spirits,
but the Pharisees believe all these things.)
9There was a great uproar, and some of the teachers of the law who were Pharisees stood
up and argued vigorously. "We find nothing wrong with this man," they said. "What if a spir-
it or an angel has spoken to him?" 10The dispute became so violent that the commander
was afraid Paul would be torn to pieces by them. He ordered the troops to go down and take
him away from them by force and bring him into the barracks.
11The following night the Lord stood near Paul and said, "Take courage! As you have tes-
tified about me in Jerusalem, so you must also testify in Rome."

The Plot to Kill Paul

12The next morning the Jews formed a conspiracy and bound themselves with an oath
not to eat or drink until they had killed Paul. 13More than forty men were involved in this
plot. 14They went to the chief priests and the elders and said, "We have taken a solemn
oath not to eat anything until we have killed Paul. 15Now then, you and the Sanhedrin pe-
tition the commander to bring him before you on the pretext of wanting more accurate in-
formation about his case. We are ready to kill him before he gets here."
16But when the son of Paul's sister heard of this plot, he went into the barracks and told
Paul.
17Then Paul called one of the centurions and said, "Take this young man to the com-
mander; he has something to tell him." 18So he took him to the commander.
The centurion said, "Paul, the prisoner, sent for me and asked me to bring this young
man to you because he has something to tell you."
19The commander took the young man by the hand, drew him aside and asked, "What
is it you want to tell me?"
20He said: "The Jews have agreed to ask you to bring Paul before the Sanhedrin tomor-
row on the pretext of wanting more accurate information about him. 21Don't give in to
them, because more than forty of them are waiting in ambush for him. They have taken
an oath not to eat or drink until they have killed him. They are ready now, waiting for your
consent to their request."
22The commander dismissed the young man with this warning: "Don't tell anyone that
you have reported this to me."

Paul Transferred to Caesarea

23Then he called two of his centurions and ordered them, "Get ready a detachment of
two hundred soldiers, seventy horsemen and two hundred spearmen[b] to go to Caesarea at
nine tonight. 24Provide horses for Paul so that he may be taken safely to Governor Felix."
25He wrote a letter as follows:

---

[a] 5 Exodus 22:28 [b] *23* The meaning of the Greek for this word is uncertain.

26 Claudius Lysias,

To His Excellency, Governor Felix:

Greetings.

27 This man was seized by the Jews and they were about to kill him, but I came with
my troops and rescued him, for I had learned that he is a Roman citizen. 28 I wanted
to know why they were accusing him, so I brought him to their Sanhedrin. 29 I found
that the accusation had to do with questions about their law, but there was no charge
against him that deserved death or imprisonment. 30 When I was informed of a plot to
be carried out against the man, I sent him to you at once. I also ordered his accusers
to present to you their case against him.

31 So the soldiers, carrying out their orders, took Paul with them during the night and
brought him as far as Antipatris. 32 The next day they let the cavalry go on with him, while
they returned to the barracks. 33 When the cavalry arrived in Caesarea, they delivered the
letter to the governor and handed Paul over to him. 34 The governor read the letter and
asked what province he was from. Learning that he was from Cilicia, 35 he said, "I will hear
your case when your accusers get here." Then he ordered that Paul be kept under guard in
Herod's palace.

Paul's Trial Before Felix

24 Five days later the high priest Ananias went down to Caesarea with some of the
elders and a lawyer named Tertullus, and they brought their charges against
Paul before the governor. 2 When Paul was called in, Tertullus presented his case
before Felix: "We have enjoyed a long period of peace under you, and your foresight has
brought about reforms in this nation. 3 Everywhere and in every way, most excellent Felix,
we acknowledge this with profound gratitude. 4 But in order not to weary you further, I
would request that you be kind enough to hear us briefly.
5 "We have found this man to be a troublemaker, stirring up riots among the Jews all
over the world. He is a ringleader of the Nazarene sect 6[7] and even tried to desecrate the
temple; so we seized him. 8 By examining him yourself you will be able to learn the truth
about all these charges we are bringing against him."
9 The other Jews joined in the accusation, asserting that these things were true.
10 When the governor motioned for him to speak, Paul replied: "I know that for a num-
ber of years you have been a judge over this nation; so I gladly make my defense. 11 You can
easily verify that no more than twelve days ago I went up to Jerusalem to worship. 12 My
accusers did not find me arguing with anyone at the temple, or stirring up a crowd in the
synagogues or anywhere else in the city. 13 And they cannot prove to you the charges they
are now making against me. 14 However, I admit that I worship the God of our ancestors as
a follower of the Way, which they call a sect. I believe everything that is in accordance with
the Law and that is written in the Prophets, 15 and I have the same hope in God as these peo-
ple themselves have, that there will be a resurrection of both the righteous and the wick-
ed. 16 So I strive always to keep my conscience clear before God and all people.
17 "After an absence of several years, I came to Jerusalem to bring my people gifts for the
poor and to present offerings. 18 I was ceremonially clean when they found me in the tem-
ple courts doing this. There was no crowd with me, nor was I involved in any disturbance.
19 But there are some Jews from the province of Asia, who ought to be here before you and
bring charges if they have anything against me. 20 Or these who are here should state what
crime they found in me when I stood before the Sanhedrin— 21 unless it was this one thing
I shouted as I stood in their presence: 'It is concerning the resurrection of the dead that I
am on trial before you today.' "
22 Then Felix, who was well acquainted with the Way, adjourned the proceedings. "When
Lysias the commander comes," he said, "I will decide your case." 23 He ordered the centu-
rion to keep Paul under guard but to give him some freedom and permit his friends to take
care of his needs.

[24]Several days later Felix came with his wife Drusilla, who was Jewish. He sent for Paul and listened to him as he spoke about faith in Christ Jesus. [25]As Paul talked about righteousness, self-control and the judgment to come, Felix was afraid and said, "That's enough for now! You may leave. When I find it convenient, I will send for you." [26]At the same time he was hoping that Paul would offer him a bribe, so he sent for him frequently and talked with him.

[27]When two years had passed, Felix was succeeded by Porcius Festus, but because Felix wanted to grant a favor to the Jews, he left Paul in prison.

Paul's Trial Before Festus

25 Three days after arriving in the province, Festus went up from Caesarea to Jerusalem, [2]where the chief priests and the Jewish leaders appeared before him and presented the charges against Paul. [3]They requested Festus, as a favor to them, to have Paul transferred to Jerusalem, for they were preparing an ambush to kill him along the way. [4]Festus answered, "Paul is being held at Caesarea, and I myself am going there soon. [5]Let some of your leaders come with me, and if the man has done anything wrong, they can press charges against him there."

[6]After spending eight or ten days with them, Festus went down to Caesarea. The next day he convened the court and ordered that Paul be brought before him. [7]When Paul came in, the Jews who had come down from Jerusalem stood around him. They brought many serious charges against him, but they could not prove them.

[8]Then Paul made his defense: "I have done nothing wrong against the Jewish law or against the temple or against Caesar."

[9]Festus, wishing to do the Jews a favor, said to Paul, "Are you willing to go up to Jerusalem and stand trial before me there on these charges?"

[10]Paul answered: "I am now standing before Caesar's court, where I ought to be tried. I have not done any wrong to the Jews, as you yourself know very well. [11]If, however, I am guilty of doing anything deserving death, I do not refuse to die. But if the charges brought against me by these Jews are not true, no one has the right to hand me over to them. I appeal to Caesar!"

[12]After Festus had conferred with his council, he declared: "You have appealed to Caesar. To Caesar you will go!"

Festus Consults King Agrippa

[13]A few days later King Agrippa and Bernice arrived at Caesarea to pay their respects to Festus. [14]Since they were spending many days there, Festus discussed Paul's case with the king. He said: "There is a man here whom Felix left as a prisoner. [15]When I went to Jerusalem, the chief priests and the elders of the Jews brought charges against him and asked that he be condemned.

[16]"I told them that it is not the Roman custom to hand over anyone before they have faced their accusers and have had an opportunity to defend themselves against the charges. [17]When they came here with me, I did not delay the case, but convened the court the next day and ordered the man to be brought in. [18]When his accusers got up to speak, they did not charge him with any of the crimes I had expected. [19]Instead, they had some points of dispute with him about their own religion and about a dead man named Jesus who Paul claimed was alive.

Knowing Yourself

24:24–27 // Character. Here's a good example of the wrong kind of seeker! Felix listened to Paul's teaching up to a point, but when a particular teaching struck a nerve, he reacted emotionally and stopped the conversation. He also had ulterior motives for listening to Paul, so his heart was in the wrong place to begin with.

Perhaps you're the kind of seeker who gets uncomfortable during a spiritual conversation. If your tendency is to react as Felix did, then say a simple prayer the next time that happens: "God, if you're real, and if any of this is true, help me to accept it without getting defensive."

[20]I was at a loss how to investigate such matters; so I asked if he would be willing to go to Jerusalem and stand trial there on these charges. [21]But when Paul made his appeal to be held over for the Emperor's decision, I ordered him held until I could send him to Caesar."

[22]Then Agrippa said to Festus, "I would like to hear this man myself."

He replied, "Tomorrow you will hear him."

Paul Before Agrippa

[23]The next day Agrippa and Bernice came with great pomp and entered the audience room with the high-ranking military officers and the prominent men of the city. At the command of Festus, Paul was brought in. [24]Festus said: "King Agrippa, and all who are present with us, you see this man! The whole Jewish community has petitioned me about him in Jerusalem and here in Caesarea, shouting that he ought not to live any longer. [25]I found he had done nothing deserving of death, but because he made his appeal to the Emperor I decided to send him to Rome. [26]But I have nothing definite to write to His Majesty about him. Therefore I have brought him before all of you, and especially before you, King Agrippa, so that as a result of this investigation I may have something to write. [27]For I think it is unreasonable to send a prisoner on to Rome without specifying the charges against him."

26 Then Agrippa said to Paul, "You have permission to speak for yourself."

So Paul motioned with his hand and began his defense: [2]"King Agrippa, I consider myself fortunate to stand before you today as I make my defense against all the accusations of the Jews, [3]and especially so because you are well acquainted with all the Jewish customs and controversies. Therefore, I beg you to listen to me patiently.

[4]"The Jewish people all know the way I have lived ever since I was a child, from the beginning of my life in my own country, and also in Jerusalem. [5]They have known me for a long time and can testify, if they are willing, that I conformed to the strictest sect of our religion, living as a Pharisee. [6]And now it is because of my hope in what God has promised our ancestors that I am on trial today. [7]This is the promise our twelve tribes are hoping to see fulfilled as they earnestly serve God day and night. King Agrippa, it is because of this hope that the Jews are accusing me. [8]Why should any of you consider it incredible that God raises the dead?

[9]"I too was convinced that I ought to do all that was possible to oppose the name of Jesus of Nazareth. [10]And that is just what I did in Jerusalem. On the authority of the chief priests I put many of the Lord's people in prison, and when they were put to death, I cast my vote against them. [11]Many a time I went from one synagogue to another to have them punished, and I tried to force them to blaspheme. I was so obsessed with persecuting them that I even hunted them down in foreign cities.

[12]"On one of these journeys I was going to Damascus with the authority and commission of the chief priests. [13]About noon, King Agrippa, as I was on the road, I saw a light from heaven, brighter than the sun, blazing around me and my companions. [14]We all fell to the ground, and I heard a voice saying to me in Aramaic,[a] 'Saul, Saul, why do you persecute me? It is hard for you to kick against the goads.'

[15]"Then I asked, 'Who are you, Lord?'

" 'I am Jesus, whom you are persecuting,' the Lord replied. [16]'Now get up and stand on your feet. I have appeared to you to appoint you as a servant and as a witness of what you

Reasons to Believe

25:16–21 // The Incomparable Jesus. Although Festus didn't believe that Jesus' resurrection had taken place, he understood that it was at the very center of Christianity.

Paul once wrote, "If you declare with your mouth, 'Jesus is Lord,' and believe in your heart that God raised him from the dead, you will be saved" (Romans chapter 10, verse 9 [page 213]). Christianity without Christ is an impossibility; but Christianity without a *risen* Christ is just as invalid and cannot lead to a saving, transforming relationship with him.

[a] 14 Or *Hebrew*

have seen and will see of me. 17I will rescue you from your own people and from the Gen-
tiles. I am sending you to them 18to open their eyes and turn them from darkness to light,
and from the power of Satan to God, so that they may receive forgiveness of sins and a
place among those who are sanctified by faith in me.'
19"So then, King Agrippa, I was not disobedient to the vision from heaven. 20First to those
in Damascus, then to those in Jerusalem and in all Judea, and then to the Gentiles, I
preached that they should repent and turn to God and demonstrate their repentance by
their deeds. 21That is why some Jews seized me in the temple courts and tried to kill me.
22But God has helped me to this very day; so I stand here and testify to small and great
alike. I am saying nothing beyond what the prophets and Moses said would happen— 23that
the Messiah would suffer and, as the first to rise from the dead, would bring the message
of light to his own people and to the Gentiles."
24At this point Festus interrupted Paul's defense. "You are out of your mind, Paul!" he
shouted. "Your great learning is driving you insane."
25"I am not insane, most excellent Festus," Paul replied. "What I am saying is true and
reasonable. 26The king is familiar with these things, and I can speak freely to him. I am
convinced that none of this has escaped his notice, because it was not done in a corner.
27King Agrippa, do you believe the prophets? I know you do."
28Then Agrippa said to Paul, "Do you think that in such a short time you can persuade
me to be a Christian?"
29Paul replied, "Short time or long—I pray to God that not only you but all who are lis-
tening to me today may become what I am, except for these chains."
30The king rose, and with him the governor and Bernice and those sitting with them.
31After they left the room, they began saying to one another, "This man is not doing any-
thing that deserves death or imprisonment."
32Agrippa said to Festus, "This man could have been set free if he had not appealed to
Caesar."

Paul Sails for Rome

27 When it was decided that we would sail for Italy, Paul and some other prisoners
were handed over to a centurion named Julius, who belonged to the Imperial Reg-
iment. 2We boarded a ship from Adramyttium about to sail for ports along the
coast of the province of Asia, and we put out to sea. Aristarchus, a Macedonian from Thes-
salonica, was with us.
3The next day we landed at Sidon; and Julius, in kindness to Paul, allowed him to go
to his friends so they might provide for his needs. 4From there we put out to sea again
and passed to the lee of Cyprus because the winds were against us. 5When we had sailed
across the open sea off the coast of Cilicia and Pamphylia, we landed at Myra in Lycia.

Knowing Yourself

26:12–15 // Sin. Farmers in Paul's time kept their oxen in line when plowing by using a sharp "goad." When the animals resisted correction, they only succeeded in hurting themselves. Jesus used this image to tell Paul that by persecuting Christians he was working against God's plan, not helping it.

Have you ever seen yourself as someone who resists God? Most of us think of ourselves as either neutral or, at best, reasonably open to hearing from God. But we all are like Paul in that we constantly do things that show we're at odds with God. We exclude him, and at times—although we know better—we do the very things of which we know a righteous and holy God would not approve.

If God seems distant from you, part of the reason is because of your resistance to him. As much as you may want to think differently, your sin has built a barrier between you and God. But God is a forgiving God, eager to take away that barrier and give you full access to him. Why not face the sin in your life—as Paul had to—and admit your need for forgiveness?

6There the centurion found an Alexandrian ship sailing for Italy and put us on board.
7We made slow headway for many days and had difficulty arriving off Cnidus. When the
wind did not allow us to hold our course, we sailed to the lee of Crete, opposite Salmo-
ne. 8We moved along the coast with difficulty and came to a place called Fair Havens,
near the town of Lasea.

9Much time had been lost, and sailing had already become dangerous because by now
it was after the Day of Atonement.[a] So Paul warned them, 10"Men, I can see that our voy-
age is going to be disastrous and bring great loss to ship and cargo, and to our own lives
also." 11But the centurion, instead of listening to what Paul said, followed the advice of the
pilot and of the owner of the ship. 12Since the harbor was unsuitable to winter in, the ma-
jority decided that we should sail on, hoping to reach Phoenix and winter there. This was
a harbor in Crete, facing both southwest and northwest.

The Storm

13When a gentle south wind began to blow, they saw their opportunity; so they weighed
anchor and sailed along the shore of Crete. 14Before very long, a wind of hurricane force,
called the Northeaster, swept down from the island. 15The ship was caught by the storm and
could not head into the wind; so we gave way to it and were driven along. 16As we passed
to the lee of a small island called Cauda, we were hardly able to make the lifeboat secure,
17so the men hoisted it aboard. Then they passed ropes under the ship itself to hold it to-
gether. Because they were afraid they would run aground on the sandbars of Syrtis, they
lowered the sea anchor[b] and let the ship be driven along. 18We took such a violent batter-
ing from the storm that the next day they began to throw the cargo overboard. 19On the
third day, they threw the ship's tackle overboard with their own hands. 20When neither sun
nor stars appeared for many days and the storm continued raging, we finally gave up all
hope of being saved.

21After they had gone a long time without food, Paul stood up before them and said: "Men,
you should have taken my advice not to sail from Crete; then you would have spared your-
selves this damage and loss. 22But now I urge you to keep up your courage, because not one
of you will be lost; only the ship will be destroyed. 23Last night an angel of the God whose I
am and whom I serve stood beside me 24and said, 'Do not be afraid, Paul. You must stand tri-
al before Caesar; and God has graciously given you the lives of all who sail with you.' 25So
keep up your courage, men, for I have faith in God that it will happen just as he told me.
26Nevertheless, we must run aground on some island."

The Shipwreck

27On the fourteenth night we were still being driven across the Adriatic[c] Sea, when about
midnight the sailors sensed they were approaching land. 28They took soundings and found
that the water was a hundred and twenty feet[d] deep. A short time later they took sound-
ings again and found it was ninety feet[e] deep. 29Fearing that we would be dashed against
the rocks, they dropped four anchors from the stern and prayed for daylight. 30In an at-
tempt to escape from the ship, the sailors let the lifeboat down into the sea, pretending they
were going to lower some anchors from the bow. 31Then Paul said to the centurion and the
soldiers, "Unless these men stay with the ship, you cannot be saved." 32So the soldiers cut
the ropes that held the lifeboat and let it drift away.

33Just before dawn Paul urged them all to eat. "For the last fourteen days," he said, "you
have been in constant suspense and have gone without food—you haven't eaten anything.
34Now I urge you to take some food. You need it to survive. Not one of you will lose a single
hair from his head." 35After he said this, he took some bread and gave thanks to God in front
of them all. Then he broke it and began to eat. 36They were all encouraged and ate some food
themselves. 37Altogether there were 276 of us on board. 38When they had eaten as much as
they wanted, they lightened the ship by throwing the grain into the sea.

---

[a] 9 That is, Yom Kippur [b] *17* Or *the sails* [c] *27* In ancient times the name referred to an area extending well south of Italy. [d] *28* Or about 37 meters [e] *28* Or about 27 meters

[39]When daylight came, they did not recognize the land, but they saw a bay with a sandy
beach, where they decided to run the ship aground if they could. [40]Cutting loose the an-
chors, they left them in the sea and at the same time untied the ropes that held the rud-
ders. Then they hoisted the foresail to the wind and made for the beach. [41]But the ship
struck a sandbar and ran aground. The bow stuck fast and would not move, and the stern
was broken to pieces by the pounding of the surf.

[42]The soldiers planned to kill the prisoners to prevent any of them from swimming away
and escaping. [43]But the centurion wanted to spare Paul's life and kept them from carrying out
their plan. He ordered those who could swim to jump overboard first and get to land. [44]The
rest were to get there on planks or on other pieces of the ship. In this way everyone reached
land safely.

Paul Ashore on Malta

28 Once safely on shore, we found out that the island was called Malta. [2]The island-
ers showed us unusual kindness. They built a fire and welcomed us all because it
was raining and cold. [3]Paul gathered a pile of brushwood and, as he put it on the
fire, a viper, driven out by the heat, fastened itself on his hand. [4]When the islanders saw the
snake hanging from his hand, they said to each other, "This man must be a murderer; for
though he escaped from the sea, the goddess Justice has not allowed him to live." [5]But Paul
shook the snake off into the fire and suffered no ill effects. [6]The people expected him to swell
up or suddenly fall dead; but after waiting a long time and seeing nothing unusual happen to
him, they changed their minds and said he was a god.

[7]There was an estate nearby that belonged to Publius, the chief official of the island.
He welcomed us to his home and showed us generous hospitality for three days. [8]His fa-
ther was sick in bed, suffering from fever and dysentery. Paul went in to see him and, af-
ter prayer, placed his hands on him and healed him. [9]When this had happened, the rest of
the sick on the island came and were cured. [10]They honored us in many ways; and when
we were ready to sail, they furnished us with the supplies we needed.

Paul's Arrival at Rome

[11]After three months we put out to sea in a ship that had wintered in the island—it was
an Alexandrian ship with the figurehead of the twin gods Castor and Pollux. [12]We put in at
Syracuse and stayed there three days. [13]From there we set sail and arrived at Rhegium. The
next day the south wind came up, and on the following day we reached Puteoli. [14]There
we found some believers who invited us to spend a week with them. And so we came to
Rome. [15]The believers there had heard that we were coming, and they traveled as far as
the Forum of Appius and the Three Taverns to meet us. At the sight of these people Paul
thanked God and was encouraged. [16]When we got to Rome, Paul was allowed to live by
himself, with a soldier to guard him.

Paul Preaches at Rome Under Guard

[17]Three days later he called together the local Jewish leaders. When they had assembled,
Paul said to them: "My brothers, although I have done nothing against our people or against
the customs of our ancestors, I was arrested in Jerusalem and handed over to the Romans.
[18]They examined me and wanted to release me, because I was not guilty of any crime deserv-
ing death. [19]The Jews objected, so I was compelled to make an appeal to Caesar. I certainly
did not intend to bring any charge against my own people. [20]For this reason I have asked to
see you and talk with you. It is because of the hope of Israel that I am bound with this chain."

[21]They replied, "We have not received any letters from Judea concerning you, and none
of our people who have come from there has reported or said anything bad about you. [22]But
we want to hear what your views are, for we know that people everywhere are talking
against this sect."

[23]They arranged to meet Paul on a certain day, and came in even larger numbers to the
place where he was staying. He witnessed to them from morning till evening, explaining
about the kingdom of God, and from the Law of Moses and from the Prophets he tried to
persuade them about Jesus. [24]Some were convinced by what he said, but others would not
believe. [25]They disagreed among themselves and began to leave after Paul had made this

final statement: "The Holy Spirit spoke the truth to your ancestors when he said through Isaiah the prophet:

[26]" 'Go to this people and say,
"You will be ever hearing but never understanding;
you will be ever seeing but never perceiving."
[27]For this people's heart has become calloused;
they hardly hear with their ears,
and they have closed their eyes.
Otherwise they might see with their eyes,
hear with their ears,
understand with their hearts
and turn, and I would heal them.'[a]

[28][29]"Therefore I want you to know that God's salvation has been sent to the Gentiles,
and they will listen!"
[30]For two whole years Paul stayed there in his own rented house and welcomed all who
came to see him. [31]He proclaimed the kingdom of God and taught about the Lord Jesus
Christ—with all boldness and without hindrance!

Reasons to Believe

28:23–28 // The Christian Experience. By the end of the book of Acts, Paul had spent many years teaching about Jesus. Here, in prison, he patiently encountered yet another mixture of belief and rejection on the part of his listeners.

Yet this time Paul's words had an ominous finality (see verse 28). The early church had been almost exclusively Jewish. But the work of Paul and the other apostles had flung open the church's doors to the whole world. Paul had decided to minister primarily to non-Jews, and was determined to pull as many as he could into that wonderful new order called the kingdom of God.

Paul's work in taking Jesus' message to the Gentiles is part of the reason Christianity became a *world* religion. Today anyone—you too!—can be included in God's family regardless of any religious or ethnic background.

Epilogue

The story of the spread of Christianity makes for fascinating reading. The reasons behind this explosive first-century reaction are complex, but clearly something about the Christian message was very compelling.

Beginning the Journey is designed to help you comprehend that powerful message by reading five books of the Bible. The final book on the list is Romans. It is a logical masterpiece that reads like a well-argued lawyer's explanation and defense of Christianity. Take your time with it. You will want to read that book slowly and with careful attention to the flow of thought. But reading it will be well worth the effort, because it is the apostle Paul's *magnum opus,* containing the best and most thorough articulation of the Christian message in the Bible.

Turn to page 198 to begin reading Romans.

[a] *27* Isaiah 6:9,10 (see Septuagint)

Seeker Stories

My parents divorced when I was seven. After living for three years with an aunt and uncle, I moved to Chicago to live with my dad and stepmother, where I stayed through high school. Those years were difficult for me; my father and his wife were alcoholics, my brother was (and still is) a homosexual, and my sisters left home at age 17. It helped that my dad was a choir director for our church. Although I hadn't given my life to Christ, I often found peace in Christian music.

I overcame all of my childhood traumas by being a superachiever and a caretaker. I thought to myself, "*I* will try harder; *I* will make everyone happy; *I* will succeed on my own! Through sheer effort and self-will, everything will be fine." From the ages of 21 to 38 I built my world on my good deeds, all the while ignoring my relationship with God. I had a good job where I was well-respected; I had a solid, 10-year marriage and two kids; I had a nice house, two cars and a cat. In retrospect, however, I can see that I was building my life on a foundation of stacked cards.

In October of 1989, my "house of cards" completely collapsed. My wife revealed to me that she had been having an affair with a neighbor for two years, and that she now wanted to marry him. I was devastated, and fear of being abandoned by my wife and children dominated both my waking and sleeping hours.

After the divorce, my ex-wife's sister gave me a call. When we talked about the affair, she explained that she felt my ex-wife's problem was that she had taken God out of his rightful place at the center of her world. At the end of our conversation, she invited me to go with her to a "seeker service" at her church, and I agreed.

As I sat at church that night, I realized that I had the exact same problem! I had been ignoring God for years. That realization was a real turning point, and the following two years were a time of healing and growing for me. During that time I learned to take responsibility for all the pain I had caused others by not being a "truth-seeking" husband. I decided to commit my life to Christ, realizing that true joy would begin in my life only when I opened the door of my heart to God and became a fully devoted follower of Christ.

God's grace is truly amazing! The fact that he'd still want me after I had turned my back on him for so many years still leaves me speechless. Although some days are still shaky and challenging, my faith has given my life a new and solid foundation, along with many new opportunities and friends. I still have a long way to go; growth in Christ seems to be a slow and gradual process, and listening to God's will is a difficult task (especially since I'd rather do my own will!). But my life is much more at peace now—more authentic, more honest, and more enjoyable! I'm just beginning to realize what it means to be free!

Romans Introduction

THE BOTTOM LINE

"Well, nobody's perfect." That's a common idiom all people—regardless of their religious beliefs—seem to agree upon. It's also the starting point of this book. In it Paul explains that, no matter how good we think we are, we still fall short of God's plan for our lives. But the good news of Romans is that God still wants to have a relationship with us in spite of our imperfections. Jesus' work on our behalf makes us acceptable in God's eyes. In chapter 8, one of the Bible's most powerful passages, Paul takes this concept a step further by describing the immense benefits of living a life directed by faith in Christ (see page 209). This book explains more clearly than perhaps any other book in the Bible how you can have that kind of life.

CENTRAL IDEAS

- Paul reveals the universality of the problem of sin.
- This book explains the message of Christ's salvation and how we can accept it by faith.
- Paul responds to persecution with patience and frankly discusses his own inner struggles.
- Paul explains the benefits of living life in the power of the Holy Spirit.
- Paul gives practical guidance on living out the Christian faith.

OUTLINE

1. **Introduction** (1:1–15)
2. **God is sinless and perfect** (1:16–17)
3. **People are imperfect** (1:18—3:20)
4. **Jesus offers us salvation** (3:21—5:21)
5. **People can have Christ's power** (chaps. 6–8)
6. **Why God rejects evil** (chaps. 9–11)
7. **The practice of the Christian life** (12:1—15:13)
8. **Conclusion** (15:14–33)
9. **Final greetings** (chap. 16)

TITLE

This book is titled after its original recipients—Christians in Rome.

AUTHOR AND READERS

Paul, the author of this book, wrote this especially to the non-Jewish believers in Rome. He was preparing the way for his eventual visit, reminding them of the basics of salvation. He also wanted to outline to his readers the relationship between the Jew and the non-Jew in the early church.

Every religion tries to answer a fundamental question, phrased in a multitude of ways, that essentially boils down to this: "What must a person do to gain eternal life?" Every world religion—except Christianity—says that eternal life must be earned.

In Buddhism the ultimate goal is enlightenment. It is called "Nirvana," or the blissful extinction of all desires. According to the Buddha's teaching, all pain and suffering originate in human desire. If desire itself can be overcome by following the Eightfold Path, one can achieve "Nirvana," which is total nothingness.

The Hindu's ultimate destiny is to discover that the individual soul is really part of the bigger world soul, which includes everything else that exists. Hindus say that people are repeatedly reborn in endless cycles of reincarnation to try to work out their "karma" (the law of reaping what you sow) so that they can eventually reach this highest state. Achieving this Hindu goal is like being a drop of water that is returned to the ocean. Individuality is lost as the self is absorbed into the world soul.

"What must a person do to gain eternal life?"

The afterlife to which followers of Islam aspire is called "Paradise"—a spiritual wonderland of sensual delights. Muslims achieve paradise by staying away from earthly sensual delights in anticipation of their heavenly reward. In addition, a Muslim must follow the Five Pillars of Islam: repeating the Islamic creed, making a pilgrimage to Mecca, giving alms to the poor, praying five times a day, and keeping the fast of the month of Ramadan. Failure to fulfill these commands jeopardizes one's chances that Allah, the Muslim god, will allow the individual into Paradise.

Note the common teaching in all of these world religions—that one can achieve the afterlife through human effort. Based on such a system, people can never know for sure where they will end up after they die. It's like taking a test in school, but never knowing if you have a passing score.

Unlike other world religions, Christianity teaches that people can know for sure that they have eternal life. The Bible teaches that Jesus took God's test in our place—and passed it. Now Jesus offers to write our names on that perfect exam, so that his "A" is applied to us. In other words, we can have eternal life based on the merits of what Jesus has done for us.

The highest goal of God's highest creation—you and me—is not to be absorbed into God, but to have a relationship with him and to enjoy him forever. The apostle Paul explains in the book of Romans how a person can know God. This book, more than any other in the Bible, discusses the basis and benefits of a relationship with God. If you're interested in knowing what you must do to have eternal life, turn to Romans chapter 10, verses 9–13 (page 213).

ROMANS

1 Paul, a servant of Christ Jesus, called to be an apostle and set apart for the gospel of
God— [2]the gospel he promised beforehand through his prophets in the Holy Scrip-
tures [3]regarding his Son, who as to his earthly life[a] was a descendant of David, [4]and
who through the Spirit of holiness was appointed the Son of God in power[b] by his resur-
rection from the dead: Jesus Christ our Lord. [5]Through him we received grace and apostle-
ship to call all the Gentiles to faith and obedience for his name's sake. [6]And you also are
among those Gentiles who are called to belong to Jesus Christ.

[7]To all in Rome who are loved by God and called to be his holy people:

Grace and peace to you from God our Father and from the Lord Jesus Christ.

Paul's Longing to Visit Rome

[8]First, I thank my God through Jesus Christ for all of you, because your faith is being re-
ported all over the world. [9]God, whom I serve in my spirit in preaching the gospel of his Son,
is my witness how constantly I remember you [10]in my prayers at all times; and I pray that
now at last by God's will the way may be opened for me to come to you.

[11]I long to see you so that I may impart to you some spiritual gift to make you strong—
[12]that is, that you and I may be mutually encouraged by each other's faith. [13]I do not want
you to be unaware, brothers and sisters, that I planned many times to come to you (but
have been prevented from doing so until now) in order that I might have a harvest among
you, just as I have had among the other Gentiles.

[14]I am obligated both to Greeks and non-Greeks, both to the wise and the foolish. [15]That
is why I am so eager to preach the gospel also to you who are in Rome.

[16]I am not ashamed of the gospel, because it is the power of God that brings salvation
to everyone who believes: first to the Jew, then to the Gentile. [17]For in the gospel the righ-
teousness of God is revealed—a righteousness that is by faith from first to last,[c] just as it
is written: "The righteous will live by faith."[d]

God's Wrath Against Sinful Humanity

[18]The wrath of God is being revealed from heaven against all the godlessness and wick-
edness of human beings who suppress the truth by their wickedness, [19]since what may be
known about God is plain to them, because God has made it plain to them. [20]For since the
creation of the world God's invisible qualities—his eternal power and divine nature—have
been clearly seen, being understood from what has been made, so that people are without
excuse.

Discovering God

1:1–7 // The God Who Is There. Have you ever experienced the beauty of a star-filled sky or a fiery sunset and been prompted to say, "God, if you're real, show yourself to me"?

Nature is one way that God shows himself to people. The Bible is another way. And this book, Paul's letter to the Romans, is a short course on the basics of the gospel message—Paul's version of "Christianity 101." If you take the time to study this book, God can use it to reveal himself to you in new ways.

Paul explains why we need God (chapter 1, verse 1—chapter 3, verse 20), what God has done so that we can know him (chapter 3, verse 21—chapter 5, verse 21), and how knowing him will change our lives (chapter 6, verse 1—chapter 16, verse 27).

Romans is not "Christianity Lite," however. It is a brilliantly argued treatise, full of rich insight and profound truth. Paul claims his book is a message from God to you (verses 5 and 6). It's at least a partial answer to those times you have called out to him, so listen well—God is trying to get through to you!

---

[a] 3 Or *who according to the flesh* [b] 4 Or *was declared with power to be the Son of God* [c] 17 Or *is from faith to faith* [d] 17 Hab. 2:4

21For although they knew God, they neither glorified him as God nor gave thanks to him,
but their thinking became futile and their foolish hearts were darkened. 22Although they
claimed to be wise, they became fools 23and exchanged the glory of the immortal God for
images made to look like mortal human beings and birds and animals and reptiles.
24Therefore God gave them over in the sinful desires of their hearts to sexual impurity
for the degrading of their bodies with one another. 25They exchanged the truth about God
for a lie, and worshiped and served created things rather than the Creator—who is forev-
er praised. Amen.
26Because of this, God gave them over to shameful lusts. Even their women exchanged
natural sexual relations for unnatural ones. 27In the same way the men also abandoned
natural relations with women and were inflamed with lust for one another. Men commit-
ted shameful acts with other men, and received in themselves the due penalty for their
error.
28Furthermore, just as they did not think it worthwhile to retain the knowledge of God,
so God gave them over to a depraved mind, so that they do what ought not to be done.
29They have become filled with every kind of wickedness, evil, greed and depravity. They
are full of envy, murder, strife, deceit and malice. They are gossips, 30slanderers, God-hat-
ers, insolent, arrogant and boastful; they invent ways of doing evil; they disobey their par-
ents; 31they have no understanding, no fidelity, no love, no mercy. 32Although they know
God's righteous decree that those who do such things deserve death, they not only contin-
ue to do these very things but also approve of those who practice them.

God's Righteous Judgment

2 You, therefore, have no excuse, you who pass judgment on someone else, for at
whatever point you judge another, you are condemning yourself, because you who
pass judgment do the same things. 2Now we know that God's judgment against
those who do such things is based on truth. 3So when you, a mere human, pass judgment
on them and yet do the same things, do you think you will escape God's judgment? 4Or
do you show contempt for the riches of his kindness, forbearance and patience, not real-
izing that God's kindness is intended to lead you to repentance?
5But because of your stubbornness and your unrepentant heart, you are storing up wrath
against yourself for the day of God's wrath, when his righteous judgment will be revealed.

Discovering God

1:16–17 // Life with God. Paul states the theme of Romans in these two verses: God will rescue women and men who turn to him in faith from the consequences of sin, regardless of their ethnic or religious background. That freedom will transform their lives here on earth and assure them of life after death.

Note especially Paul's explanation of how salvation is obtained: by trusting Jesus Christ. Paul declared that people who are right with God get that way *by faith*. He challenged the popular religious assumption that God bases admission into heaven on a person's good deeds. Instead, Paul proclaimed that Jesus Christ has already done the work of saving people, and that the proper response is to receive that gift and live in the reality of Jesus' forgiveness.

Addressing Questions

1:18–32 // Human Experience. In this passage, Paul emphasizes that God makes himself known to all people through his glory in creation. People are "without excuse"; there is no reason for anyone to deny that God exists.

Still, people live as if there is no God at all. In the next few verses Paul outlines some of the activities in which people engage, willfully distorting God's created order.

The list is quite comprehensive; it mirrors human nature itself. By making us look at ourselves in this mirror, Paul reveals that, without God's intervention, we're all hopelessly—though justifiably—lost. But keep reading . . . there's good news coming.

[6]God "will repay everyone according to what they have done."[a] [7]To those who by persis-
tence in doing good seek glory, honor and immortality, he will give eternal life. [8]But for
those who are self-seeking and who reject the truth and follow evil, there will be wrath and
anger. [9]There will be trouble and distress for every human being who does evil: first for
the Jew, then for the Gentile; [10]but glory, honor and peace for everyone who does good:
first for the Jew, then for the Gentile. [11]For God does not show favoritism.
[12]All who sin apart from the law will also perish apart from the law, and all who sin
under the law will be judged by the law. [13]For it is not those who hear the law who are
righteous in God's sight, but it is those who obey the law who will be declared righteous.
[14](Indeed, when Gentiles, who do not have the law, do by nature things required by the
law, they are a law for themselves, even though they do not have the law. [15]They show
that the requirements of the law are written on their hearts, their consciences also bear-
ing witness, and their thoughts now accusing, now even defending them.) [16]This will
take place on the day when God judges everyone's secrets through Jesus Christ, as my
gospel declares.

The Jews and the Law

[17]Now you, if you call yourself a Jew; if you rely on the law and boast in God; [18]if you
know his will and approve of what is superior because you are instructed by the law; [19]if you
are convinced that you are a guide for the blind, a light for those who are in the dark, [20]an
instructor of the foolish, a teacher of infants, because you have in the law the embodiment
of knowledge and truth— [21]you, then, who teach others, do you not teach yourself? You
who preach against stealing, do you steal? [22]You who say that people should not commit
adultery, do you commit adultery? You who abhor idols, do you rob temples? [23]You who
boast in the law, do you dishonor God by breaking the law? [24]As it is written: "God's name
is blasphemed among the Gentiles because of you."[b]
[25]Circumcision has value if you observe the law, but if you break the law, you have be-
come as though you had not been circumcised. [26]If those who are not circumcised keep the
law's requirements, will they not be regarded as though they were circumcised? [27]The one
who is not circumcised physically and yet obeys the law will condemn you who, even
though you have the[c] written code and circumcision, are a lawbreaker.
[28]A person is not a Jew who is one only outwardly, nor is circumcision merely outward
and physical. [29]No, a person is a Jew who is one inwardly; and circumcision is circumcision
of the heart, by the Spirit, not by the written code. Such a person's praise is not from oth-
er people, but from God.

God's Faithfulness

3 What advantage, then, is there in being a Jew, or what value is there in circumci-
sion? [2]Much in every way! First of all, the Jews have been entrusted with the very
words of God.

Knowing Yourself

2:1–16 // Sin. Black sheep. Bad seed. Rebel. Criminal.

Have any of these labels ever been applied to you? If so, perhaps you feel like God is farther away from you than from other people. If not, perhaps you feel closer to God because you try to live right. Whatever your response, Paul has news for you: *In God's eyes, we're all the same.*

There's not a person on earth who can live up to God's perfect moral code. Those who look down their noses and accuse others of being hopelessly corrupt need to start looking in the mirror at some of their own thoughts, desires and motives. Paul says that no matter what kind of evil we've done or how good we've tried to be in our lives, we all stand under God's judgment and in need of his forgiveness.

---

[a] 6 Psalm 62:12; Prov. 24:12 [b] 24 Isaiah 52:5 (see Septuagint); Ezek. 36:20,22 [c] 27 Or *who, by means of a*

3What if some were unfaithful? Will their unfaithfulness nullify God's faithfulness? 4Not
at all! Let God be true, and every human being a liar. As it is written:

"So that you may be proved right when you speak
and prevail when you judge."[a]

5But if our unrighteousness brings out God's righteousness more clearly, what shall we
say? That God is unjust in bringing his wrath on us? (I am using a human argument.) 6Cer-
tainly not! If that were so, how could God judge the world? 7Someone might argue, "If my
falsehood enhances God's truthfulness and so increases his glory, why am I still condemned
as a sinner?" 8Why not say—as we are being slanderously reported as saying and as some
claim that we say—"Let us do evil that good may result"? Their condemnation is just!

No One Is Righteous

9What shall we conclude then? Do we have any advantage? Not at all! We have already
made the charge that Jews and Gentiles alike are all under the power of sin. 10As it is written:

"There is no one righteous, not even one;
11 there is no one who understands;
there is no one who seeks God.
12 All have turned away,
they have together become worthless;
there is no one who does good,
not even one."[b]
13 "Their throats are open graves;
their tongues practice deceit."[c]
"The poison of vipers is on their lips."[d]
14 "Their mouths are full of cursing and bitterness."[e]
15 "Their feet are swift to shed blood;
16 ruin and misery mark their ways,
17 and the way of peace they do not know."[f]
18 "There is no fear of God before their eyes."[g]

19Now we know that whatever the law says, it says to those who are under the law, so
that every mouth may be silenced and the whole world held accountable to God. 20There-
fore no one will be declared righteous in God's sight by observing the law; rather, through
the law we become conscious of our sin.

Righteousness Through Faith

21But now apart from the law the righteousness of God has been made known, to which
the Law and the Prophets testify. 22This righteousness is given through faith in[h] Jesus
Christ to all who believe. There is no difference between Jew and Gentile, 23for all have
sinned and fall short of the glory of God, 24and all are justified freely by his grace through

Knowing Yourself

2:17—3:8 // Sin. In this passage Paul says that even the most religious people among us break God's laws. To illustrate, Paul specifically points to the religious Jews of his day. They knew all about God. They practiced the religious ceremonies God had prescribed. Others looked to them for guidance. Yet Paul notes that while they told others to uphold God's law, they themselves broke it.

The message is clear. Even the most religious people aren't without fault, because they don't perfectly obey their own religious codes. Any person who has an honest view of his or her fidelity toward God will readily admit that he or she often fails and needs God's forgiveness.

[a] *4* Psalm 51:4 [b] *12* Psalms 14:1-3; 53:1-3; Eccles. 7:20 [c] *13* Psalm 5:9 [d] *13* Psalm 140:3 [e] *14* Psalm 10:7 (see Septuagint) [f] *17* Isaiah 59:7,8 [g] *18* Psalm 36:1 [h] *22* Or *through the faithfulness of*

the redemption that came by Christ Jesus. 25God presented Christ as a sacrifice of atone-
ment,[a] through the shedding of his blood—to be received by faith. He did this to demon-
strate his justice, because in his forbearance he had left the sins committed beforehand
unpunished— 26he did it to demonstrate his justice at the present time, so as to be just
and the one who justifies those who have faith in Jesus.
27Where, then, is boasting? It is excluded. Because of what law? The law that requires
works? No, because of the "law" that requires faith. 28For we maintain that a person is jus-
tified by faith apart from observing the law. 29Is God the God of Jews only? Is he not the
God of Gentiles too? Yes, of Gentiles too, 30since there is only one God, who will justify the
circumcised by faith and the uncircumcised through that same faith. 31Do we, then, nulli-
fy the law by this faith? Not at all! Rather, we uphold the law.

Abraham Justified by Faith

4 What then shall we say that Abraham, the forefather of us Jews, discovered in this
matter? 2If, in fact, Abraham was justified by works, he had something to boast
about—but not before God. 3What does Scripture say? "Abraham believed God, and
it was credited to him as righteousness."[b]
4Now to anyone who works, their wages are not credited to them as a gift, but as an ob-
ligation. 5However, to anyone who does not work but trusts God who justifies the ungod-
ly, their faith is credited as righteousness. 6David says the same thing when he speaks of
the blessedness of those to whom God credits righteousness apart from works:

7"Blessed are those
whose transgressions are forgiven,
whose sins are covered.
8Blessed are those
whose sin the Lord will never count against them."[c]

9Is this blessedness only for the circumcised, or also for the uncircumcised? We have
been saying that Abraham's faith was credited to him as righteousness. 10Under what cir-
cumstances was it credited? Was it after he was circumcised, or before? It was not after,
but before! 11And he received circumcision as a sign, a seal of the righteousness that he
had by faith while he was still uncircumcised. So then, he is the father of all who believe

Discovering God

3:21–31 // Life with God. As Paul has demonstrated, we're all sinful and deserving of God's judgment (chapter 1, verse 18 through chapter 3, verse 21). But since we can't earn God's favor, is life just a cruel joke? Is Paul holding up a goal that's impossible for any of us to achieve?

No. Paul's discussion is meant to drive us to the realization that we need a gift from God, not an opportunity to earn a spiritual merit badge.

Paul says in verse 24 that we are justified by God's grace. The word "justified" refers to the act by which God, the righteous Judge, declares sinful people righteous, or "right" with him.

Consider this illustration: Sin is like a speeding ticket that we receive after breaking the law (as we all do). God is the judge who recognizes that the speeding ticket is valid (fair and justly given), but then declares it "paid in full"—and takes care of the payment himself.

In past ages, the payment for wrongdoing was the blood of animals (Leviticus chapter 1, verses 3–5). At one point in history, however, Jesus died as the once-and-for-all sin sacrifice *par excellence*. Now, because Jesus' blood has paid for our sin, God can declare us righteous. Those who put their trust in Jesus will never say, "I know God because I've lived a good life." On the contrary, they'll say, "I deserve God's judgment, but he has forgiven me on the basis of Jesus' blood.

[a] *25* The Greek for *sacrifice of atonement* refers to the atonement cover on the ark of the covenant (see Lev. 16:15,16). [b] *3* Gen. 15:6; also in verse 22 [c] *8* Psalm 32:1,2

but have not been circumcised, in order that righteousness might be credited to them.
[12]And he is then also the father of the circumcised who not only are circumcised but who
also follow in the footsteps of the faith that our father Abraham had before he was circum-
cised.
[13]It was not through the law that Abraham and his offspring received the promise that he
would be heir of the world, but through the righteousness that comes by faith. [14]For if those
who depend on the law are heirs, faith means nothing and the promise is worthless, [15]be-
cause the law brings wrath. And where there is no law there is no transgression.
[16]Therefore, the promise comes by faith, so that it may be by grace and may be guaran-
teed to all Abraham's offspring—not only to those who are of the law but also to those who
have the faith of Abraham. He is the father of us all. [17]As it is written: "I have made you a
father of many nations."[a] He is our father in the sight of God, in whom he believed—the
God who gives life to the dead and calls into being things that were not.
[18]Against all hope, Abraham in hope believed and so became the father of many nations,
just as it had been said to him, "So shall your offspring be."[b] [19]Without weakening in his
faith, he faced the fact that his body was as good as dead—since he was about a hundred
years old—and that Sarah's womb was also dead. [20]Yet he did not waver through unbelief
regarding the promise of God, but was strengthened in his faith and gave glory to God,
[21]being fully persuaded that God had power to do what he had promised. [22]This is why "it
was credited to him as righteousness." [23]The words "it was credited to him" were written
not for him alone, [24]but also for us, to whom God will credit righteousness—for us who
believe in him who raised Jesus our Lord from the dead. [25]He was delivered over to death
for our sins and was raised to life for our justification.

Peace and Hope

5 Therefore, since we have been justified through faith, we[c] have peace with God
through our Lord Jesus Christ, [2]through whom we have gained access by faith into
this grace in which we now stand. And we[d] boast in the hope of the glory of God.
[3]Not only so, but we[d] also glory in our sufferings, because we know that suffering pro-
duces perseverance; [4]perseverance, character; and character, hope. [5]And hope does not
put us to shame, because God's love has been poured out into our hearts through the Holy
Spirit, who has been given to us.
[6]You see, at just the right time, when we were still powerless, Christ died for the ungod-
ly. [7]Very rarely will anyone die for a righteous person, though for a good person someone

Discovering God

4:1–25 // Life with God. To validate his statement that faith is the link that connects us with God, Paul uses an illustration that his Jewish readers readily understood. Almost 2000 years before Christ, a man named Abraham became the father of a new nation later named Israel. He had a very close relationship with God that Jewish people desired to imitate.

Paul discusses how this relationship between Abraham and God began, pointing out that Abraham was connected to God through simple belief (faith) before he received the religious rite of circumcision, and long before God gave people the law of Moses (verses 13–22). Abraham's faith, not his good works or participation in religious rituals, cemented his relationship with God. To many of Paul's fellow Jews, this was probably a startling realization. Circumcision and the law were the cornerstones of Jewish religious practice, yet here Paul asserts that neither saved Abraham, nor can they save anybody else!

If you're a seeker, Paul's point is good news for you. Salvation isn't based on something you must do for God. Religious rituals don't impress him. Good deeds won't win his favor. Rather, he wants you to believe (trust) in what he has already done for you through his Son, Jesus Christ. Then, as a forgiven son or daughter of God, you'll naturally want to serve him and others around you—not to earn anything, but out of a heart filled with gratitude for what God has done.

[a] *17* Gen. 17:5 [b] *18* Gen. 15:5 [c] *1* Many manuscripts *let us* [d] *2,3* Or *let us*

might possibly dare to die. [8]But God demonstrates his own love for us in this: While we
were still sinners, Christ died for us.

[9]Since we have now been justified by his blood, how much more shall we be saved from
God's wrath through him! [10]For if, while we were God's enemies, we were reconciled to
him through the death of his Son, how much more, having been reconciled, shall we be
saved through his life! [11]Not only is this so, but we also boast in God through our Lord Jesus
Christ, through whom we have now received reconciliation.

Death Through Adam, Life Through Christ

[12]Therefore, just as sin entered the world through one man, and death through sin, and
in this way death came to all people, because all sinned—

[13]To be sure, sin was in the world before the law was given, but sin is not charged against
anyone's account where there is no law. [14]Nevertheless, death reigned from the time of
Adam to the time of Moses, even over those who did not sin by breaking a command, as
did Adam, who is a pattern of the one to come.

[15]But the gift is not like the trespass. For if the many died by the trespass of the one man,
how much more did God's grace and the gift that came by the grace of the one man, Jesus
Christ, overflow to the many! [16]Nor can the gift of God be compared with the result of one
man's sin: The judgment followed one sin and brought condemnation, but the gift followed
many trespasses and brought justification. [17]For if, by the trespass of the one man, death
reigned through that one man, how much more will those who receive God's abundant provision of grace and of the gift of righteousness reign in life through the one man, Jesus Christ!

[18]Consequently, just as one trespass resulted in condemnation for all people, so also
one righteous act resulted in justification and life for all. [19]For just as through the disobedience of the one man the many were made sinners, so also through the obedience of the
one man the many will be made righteous.

[20]The law was brought in so that the trespass might increase. But where sin increased,
grace increased all the more, [21]so that, just as sin reigned in death, so also grace might
reign through righteousness to bring eternal life through Jesus Christ our Lord.

Reasons to Believe

5:1–11 // The Christian Experience. Are there any practical benefits to following Christ? Paul lists three in these verses: peace with God, hope in affliction, and love that's unconditional.

When Jesus said, "Whoever loses their life for me will find it" (Matthew chapter 16, verse 25), he didn't mean that our lives would become empty when we made the trade. Paul helps us see some of the wonderful blessings that fill our lives when we make that exchange.

Life is full of peaks and valleys. Christ-followers make it through both the good times and the tough times by clinging to promises such as these that God has made.

Knowing Yourself

5:12–21 // Sin. None of us has ever had to be taught how to be sinful—it's an inbred "skill."

Maybe you've wondered where the human tendency to do wrong comes from. Paul doesn't dance around the issue. He says each of us has inherited the tendency from our distant forefather Adam. When Adam sinned, he was infected with a spiritual disease, which he passed on to his offspring (see Genesis chapter 3 [page 8]). Every child of Adam, without exception, is born with a nature that seeks gratification and fulfillment apart from God. And every child of Adam, without exception, commits sin and will therefore die.

Thankfully, the story doesn't end there. Paul mentions Adam so that he can contrast the widespread effect of Adam's actions with Christ's. One man's sin brought death; so too, one man's righteousness brings life. Paul doesn't say that everybody automatically has this life. Whereas sin is passed on by being born, salvation is passed on by being "born again" (see John chapter 3 [page 121]). Only those who personally pledge to trust in God for their salvation receive the benefits of Christ's sacrifice.

Dead to Sin, Alive in Christ

6 What shall we say, then? Shall we go on sinning so that grace may increase? [2]By no
means! We are those who have died to sin; how can we live in it any longer? [3]Or
don't you know that all of us who were baptized into Christ Jesus were baptized into
his death? [4]We were therefore buried with him through baptism into death in order that,
just as Christ was raised from the dead through the glory of the Father, we too may live a
new life.
[5]If we have been united with him in a death like his, we will certainly also be united
with him in a resurrection like his. [6]For we know that our old self was crucified with him
so that the body ruled by sin might be done away with,[a] that we should no longer be slaves
to sin— [7]because anyone who has died has been set free from sin.
[8]Now if we died with Christ, we believe that we will also live with him. [9]For we know that
since Christ was raised from the dead, he cannot die again; death no longer has mastery
over him. [10]The death he died, he died to sin once for all; but the life he lives, he lives to
God.
[11]In the same way, count yourselves dead to sin but alive to God in Christ Jesus. [12]There-
fore do not let sin reign in your mortal body so that you obey its evil desires. [13]Do not of-
fer any part of yourself to sin as an instrument of wickedness, but rather offer yourselves
to God as those who have been brought from death to life; and offer every part of yourself
to him as an instrument of righteousness. [14]For sin shall no longer be your master, because
you are not under the law, but under grace.

Slaves to Righteousness

[15]What then? Shall we sin because we are not under the law but under grace? By no
means! [16]Don't you know that when you offer yourselves to someone as obedient slaves,
you are slaves of the one you obey—whether you are slaves to sin, which leads to death,
or to obedience, which leads to righteousness? [17]But thanks be to God that, though you
used to be slaves to sin, you have come to obey from your heart the pattern of teaching that
has now claimed your allegiance. [18]You have been set free from sin and have become slaves
to righteousness.
[19]I am using an example from everyday life because of your human limitations. Just as
you used to offer yourselves as slaves to impurity and to ever-increasing wickedness, so

Addressing Questions

6:1–14 // Human Experience. The idea that salvation is a free gift may have raised this question in your mind: *If I don't have to do anything to win God's favor, what's to keep me from living a wild life after I accept Christ?*

Paul anticipated that question and gave a profound answer. When people trust Jesus to rescue them from their sin, an amazing transaction occurs: They are spiritually identified—tied together—with Christ. Since sin has no power over Christ, those who are united with Christ have also been delivered from the power of sin.

Paul also points out that it doesn't make sense to come to Jesus with the intention of disobeying him. That's like getting married with the intention of regularly committing adultery—possible, but utterly foolish and completely at odds with the purpose of the relationship.

Imagine a ceiling fan with blades driven by a belt connected to an electric motor. If someone disconnects the belt, the electric motor will still operate, but it won't be able to turn the blades. Similarly, when we come to Christ, the belt on the motor that drives us to sin gets disconnected. It's still there, and we unfortunately choose to reengage it at times, but we don't have to sin the way we did before we became Christ-followers.

The more we realize that we've been liberated from the power of sin, the more we want to live free from its destructive effects. Jesus' gift of salvation sets us free *from* sin, not free *to* sin!

---

[a] 6 Or *be rendered powerless*

now offer yourselves as slaves to righteousness leading to holiness. [20]When you were slaves
to sin, you were free from the control of righteousness. [21]What benefit did you reap at that
time from the things you are now ashamed of? Those things result in death! [22]But now
that you have been set free from sin and have become slaves of God, the benefit you reap
leads to holiness, and the result is eternal life. [23]For the wages of sin is death, but the gift
of God is eternal life in[a] Christ Jesus our Lord.

Released From the Law, Bound to Christ

7 Do you not know, brothers and sisters—for I am speaking to those who know the
law—that the law has authority over someone only as long as that person lives? [2]For
example, by law a married woman is bound to her husband as long as he is alive, but
if her husband dies, she is released from the law that binds her to him. [3]So then, if she
marries another man while her husband is still alive, she is called an adulteress. But if her
husband dies, she is released from that law and is not an adulteress if she marries anoth-
er man.

[4]So, my brothers and sisters, you also died to the law through the body of Christ, that
you might belong to another, to him who was raised from the dead, in order that we might
bear fruit for God. [5]For when we were controlled by our sinful nature,[b] the sinful passions
aroused by the law were at work in us, so that we bore fruit for death. [6]But now, by dying
to what once bound us, we have been released from the law so that we serve in the new
way of the Spirit, and not in the old way of the written code.

Reasons to Believe

7:1–25 // The Incomparable Jesus. Perhaps one thing that has kept you from following Christ is your belief that you could never live up to God's expectations. You don't want to be a hypocrite, so you don't even bother trying to live up to standards that you know you'll never achieve.

In a way, you're right. Only one person has ever lived the Christian life perfectly—Jesus. So you're not alone in your belief that you can't hack it. God's commands are impossible to follow—not because he is unreasonable, but because we're sinful. In fact, Paul says that one of the reasons why God gave us his commandments is so we'll stop believing that we're "good." Through the law we see that we can't fully obey God. That's why we need to rely on Jesus for forgiveness.

Paul notes three purposes for the law. First, *it reveals sin* (verse 7). A driver doesn't know he's speeding until he passes a speed-limit sign and compares it with his speedometer. Similarly, we don't know that some things are wrong until God points them out.

Second, *God's law provokes sin so that it comes into full view* (verses 8–13). To illustrate: What's your first response to a sign that says "Wet Paint—Do Not Touch"? Making something off limits actually increases our desire to disobey. That doesn't make God's law evil. It just points out how evil we are—how ready we are to do wrong.

Third, *God's law spells out the consequences of sin* (verse 13). If we're caught speeding, we get a ticket—that's the law. If we continually refuse to admit our sins to God and ask for his forgiveness, we pay the penalty and die spiritually.

Even the apostle Paul, as spiritually mature as he was, despaired that he ended up doing the very things he didn't want to do (verses 15–23). His cry in verse 25 and his immediate response in verse 26 demonstrate the principle that he discusses in this chapter. Even though we live in a sinful world and experience sin's effects, we can look to Jesus for release from our bondage to sin. When we give our lives to Christ, we trust him to change us from the inside as we mature spiritually. It's a matter of growing into obedience—*training* to be like Jesus over time instead of *trying* to be like him in our own power.

[a] *23* Or *through*   [b] *5* Or *by the flesh*

The Law and Sin

7What shall we say, then? Is the law sinful? Certainly not! Nevertheless, I would not
have known what sin was had it not been for the law. For I would not have known what cov-
eting really was if the law had not said, "You shall not covet."[a] 8But sin, seizing the oppor-
tunity afforded by the commandment, produced in me every kind of coveting. For apart
from the law, sin was dead. 9Once I was alive apart from the law; but when the command-
ment came, sin sprang to life and I died. 10I found that the very commandment that was
intended to bring life actually brought death. 11For sin, seizing the opportunity afforded by
the commandment, deceived me, and through the commandment put me to death. 12So
then, the law is holy, and the commandment is holy, righteous and good.

13Did that which is good, then, become death to me? By no means! Nevertheless, in or-
der that sin might be recognized as sin, it used what is good to bring about my death, so
that through the commandment sin might become utterly sinful.

14We know that the law is spiritual; but I am unspiritual, sold as a slave to sin. 15I do not
understand what I do. For what I want to do I do not do, but what I hate I do. 16And if I do
what I do not want to do, I agree that the law is good. 17As it is, it is no longer I myself who
do it, but it is sin living in me. 18I know that good itself does not dwell in me, that is, in my
sinful nature.[b] For I have the desire to do what is good, but I cannot carry it out. 19For I do
not do the good I want to do, but the evil I do not want to do—this I keep on doing. 20Now
if I do what I do not want to do, it is no longer I who do it, but it is sin living in me that
does it.

21So I find this law at work: Although I want to do good, evil is right there with me. 22For
in my inner being I delight in God's law; 23but I see another law at work in me, waging war
against the law of my mind and making me a prisoner of the law of sin at work within me.
24What a wretched man I am! Who will rescue me from this body of death? 25Thanks be to
God, who delivers me through Jesus Christ our Lord!

So then, I myself in my mind am a slave to God's law, but in my sinful nature[c] a slave
to the law of sin.

Life Through the Spirit

8 Therefore, there is now no condemnation for those who are in Christ Jesus, 2because
through Christ Jesus the law of the Spirit who gives life has set you[d] free from the law
of sin and death. 3For what the law was powerless to do because it was weakened by the
sinful nature,[e] God did by sending his own Son in the likeness of sinful humanity to be a sin
offering.[f] And so he condemned sin in human flesh, 4in order that the righteous requirement
of the law might be fully met in us, who do not live according to the sinful nature but accord-
ing to the Spirit.

5Those who live according to the sinful nature have their minds set on what that nature
desires; but those who live in accordance with the Spirit have their minds set on what the
Spirit desires. 6The mind controlled by the sinful nature[g] is death, but the mind controlled
by the Spirit is life and peace. 7The sinful mind[h] is hostile to God; it does not submit to
God's law, nor can it do so. 8Those controlled by the sinful nature cannot please God.

9You, however, are not controlled by the sinful nature but are in the Spirit, if indeed the
Spirit of God lives in you. And if anyone does not have the Spirit of Christ, they do not be-
long to Christ. 10But if Christ is in you, then even though your body is subject to death be-
cause of sin, the Spirit gives life[i] because of righteousness. 11And if the Spirit of him who
raised Jesus from the dead is living in you, he who raised Christ from the dead will also
give life to your mortal bodies because of[j] his Spirit who lives in you.

12Therefore, brothers and sisters, we have an obligation—but it is not to the sinful na-
ture, to live according to it. 13For if you live according to the sinful nature, you will die; but
if by the Spirit you put to death the misdeeds of the body, you will live.

---

[a] *7* Exodus 20:17; Deut. 5:21 [b] *18* Or *my flesh* [c] *25* Or *in the flesh* [d] *2* The Greek is singular; some manuscripts *me* [e] *3* Or *the flesh*; also in verses 4, 5, 8, 9, 12 and 13 [f] *3* Or *humanity, for sin* [g] *6* Or *mind set on the flesh* [h] *7* Or *the mind set on the flesh* [i] *10* Or *you, your body is dead because of sin, yet your spirit is alive* [j] *11* Some manuscripts *bodies through*

14For those who are led by the Spirit of God are the children of God. 15The Spirit you re-
ceived does not make you slaves, so that you live in fear again; rather, the Spirit you re-
ceived brought about your adoption to sonship.[a] And by him we cry, *"Abba,*[b] Father." 16The
Spirit himself testifies with our spirit that we are God's children. 17Now if we are children,
then we are heirs—heirs of God and co-heirs with Christ, if indeed we share in his suffer-
ings in order that we may also share in his glory.

Present Suffering and Future Glory

18I consider that our present sufferings are not worth comparing with the glory that will
be revealed in us. 19The creation waits in eager expectation for the children of God to be re-
vealed. 20For the creation was subjected to frustration, not by its own choice, but by the will
of the one who subjected it, in hope 21that[c] the creation itself will be liberated from its bond-
age to decay and brought into the freedom and glory of the children of God.

22We know that the whole creation has been groaning as in the pains of childbirth right
up to the present time. 23Not only so, but we ourselves, who have the firstfruits of the Spir-
it, groan inwardly as we wait eagerly for our adoption, the redemption of our bodies. 24For
in this hope we were saved. But hope that is seen is no hope at all. Who hopes for what they
already have? 25But if we hope for what we do not yet have, we wait for it patiently.

26In the same way, the Spirit helps us in our weakness. We do not know what we ought
to pray for, but the Spirit himself intercedes for us through wordless groans. 27And he who
searches our hearts knows the mind of the Spirit, because the Spirit intercedes for God's
people in accordance with the will of God.

28And we know that in all things God works for the good of those who love him, who[d]
have been called according to his purpose. 29For those God foreknew he also predestined
to be conformed to the image of his Son, that he might be the firstborn among many broth-
ers and sisters. 30And those he predestined, he also called; those he called, he also justified;
those he justified, he also glorified.

Discovering God

8:1–11 // Life with God. Trying harder. It's a well-worn path. Tired, frustrated people take it when they resolve to live their lives differently. Unfortunately, that uphill path is just as worn with footprints moving in the opposite direction. People who resolve to "pull themselves up by the bootstraps" and change their lives for the better often find themselves in the same predicament within a few days, weeks, or months.

But it doesn't have to be that way. In this chapter, Paul spells out God's plan for us to experience the inner transformation that results in a changed lifestyle.

First, he says that we must *recognize that God will accept us completely in Christ* (verse 1). Even though repeated sin might make us feel guilty, God's condemnation becomes a thing of the past when we receive Christ as our forgiver and leader.

Second, we need to *recognize the freedom we have available in Christ* (verses 2–4). Through his Spirit, Jesus wants to liberate us from the downward spiral of sin. Just as aerodynamics, when properly applied, overcome the effects of gravity, so the Spirit frees us from the "gravity" of sin, allowing us to soar above the limitations of our sinful appetites and to please God.

Third, we must *remember that we now have a choice whether to be controlled by our sinful desires or by God's Spirit* (verses 5–11). Controlled by sin, we're rebellious and obsessed with gratifying our own self-seeking agendas. But when we're directed by God's Spirit, we're empowered by a new impulse to please him.

---

[a] 15 The Greek word for *adoption to sonship* is a term referring to the full legal standing of an adopted male heir in Roman culture. [b] 15 Aramaic for *Father* [c] 20,21 Or *subjected it in hope.* 21For
[d] 28 Or *that all things work together for good to those who love God, who;* or *that in all things God works together with those who love him to bring about what is good—with those who*

More Than Conquerors

[31]What, then, shall we say in response to these things? If God is for us, who can be against
us? [32]He who did not spare his own Son, but gave him up for us all—how will he not also,
along with him, graciously give us all things? [33]Who will bring any charge against those
whom God has chosen? It is God who justifies. [34]Who then can condemn? No one. Christ
Jesus who died—more than that, who was raised to life—is at the right hand of God and is
also interceding for us. [35]Who shall separate us from the love of Christ? Shall trouble or
hardship or persecution or famine or nakedness or danger or sword? [36]As it is written:

> "For your sake we face death all day long;
> we are considered as sheep to be slaughtered."[a]

[37]No, in all these things we are more than conquerors through him who loved us. [38]For I am
convinced that neither death nor life, neither angels nor demons,[b] neither the present nor
the future, nor any powers, [39]neither height nor depth, nor anything else in all creation,
will be able to separate us from the love of God that is in Christ Jesus our Lord.

Paul's Anguish Over Israel

9 I speak the truth in Christ—I am not lying, my conscience confirms it through the
Holy Spirit— [2]I have great sorrow and unceasing anguish in my heart. [3]For I could
wish that I myself were cursed and cut off from Christ for the sake of my people,
those of my own race, [4]the people of Israel. Theirs is the adoption; theirs the divine glory,
the covenants, the receiving of the law, the temple worship and the promises. [5]Theirs are
the patriarchs, and from them is traced the human ancestry of the Messiah, who is God
over all, forever praised![c] Amen.

Discovering God

8:28–30 // Life with God. Imagine putting together a large puzzle without being able to look at the picture on the cover of the box. It would be next to impossible, wouldn't it? You might successfully get the edges together. You might even make some progress on small sections. But your work would be painfully slow and frustrating as you held up each piece and wondered, *Where does this fit in?*

The same is true in life. Some pieces of the puzzle don't make sense when seen by themselves. We wonder where our disappointments, failures, and losses fit in. We want the box top—the "big picture" that assures us that all our experiences have a purpose.

God doesn't provide a box-top view of our lives, but he does give his followers a promise: Every experience in life's puzzle will be used for some good. While that doesn't mean that everything that happens to us will be good in and of itself, it does mean that, in the end, there will be no missing or useless pieces. God promises that he'll work to fit our experiences together, making even the painful and confusing times into a beautiful picture that has purpose and makes sense. That's a promise that "those who love him" can count on (verse 28).

Addressing Questions

8:31–39 // Human Experience. As a seeker you may wonder, *If I become a true Christ-follower, can I ever lose his forgiveness and the eternal life he gives me?*

According to this passage, if you choose to trust Christ, you'll receive a salvation that can never be taken from you. Paul goes so far as to say that *nothing in all creation* can separate you from the love of God in Christ.

Whenever you sin, Jesus Christ is your defense attorney (verse 34). He died for your sins—released you from them—and his resurrection proves you've been acquitted. When you're united with Jesus, the outcome of your case is not pending—it's *over.* If anyone—even you—tries to reopen the case against you, Jesus tells them you've already been forgiven.

That is true freedom!

---

[a] 36 Psalm 44:22 [b] 38 Or *nor heavenly rulers* [c] 5 Or *Messiah, who is over all. God be forever praised!* Or *Messiah. God who is over all be forever praised!*

God's Sovereign Choice

6It is not as though God's word had failed. For not all who are descended from Israel are
Israel. 7Nor because they are his descendants are they all Abraham's children. On the con-
trary, "It is through Isaac that your offspring will be reckoned."[a] 8In other words, it is not
the natural children who are God's children, but it is the children of the promise who are
regarded as Abraham's offspring. 9For this was how the promise was stated: "At the ap-
pointed time I will return, and Sarah will have a son."[b]

10Not only that, but Rebekah's children were conceived at the same time by our father
Isaac. 11Yet, before the twins were born or had done anything good or bad—in order that
God's purpose in election might stand: 12not by works but by him who calls—she was told,
"The older will serve the younger."[c] 13Just as it is written: "Jacob I loved, but Esau I hated."[d]

14What then shall we say? Is God unjust? Not at all! 15For he says to Moses,

> "I will have mercy on whom I have mercy,
> and I will have compassion on whom I have compassion."[e]

16It does not, therefore, depend on human desire or effort, but on God's mercy. 17For Scrip-
ture says to Pharaoh: "I raised you up for this very purpose, that I might display my power in
you and that my name might be proclaimed in all the earth."[f] 18Therefore God has mercy on
whom he wants to have mercy, and he hardens whom he wants to harden.

19One of you will say to me: "Then why does God still blame us? For who is able to resist
his will?" 20But who are you, a mere human being, to talk back to God? "Shall what is formed
say to the one who formed it, 'Why did you make me like this?' "[g] 21Does not the potter have
the right to make out of the same lump of clay some pottery for noble purposes and some
for disposal of refuse?

22What if God, although choosing to show his wrath and make his power known, bore
with great patience the objects of his wrath—prepared for destruction? 23What if he did
this to make the riches of his glory known to the objects of his mercy, whom he prepared
in advance for glory— 24even us, whom he also called, not only from the Jews but also from
the Gentiles? 25As he says in Hosea:

> "I will call them 'my people' who are not my people;
> and I will call her 'my loved one' who is not my loved one,"[h]

26and,

> "In the very place where it was said to them,
> 'You are not my people,'
> they will be called 'children of the living God.' "[i]

27Isaiah cries out concerning Israel:

> "Though the number of the Israelites be like the sand by the sea,
> only the remnant will be saved.
> 28For the Lord will carry out
> his sentence on earth with speed and finality."[j]

Addressing Questions

9:1–8 // God. Paul grieved that the Jewish people had turned from their Messiah, Jesus Christ (the word "Christ" means "Messiah"). Even though historically Israel had a special relationship with God, most of the Israelites rejected Christ. Paul therefore focused his ministry on non-Jews who were willing to believe in Jesus as the Jewish Messiah and receive the benefits of that belief.

Paul argued that the true Israel consists of all people who share in Abraham's faith, rather than his direct ancestry. That includes both Jews and non-Jews, and it can include *you* if you respond to God in faith, as Abraham did.

[a] *7* Gen. 21:12 [b] *9* Gen. 18:10,14 [c] *12* Gen. 25:23 [d] *13* Mal. 1:2,3 [e] *15* Exodus 33:19
[f] *17* Exodus 9:16 [g] *20* Isaiah 29:16; 45:9 [h] *25* Hosea 2:23 [i] *26* Hosea 1:10
[j] *28* Isaiah 10:22,23 (see Septuagint)

[29]It is just as Isaiah said previously:

> "Unless the Lord Almighty
> had left us descendants,
> we would have become like Sodom,
> we would have been like Gomorrah."[a]

Israel's Unbelief

[30]What then shall we say? That the Gentiles, who did not pursue righteousness, have ob-
tained it, a righteousness that is by faith; [31]but the people of Israel, who pursued the law
as the way of righteousness, have not attained their goal. [32]Why not? Because they pur-
sued it not by faith but as if it were by works. They stumbled over the stumbling stone.
[33]As it is written:

> "See, I lay in Zion a stone that causes people to stumble
> and a rock that makes them fall,
> and the one who believes in him will never be put to shame."[b]

10 Brothers and sisters, my heart's desire and prayer to God for the Israelites is that
they may be saved. [2]For I can testify about them that they are zealous for God,
but their zeal is not based on knowledge. [3]Since they did not know the righteous-
ness of God and sought to establish their own, they did not submit to God's righteousness.
[4]Christ is the culmination of the law so that there may be righteousness for everyone who
believes.
[5]Moses writes this about the righteousness that is by the law: "Whoever does these
things will live by them."[c] [6]But the righteousness that is by faith says: "Do not say in your
heart, 'Who will ascend into heaven?' "[d] (that is, to bring Christ down) [7]"or 'Who will de-
scend into the deep?' "[e] (that is, to bring Christ up from the dead). [8]But what does it say?
"The word is near you; it is in your mouth and in your heart,"[f] that is, the message concern-
ing faith that we proclaim: [9]If you declare with your mouth, "Jesus is Lord," and believe in
your heart that God raised him from the dead, you will be saved. [10]For it is with your heart
that you believe and are justified, and it is with your mouth that you profess your faith and
are saved. [11]As Scripture says, "Anyone who believes in him will never be put to shame."[g]
[12]For there is no difference between Jew and Gentile—the same Lord is Lord of all and rich-
ly blesses all who call on him, [13]for, "Everyone who calls on the name of the Lord will be
saved."[h]

Discovering God

10:9–13 // Life with God. The smartly dressed couple stands in front of family and friends, nervous but excited. Although an invisible attraction has brought them to this moment, their unseen love is about to become a matter of public record. The words and phrases that accompany this public ceremony are simple, yet the commitment behind those words is profoundly deep and life-changing.

Starting a new life with God is not all that different from beginning a marriage. According to Paul's words in this passage, that commitment is expressed by affirming the name that is higher and more important than all others. Like a bride uniting with her husband, we unite with Jesus, and his riches become ours through that marriage.

If you're a seeker, this is the place to come when you're ready to say, "I want to live forever with Jesus." You must acknowledge who Jesus is (Lord, Master, Leader) and be convinced that he rose from the dead and is alive right now. God's promise to you is that when you forsake all others and give yourself to him who conquered death for you, *you will be rescued.* Not maybe. Not possibly. But *absolutely.*

This is the "gospel" that Paul devoted his life to telling others about. This is the core assurance of Christianity. It can be yours too—if you just say, "I do."

---

[a] *29* Isaiah 1:9 [b] *33* Isaiah 8:14; 28:16 [c] *5* Lev. 18:5 [d] *6* Deut. 30:12 [e] *7* Deut. 30:13
[f] *8* Deut. 30:14 [g] *11* Isaiah 28:16 (see Septuagint) [h] *13* Joel 2:32

14How, then, can they call on the one they have not believed in? And how can they be-
lieve in the one of whom they have not heard? And how can they hear without someone
preaching to them? 15And how can anyone preach unless they are sent? As it is written:
"How beautiful are the feet of those who bring good news!"[a]
16But not all the Israelites accepted the good news. For Isaiah says, "Lord, who has be-
lieved our message?"[b] 17Consequently, faith comes from hearing the message, and the
message is heard through the word about Christ. 18But I ask: Did they not hear? Of course
they did:

> "Their voice has gone out into all the earth,
> their words to the ends of the world."[c]

19Again I ask: Did Israel not understand? First, Moses says,

> "I will make you envious by those who are not a nation;
> I will make you angry by a nation that has no understanding."[d]

20And Isaiah boldly says,

> "I was found by those who did not seek me;
> I revealed myself to those who did not ask for me."[e]

21But concerning Israel he says,

> "All day long I have held out my hands
> to a disobedient and obstinate people."[f]

The Remnant of Israel

11 I ask then: Did God reject his people? By no means! I am an Israelite myself, a de-
scendant of Abraham, from the tribe of Benjamin. 2God did not reject his people,
whom he foreknew. Don't you know what Scripture says in the passage about Eli-
jah—how he appealed to God against Israel: 3"Lord, they have killed your prophets and
torn down your altars; I am the only one left, and they are trying to kill me"[g]? 4And what
was God's answer to him? "I have reserved for myself seven thousand who have not bowed
the knee to Baal."[h] 5So too, at the present time there is a remnant chosen by grace. 6And
if by grace, then it cannot be based on works; if it were, grace would no longer be grace.
7What then? What the people of Israel sought so earnestly they did not obtain. The elect
among them did, but the others were hardened, 8as it is written:

> "God gave them a spirit of stupor,
> eyes that could not see
> and ears that could not hear,
> to this very day."[i]

Discovering God

11:1–36 // The God Who Is There. Does God sometimes seem far away or hidden in a thick cloud? Let this passage assure you that you're never beyond his reach.

Here Paul discusses some who seemed beyond God's reach—Jewish people who refused to accept Jesus as their leader and forgiver. That number made up the majority of the Jews in Paul's time, as it does still today. But that won't always be true. Many scholars believe that this passage implies that one day a great spiritual awakening will take place among the Jewish people and that many will turn to their Messiah, Jesus. That prospect caused Paul, a Jew himself, to praise God (verses 33–36).

Don't ever give up hope that God can get through the barriers that separate people from him. He can do it for individuals, groups of people and even nations. But, more specifically, he can do it for *you!*

---

[a] *15* Isaiah 52:7 [b] *16* Isaiah 53:1 [c] *18* Psalm 19:4 [d] *19* Deut. 32:21 [e] *20* Isaiah 65:1
[f] *21* Isaiah 65:2 [g] *3* 1 Kings 19:10,14 [h] *4* 1 Kings 19:18 [i] *8* Deut. 29:4; Isaiah 29:10

[9]And David says:

> "May their table become a snare and a trap,
> a stumbling block and a retribution for them.
> [10]May their eyes be darkened so they cannot see,
> and their backs be bent forever."[a]

Ingrafted Branches

[11]Again I ask: Did they stumble so as to fall beyond recovery? Not at all! Rather, because
of their transgression, salvation has come to the Gentiles to make Israel envious. [12]But if
their transgression means riches for the world, and their loss means riches for the Gentiles, how much greater riches will their fullness bring!
[13]I am talking to you Gentiles. Inasmuch as I am the apostle to the Gentiles, I make
much of my ministry [14]in the hope that I may somehow arouse my own people to envy and
save some of them. [15]For if their rejection brought reconciliation to the world, what will
their acceptance be but life from the dead? [16]If the part of the dough offered as firstfruits
is holy, then the whole batch is holy; if the root is holy, so are the branches.
[17]If some of the branches have been broken off, and you, though a wild olive shoot, have
been grafted in among the others and now share in the nourishing sap from the olive root,
[18]do not consider yourself to be superior to those other branches. If you do, consider this:
You do not support the root, but the root supports you. [19]You will say then, "Branches were
broken off so that I could be grafted in." [20]Granted. But they were broken off because of unbelief, and you stand by faith. Do not be arrogant, but tremble. [21]For if God did not spare
the natural branches, he will not spare you either.
[22]Consider therefore the kindness and sternness of God: sternness to those who fell, but
kindness to you, provided that you continue in his kindness. Otherwise, you also will be cut
off. [23]And if they do not persist in unbelief, they will be grafted in, for God is able to graft
them in again. [24]After all, if you were cut out of an olive tree that is wild by nature, and
contrary to nature were grafted into a cultivated olive tree, how much more readily will
these, the natural branches, be grafted into their own olive tree!

All Israel Will Be Saved

[25]I do not want you to be ignorant of this mystery, brothers and sisters, so that you may
not think you are superior: Israel has experienced a hardening in part until the full number of the Gentiles has come in, [26]and in this way[b] all Israel will be saved. As it is written:

> "The deliverer will come from Zion;
> he will turn godlessness away from Jacob.
> [27]And this is[c] my covenant with them
> when I take away their sins."[d]

[28]As far as the gospel is concerned, they are enemies for your sake; but as far as election
is concerned, they are loved on account of the patriarchs, [29]for God's gifts and his call are
irrevocable. [30]Just as you who were at one time disobedient to God have now received mercy as a result of their disobedience, [31]so they too have now become disobedient in order that
they too may now[e] receive mercy as a result of God's mercy to you. [32]For God has bound
everyone over to disobedience so that he may have mercy on them all.

Doxology

> [33]Oh, the depth of the riches of the wisdom and[f] knowledge of God!
> How unsearchable his judgments,
> and his paths beyond tracing out!
> [34]"Who has known the mind of the Lord?
> Or who has been his counselor?"[g]

---

[a] *10* Psalm 69:22,23 [b] *26* Or *and so* [c] *27* Or *will be* [d] *27* Isaiah 59:20,21; 27:9 (see Septuagint); Jer. 31:33,34 [e] *31* Some manuscripts do not have *now.* [f] *33* Or *riches and the wisdom and the* [g] *34* Isaiah 40:13

35 “Who has ever given to God,
that God should repay them?”[a]
36 For from him and through him and to him are all things.
To him be the glory forever! Amen.

A Living Sacrifice

12 Therefore, I urge you, brothers and sisters, in view of God’s mercy, to offer your
bodies as a living sacrifice, holy and pleasing to God—this is true worship. 2 Do
not conform to the pattern of this world, but be transformed by the renewing of
your mind. Then you will be able to test and approve what God’s will is—his good, pleas-
ing and perfect will.

Humble Service in the Body of Christ

3 For by the grace given me I say to every one of you: Do not think of yourself more high-
ly than you ought, but rather think of yourself with sober judgment, in accordance with
the faith God has distributed to each of you. 4 For just as each of us has one body with many
members, and these members do not all have the same function, 5 so in Christ we, though
many, form one body, and each member belongs to all the others. 6 We have different gifts,
according to the grace given to each of us. If your gift is prophesying, then prophesy in ac-
cordance with your[b] faith; 7 if it is serving, then serve; if it is teaching, then teach; 8 if it is
to encourage, then give encouragement; if it is giving, then give generously; if it is to lead,[c]
do it diligently; if it is to show mercy, do it cheerfully.

Love in Action

9 Love must be sincere. Hate what is evil; cling to what is good. 10 Be devoted to one an-
other in love. Honor one another above yourselves. 11 Never be lacking in zeal, but keep
your spiritual fervor, serving the Lord. 12 Be joyful in hope, patient in affliction, faithful in
prayer. 13 Share with the Lord’s people who are in need. Practice hospitality.
14 Bless those who persecute you; bless and do not curse. 15 Rejoice with those who rejoice;
mourn with those who mourn. 16 Live in harmony with one another. Do not be proud, but
be willing to associate with people of low position.[d] Do not think you are superior.
17 Do not repay anyone evil for evil. Be careful to do what is right in the eyes of everyone.
18 If it is possible, as far as it depends on you, live at peace with everyone. 19 Do not take re-
venge, my dear friends, but leave room for God’s wrath, for it is written: “It is mine to
avenge; I will repay,”[e] says the Lord. 20 On the contrary:

“If your enemy is hungry, feed him;
if he is thirsty, give him something to drink.
In doing this, you will heap burning coals on his head.”[f]

21 Do not be overcome by evil, but overcome evil with good.

Discovering God

12:1–8 // Life with God. What difference does being a Christ-follower make in our day-to-day lives? A huge one! Paul takes the rest of the book of Romans (chapters 12–16) to tell us about it.

When we accept Christ’s leadership in our lives, we experience an entire change in life focus. To use Paul’s illustration, an animal lying on the altar has basically one purpose, and very few earthly concerns. In the same way our lives, once given to God, are now totally at his disposal; our talents and our selfish former agenda are now surrendered to his purpose. And the more we give of ourselves to him, the more he will empower, bless and use us.

---

[a] *35* Job 41:11 [b] *6* Or *the* [c] *8* Or *to provide for others* [d] *16* Or *willing to do menial work*
[e] *19* Deut. 32:35 [f] *20* Prov. 25:21,22

Submission to Governing Authorities

13 Let everyone be subject to the governing authorities, for there is no authority ex-
cept that which God has established. The authorities that exist have been estab-
lished by God. [2]Consequently, whoever rebels against the authority is rebelling
against what God has instituted, and those who do so will bring judgment on themselves.
[3]For rulers hold no terror for those who do right, but for those who do wrong. Do you want
to be free from fear of the one in authority? Then do what is right and you will be com-
mended. [4]For the one in authority is God's servant for your good. But if you do wrong, be
afraid, for rulers do not bear the sword for no reason. They are God's servants, agents of
wrath to bring punishment on the wrongdoer. [5]Therefore, it is necessary to submit to the
authorities, not only because of possible punishment but also as a matter of conscience.
[6]This is also why you pay taxes, for the authorities are God's servants, who give their
full time to governing. [7]Give to everyone what you owe: If you owe taxes, pay taxes; if rev-
enue, then revenue; if respect, then respect; if honor, then honor.

Love Fulfills the Law

[8]Let no debt remain outstanding, except the continuing debt to love one another, for
whoever loves others has fulfilled the law. [9]The commandments, "You shall not commit
adultery," "You shall not murder," "You shall not steal," "You shall not covet,"[a] and what-
ever other command there may be, are summed up in this one command: "Love your
neighbor as yourself."[b] [10]Love does no harm to its neighbor. Therefore love is the fulfill-
ment of the law.

The Day Is Near

[11]And do this, understanding the present time. The hour has already come for you to
wake up from your slumber, because our salvation is nearer now than when we first be-
lieved. [12]The night is nearly over; the day is almost here. So let us put aside the deeds of
darkness and put on the armor of light. [13]Let us behave decently, as in the daytime, not in
carousing and drunkenness, not in sexual immorality and debauchery, not in dissension
and jealousy. [14]Rather, clothe yourselves with the Lord Jesus Christ, and do not think about
how to gratify the desires of the sinful nature.[c]

Addressing Questions

13:1–7 // Human Experience. While we may not agree with everything our government does, God, through Paul, commands us to subject ourselves to government. Why? Because God establishes government as a way to control society and to limit evil in the world. The only exception to this principle is when the government asks us to do something that directly violates the teaching of the Bible. In that case, the right thing to do is to respectfully refuse to obey human authority so that we can obey God (see Acts chapter 5, verse 29 [page 165]).

In general, however, submitting to governing authorities is a visible way to show our submission to God.

Strengthening Relationships

13:8–14 // Social. The kind of love that Paul talks about here doesn't always come easily. How can we express Christ's love when our emotions are running high or when we're faced with some sort of injustice? One approach is to clench our fists, grit our teeth, and say, "I'll love you in spite of what a louse you are!" But that act doesn't fool anybody.

A better way is to admit our "love limits" and ask God for his help. Ask yourself, "What would a truly loving person do in such a situation?" Then rely on Jesus to clothe you with his love (verse 14), so that you can show it to others.

---

[a] 9 Exodus 20:13-15,17; Deut. 5:17-19,21 [b] 9 Lev. 19:18 [c] 14 Or *the flesh*

The Weak and the Strong

14 Accept those whose faith is weak, without quarreling over disputable matters.
2One person's faith allows them to eat everything, but another person, whose faith
is weak, eats only vegetables. 3The one who eats everything must not treat with
contempt the one who does not, and the one who does not eat everything must not judge
the one who does, for God has accepted that person. 4Who are you to judge someone else's
servant? To their own master they stand or fall. And they will stand, for the Lord is able to
make them stand.

5Some consider one day more sacred than another; others consider every day alike. Ev-
eryone should be fully convinced in their own mind. 6Those who regard one day as special
do so to the Lord. Those who eat meat do so to the Lord, for they give thanks to God; and those
who abstain do so to the Lord and give thanks to God. 7For we do not live to ourselves alone
and we do not die to ourselves alone. 8If we live, we live to the Lord; and if we die, we die to
the Lord. So, whether we live or die, we belong to the Lord. 9For this very reason, Christ died
and returned to life so that he might be the Lord of both the dead and the living.

10You, then, why do you judge your brother or sister? Or why do you treat your brother or
sister with contempt? For we will all stand before God's judgment seat. 11It is written:

> " 'As surely as I live,' says the Lord,
> 'every knee will bow before me;
>   every tongue will confess to God.' "[a]

12So then, we will all give an account of ourselves to God.

13Therefore let us stop passing judgment on one another. Instead, make up your mind
not to put any stumbling block or obstacle in the way of a brother or sister. 14I am con-
vinced, being fully persuaded in the Lord Jesus, that nothing is unclean in itself. But if any-
one regards something as unclean, then for that person it is unclean. 15If your brother or
sister is distressed because of what you eat, you are no longer acting in love. Do not by
your eating destroy your brother or sister for whom Christ died. 16Therefore do not let what
you know is good be spoken of as evil. 17For the kingdom of God is not a matter of eating
and drinking, but of righteousness, peace and joy in the Holy Spirit, 18because anyone who
serves Christ in this way is pleasing to God and receives human approval.

19Let us therefore make every effort to do what leads to peace and to mutual edifica-
tion. 20Do not destroy the work of God for the sake of food. All food is clean, but it is wrong

Strengthening Relationships

14:1–12 // Social. If you're a seeker, perhaps one thing that has kept you from Christ is the fear that the Bible's rules will take away your freedom. Actually, Paul says just the opposite: We have so much freedom as Christians, we need to be careful how we handle it.

In this passage, Paul talks about two kinds of Christ-followers. Some believers feel that certain issues (in this case, eating meat that had been sacrificed to idols) don't affect a person's relationship with God. Others, because of their backgrounds (Jews were specifically forbidden to eat such meat), believe certain things are off-limits.

Paul's discussion is specifically tied to the cultural situation in which he wrote. In our day, and even in your own community, these issues are different. For example, one family may feel strongly that drinking alcoholic beverages should be strictly off-limits to Christians. The family next door may not subscribe to such restrictions. Paul's advice in such situations is straightforward: Be careful not to criticize, and don't be condescending. Ultimately, each of us must answer to God, not to each other.

What's the practical implication of Paul's advice? When the two families get together for dinner, the one family shouldn't offer wine with the meal, and the other family shouldn't write their neighbors off as "sinners" when they see full wine rack in the kitchen. Believers need to exercise their Christian freedom in a way that builds others up. The freest people are those who act compassionately, not compulsively, toward other people, seeking to build them up and encourage them in their walk with God.

[a] *11* Isaiah 45:23

for a person to eat anything that causes someone else to stumble. 21It is better not to eat
meat or drink wine or to do anything else that will cause your brother or sister to fall.
22So whatever you believe about these things keep between yourself and God. Blessed
are those who do not condemn themselves by what they approve. 23But those who have
doubts are condemned if they eat, because their eating is not from faith; and everything
that does not come from faith is sin.

15 We who are strong ought to bear with the failings of the weak and not to please
ourselves. 2We should all please our neighbors for their good, to build them up.
3For even Christ did not please himself but, as it is written: "The insults of those
who insult you have fallen on me."[a] 4For everything that was written in the past was writ-
ten to teach us, so that through the endurance taught in the Scriptures and the encour-
agement they provide we might have hope.
5May the God who gives endurance and encouragement give you the same attitude of
mind toward each other that Christ Jesus had, 6so that with one mind and one voice you
may glorify the God and Father of our Lord Jesus Christ.
7Accept one another, then, just as Christ accepted you, in order to bring praise to God.
8For I tell you that Christ has become a servant of the Jews[b] on behalf of God's truth, so that
the promises made to the patriarchs might be confirmed 9and, moreover, that the Gen-
tiles might glorify God for his mercy. As it is written:

> "Therefore I will praise you among the Gentiles;
> I will sing the praises of your name."[c]

10Again, it says,

> "Rejoice, you Gentiles, with his people."[d]

11And again,

> "Praise the Lord, all you Gentiles;
> let all the peoples extol him."[e]

12And again, Isaiah says,

> "The Root of Jesse will spring up,
> one who will arise to rule over the nations;
> in him the Gentiles will hope."[f]

13May the God of hope fill you with all joy and peace as you trust in him, so that you
may overflow with hope by the power of the Holy Spirit.

Paul the Minister to the Gentiles

14I myself am convinced, my brothers and sisters, that you yourselves are full of good-
ness, filled with knowledge and competent to instruct one another. 15Yet I have written you
quite boldly on some points to remind you of them again, because of the grace God gave
me 16to be a minister of Christ Jesus to the Gentiles. He gave me the priestly duty of pro-
claiming the gospel of God, so that the Gentiles might become an offering acceptable to
God, sanctified by the Holy Spirit.

Discovering God

15:1–13 // Life with God. Followers of Christ don't measure success by how much money they make or how much power they acquire. A Christian's goal is simply to clearly reflect the life of Jesus—to do what Jesus would do if he were in our body.

In this passage, Paul outlines some specific ways his readers can reflect the life of Jesus: Be considerate of others who are at different points in their spiritual journey; diligently seek to please others instead of yourself; accept people who are different from you.

This is a tall order, since only Christ himself is strong enough to live this way. But people who follow Christ live in his strength, and the Spirit that lives within them gives them the power to treat others as Jesus would.

---

[a] *3* Psalm 69:9 [b] *8* Greek *circumcision* [c] *9* 2 Samuel 22:50; Psalm 18:49 [d] *10* Deut. 32:43
[e] *11* Psalm 117:1 [f] *12* Isaiah 11:10 (see Septuagint)

17 Therefore I glory in Christ Jesus in my service to God. 18 I will not venture to speak of
anything except what Christ has accomplished through me in leading the Gentiles to obey
God by what I have said and done— 19 by the power of signs and wonders, through the pow-
er of the Spirit of God. So from Jerusalem all the way around to Illyricum, I have fully pro-
claimed the gospel of Christ. 20 It has always been my ambition to preach the gospel where
Christ was not known, so that I would not be building on someone else's foundation. 21 Rath-
er, as it is written:

> "Those who were not told about him will see,
> and those who have not heard will understand."[a]

22 This is why I have often been hindered from coming to you.

Paul's Plan to Visit Rome

23 But now that there is no more place for me to work in these regions, and since I have
been longing for many years to visit you, 24 I plan to do so when I go to Spain. I hope to see
you while passing through and to have you assist me on my journey there, after I have en-
joyed your company for a while. 25 Now, however, I am on my way to Jerusalem in the ser-
vice of the Lord's people there. 26 For Macedonia and Achaia were pleased to make a
contribution for the poor among the Lord's people in Jerusalem. 27 They were pleased to do
it, and indeed they owe it to them. For if the Gentiles have shared in the Jews' spiritual
blessings, they owe it to the Jews to share with them their material blessings. 28 So after I
have completed this task and have made sure that they have received this fruit, I will go
to Spain and visit you on the way. 29 I know that when I come to you, I will come in the full
measure of the blessing of Christ.

30 I urge you, brothers and sisters, by our Lord Jesus Christ and by the love of the Spir-
it, to join me in my struggle by praying to God for me. 31 Pray that I may be kept safe from
the unbelievers in Judea and that the contribution I take to Jerusalem may be favorably
received by the Lord's people there, 32 so that by God's will I may come to you with joy
and together with you be refreshed. 33 The God of peace be with you all. Amen.

Personal Greetings

16 I commend to you our sister Phoebe, a deacon[b] of the church in Cenchreae. 2 I ask
you to receive her in the Lord in a way worthy of his people and to give her any
help she may need from you, for she has been the benefactor of many people, in-
cluding me.

Strengthening Relationships

15:14–33 // Leadership. If you've ever wondered how a great leader treats his followers, take a close look at the apostle Paul. These few verses in the second half of chapter 15 offer some important clues.

First, Paul affirms these people (verse 14). He tells them that he is aware of their insight and knowledge. Great leaders know their people's strengths and remind them often of that awareness.

Next, he exhorts them (verses 15–16). Time and again in his letter to the Romans, Paul encourages his readers to live in a way that reflects the life of Christ. Great leaders are not afraid to challenge their followers to high standards of conduct.

Finally, Paul submits himself to meeting their needs (verses 17–21). As a Jewish scholar, Paul probably could have had an honored ministry among the Jews. Yet he ministered to those who weren't impressed by his training. Great leaders often have abilities that are never fully displayed in public, because they build up those they lead instead of themselves.

If you're a leader, Paul's example is a good one to follow.

---

[a] *21* Isaiah 52:15 (see Septuagint)   [b] *1* Or *servant*

[3]Greet Priscilla[a] and Aquila, my co-workers in Christ Jesus. [4]They risked their lives for me. Not only I but all the churches of the Gentiles are grateful to them.
[5]Greet also the church that meets at their house.
Greet my dear friend Epenetus, who was the first convert to Christ in the province of Asia.
[6]Greet Mary, who worked very hard for you.
[7]Greet Andronicus and Junia, my fellow Jews who have been in prison with me. They are outstanding among the apostles, and they were in Christ before I was.
[8]Greet Ampliatus, my dear friend in the Lord.
[9]Greet Urbanus, our co-worker in Christ, and my dear friend Stachys.
[10]Greet Apelles, whose fidelity to Christ has stood the test.
Greet those who belong to the household of Aristobulus.
[11]Greet Herodion, my fellow Jew.
Greet those in the household of Narcissus who are in the Lord.
[12]Greet Tryphena and Tryphosa, those women who work hard in the Lord.
Greet my dear friend Persis, another woman who has worked very hard in the Lord.
[13]Greet Rufus, chosen in the Lord, and his mother, who has been a mother to me, too.
[14]Greet Asyncritus, Phlegon, Hermes, Patrobas, Hermas and the other brothers and sisters with them.
[15]Greet Philologus, Julia, Nereus and his sister, and Olympas and all the Lord's people who are with them.
[16]Greet one another with a holy kiss.
All the churches of Christ send greetings.

[17]I urge you, brothers and sisters, to watch out for those who cause divisions and put obstacles in your way that are contrary to the teaching you have learned. Keep away from
them. [18]For such people are not serving our Lord Christ, but their own appetites. By smooth talk and flattery they deceive the minds of naive people. [19]Everyone has heard about your obedience, so I rejoice because of you; but I want you to be wise about what is good, and innocent about what is evil.

[20]The God of peace will soon crush Satan under your feet.

The grace of our Lord Jesus be with you.

[21]Timothy, my co-worker, sends his greetings to you, as do Lucius, Jason and Sosipater, my fellow Jews.

[22]I, Tertius, who wrote down this letter, greet you in the Lord.

[23][24]Gaius, whose hospitality I and the whole church here enjoy, sends you his greetings.

Erastus, who is the city's director of public works, and our brother Quartus send you their greetings.[b]

[25]Now to him who is able to establish you in accordance with my gospel, the message I proclaim about Jesus Christ, in keeping with the revelation of the mystery hidden for long
ages past, [26]but now revealed and made known through the prophetic writings by the command of the eternal God, so that all the Gentiles might come to faith and obedience— [27]to
the only wise God be glory forever through Jesus Christ! Amen.

Addressing Questions

16:1–24 // Human Experience. Paul's personal connection with his readers is evident in that he greets 35 people by name at the end of this letter. This great theological treatise is *personal*. It was written to individuals.

Don't miss an important implication. If you're a seeker, you're not just a face in the crowd. Nothing would delight God more than including your name on the list of his children. He already knows your name. All you have to do is say yes to his invitation.

[a] 3 Greek *Prisca*, a variant of *Priscilla* [b] 23 Some manuscripts *their greetings.* [24]*May the grace of our Lord Jesus Christ be with all of you. Amen.*

Epilogue

The book of Romans is the last one in *Beginning the Journey.* If you've read all five books, you have a good bird's-eye view of the Bible's main themes.

By now you probably have a sense of what aspects you agree with and what questions still remain. The next step is to keep reading—there's so much more to be found in a complete Bible. Read more of Paul's letters—1 Corinthians, for example. When you're ready for a break, go back and check out the other three books that recount the life of Jesus: Matthew, Mark and Luke. In the Old Testament, the Psalms contain rich reflections on life with God; and the practical, down-to-earth wisdom of the Proverbs is a favorite among beginners as well as Bible-study veterans.

If you haven't done so already, find a small group of Christians who you can talk to about your questions and who can guide you into a greater understanding of the Bible's truths. Learning is both an individual and a collective process, and you'll make better progress if you have others around who you can learn from, and vice-versa.

Whatever roadblocks you experience, Christ promises that you'll find your way around them if you keep seeking. He earnestly desires to have a saving, life-transforming relationship with you. He wants to show himself to you as the unique Son of God, the One who died to give you new life.

Seeker Stories

Before I decided to trust Christ, my life was focused on earthly matters. I was very materialistic. To feed that craving I devoted most of my energy to my career rather than to my marriage. My marriage fell apart as a result, and the cumulative financial rewards from my successful career were consumed entirely by the legal process of divorce.

I decided to trust Christ alone for my salvation when I participated in a support group for divorced persons. Prior to my divorce I believed that I could handle anything on my own, without God's help. The divorce brought me to my knees, and I learned that I needed to place my faith in Christ in order to survive.

The decision to trust Christ has transformed my life. I am much happier now that I've changed the focus of my life to following Christ on a daily basis. I've turned away from my past ways, and am trying to conduct my life in a way that pleases God.

Although I was raised as a "good little Christian boy" from birth, it was a far different kind of Christianity than I now know. I was baptized at age seven in our fear-based church, and when my mother remarried, I was baptized again at age 15 in a church that was even more "shame and punishment" focused.

Ten years in a 12-step recovery group and more than three years at my current church have brought me along a journey of faith and surrender, a journey from pride to greater humility. The world tells me that "there is no free lunch," but the Holy Spirit tells me that grace and forgiveness are not only free, but that they delight and honor the Giver.

Along this journey there have been many times when I have committed myself to Jesus, God's Son, on a deeper and deeper level. I am sure that he will call me closer and closer to him in the future. Now the reality of God's grace and unconditional love overwhelms the "logic" of the world that tells me I need to earn my salvation. And while my life hasn't gotten any easier, it now has definite purpose and direction.

Appendix I: Table of Weights and Measures

	BIBLICAL UNIT	APPROXIMATE AMERICAN EQUIVALENT	APPROXIMATE METRIC EQUIVALENT
WEIGHTS	talent (60 minas)	75 pounds	34 kilograms
	mina (50 shekels)	1 1/4 pounds	0.6 kilogram
	shekel (2 bekas)	2/5 ounce	11.5 grams
	pim (2/3 shekel)	1/3 ounce	9.5 grams
	beka (10 gerahs)	1/5 ounce	5.5 grams
	gerah	1/50 ounce	0.6 gram
LENGTH	cubit	18 inches	0.5 meter
	span	9 inches	23 centimeters
	handbreadth	3 inches	8 centimeters
CAPACITY			
Dry Measure	cor [homer] (10 ephahs)	6 bushels	220 liters
	lethek (5 ephahs)	3 bushels	110 liters
	ephah (10 omers)	3/5 bushel	22 liters
	seah (1/3 ephah)	7 quarts	7.7 liters
	omer (1/10 ephah)	2 quarts	2 liters
	cab (1/18 ephah)	1 quart	1 liter
Liquid Measure	bath (1 ephah)	6 gallons	4 liters
	hin (1/6 bath)	22 liters	1/3 quart
	log (1/72 bath)	4 quarts	0.3 liter

The figures of the table are calculated on the basis of a shekel equaling 11.5 grams, a cubit equaling 18 inches and an ephah equaling 22 liters. The quart referred to is either a dry quart (slightly larger than a liter) or a liquid quart (slightly smaller than a liter), whichever is applicable. The ton referred to in the footnotes is the American ton of 2,000 pounds. Since most readers are more familiar with dry measures being given in weight rather than capacity (bushel, quart), dry measures have been converted in the footnotes to approximate weights.

This table is based upon the best available information, but it is not intended to be mathematically precise; like the measurement equivalents in the footnotes, it merely gives approximate amounts and distances. Weights and measures differed somewhat at various times and places in the ancient world. There is uncertainty particularly about the ephah and the bath; further discoveries may shed more light on these units of capacity.

Appendix II: Revised Spelling of Proper Names

NIV	TNIV
Abib	Aviv
Abimelech	Abimelek
Achbor	Akbor
Acco	Akko
Acsah	Aksah
Acshaph	Akshaph
Aczib	Akzib
Adrammelech	Adrammelek
Ahimelech	Ahimelek
Ahisamach	Ahisamak
Allammelech	Allammelek
Anammelech	Anammelek
Asshur	Ashur
Asshurites	Ashurites
Athach	Athak
Baca	Baka
Bacuth	Bakuth
Becorath	Bekorath
Beracah	Berakah
Beth Car	Beth Kar
Bicri	Bikri
Cabbon	Kabbon
Cabul	Kabul
Calcol	Kalkol
Calno	Kalno
Calneh	Kalneh
Canneh	Kanneh
Carshena	Karshena
Carcas	Karkas
Carmi	Karmi
Casiphia	Kasiphia
Casluhites	Kasluhites
Cenchrea	Cenchreae
Col-Hozeh	Kol-Hozeh
Colosse	Colossae
Conaniah	Konaniah
Cozbi	Kozbi
Cozeba	Kozeba
Cun	Kun
Cuthah	Kuthah
Ebed-Melech	Ebed-Melek
Elimelech	Elimelek
Erech	Uruk

NIV	TNIV
Eshcol	Eshkol
Eshtarah	Eshterah
Evil-Merodach	Awel-Marduk
Goiim	Goyim
Hacaliah	Hakaliah
Hacmoni	Hakmoni
Hadrach	Hadrak
Hanoch	Hanok
Hathach	Hathak
Haran	Harran
Hatticon	Hattikon
Hazazon Tamar	Hazezon Tamar
Helech	Helek
Iim	Iyim
Iscah	Iskah
Isshiah	Ishiah
Jaakanites	Bene Jaakan
Jacan	Jakan
Jecoliah	Jekoliah
Jehucal	Jehukal
Josech	Josek
Kittim	Kittites
Korazin	Chorazin
Lecah	Lekah
Maacah	Maakah
Macbannai	Makbannai
Macbenah	Makbenah
Macnadebai	Maknadebai
Malcam	Malkam
Malluch	Malluk
Maoch	Maok
Marcaboth	Markaboth
Meconah	Mekonah
Melech	Melek
Memucan	Memukan
Merodach-Baladan	Marduk-Baladan
Meshech	Meshek
Mica	Mika
Micmash	Mikmash
Micmethah	Mikmethah
Micri	Mikri
Milcah	Milkah
Milcom	Milkom

NIV	TNIV
Mithcah	Mithkah
Mizraim	Egypt
Molech	Molek
Nacon	Nakon
Nathan-Melech	Nathan-Melek
Neco	Necho
Nisroch	Nisrok
Ocran	Okran
Parnach	Parnak
Pasach	Pasak
Racal	Rakal
Recab	Rekab
Recabites	Rekabites
Recah	Rekah
Regem-Melech	Regem-Melek
Rodanim	Rodanites
Sabteca	Sabteka
Sacar	Sakar
Salecah	Salekah
Secacah	Sekakah
Secu	Seku
Shecaniah	Shekaniah
Sheshach	Sheshak
Shobach	Shobak
Shophach	Shophak
Sibbecai	Sibbekai
Soco	Soko
Socoh	Sokoh
Succoth	Sukkoth
Ucal	Ukal
Zaccai	Zakkai
Zaccur	Zakkur
Zeboiim	Zeboyim
Zicri	Zikri

A Word to the Reader

Today's New International Version (TNIV) is a revision of the New International Version (NIV). Among the many English versions of the Bible that appeared in the twentieth century, the NIV (1973, 1978, 1984) has gained the widest readership in all parts of the English-speaking world. It was a completely new translation made by over a hundred scholars working directly from the best available Hebrew, Aramaic and Greek texts. The fact that participants from the United States, Great Britain, Canada, Australia and New Zealand worked together gave the project its international scope. That they were from many denominations—including Anglican, Assemblies of God, Baptist, Brethren, Christian Reformed, Church of Christ, Evangelical Covenant, Evangelical Free, Lutheran, Mennonite, Methodist, Nazarene, Presbyterian, Wesleyan and other churches—helped to safeguard the translation from sectarian bias. Responsibility for the NIV text, and now also for the text of the TNIV, is held by a self-governing body, the Committee on Bible Translation (CBT), composed of Biblical scholars from colleges, universities and seminaries. During the revision process, many of the original members of CBT have been replaced by other scholars owing to retirement and other causes, but a similar geographical and denominational mix has been maintained.

From the beginning the translators have been united in their commitment to the authority and infallibility of the Bible as God's Word in written form. For them, the Bible contains the divine answer to the deepest needs of humanity, sheds unique light on our path in a dark world and sets forth the way to our eternal well-being. Out of this deep conviction, the Committee has held to certain goals for the NIV and for the present revision: that it would be an accurate translation and one that would have clarity and literary quality and so prove suitable for public and private reading, teaching, preaching, memorizing and liturgical use. The Committee has also sought to preserve a measure of continuity with the long tradition of translating the Scriptures into English.

There is a sense in which the work of translating the Bible is never finished. This very fact has prompted the Committee to engage in an ongoing review of the text of the NIV with the assistance of many other scholars. The chief goal of this review has always been to bring the text of the NIV abreast of contemporary Biblical scholarship and of shifts in English idiom and usage. Already in 1978 and again in 1984 various corrections and revisions to the NIV text were made. In the TNIV the Committee offers to the reading public the latest fruits of its review.

The first concern of the translators has continued to be the accuracy of the translation and its faithfulness to the intended meaning of the Biblical writers. This has moved the translators to go beyond a formal word-for-word rendering of the original texts. Because thought patterns and syntax differ from language to language, accurate communication of the meaning of the Biblical authors demands constant regard for varied contextual uses of words and idioms and for frequent modifications in sentence structures.

To achieve clarity the translators have sometimes supplied words not in the original texts but required by the context. In a few instances, where some uncertainty about such material remained, it is enclosed in corner brackets. As an aid to the reader, italicized sectional headings have been inserted. They are not to be regarded as part of the Biblical text and are not intended for oral reading. It is the Committee's hope that these headings may prove more helpful to the reader than the traditional chapter divisions (which were introduced in the thirteenth century).

For the Old Testament the standard Hebrew text, the Masoretic Text as published in the latest editions of *Biblia Hebraica*, has been used throughout. The Masoretic Text tradition contains marginal notations that offer variant readings. These have sometimes been followed instead of the text itself. Because such instances involve variants within the Masoretic tradition, they have not been indicated in the textual notes. In a few cases, words in the basic consonantal text have been divided differently than in the Masoretic Text. Such cases are usually indicated in the textual footnotes. The Dead Sea Scrolls contain Biblical texts that represent an earlier stage of the transmission of the Hebrew text. They have been consulted, as have been the Samaritan Pentateuch and the ancient scribal traditions concerning deliberate textual changes. The translators also consulted the more important early versions-the Greek Septuagint, Aquila, Symmachus and Theodotion, the Latin Vulgate, the Syriac Peshitta, the Aramaic Targums, and for the Psalms the *Juxta Hebraica* of Jerome. Readings from the Dead Sea Scrolls, the scribal traditions and these versions were occasionally followed where the Masoretic Text seemed doubtful and where accepted principles of textual criticism showed that one or more of these textual witnesses appeared to provide the correct reading. In rare cases, the translators have emended the Hebrew text where it appears to have become corrupted at an even earlier stage of its transmission. These departures from the Masoretic Text are also indicated in the textual footnotes. Sometimes the vowel indicators (which are later additions to the basic consonantal text) found in the Masoretic Text did not, in the judgment of the translators, represent the correct vowels for the original text. Accordingly, some words have been read with a different set of vowels. These instances are usually not indicated in the footnotes.

The Greek text used in translating the New Testament has been an eclectic one, based on the latest editions of the Nestle-Aland / United Bible Societies' Greek New Testament. The translators have made their choices among the variant readings in accordance with widely accepted principles of New Testament textual criticism. Footnotes call attention to places where uncertainty remains.

The New Testament authors, writing in Greek, often quote the Old Testament from its ancient Greek version, the Septuagint. This is one reason why some of the Old Testament quotations in the TNIV New Testament are not identical to the corresponding passages in the TNIV Old Testament. Such quotations in the New Testament are indicated with the footnote "(see Septuagint)."

Other footnotes in this version are of several kinds, most of which need no explanation. Those giving alternative translations begin with "Or" and generally introduce the alternative with the last word preceding it in the text, except when it is a single-word alternative. In poetry quoted in a footnote a slash mark indicates a line division.

It should be noted that references to diseases, minerals, flora and fauna, architectural details, clothing, jewelry, musical instruments and other articles cannot always be identified with precision. Also, linear measurements and measures of capacity can only be approximated (see Appendix I). The manner in which Hebrew proper names are to be represented in English has not become fully standardized. In the TNIV the spelling of many names has been revised to conform more closely to current scholarly practice and to the phonetics of the Hebrew originals. A list of such changes can be found in Appendix II, following the Biblical text. A parallel list provides the spelling of these names in the NIV. Although *Selah*, used mainly in the Psalms, is probably a musical term, its meaning is uncertain. Since it may interrupt reading and distract the reader, this word has not been kept in the English text, but every occurrence has been signaled by a footnote.

Three changes of special note in the TNIV are the frequent substitution of "Messiah" for the more traditional "Christ," the replacement of "saints" in most cases with alternative renderings, and a greater sensitivity to shifts in English idiom. A word about each is in order.

While "Messiah" (from the Hebrew) and "Christ" (from the Greek) both mean "Anointed One," what began as a title full of meaning to the early Jewish hearers of the gospel tended in the later Greek-speaking churches to become just another name for Jesus. So where the term is clearly used to designate the God-sent deliverer of Jewish expectations (primarily in the Gospels and Acts), it was judged more appropriate to use "Messiah." However, where this sense seems less prominent (primarily in the Epistles), the transliteration of the Greek word ("Christ") has been retained.

Concerning "saints," current usage (as reflected in major dictionaries of the English language) burdens it with meanings that lie outside the sense of the original-language words. The main Old Testament term that has traditionally been rendered "saints" refers to those who are faithful to God. The New Testament term primarily designates those who have become followers of the Christian Way as people consecrated to God and thus belonging to the Lord in a special sense.

Although a basic core of the English language remains relatively stable, many diverse and complex cultural forces continue to bring about subtle shifts in the meanings and/or connotations of even old, well-established words and phrases. Among the more programmatic changes in the TNIV are the removal of nearly all vocative "O"s and the elimination of most instances of the generic use of masculine nouns and pronouns. Relative to the second of these, the so-called singular "they/their/them," which has been gaining acceptance among careful writers and which actually has a venerable place in English idiom, has been employed to fill in the vocabulary gap in generic nouns and pronouns referring to human beings. Where an individual emphasis is deemed to be present, "anyone" or "everyone" or some other equivalent is generally used as the antecedent of such pronouns.

Sometimes the chapter and/or verse numbering in English translations of the Old Testament differs from that found in published Hebrew texts. This is particularly the case in the Psalms, where the traditional titles are included in the Hebrew verse numbering. Such differences are marked by asterisks (*) in the text and informative footnotes set off in a separate line (or lines) at the bottom of the page. In the New Testament, verse numbers that marked off portions of the traditional English text not supported by the best Greek manuscripts are now set alongside the immediately preceding verse numbers and placed in brackets (see, for example, Matthew 17:20[21]).

Mark 16:9–20 and John 7:53—8:11, although long accorded virtually equal status with the rest of the Gospels in which they stand, have a very questionable—and confused—standing in the textual history of the New Testament, as noted in the bracketed annotations with which they are set off. A different typeface has now been chosen for these passages to indicate even more clearly their uncertain status.

Basic formatting of the text, such as lining the poetry, paragraphing (both prose and poetry), setting up of (administrative-like) lists, indenting letters and lengthy prayers within narratives and the insertion of sectional headings, has been the work of the Committee. However, the choice between single-column and double-column formats has been left to the publishers. Also the issuing of "red-letter" editions is a publisher's choice—one that the Committee does not endorse.

The Committee has again been reminded that every human effort is flawed-including this revision of the NIV. We trust, however, that many will find in it an improved representation of the Word of God, through which they hear his call to faith in our Lord Jesus Christ and to service in his kingdom. We offer this version of the Bible to him in whose name and for whose glory it has been made.

The Committee on Bible Translation
August 2003

Colophon page

Beginning the Journey

General Editor
Judson Poling, Willow Creek Association

Project Management
Ben Irwin, Zondervan

Development Team
Judson Poling, general editor and writer, Willow Creek Association
Bill Perkins, writer
Mark Mittelberg, contributing editor, Willow Creek Associatoin
Mike Vander Klipp, editor, Zondervan

Production Management
Phil Herich, Zondervan

Art Direction, Cover Design and Interior Design
Rob Monacelli, Zondervan

Proofreading
Peachtree Editorial and Proofreading Service, Peachtree, GA

Interior Typesetting
Ruth Bandstra, Zondervan

Printing and Binding
R.R. Donnelley & Sons